"THOSE DAMN HORSE SOLDIERS"

* *

BOOKS BY GEORGE WALSH

"Those Damn Horse Soldiers":
*True Tales of the Civil War Cavalry**

"Whip the Rebellion":
*Ulysses S. Grant's Rise to Command**

"Damage Them All You Can":
*Robert E. Lee's Army of Northern Virginia**

Public Enemies:
The Mayor, the Mob, and the Crime That Was

Gentleman Jimmy Walker:
Mayor of the Jazz Age

*denotes a Forge Book

"THOSE DAMN HORSE SOLDIERS"

* *

TRUE TALES OF THE CIVIL WAR CAVALRY

GEORGE WALSH

A TOM DOHERTY ASSOCIATES BOOK

NEW YORK

A Forge Book
Published by Tom Doherty Associates, LLC
175 Fifth Avenue
New York, NY 10010

www.tor.com

Forge® is a registered trademark of Tom Doherty Associates, LLC.

Library of Congress Cataloging-in-Publication Data

Walsh, George, 1931–
    Those damn horse soldiers : true tales of the Civil War cavalry /
George Walsh.—1st. hardcover ed.
        p. cm.
    "A Tom Doherty Associates Book."
    ISBN-13: 978-0-765-31270-9
    ISBN-10: 0-765-31270-0
        1. United States—History—Civil War, 1861–1865—Cavalry operations—
Anecdotes.   2. United States. Army. Cavalry—History—Civil War, 1861–1865—
Anecdotes.   3. Confederate States of America. Army. Cavalry—History—
Anecdotes.   I. Title.

    E492.5.W35   2006
    973.7'4—dc22

                                                                    2006004877

First Edition: December 2006

Printed in the United States of America

0   9   8   7   6   5   4   3   2   1

For Mahon, Declan, and Daniel

CONTENTS

PROLOGUE

Our story begins in 1862, one year after the shelling of Fort Sumter, South Carolina, touched off the Civil War, with the leadership of the Southern cavalry largely in place, and its hard-riding troopers clearly besting their adversaries. In the East, Turner Ashby in the Shenandoah is making himself a mythic figure, while General Robert E. Lee is entrusting the mounted arm of the Army of Northern Virginia to the flamboyant James Ewell Brown "Jeb" Stuart, whose lieutenants include Fitzhugh Lee and, later, Wade Hampton. In the West, the vast area stretching from the Alleghenies to the Mississippi, the raiders Nathan Bedford Forrest and John Hunt Morgan, soon to be joined by Joseph Wheeler, are becoming equally fearsome.

The Union horsemen meanwhile are still searching for their identity. Divided into small units and reporting to individual infantry commanders, they have no clear-cut leadership of their own and few responsibilities other than establishing picket lines and protecting wagon trains. "The enemy has shown more wisdom respecting his cavalry than we," acknowledged General Ulysses S. Grant. "Instead of wasting its strength . . . he, at an early day, had organized his mounted force into compact masses, and plainly made it a favorite."

Compounding this contrast is the experience factor. Southerners were born to the saddle, becoming superb riders while still in their teens. To most Northerners, however, horses were mere draft animals, useful for pulling plows and carriages. Rebel cavalrymen looked down upon their rivals, and their confidence gave them the edge before the battle even was joined. "The young bloods of the South . . . men who never did work and never will," General William Tecumseh Sherman huffed. "War suits them, and the rascals are brave, fine riders, bold to rashness. . . . They hate Yankees per se, and don't bother their brains about the past, present or future. As long as they have good horses, plenty of forage, and an open country, they are happy. This is a larger class than most men suppose. . . . [They] must all be killed . . . before we can hope for peace."[1]

Rebel horse soldiers in 1862 relished their roles. "The duty of cavalry after battle is joined," enthused one of Stuart's officers, "is to cover the flanks to prevent the enemy from turning them. If victorious, it improves upon the victory by rapid pursuit. If defeated, it covers the rear and makes vigorous charges to delay the advance of the enemy—or in the supreme movement . . . when the reserves are brought into action and the death struggle had come, *then* the cavalry comes down like an avalanche, upon the flanks of troops already engaged, with splendid effect."

All this was true, and more. In the lulls between battles, the Confederate cavalry proved expert at screening the infantry's movements from the Federals while simultaneously probing to learn the foe's intent. The Rebels also introduced the tactic of raids in force behind enemy lines—cutting telegraph and rail lines, capturing and destroying supplies, and generally creating havoc. They likewise adapted to riding to danger points and fighting on foot, with every fourth man holding the horses in the rear, and the rest felling trees to set up instant barricades. "We boys of the cavalry were not much on using spades and shovels," noted one of Fitz Lee's men, "but we could use axes very well."[2]

By 1863, of course, the Union cavalry was copying and even improving upon these tactics. Using newly granted authority, commanders like Alfred Pleasanton, John Buford, and David McMurtrie Gregg were going on the offensive themselves, conducting raids of their own and, on the first day at Gettysburg, fighting a dismounted battle that arguably prevented a premature rout.

It would not be until the spring of 1864, however, when Grant made the intense Philip Henry Sheridan commander of the Army of the Potomac's cavalry, that the Federals in the East came into their own. The Confederates would suffer a devastating loss at Yellow Tavern, the Shenandoah would be pacified, and Rebel troopers would find themselves outgunned and outnumbered. Union superiority in the West was more problematical. Even as Sherman advanced through Georgia, he fretted incessantly that the raiders in his rear would destroy his supply lines. His orders about Forrest—his particular bête noire—were terse: "Follow [him] to the death, if it costs 10,000 lives and breaks the [Federal] Treasury."[3]

The South's initial domination was achieved despite severe handicaps. Chief among these was that Johnny Reb had to supply his own mount, for which he was paid perhaps fifty cents a day. While he would be reimbursed for the horse's value if it was killed in battle, it was the owner's loss if the animal broke down or fell sick, as by far the greater number did. Besides this financial burden, there was the problem of replacing the steed. Virginians had the best chance of going home, refitting, and returning to the ranks within a reasonable time, but men from the Carolinas had much longer treks. In the West, troopers led by Forrest and Morgan, fighting and riding through wide swaths of Tennessee, Kentucky, and Mississippi, experienced lesser but similar difficulties. Perhaps as many as one-third of all Rebels, looking for mounts, were unavailable for duty at any given time.

Then there was the matter of weaponry. Though sabers were used both East and West in thundering charges, they proved less than effective in the hand-to-hand combat that followed. Small arms—muskets, rifles, shotguns, and handguns—evolved as the armament of choice, but at the outbreak of war almost all these weapons were produced in northern factories. Southern troopers met the challenge by relying on firearms captured from federal arsenals in the seceding states and later on weapons seized on the battlefield from a still raw and hapless enemy. Colt six-shooters were specially prized, but muzzle-loaders, cumbersome though they might be, also were welcomed—largely for use when dismounted.

By late 1863, however, with almost all the Yankee cavalry outfitted with breechloaders, the armament picture changed. The single-shot breechloader sharply increased the bluecoat's rate of fire, while the seven-shot carbine provided him with a weapon the Confederates could not match. Even when the Rebels did capture such arms, they often found they required metallic cartridges—not the usual paper-and-linen kind—and could be used only while the seized ammunition lasted.

The last problem for the South, which intensified as the war progressed, was the habitual lack of fodder—a need the well-supplied North rarely endured. Rebels East and West were accustomed to hunger, and could survive for days on virtually empty stomachs. Not so their mounts. Though daily rations called for six quarts of corn and six of grain, fodder often fell to less than half that quantity. "The unsatisfied craving . . . produces a morbid appetite, and the horse will then greedily seize and swallow almost anything to distend its stomach," wrote an observer. "Where a camp had been located for a few days one would notice the trees to which the horses had been fastened stripped of bark from the ground to as high up as the animals could reach. . . . Empty bags, scraps of paper and similar things often would be voraciously devoured. . . . All of this was lamentable . . . an immense injury to the efficiency of the cavalry."[4]

Horse soldiers in the Civil War often are referred to as romantic cavaliers—perhaps the last of their kind. But they were likewise flesh and blood, and in this narrative we see their diverse strengths and weaknesses. Consider three of the leading cavalry commanders of the war: the Confederacy's Jeb Stuart and Nathan Forrest, and the Union's Phil Sheridan. Stuart, who loved music, dancing, and pretty women, could do little wrong in 1862 and early 1863, but then before Gettysburg his high spirits led to folly, costing Lee the eyes and ears of his cavalry. Forrest, the most implacable of men, possessed a mind-set that led to the debacle at Fort Pillow, when he permitted the massacre of black Union soldiers. The dutiful Sheridan, whose recall to Washington nearly resulted in disaster at Cedar Creek in 1864, returned just in time to stage one of the war's great rallies.

Our list goes on: Earl Van Dorn, who failed as an infantryman but whose raid on Holly Springs, Mississippi, kept Grant from capturing Vicksburg for another year. William Averell—his sortie at Kelly's Ford in March 1863 signaled the awakening of the Union cavalry. The partisan John Singleton Mosby, whose men rarely wore uniforms and in some instances were hung by the Federals as outlaws. Benjamin H. Grierson, scarred as a youngster by a horse's kick and no lover of horseflesh, who led through Mississippi the most important Union expedition of the war. William Henry Fitzhugh "Rooney" Lee, Robert's dutiful middle son—always in the shadow of his cousin Fitzhugh. George Stoneman, who some believe departed on an errant ride before Chancellorsville, opening the way for Thomas "Stonewall" Jackson's flank attack. The Union's Hugh Judson Kilpatrick—womanizer, braggart, outright liar—but highly valued by Sherman during and after the Atlanta Campaign. The cerebral James H. Wilson and the impetuous George Armstrong Custer—young Federal officers intent, perhaps too much so, on quickly gaining rank. Cool and competent Thomas Munford, who served with the Confederacy from the First Shenandoah to the siege of Petersburg, but was a secondary figure to the last . . .

Here in this narrative you will encounter these commanders and others, rejoice in their triumphs, and mourn their defeats. Horse soldiers indeed were the last of the cavaliers, men who valued their honor as much as their cause. Jeb Stuart summed up their creed. "Remember," he would admonish his troopers, "cavalry gallops at the enemy, but trots away! *No other gait is worthy!*"[5]

1862

ONE

* * * *

THE EAST, MARCH 23–JUNE 6: ASHBY IN THE SHENANDOAH

Thirty-three-year-old, soft-spoken Turner Ashby, whose forebears had fought with distinction in all of America's wars, would himself come to fame during a few short months in 1862 as the daring commander of the 7th Virginia Cavalry during Stonewall Jackson's Valley Campaign. But on this fateful March 23, as the Confederates neared the hamlet of Kernstown, just south of Winchester, he was unwittingly leading his chief into disaster. Jackson with his badly outnumbered force earlier had withdrawn from Winchester before the Federal advance. Now he was under pressure to counterattack in order to hold General Nathaniel Banks and his 38,000 men in the Shenandoah and keep them from the gathering assault on Richmond. So when Ashby reported that James Shields, one of Banks's division heads, was withdrawing from the Kernstown-Winchester area, Jackson with 3,500 men pushed forward, thinking he would overwhelm Shields's rear guard. Instead Jackson blundered into Shields's entire division—some 7,000 strong.

Ashby had been misled. Following a series of skirmishes, his scouts had slipped into Winchester and talked to sympathizers, who told them that the enemy was evacuating. But the departure was only a sham. Shields had anticipated that Jackson would be attacking, and had ordered the greater part of his force to remain concealed around Kernstown. Though the Confederates fought desperately during the ensuing battle, they had little chance against the long odds. The chagrined Ashby, smarting over his intelligence lapse, was everywhere on the field, making able use of his horse artillery and, late in the afternoon, launching a charge that enjoyed initial success. But by nightfall the storied Stonewall Brigade had fallen back, the Confederates were in full retreat, and Jackson had suffered his only defeat of the war.

During this second withdrawal and in subsequent weeks as Jackson moved his troops up the Valley, first to Strasburg and Mount Jackson and then Harrisonburg and Conrad's Store, Ashby was conspicuous in directing the rear guard, delaying and harassing the pursuit. Day after day he would swoop down on scouts and foragers, ambush small units, and with his mobile artillery, shell enemy columns from ever-changing hilltop positions. One Union officer credited him with seizing "every opportunity to annoy us and impede our progress," and was grateful for a Sunday interlude when "Ashby failed to give us his report." Reflected Jackson mapmaker Jedediah Hotchkiss: "Ashby . . . always keeps the enemy at bay. I hope he may be preserved."[1]

Though Jackson did not know it at the time, Abraham Lincoln and the Union high command, believing that the Confederates would not have attacked unless they were in much greater numbers, were thrown into panic. They soon canceled Banks's withdrawal from the Shenandoah, keeping his troops from aiding in the assault on Richmond and giving Stonewall a strategic triumph.

There would be many tactical wins as well, great and small, in the Valley Campaign to come. The demanding Jackson knew full well that Ashby was charismatic and without fear, utterly dedicated, and the only man who could—at least to some degree—control the rowdy and rambunctious Valley cavalry. In the aftermath of Kernstown, therefore, Jackson never made an issue of the breakdown in intelligence. Indeed, despite his reservations about Ashby's abilities as a disciplinarian, he would acknowledge and even laud his lieutenant's personal traits: "His power of endurance [was] almost incredible, his tone of character heroic, and his sagacity almost intuitive in divining the purposes and movements of the enemy."

Henry Kyd Douglas, one of Jackson's aides, would describe Ashby as having "a striking personal appearance, about five feet ten inches, graceful and compact, black eyes, black hair, and a flowing black beard. His complexion was of the darkest brunette. . . . His face was placid not stern; even his smile was shadowed with a tinge of melancholy."

The Federals had slain one of Ashby's brothers during a bloody skirmish in the Valley the year before, bayoneting him while he lay unhorsed and helpless, and the loss had increased Ashby's resolve. "His face did not flush in battle . . . ," Douglas continued, "only the melancholy passed away. . . . As a colonel with an independent command he was active, vigilant, energetic, never at rest. . . . The statements of Ashby with regard to the strength and position of the enemy were singularly accurate: [only] once, at Kernstown, was he deceived. [But] his idea that [the volunteer] should not be subjected to very much starch and drill . . . caused the only failures he ever made."[2]

That he was an inspirational leader was plain. "One glance at the features of Ashby confirmed the high estimate that I had formed of him," said one of his troopers after their first meeting. "I said to myself, 'If I follow you, I go far.'" Reported an awed Valley contemporary: "He told me that he had been under fire for sixty consecutive days. . . . But he found no inconvenience from it. 'I eat a few apples, drink some spring water, and draw up my swordbelt a hole or two tighter, and I'm all right. It's just as good as eating.'"[3]

But Ashby did not lead by speechifying. Just after the Kernstown affair, noted Jedediah Hotchkiss, "a Federal sharpshooter, in Edinburg, fired at him but hit . . . and killed the horse that a little boy they called Dixie, who was following Ashby, was riding. As the horse fell Dixie tumbled off, then jumped to his feet to run. Ashby called him back to get his saddle and coolly waited for him under a continuing fire from sharpshooters." More than once, indifferent to danger, he would sit on his mount, eating a hardboiled egg or a crust of bread while balls whizzed by him. "Never mind [the bullets]," he would say to companions, "I am very hungry." These casual heroics were not lost upon his troopers.

Historian Douglas Southall Freeman summed up the man and his leadership thus: "Away from bugles and battle smoke, Turner Ashby's mien was that of a mild, affable and modest gentleman, to whom men and women were equally attracted. Like (Jeb) Stuart, he was rigid though not ostentatious in morals and in speech similarly clean; but, unlike Stuart, he had no banter and probably little humor. Those admirers who always remembered how he looked [rarely] recalled anything he said. He spoke best with his sword."[4]

The third of six children, Turner Ashby was born on October 23, 1828, in Fauquier County, Virginia, just east of the Blue Ridge Mountains, the son of a prosperous merchant who owned Rose Bank, a comfortable 15-acre estate, and who leased an additional 800 nearby acres for farming. Ashby's father died when he was seven, however, and thereafter the family suffered through a slow financial decline, losing Rose Bank in the process. Young Ashby nonetheless emerged as a popular figure in the area, gaining fame in local hunts and in riding tournaments. A cousin would write that he exhibited "a dash and fire few young men have ever possessed . . . for it was seldom that he failed to carry off first honors. . . . His superb management of his horse . . . and his grace were the marvel of his day."[5]

During the 1850s Ashby, then in his mid-twenties, went into the mercantile business himself, opening a store that catered to the immigrant Irish laborers who were extending the Manassas Gap Railroad. The venture proved a success, and it gave him a degree of financial security, enabling him to buy a home he called Wolf's Crag. He also became the captain of a mounted militia, formed to keep order in the community, which attracted the adventurous and well born and gave him considerable prestige. When John Brown struck Harpers Ferry, Virginia, in 1859, intent on seizing a federal arsenal, arming slaves, and fostering an uprising, Ashby and his troopers rushed to the scene and assisted in Brown's capture.

The Virginian was no rabid secessionist, however, and he continued to hope that war could be averted. Some months later, he showed his restraint and innate sense of civility firsthand. The occasion was a large and well-attended evening reception that Ashby, a bachelor, was giving at Wolf's Crag for some neighbors, their daughter, and a visiting Northerner who was courting her. While the host was off enjoying the party, a rejected suitor approached the young couple and made an insulting remark.

"Isn't it a sublime piece of impudence for a Yankee and a Black Republican to come down here and accept the hospitality of a Virginia gentleman?" he asked.

"You should be the last person to criticize . . . ," the young woman retorted. "You have profited by [my father's] indisposition to draw social lines too sharply. You have been received by him as a guest on several occasions."

Thinking he would save everyone embarrassment, her fiancé decided to leave Ashby's home. But the matter did not end there. The troublemaker followed him into the cloakroom and continued the confrontation.

"What I have just said had reference to you and was *meant* to be insulting," he persisted.

The Northerner had no desire for a duel, but neither did he wish his fiancée to think him a coward. A challenge was given and accepted, and arrangements were made to go out in the darkness and settle the matter with pistols by torchlight.

Here Ashby entered the cloakroom, his outrage concealed by a calm and deliberate manner. "What is the time set for our meeting?" he said, addressing the troublemaker.

"I am to fight Mr. _____ immediately."

"Mr. _____ has nothing to do with this affair," Ashby said. "He came to my house tonight as my guest. . . . The invitation was Turner Ashby's word of honor that he should be treated as a gentleman. . . . I am sorry to have to explain these points of good breeding to you . . . but you have shown your ignorance of them. . . . The insult is mine, not his, to resent. . . . If you are not prepared to make a proper and satisfactory apology, both to my guest and me, you must fight Turner Ashby. . . ."

The man backed down immediately, saying he had been drinking and making profuse apologies.[6]

Once the war was joined in April 1861, Ashby and his militia reported to Harpers Ferry, where the Rebels had seized the Federal arsenal. In the ensuing weeks there and elsewhere around the Shenandoah, he enhanced his reputation, moving the Confederate inspector general to state: "I visited the position opposite the Point of Rocks, distant twelve miles from [Harpers Ferry], where Captain Ashby of the Virginia cavalry, an excellent officer is stationed. . . . His cavalry is employed in active reconnaissance." In June his troop and others were formed into the 7th Virginia under the ailing Colonel Angus W. McDonald, a sixty-two-year-old West Pointer. Ashby, promoted to lieutenant colonel and second-in-command, would soon move up a notch in rank and replace McDonald.

Ashby's unit saw no action at First Manassas, but remained in the Valley. There in October, while conducting an assault on Bolivar Heights in the rear of Harpers Ferry, he foresaw the value of mobile artillery—light cannon drawn by horses and serviced by cannoneers on horseback. He organized the first such unit and, though he knew nothing of artillery himself, was fortunate in the men who staffed it. They were young, as many cannoneers were, but also graduates of the Virginia Military Institute, and well versed in the mathematics of bombardment. Their leader was Captain R. Preston Chew, eighteen, who before the war ended would command all the horse artillery in Lee's army. Chew would say that his chief, whom he would observe in some one hundred engagements, "was with us constantly on the battlefield," and always "without consciousness of danger . . . and ever alert and quick as lightning to take advantage of any mistake of the enemy."[7]

Two months later, Lieutenant William Poague of Jackson's Rockbridge Artillery, during a sortie to disrupt Union troop movements on the Chesapeake and Ohio Canal, would see Ashby in action for the first time. "The enemy seemed to be searching the whole region with his fire . . . ," he marveled. "Did I dodge? Yes: just as low as my saddle pommel would allow. But who was that man out there walking slowly back and forth . . . with arms folded apparently enjoying a quiet promenade, totally indifferent to the hellish fire. . . . That was Turner Ashby—a man of the coolest courage and finest nerve I ever knew."

Robert L. Dabney, a Presbyterian minister soon to be Jackson's chief of staff, attributed the cavalryman's risk taking to deep sorrow over his brother's death. "He evidently regarded his life as no longer his own . . . wherever death flew thickest, thither he hastened." His seeming immunity to wounds "filled the Federal soldiers with a species of superstitious dread. At the sound of his well-known yell, and the shout of 'Ashby' from his men, they relinquished every thought of resistance and usually fled without pausing to count the odds in their favor." To the residents of the Shenandoah, he was the stuff of legend. "Especially was the enthusiasm of the people stimulated by the chivalrous and modest courage of Ashby, whose name roused the hearts of the youth, like the peal of a clarion."[8]

By late April 1862, just weeks after Kernstown, serious trouble was brewing between Jackson and Ashby. Two events triggered the contretemps. In one instance a company of troopers, perhaps fifty men, were captured when they neglected to post a nighttime guard. In another disaster a second company, sent off on a bridge-burning raid, failed dismally in their mission when most of the men found some applejack and got drunk.

Jed Hotchkiss, who observed the latter fiasco, would say, "I never saw a more disgraceful affair—all owing . . . to the want of discipline. . . . When Ashby's men are with him, they behave gallantly, but when they are away they lack the inspiration of his presence, and being undisciplined they often fail to do any good." Jackson aide Kyd Douglas was more sympathetic: "Had [Ashby] been as full of discipline as he was of leadership his success would have been more fruitful and his reputation still greater. Yet it should be remembered that he had little time for instruction of any kind. From the beginning his only drill ground was the field of battle. . . . He was compelled to organize his troops while on the gallop."

The ordinarily rigid Stonewall, who knew how much he needed Ashby's leadership, was between a rock and a hard place. The problem was that the cavalryman did not see there *was* a problem. He regarded his troopers as an extended Valley family, and had little patience with military structure, fearing it would "cramp, if not crush, [their] spirit." His command now consisted of twenty-one widely scattered companies, each headed by a captain reporting directly to Ashby but otherwise making individual decisions—a recipe for chaos.[9]

Jackson's solution was to assign the 7th Virginia to two of his infantry brigades, so the unit could receive strict and immediate training. Ashby would continue to head his troopers, but in effect would have to ask the brigade commanders, if the army was in advance or in retreat, to *lend* him his men. His reaction was mercurial. He hauled in the support of all the Valley politicians he could reach, basically told his men to go home, and in a stormy meeting in Jackson's tent, submitted his resignation. Then he joined Captain Chew and other officers, telling them, according to Chew, that he would "organize an independent command and operate in the lower Valley and the Piedmont country. All the officers present declared their intention to go with him."

Within hours Jackson would swallow hard and capitulate, revoking his order and restoring the status quo. The next phase of the Valley Campaign was soon to come, and Ashby's talents would be sorely needed. "I became well satisfied that if I persisted in my attempt to increase the efficiency of the cavalry," Jackson later wrote General Lee, "it would produce the contrary effect, as Colonel Ashby's influence, who is very popular with his men, would be thrown against me."[10]

Meanwhile, during these April weeks and into May, the cautious Nathaniel Banks, perhaps fearful of being flanked, was giving Jackson all the slack he could wish. A political appointee and former governor of Massachusetts, he had not pressed Shields's success at Kernstown, instead halting the advance between Harrisonburg and New Market. Thanks to the aggressive efforts of Ashby's cavalry, Banks had no knowledge of where precisely Jackson was in the Conrad's Store area, or where he might be heading. Even worse, he would find that the War Department was taking the bulk of his army, including Shields's division, and sending it elsewhere.

A word is in order here about the topography of the Shenandoah. Lying between the Alleghenies to the west and the Blue Ridge to the east, the Valley extends from Harpers Ferry on the Potomac in the north to Lexington in the south, including such townships as Winchester, Strasburg, and

Harrisonburg. About 165 miles long and 25 miles wide, the Valley is split for some 50 miles by the Massanutten Mountains, which extend from Strasburg to Harrisonburg. At their northern end Strasburg connects with Front Royal to the east, and at their southern end Harrisonburg connects with Conrad's Store. But the Massanuttens are passable only at their midpoint, from New Market to Luray in the east. They divide the Shenandoah into two 50-mile corridors, the wider Great Valley with its vastly better turnpike to the west, and the smaller Luray Valley to the east.

To Jackson the tactical implication of the two corridors was obvious. An army in the Great Valley that did not control the New Market–to–Luray passage across the Massanuttens could move only north or south. But an army in the Luray Valley could still move east through the gaps in the Blue Ridge. Lastly, a force moving up the Great Valley on the turnpike was vulnerable to a foe moving down the Luray Valley and falling on its rear. Helped by the ceaseless demonstrations of Ashby and his troopers, Jackson would be taking full advantage of these corridors.

What Stonewall decided to do first, however, was forestall the possibility that Banks would be reinforced by Union general John C. Fremont, who was operating in the Alleghenies. Stonewall did this by marching west from Conrad's Store in a circuitous route, winning the battle of McDowell on May 8, and driving lead elements of the demoralized Federals back into the mountains. Belatedly hearing this news, Banks—with his now depleted force of 8,000—withdrew down the Valley to Strasburg.

By mid-May Jackson was back at Harrisonburg, ready to reclaim the Shenandoah. His column advanced down the Great Valley toward Strasburg, then—ably screened as always by Ashby's cavalry—crossed the Massanuttens at New Market and entered the Luray Valley. There Jackson was joined by Richard Ewell's division, which previously had been placed under his command. With other reinforcements, his army now was 16,000 strong, giving him a two-to-one advantage over the Federals.

On May 23, the Confederates rushed into Front Royal, overwhelming the surprised garrison and placing them in position to cut off Banks from further retreat. During this operation Ashby swung to the northwest, cutting the Manassas Gap Railroad at Buckton Station. Two spirited charges drove back the Union defenders, allowing him to cut the telegraph lines to Strasburg and burn the station, but the enemy then entrenched, guarding the railroad bridge. Here Ashby, typically reckless and intent on destroying the bridge as well, ordered a third charge and then a fourth—to no avail.

"Forward, boys, forward!" he shouted. "We will get every mother's son of them!"

The casualties were severe, and at least one Rebel believed them needless. "It would have been well if he had retired instead. . . . To charge a covered position under any circumstances is sufficiently dangerous, but doubly so with mounted men."

Ashby's chief regret, however, was that Chew and the horse artillery, off elsewhere, were not in the engagement. "If my little Blakely [gun] were here, these people should not escape."[11]

From Front Royal, Jackson with Ashby in the van moved northwest the next day toward Middletown and the Valley pike, hoping to cut off Banks before he could abandon Strasburg and retreat toward the Potomac. Major Robert Dabney, Jackson's chief of staff, remembered the scene: "When the little village of Middletown came into view, across the broad and level fields, the highway passing through it . . . was seen canopied with a vast cloud of gray dust, and crowded beneath, as far as the eye could reach, with a column of troops. At the sight, the artillery rushed forward in a gallop for a rising ground, whence to tear their ranks with shell. Ashby swooped down upon the right like an eagle; cut through their path; and arrested their escape on that side. . . . In one moment, the way was encumbered by dying horses and men."

Dense columns of enemy infantry and long lines of supply wagons, Jackson soon learned, had been on the pike for hours. "The Federal column was pierced," he said, "but what proportion of its strength had passed north toward Winchester, I had then no means of knowing. Among [their] surviving cavalry the wildest confusion ensued, and they scattered in disorder in various directions, leaving, however, some 200 prisoners, with their equipment, in our hands. A train of wagons was seen disappearing in the distance toward Winchester, and Ashby with his cavalry, some artillery, and a supporting infantry force . . . was sent in pursuit."

The pursuit proved brief. Catching up with the freshly deserted wagons, to which were tethered many spare mounts, the troopers stopped to plunder. "Some of Ashby's men [were seen]," said Dabney bitterly, "with a quickness more suitable to horse-thieves than soldiers, breaking from their ranks, seizing each two or three of the captured horses, and making off across the fields. Nor did these men pause until they had carried their illegal booty to their homes."

Colonel Thomas Munford, leading the 2nd Virginia Cavalry in Dick Ewell's division, was more understanding, pointing out that there were good reasons for the troopers to covet the mounts: "A spavined or jammed horse, or when wounded, cannot carry a sound or an impetuous man. A dead horse cannot be replaced without money, which the man could not procure and the Government failed to supply. The man felt that any moment he was liable to lose his horse."[12]

Jackson must have been seething, but there is no record that he confronted Ashby in this instance for losing control of his men. He undoubtedly had decided he must accept him for what he was—a brilliant but idiosyncratic commander. The next morning, May 25, the Confederates stormed and took Winchester, sending Banks fleeing toward Harpers Ferry and the north bank of the Potomac. Here the situation again called for aggressive cavalry pursuit, but Ashby's men were scattered far and wide with their plunder and had not yet returned, and Ewell's cavalry, due to a misunderstanding, became involved too late. "Never have I seen an opportunity when it was in the power of the cavalry to reap a richer harvest," Jackson would say. "There is good reason for believing, had the cavalry played its part . . . but a small portion of Banks's army would have made its escape to the Potomac."[13]

For the next few days Jackson demonstrated around Harpers Ferry, feinting an invasion of Maryland. During this time, persistent Valley politicians were at last successful in having Ashby named a brigadier general. Despite the Federals' escape, however, Stonewall had achieved a stunning victory. Banks had lost half of his command in killed, wounded, and captured, and he left behind 9,000 small arms, 500,000 rounds of ammunition, two rifled cannon, and immense supplies of food and medicine.

Lincoln and the War Department were alarmed even more by Jackson's triumph at Winchester than they had been by his defeat at Kernstown. Frantic for the safety of Washington, they turned their attention from the coming siege of Richmond and began flooding soldiers into the Shenandoah. Fremont, with 15,000 men, was pressing down from the Alleghenies in the west. Shields, with 10,000, was approaching Manassas Gap in the east; two other divisions, another 20,000, were close behind him. Banks, reinforced to 15,000, was moving up from the Potomac. Some 60,000 Federals were on the chase.

Amid sporadic but heavy rainfall, Jackson now began withdrawing at a rapid pace up the Valley, leaving behind Ashby's cavalry and the Stonewall Brigade to guard the rear. By the afternoon of May 31, virtually all of his seven-mile-long column, wagons filled with spoil in the lead, had cleared Winchester and was on the way to Strasburg. His immediate concern was to pass through that town before Fremont and Shields, assailing the turn-pike from the west and the east, could squeeze him between them. This he did, to some extent because the enemy believed him stronger than he was, but mostly because of Ashby, whose promotion to brigadier had only in-creased his appetite for battle. "On every hill . . . at every bridge," said one Rebel, "he swore to hold his ground or die. He played with death, and dared it everywhere." Sensing his resolve, Jackson now put all the cavalry, including Ewell's, under his command.

On June 2, as Ashby's troopers passed through New Market, they de-stroyed the bridges that connected that town with Luray at the Massanut-tens' midpoint, insuring that Fremont, now pursuing the Rebels up the Great Valley, and Shields, chasing them up the Luray, would not be able to converge. "To prevent Shields from crossing at these two bridges," ex-plained another Confederate, "was . . . to keep him from making any ef-fort to 'head off' Jackson short of Harrisonburg, as well as condemn him to a march of sixty miles over muddy roads to reach a point fifty miles dis-tant from [us], and which [we] were approaching by a good MacAdam road."

The pressure on the pike, however, was incessant. Fremont's van at one juncture came within artillery range of the rear guard, raining down shells and threatening a rout. "This led General Ashby to one of those acts of personal heroism and prompt resources which strikingly marked his char-acter," said Jackson, recounting how his subordinate had leapt from his horse, rallied the survivors, and lay in wait in the woods for the oncoming Federal cavalry. "As they approached within easy range," continued Stonewall, "he poured such an effective fire into their ranks as to empty a number of saddles and check their pursuit."[14]

On June 3, once Jackson's column crossed the North Fork of the Shenandoah, Ashby again distinguished himself, burning the bridge in the face of the enemy. "Before this task was completed," said Major Dabney, "the Federals appeared on the opposite bank, and a skirmish ensued, in which his horse was struck dead, and he himself narrowly escaped. The necessity of replacing this bridge arrested Fremont for a day, and gave the tired Confederates a respite, which they employed in retiring, slowly and unmolested, to Harrisonburg." Here Jackson with the main body left the pike and turned east toward Port Republic, a hamlet on the South Fork of the Shenandoah, as usual leaving Ashby in the rear.[15]

Trotting out of Harrisonburg on June 6, Colonel Sir Percy Wyndham of the 400-man 1st New Jersey Cavalry, accompanied by elements of several other regiments, had one object in mind: capturing or killing Turner Ashby and smashing his command. Wyndham was a British soldier of fortune, a fop who wore his hair in long locks and affected gold lace and "every ornament permissible under regulations," but he was also, on most occasions, a gifted leader. One Valley woman sniffed that the interloper "was a blaze of diamonds, but looked as mean as the rest [of the Yankees]; he is a celebrated cavalry officer & old Abe sent for him to come over to take Ashby."

The Englishman had been boasting that he would best the Shenandoah's idol, and on this day, his emotions must have impaired his judgment. Seeing a line of gray-clad cavalrymen waiting motionless behind a winding stream, he ordered an all-out charge without first reconnoitering. The outcome was predictable. Even as the two lines were meeting head-on, the bulk of Ashby's command emerged from the nearby woods and enveloped the Federals, raking them with enfilading fire and sending them reeling. Wrote a *New York Times* correspondent traveling with Wyndham: "Such an utter scene of rout and demoralization . . . I never before witnessed." In the center of the melee, of course, was Ashby, heedless of the bullets whizzing by. "No use to dodge, boys," he had cried out to his troopers at one point, "they will not one in ten thousand hit you!" The engagement was over in minutes, with the enemy survivors galloping off in complete disorder, leaving behind some sixty prisoners.[16]

Watching the rout, powerless and aghast, was Sir Percy, who soon himself became a prisoner—and the butt of much derision. "Looky yonder, boys!" one threadbare Confederate yelled, pointing in mock wonder at the elegantly dressed Englishman. "There's a Yankee colonel!" By all accounts Wyndham was fuming so much he could hardly speak, but this last comment unloosed an oath-laced protest: "I'm not a Yankee, you _____ Rebel fool!" One of his fellow captives was more subdued: "Percy Wyndham met the man he had so long sought, and I didn't think he'd care about seeing him so again, for we've been smashed all to flinders."

Courtly as ever, Ashby soon quieted his troopers and restored Wyndham's sense of dignity, sending him under guard to Jackson's headquarters.[17]

It was now shortly after 4 p.m., and Ashby knew the Federals in Harrisonburg, once they heard of the debacle, would be sending an even stronger force against him. Rather than withdrawing, he decided to take them on. "General," said Colonel Munford, "you've done a handsome thing already. Do you think they will be as easily fooled again?"

"They have had it their way long enough," was the reply. "I am tired [of] *being crowded* and will make them stop it."

Leaving two guns with a small detachment of Munford's cavalry as a lure on the Port Republic Road, and hiding the rest of the cavalry nearby, Ashby moved with an additional force of some 500 infantrymen through the woods to the right. His plan was to take the Federals in flank when they rushed the guns, and then have Munford complete the job with a charge.

On the enemy came, the 1st Pennsylvania Cavalry supported by the 1st Pennsylvania "Bucktail" Rifles, seemingly according to script. Bradley Johnson, commanding the 1st Maryland Infantry and standing close to Ashby, recalled that the cavalryman's "dark face [was] afire with enthusiasm. His hair and head were as black as a crow. . . . He was pointing out the positions and topography, swinging his arm right and left."

"Look at Ashby enjoying himself," Johnson said to an aide.

Now the script changed for the worse. The Bucktails did not, for the most part, come down the Port Republic Road; they came through the same woods where the would-be Rebel flankers were concealed. The surprise was mutual. Soon the well-disciplined Bucktails took cover behind a protective fence, laying down a heavy fire and turning the tables on their tormentors. "Ashby, seeing at a glance [his men's] disadvantage, galloped to the front and ordered them to charge, and drive the Federals from their vantage ground," said Dabney. "At this moment the horse fell; but extricating himself from the dying animal, and leaping to his feet, he saw his men wavering.

"He shouted, 'Charge men; for God's Sake, charge!' and waved his sword; when a bullet pierced him full in the breast, and he fell dead."[18]

Ashby's prodding nonetheless had the desired result. The Confederates took the fence, poured volley after volley into the retreating foe, and for the second time that day, were triumphant.

Ashby's body was borne to Port Republic athwart the back of a horse, accompanied by a cavalry escort, "crying, most of them, like children." Some women of the town prepared the corpse for burial, pinning a rose over the bullet hole in his chest and his torn jacket. Someone else took a photograph, perhaps the only such likeness taken of a Confederate general killed in action. Jackson took the news of Ashby's death hard. He closed the door to his room, paced about, and doubtless offered silent prayers. "As a partisan officer," he would say, "I never knew his superior."[19]

On June 8 and 9, Jackson culminated his Valley Campaign with decisive victories at Cross Keys and Port Republic. With never more than 16,000 men, he had baffled, outmaneuvered, and bested four times that number of the enemy, giving the Confederates around Richmond precious weeks to prepare their defense of the capital. How much Stonewall owed the difficult and strong-willed Ashby for his startling success cannot be overstated.

TWO
* * * *

THE EAST, JUNE 12–15: STUART'S RIDE AROUND MCCLELLAN

Robert E. Lee, newly in charge of the Army of Northern Virginia, had known twenty-nine-year-old Jeb Stuart since 1852, when Lee was superintendent at West Point and Stuart was a cadet. Now Stuart was his brigadier of cavalry, Richmond was being besieged by George McClellan's Army of the Potomac from the east on both sides of the Chickahominy River, and Lee desperately needed intelligence. He intended to assault and overwhelm the single corps McClellan had north of the Chickahominy (the other four were south of the river) with the bulk of his own command, but first he had to know how far the Federal right flank extended, and how strongly it was fortified.

Following a discussion, Lee commissioned Stuart to make a reconnaissance in force north of the Chickahominy, but, he wrote, the cavalryman was "not to hazard unnecessarily your command, or to attempt what your judgment may not approve . . . but be content to accomplish all the good you can." Stuart had already proven himself as a leader and fighter, but he possessed a larger-than-life personality—and Lee did not want him taking needless chances. "Ardent, impetuous . . . with the headlong courage of a high-spirited boy," was the way one aide described him, "fond of bright colors, of rippling flags, of martial music, and the clash of sabers." But the same aide recognized Jeb as a born soldier. "He had the instinctive power of penetrating his enemy's design, an eye consummate in the choice of ground for fighting . . . and, while reckless, apparently, in attacking, knew well when he ought to retreat."[1]

For the mission Stuart chose the 1st Virginia Cavalry under Colonel Fitzhugh Lee and the 9th Virginia under William Henry Fitzhugh "Rooney" Lee, bolstered by elements of the 4th Virginia and troopers from the Jeff Davis Legion. The force, which included two guns from the horse artillery under Lieutenant James Breathed (Stuart had formed his own mobile artillery a month or two after Ashby), totaled 1,200 men. Jovial Fitz Lee, who had narrowly escaped expulsion from West Point for carousing, was Robert E. Lee's nephew. The burly and handsome Rooney Lee was Lee's second son. Among Jeb's aides were John Singleton Mosby, who would later make a name for himself as an elusive partisan; Heros von Borcke, a Prussian officer on leave as an observer; and John Esten Cooke, a cousin of Stuart's wife.

Born in 1833 in southwestern Patrick County, Virginia, James Ewell Brown "Jeb" Stuart was one of ten children of Elizabeth Pannill, who was fond of moralizing, and Archibald Stuart, a lawyer perhaps overly fond of liquor. His mother would ask each of her sons on his twelfth birthday to swear not to touch alcohol. This young James did, and he remained a teetotaler all his life, as well as a dedicated Christian. Growing up, he was as physical as a boy could be—riding, hunting, and using his fists if necessary. But he showed a sensitive side as well, and enjoyed literature, music, and poetry.

At West Point, Stuart earned an endearing nickname. " 'Beauty Stuart,' he was then universally called," Fitzhugh Lee would say, ". . . . his comrades bestowed that appellation upon him to express their idea of his personal comeliness in inverse ratio to the term employed." Homely he might have been, but lacking in soldierly qualities he was not. By senior year he was second captain of the corps and renowned for his horsemanship. "I well recall his distinguishing characteristics," Fitz Lee continued, "which were a strict attention to his military duties . . . an immediate and almost thankful acceptance of a challenge to fight from any cadet who might in any way find himself aggrieved, and a clear, metallic, ringing voice."[2]

Following graduation in 1854, Stuart met and married Flora Cooke, the daughter of then Lieutenant Colonel Philip St. John Cooke of Virginia. He fought for several years against the Cheyenne, and later helped Robert E. Lee put down John Brown's insurrection at Harpers Ferry.

When Virginia seceded, he offered his services to the Confederacy, and soon was colonel of the 1st Virginia Cavalry. At First Manassas in 1861, a battle that was unsuited for mounted action, Stuart showed his initiative by borrowing an artillery battery and blocking the enemy attempt to turn the Rebel left, contributing mightily to the victory.

There would be plenty of time for Jeb to establish his cavalry credentials, however, in the months to come. Promoted to brigadier, he would be leading his troopers in action after action. "He was so brave a man himself," said one comrade-in-arms, "that he never seemed to attribute unworthy motives to his men, and this was one of the secrets of his great influence over them in action. They were ashamed to be anything but brave where he was."

Stuart in his personal life, meanwhile, was in a fury. His father-in-law had elected to stay with the Union and, in so doing, Jeb felt, sullied the family's honor. To Flora's brother, Confederate officer John R. Cooke, he would write, "He will regret it but once, and that will be continually." Nor could he bear that his son, who had been named for his grandfather, "should keep any part of his previous Christian name." Philip St. George Cooke Stuart would henceforth be known as James Ewell Brown Stuart Jr.[3]

Leaving the Richmond area early on the morning of June 12, Stuart's column headed first to the northwest, ostensibly to join Jackson in the Valley. Jeb as usual cut a splendid figure in the saddle. "If ever human being *looked* his character," said Esten Cooke, "it was Stuart, in his short fighting jacket, heavy with gold braid, his huge gauntlets, and boots reaching to the knees, his hat with its black feather, his saber and pistol, his rattling spurs, and his gay, alert, off-hand bearing."[4]

Soon the Confederates swerved to the northeast and, after covering more than twenty miles, camped at Ashland, near the Pamunkey River. Before dawn the next day they turned east, plunging into enemy territory. Stuart at this juncture, just before reaching Hanover Court House, sent Mosby and two scouts ahead. There they encountered a small contingent of blue-clad troopers, who quickly wheeled and made off. When Stuart heard this, he ordered Fitz Lee around the courthouse in a wide detour, hoping to cut them off before they spread the alarm. But Lee got bogged down in swampland, and the enemy escaped, heading south toward Mechanicsville.

Moving now southeast, parallel to the Pamunkey, the column passed through Hanover Court House and then Enon Church—deeper into territory guarded, ironically, by the cavalry of General Philip St. George Cooke. But Cooke would accept wild reports that Stuart's cavalry had been bolstered by several brigades of infantry; he would procrastinate before organizing a pursuit, and would not be a factor. "A vigorous pursuit might greatly have embarrassed Stuart," admitted Major H. B. McClellan, who would become Stuart's adjutant [and who incidentally was a cousin of the Union general], "but he was favored by the uncertainty of the Federal officers as to the character of his command."[5]

Not until the afternoon, fourteen miles past Hanover at Totopotomoy Creek, did the Confederates encounter any real resistance. Rooney Lee's 9th Virginia was in the lead, with a squadron under Captain William Latane at the point. No sooner had the men crossed the stream when they encountered some 100 Federal troopers blocking the road.

Stuart unhesitatingly gave the order: "Form fours! Draw sabers! Charge!" Latane, a twenty-nine-year-old doctor and plantation owner, headed straight for his opposite number, Union Captain William Royall. Latane was killed, pierced by several bullets; Royall went down, severely wounded by Latane's saber. The wild melee lasted only a few minutes. "Swords clashed, pistols and carbines banged, yells, shouts, cheers resounded," said a participant. "Then the Federal line was seen to give back, and take to headlong flight. . . . The men went wild with this—to many of them—their first fight."[6]

Fitz Lee's 1st Virginia, now moving to the fore, pushed on to the village of Old Church, where they took possession of the enemy camp and captured some members of his regiment in the peacetime army, the old U.S. 2nd Cavalry. The prisoners called Fitz "Lieutenant," and inquired about comrades serving with the Confederacy. Their captor, just as friendly and curious, likewise made small talk and asked about old friends—almost as if he was at a reunion—even as his men were destroying the camp and burning whatever they could not take with them.

Stuart knew at this point what he had been sent to find out: the Federal right flank near the Pamunkey was in the air and vulnerable. "The infantry posts did not extend to within several miles of the river," said John Mosby. "For a considerable distance on his right, therefore, McClellan's communications were not covered by his infantry." But Stuart had no intention of returning the way he had come. Instead he would keep on riding, cutting telegraph lines and burning bridges behind him, circling the entire Federal army! *That* would be glorious sport!

"The danger was all in front; not behind us," Mosby said approvingly. "A man of mediocrity would have been satisfied with what he had done; [but] to have gone back would have been a grand anti-climax to such a beginning."[7]

Mosby's point is not entirely accurate—the danger was everywhere. To the south and west of Stuart lay the camps of McClellan's army, and by now the Federals must have been aroused in earnest. To retrace his route through Hanover Court House, even if he escaped their infantry, made it all but certain he would face large numbers of cavalry. Far better, Jeb must have thought, to ride ahead of the pursuit, southeast to Tunstall's Station and then directly south to the Chickahominy, crossing the river at one of the lower fords.

"I think the quicker we move now the better," said Esten Cooke when he heard Stuart's decision. Daylight on June 13 was fast fading.

"Right," said Stuart, "tell the column to move on at a trot."

Nearing Tunstall's Station on the Richmond & York Railroad, McClellan's main supply line, one of Lieutenant Breathed's guns became mired in mud. The troopers pushed on, leaving him to extricate the piece. Barely had Stuart swept into the station, overwhelming the garrison and cutting the wires, when a locomotive approached. The Confederates threw up a hasty barricade on the tracks, but their rifle fire had little effect, and temporarily lacking Breathed's cannon, they could not stop the train. They contented themselves with torching the station and numerous supply wagons, and then turned south to spend the rest of the night at Talleysville.

In the midst of the ride, Stuart, ever conscientious behind his carefree manner, began to worry that some of his men may have lost their way in the darkness. "Where is Rooney Lee?" he asked Cooke at one point.

"I think he moved on, General."

"Do you *know* it?"

"No, but I believe it."

"Will you *swear* to it? He may take the wrong road, and the column will get separated."

Cooke galloped on ahead to find Rooney, and learned that all was well.

"Good!" said Stuart when he received the news. Remarked Cooke, "I never heard in human accents such an expression of relief."

In Talleysville the Confederates found huge supplies of stores, to which they helped themselves with glee. The repast included canned meats, sausages, pickles, preserves, fruits, cakes, crackers, and candy, not to mention wine and spirits. Heros von Borcke, a 250-pound gourmand with a girth to match, was in his element. "My parched tongue was cleaving to the roof of my mouth, when one of our men galloped up to me and held out a bottle of champagne. . . . Never in my life have I enjoyed a bottle of wine so much," he would say.[8]

Shortly after midnight on June 14, the column again was under way, and by dawn it had reached Christian's Ford on the Chickahominy. Here Rooney Lee in the van discovered that recent rains had swollen and engorged the river. "Accompanied by a few of his men," wrote Major H. B. McClellan, "[Lee] entered the angry water and essayed to reach the opposite side by swimming. He did reach it, but only after encountering imminent peril. . . . Colonel Lee would not consent to be separated from his regiment, and recrossed the river." Axes were found, and trees were felled in an effort to create a temporary bridge. To no avail. "As their tops reached the water, the current swept them down the stream as if they had been reeds."

Cooke approached Lee, who was sitting exhausted on the riverbank. "What do you think?" he asked.

"Well, Captain," Rooney replied, "I think we are caught."

At this juncture Stuart reached the ford. "Every face showed anxious care, save that of Stuart himself," said McClellan, "who sat upon his horse, stroking his long beard, as was his custom in moments of serious thought." Jeb soon learned of a possible alternate crossing, the remains of an old bridge a mile downstream. "Enough of the debris of the old bridge remained to facilitate the construction of another," continued McClellan. "A large, abandoned warehouse stood near at hand, and a party was at once set to work . . . to tear down this house and convey the timbers to the river. Never did men work with more alacrity. . . . Within three hours [the bridge] was ready for cavalry and artillery and by 1 p.m. the whole command had crossed."

The Confederates quickly set the jerry-built structure afire. Ten minutes later, while it was still burning, the first of the Federal pursuers loomed on the north bank.

"That was a tight place at the river, General," Cooke would tell Stuart. "If the enemy had come down on us, you would have been compelled to have surrendered."

"No," Stuart replied, "one other course was left."

"What was that?"

"To die game."[9]

Stuart now led his weary men to Charles City Court House and thence the 35 miles to Richmond, sweeping around the enemy's left flank and completing the 150-mile "Ride Around McClellan." On the morning of June 15, Jeb reported his findings to Lee. The next day his exploit would be hailed in the Southern papers, to his unabashed delight, with such head-lines as "Brilliant Reconnaissance" and "Unparalleled Maneuver."

In truth Stuart owed much of his success to the bumbling of his father-in-law, General Cooke. The latter would see no further field service, and would enjoy a long life, not dying until 1894 at age eighty-five. In stark contrast was the violent end of young William Latane, the sole Confeder-ate killed during the ride. His death inspired a painting called the *Burial of Latane*, which depicted grieving women praying over his body in a peace-ful glen. Engravings made from the picture later could be found in count-less Southern homes.

Buoyed by Stuart's report, Robert E. Lee would launch his offensive north of the Chickahominy on June 26, triggering a series of clashes that came to be known as the Seven Days battles. His attempt to destroy the single en-emy corps north of the river with a crushing blow did not materialize, in part because of Stonewall Jackson's tardiness, but it did result in lifting the siege of Richmond and forcing McClellan to make a humiliating retreat.

THREE
* * * *

THE WEST, JULY 6-27: FORREST'S FIRST TENNESSEE RAID

Nathan Bedford Forrest joined the Confederate army as a private in 1861, just before his fortieth birthday. An affluent, self-made plantation owner and city alderman in Memphis, Tennessee, he had made most of his money in slave trading, a not entirely respectable pursuit among the city's elite. His most notable features were his eyes—narrow, dark, and penetrating—and his solid, determined jaw. He stood six-foot-two, weighed 180 pounds, and possessed great strength. Ordinarily he was re-served and soft-spoken—until he was crossed or felt threatened, either by an individual or Federal troops. Then he would unleash his wrath with a controlled violence all the more frightening for the intelligence behind it.

Within a year of his enlistment Forrest was a colonel of cavalry, and had distinguished himself in several engagements. He did not drink or smoke, but in camp or battle could swear a blue streak. His orders were short and to the point, and he did not brook contradiction or excuses. "Shoot any man who won't fight!" he would tell his troopers, who knew he would set the example. His tactics, an acquaintance would say, called for hurling "his entire force against [the enemy] in the fiercest and most warlike manner possible. He would thus overawe and demoralize . . . at the very start" and finish off his adversaries "by a constant repetition of blows."[1]

Before the war ended, he would be wounded four times, have twenty-nine mounts shot from under him, and, he claimed, kill at least thirty men in hand-to-hand combat. Though his boyhood schooling was scant—no more than six months—and his military education nonexistent, he proved an instinctive leader. "Get there first with the most men," he would say, and the words became his mantra.[2]

Born on July 13, 1821, in a remote settlement in Bedford County, Tennessee, the aptly named Nathan Bedford Forrest was the eldest son of William, a sturdy blacksmith, and Mariam Beck, by all accounts a remarkably strong-willed woman. He was one of twins, the other being his sister Fanny, and eventually he would have eight brothers and three sisters, although two of his brothers and all his sisters succumbed early on to typhoid fever. When he was thirteen, the family—in reduced circumstances—moved from middle Tennessee to even more remote Tippah County in northern Mississippi, where they scratched out a living on some leased farmland. In 1837 his father died, and Nathan found himself the head of the household.

For the next few years he, his mother, and his siblings continued to labor from predawn into the late night, clearing land, planting corn and wheat and oats, and fashioning and sewing buckskin clothing and shoes. Through thrift and backbreaking work, their fortunes slowly improved, and they began acquiring and raising modest numbers of cattle and horses. By 1842, with his mother about to remarry, Nathan felt he could strike out on his own, and he entered into a partnership with his uncle Jonathan, who had a livestock business in Hernando, a town in northern Mississippi. From the start he did well, showing a shrewd talent for buying and trading at a profit, and building a reputation for honesty and diligence.

In 1845 he became involved in a quarrel that showed his mettle. Three members of a planter family, the Matlocks, together with their overseer, decided to settle a grievance with Jonathan Forrest by using their guns. Before they were halfway across the Hernando town square, everyone knew there would be trouble. Jonathan faced them, but his nephew straightaway came to his side, telling the Matlocks, in the words of a biographer, "that the quarrel was none of his, but that four men against one was not fair. . . . His voice was gentle, so gentle that one might wonder why it was not muffled by the stone-like [set] of his jaw."

One of the callers shot at Nathan but missed, probably hitting his uncle, who went down with a mortal wound. In the ensuing fusillade, the young man "emptied the two barrels of his pocket pistol, and two Matlocks dropped. . . . Only the third Matlock and [the overseer] were left to send hot lead. . . . One of the balls struck him, but not hard enough to take him off his feet. . . . Empty-handed, [he] now faced the two remaining assailants. There was no time to reload."

Here one of the bystanders threw Nathan a razor-sharp Bowie knife. "[He] took it in his left hand and charged his enemies. Their nerve had been badly shaken, and for [someone] to hold them, armed with pistols, in such contempt disturbed it further. Before they could rally . . . he had slashed and disabled the third Matlock. [The overseer] did not wait his turn . . . and faced his feet in the opposite direction." Incredibly, Jonathan Forrest was the only fatality. The Matlocks were tried for murder and imprisoned for some time. Nathan, pleading self-defense, received no punishment; indeed, his stock among the townspeople rose all the more, with the result that he was named town constable.[3]

That same year, following the briefest of courtships in which he confronted and even threatened rival suitors, he won the hand of Mary Ann Montgomery, eighteen, a genteel and well-educated young woman whom he met while she and her carriage were mired in a mud-hole. Carrying her to dry land, Nathan asked if he might call; two visits later, they became engaged. Despite his acceptance in the Hernando community, there was family resistance to the betrothal. The bride-to-be's uncle and guardian, the Rev. Samuel Montgomery Cowan, put his reservations bluntly.

"Why, Bedford, I couldn't consent," he said. "You cuss and gamble, and Mary Ann is a Christian girl."

The rough-spoken Nathan, who always tried to better himself, rode over the objection. "I know it," he replied, "and that's just why I want her."[4]

The Rev. Cowan performed the ceremony.

Nathan Forrest's business interests in the town progressed from livestock to real estate and slave trading, and despite occasional setbacks, with each passing year he became increasingly successful. During this period he and Mary Ann would have two children, a boy named William and a girl named Fanny—the latter, like his twin sister, dying early of illness.

In 1851 Forrest and his wife recrossed the Mississippi-Tennessee border and relocated to Memphis, an expanding and bustling steamboat city where, despite Mary Ann's reservations, he concentrated on slave trading.

Years later a colleague, trying to justify Forrest's headlong participation in the buying and selling of human beings, illustrated the self-deluding attitude of the day. "[He] was kind, humane and extremely considerate of his slaves," the man said. ". . . He seemed to exercise the same influence over these creatures that in a greater degree he exercised over the soldiers who served him as devotedly. . . . When a slave was purchased for him his first act was to turn him over to his Negro valet . . . with instructions to wash him thoroughly and put clean clothes on him from head to foot. . . . The slaves who were thus transformed were proud of belonging to him."[5]

Though slave trading—as opposed to slave owning—was still looked down upon by the Memphis establishment, Forrest by 1857 nonetheless had become a prominent resident of the city. His business was giving him an income of some $100,000 annually, a huge sum at the time. When a gambler named John Able shot down an unarmed man on the street, therefore, it was understandable that the mayor, perhaps remembering Forrest's service as a Hernando constable, should name him to a committee of vigilance. The group was charged with keeping the peace until the prisoner could be brought to trial. Heedless of his own safety, Forrest took the lead in this effort, challenging a mob and foiling attempts to lynch the man.

Elected and reelected to the board of aldermen the next two years, the intense Forrest plunged into the arcana of the part-time job, showing a strong progressive streak. He took on the blue laws so that livery stables could remain open on Sundays; pushed for a new bridge because the old one would "fall down in three weeks"; and declared that the high cost of maintaining the roads meant that some politicians "were in league with local gravel contractors." Commented the mayor, "When he was an official he never offered a resolution . . . on any subject, no matter how unpopular it might be at first, that he did not stick to it and work at it until he carried it triumphantly through."[6]

In 1860 Forrest shut down his slave-trading concern in Memphis—perhaps he was ready for a less controversial career—and devoted himself to growing cotton on his plantations in Coahoma County, Mississippi—land he had acquired over the years. Soon he was raising a thousand bales annually and showing a profit of $30,000, small change compared to his previous income, but still an impressive sum. Then came secession, his enlistment as a private—together with his youngest brother Jeffrey and fifteen-year-old son Willie—and the war that brought him fame.

Forrest's tenure as an enlisted man was brief. The governor of Tennessee soon authorized him to raise a command, and by October 1861, at his own expense, he had outfitted a mounted battalion. This unit participated in several engagements in southern Kentucky, which at this juncture had not taken sides in the conflict. The most notable of these cavalry skirmishes, involving no more than a couple of hundred men on each side, occurred in December near the village of Sacramento. Here Forrest first employed the technique in battle he often would use, dismounting troopers in his front to fight on foot, thus keeping the foe engaged while the rest of his men turned the flanks. Then when the enemy was sufficiently confused, he remounted his troopers, sounded the cry "Charge!" and closed the pincers.

In the forefront of the attack, of course, was Forrest. "Seeing the movement upon their flanks," wrote two contemporaries of the Sacramento affair, ". . . the Federals could not be made to stand the brunt of the Confederate charge, but broke in the utmost disorder." For three miles the pursuit continued, until one enemy squadron turned to give battle. Forrest, in advance of his men, galloped toward a private and two officers. "Shooting the trooper, whose ball had passed through his collar, Forrest was assaulted simultaneously by the two officers with their sabers; but, eluding the full force of their thrusts by bending his body . . . their swordpoints only touched his shoulder." He promptly shot the one and thrust his saber into the other, sending them crashing to the ground. Though unhorsed himself in the melee, he suffered no injury.

Forrest's men now were up, finishing off the rest of the enemy squadron, whose resistance had ensured their comrades' escape. One of his officers would marvel at the change his superior underwent in combat. "It was the first time I had seen the Colonel in the face of the enemy," he said, "and when he rode up to me in the thick of the action I could scarcely believe him to be the same man. . . . His face flushed till it bore a striking resemblance to a painted Indian warrior's, and his eyes. . . . were blazing with the intense glare of a panther's springing upon its prey."[7]

In February 1862 Forrest and his cavalry were dispatched to Fort Donelson on the Cumberland River in northwest Tennessee, where they performed valiantly as Ulysses S. Grant sought to tighten the noose around the stronghold. There one evening his commanders told him that the enemy's campfires indicated the fort was encircled and they had no choice but to surrender the 15,000-man command. Forrest, because he knew the Federals had left open a road down which a withdrawal might be made, made no attempt to conceal his disgust. He had sent out scouts who, "going by the road up the bank of the river, returned without seeing any of the enemy, only fires, which I believe to be the old campfires . . .

the wind, being very high, had fanned them into a blaze." Surrendering was not in his lexicon and never would be.

Reported a Union officer who later learned of the council of war: "The bold trooper had no qualms upon the subject. He assembled his men, all as hardy as himself, and [within hours] . . . moved out and plunged into a slough formed by backwater from the river. An icy crust covered its surface, the wind blew fiercely, and the darkness was unrelieved by a star. There was fearful floundering as the command followed him. At length he struck dry land, and was safe. He was next heard of at Nashville."[8]

April 6 found Forrest at Shiloh Church on the Tennessee River in the southwest of the state, again chaffing under commanders who, he felt, were less than gifted. Though the first day's fighting had favored the Confederates, his scouting during the night made it clear that the Federals were being heavily reinforced. "I have been way down along the riverbank, close to the enemy," he would say. "They are receiving reinforcements by the thousands, and if this army does not move and attack them [before daylight] . . . it will be whipped like hell before ten-o'clock tomorrow."

He was paid no heed, with the predictable result that dawn saw 45,000 Federals surging forward in an irresistible wave. Forrest, guarding the right flank, was heavily engaged but could do little.

The next day, the 8th, while the army was withdrawing to Corinth, Mississippi, he was given the task of guarding the rear. When an Illinois cavalry unit became disorganized while crossing a stream, he was watchful and ready. Forrest led 350 troopers into their midst, melting the command and sending it back into the ranks of supporting infantry, which in turn dissolved. "At twenty paces the Confederates gave a volley with their shotguns, a formidable weapon at that short distance, and rushed in with pistols and sabers," wrote his military biographers. "The Federal cavalry broke in disorder . . . running over their own infantry in their panic . . . all around was a medley of cavalry and infantry, scattering and running to and fro. . . . The slaughter was considerable."

Forrest's ardor, however, almost was his undoing. His hell-for-leather charge brought him, alone, within fifty yards of the main enemy body, even while his men were falling back with their prisoners. Shots rang from all sides, and one struck him on the left side, above the hip, and penetrated almost to the spine. "His right leg, benumbed by the blow . . . was left hanging useless in the stirrup." Bluecoats were screaming for blood, shouting, "Kill him!" "Shoot him!" "Stick him!" "Knock him off his horse!" His horse, too, was wounded—mortally as it turned out—but Forrest somehow turned the mount about, cleared the way with well-aimed pistol shots, and galloped to safety. His painful wound would not heal for the next two months. The bullet, not immediately found, would be removed by his regimental surgeon—without anesthesia.[9]

On July 6, in an effort to forestall and frustrate Union general Don Carlos Buell's efforts to move south from Nashville and take Chattanooga, Forrest launched an audacious cavalry raid into middle Tennessee, intending to disrupt communications and create general havoc behind enemy lines. He had just been nominated for the rank of brigadier, and this new assignment marked the first of his ventures into semi-independent command, a role that perfectly suited his temperament. (About the same time, with the same purpose, the raider Colonel John Hunt Morgan led a similar incursion into central Kentucky; that story will be told in the next chapter.)

Forrest's cavalry, a mixed bag, consisted of the 8th Texas, the 1st and 2nd Georgia, a battalion of Tennesseans, and two companies of Kentuckians—some 1,400 men in all. Perhaps the toughest of these units was the 8th Texas, known as Terry's Rangers, composed of lean, laconic cattlemen who from their earliest years had been schooled in the care of horses and the use of firearms. With this handful of troopers, Forrest proposed to delay the advance of Buell's 40,000-man army.

Leaving Chattanooga, his small force moved north across the Tennessee River, passed through Altamont near the summit of the Cumberlands, then McMinnville, and late on July 12 stopped for food and fodder at Woodbury, 18 miles away from the raid's first target, the rail town of Murfreesboro. It was there that Forrest learned from frantic women residents that most of their menfolk, accused of aiding the Confederacy, had earlier been seized by Union soldiers and brought to Murfreesboro. He promptly informed the women that they were not to worry; they would soon have their men back.[10]

Before swooping down on Murfreesboro the next morning, Forrest learned from scouts that the enemy was bedded down in three camps. Forrest divided his own force accordingly. The Texans were to engage the 9th Michigan and the 7th Pennsylvania Cavalry to the right of the town; he with the 2nd Georgia would storm into its center, aiming to take the jail, courthouse, and hotel; the rest of his troopers were to gallop through the streets and confront the 3rd Minnesota beyond the village.

Captain William Richardson was in the jail on the 13th, sharing a cell with a spy named James Paul, and both prisoners were awaiting execution. Suddenly he heard "a strange noise like the roar of an approaching storm. . . . In a very few seconds we were sure we could discern the clatter of horses' feet upon the hard turnpike. . . . in a moment more there could be no doubt as to the riders. . . . There came to our ears with heartfelt welcome the famous Rebel yell." The guards fled, but before leaving, some Union soldiers fired at the inmates and one lit a bundle of papers and started a fire. "To our horror we realized he was determined to burn us to death before the rescuing party could break open the door. . . . It was not until some of our men came in with a heavy iron bar that the grating was bent back sufficiently . . . to permit us to be dragged through."

Forrest appeared, asking if the prisoners were safe. He was told they were, but that the fire had been deliberately set, and the guards had taken refuge in the courthouse.

"Never mind, we'll get them!" he rasped.

Richardson was transfixed by his zeal. "His eyes were flashing as if on fire, his face was deeply flushed."[11]

Following a lengthier struggle, the courthouse and hotel likewise were taken. Caught by surprise and captured, together with members of his staff, was General Thomas Crittenden.

Forrest now turned his attention to other fronts. The 7th Pennsylvania had been overrun, but the 9th Michigan had rallied, and behind makeshift barricades, it was giving the Texans all they could handle. The 3rd Minnesota beyond the town, though much reduced, also had dug in. "It was now about 1 p.m.," wrote Forrest's military chroniclers, and ". . . among many of his officers there was manifest a perilous want of confidence. . . . Some officers urged [him] to rest content with what had been accomplished and quit the field." Forrest would have none of this second-guessing. Dismounting all the men he could spare and sending them to the Texans' aid, he ordered them to lay down such a heavy fire that the 9th Michigan would overestimate their numbers. Then he sent the Federal commander a dire and terse ultimatum: "Colonel—I must demand an unconditional surrender . . . or I will have every man put to the sword. You are aware of the overpowering force I have at my command. This demand is made to prevent the further effusion of blood."[12]

The bluff worked, and the 9th Michigan surrendered. Forrest then sent the same threat to the 3rd Minnesota—with identical results.

There was one order of business though before leaving Murfreesboro. "After the fighting had ceased and the Federal prisoners were brought together," said Captain Richardson, ". . . Forrest came to me and said: 'They tell me these men treated you inhumanly while in jail. Point them out to me.'

"I told him there was but one man I wished to call his attention to, and that was the one who had set fire to the jail. Forrest asked me to go along the line with him and point the man out. . . .

"A few hours later, when the list of the private soldiers was being called, the name of this man was heard and no one answered.

"Forrest said: 'Pass on, it's all right.' "[13]

The raid thus far had been hugely successful. Read the official report: "Forrest . . . captured two brigadier generals [besides Crittenden, acting brigadier W. W. Duffield], staff and field officers, and 1,200 men; burned $200,000 worth of stores; captured sufficient stores with those burned to amount to $500,000; 60 wagons; 300 mules; 150 or 200 horses; and field battery of four pieces; destroyed the railroad and depot. Had to retreat to McMinnville owing to large number of prisoners to be guarded. Loss 16 or 18 killed, 25 or 30 wounded."

Falling back, Forrest solved the prisoner problem with dispatch. "Separating the Federal officers from their men, and putting the former in motion for McMinnville, escorted by a company of cavalry," said his campaign historians, "he drew up the [rest], and promised, if enough would volunteer as drivers of the wagon-train and artillery as far as McMinnville, that he would there parole the whole band and let them make their way homeward to see their families. This proposition was received with hearty cheers." The officers, meanwhile, were sent subsequently with a small guard to Rebel headquarters in Knoxville.[14]

Following a few days of rest, on July 18 Forrest advanced once more, north to Lebanon, Tennessee, hoping likewise to take that garrison by surprise. But the bluecoats there learned of his coming, and retreated to heavily fortified Nashville. He kept at their heels, however, following and tearing up the tracks of the Nashville & Chattanooga Railroad, destroying three rail bridges and a depot, and on July 21 throwing the city into panic by demonstrating within sight of its ramparts. Then, his mission accomplished, he calmly withdrew toward Murfreesboro.

Union general Buell, all but apoplectic, had put General William Nelson on Forrest's trail, but Nelson, closing in on Murfreesboro days later, found that his adversary had evaded the trap and retreated still farther south to McMinnville. "Mr. Forrest shall have no rest," Nelson promised. "I will hunt him myself." His vow would not be kept. On July 27, with Nelson nearing McMinnville, Forrest simply moved south and west to harass Manchester, attacking the garrison there and keeping one jump ahead of pursuit before ending his raid. Nelson simply could not keep up. His foot soldiers were spent—and his cavalry ineffectual. "With infantry in this hot weather," he would admit, "it is a hopeless task to chase Forrest's command mounted on race horses."[15]

FOUR
* * * *

THE WEST, JULY 4–22:
MORGAN'S FIRST KENTUCKY RAID

John Hunt Morgan, unlike the more heavy-handed Forrest, made his reputation as the quintessential guerrilla, employing methods that could be both terrifying and theatrical. His harassment of pickets is a case in point. Early in the war, most commanders had an unspoken agreement not to fire on each other's sentries unless a general attack was under way. Northern pickets, in fact, often exchanged coffee with their Southern counterparts, who bartered with tobacco.

Morgan would have none of this. He and his men commonly rode through the night, crept up on enemy pickets before dawn, and then blasted them with shotguns. "Every flash [of a gun] was followed by a groan," said Basil Duke, his brother-in-law and second-in-command, "and, by the quick, vivid light, we could see the men we hit writhing on the ground." Wrote a Northern reporter: "Skulking freebooters who thus come within our lines, committing robbery and murder, and making observation of our position, are spies, and should, when taken, be promptly put to death."

The cavalryman equally relished the theatrical, sometimes putting on civilian clothes or dressing himself and his troopers in blue uniforms, and then using such subterfuges to capture supply trains or disarm enemies. On one occasion, posing as a Union officer, Morgan confronted six Federals and, on a pretext, ordered them to surrender their weapons. When one of them learned he was now a prisoner, he was outraged.

"I can whip you sure!" he sputtered.

"Never mind, we will take good care of you," the ever-courtly Morgan replied. "Your pay will go on, and you will run no risk of being killed."[1]

Often it seemed that he felt the war was a game—a lethal one, of course, but one in which he was the principal player. With the help of aide Richard Ellsworth, he became expert in raiding train stations, tapping the telegraph wires, and intercepting and contradicting enemy orders. Nor could he resist gloating, once sending Union General Jeremiah T. Boyle, commander of the District of Kentucky, the following: "Good morning, Jerry! This telegraph is a great institution. My friend Ellsworth has in his portfolio all your dispatches. . . . Do you want copies?"

Before the infuriated Boyle could rush troops to the station, Morgan had sent a second wire and moved on. "Goodbye, Jerry. Regards to Mrs. Boyle."

Returning with captives another time, Morgan cantered into then Southern-controlled Murfreesboro, Tennessee, and like an accomplished actor, amid "heartfelt cheers and waving of handkerchiefs" he bowed and addressed the woman whom he was courting and who soon would be his bride. "I present you with your prisoners," he said. "What disposal should be made of them?"

The young lady was equal to the scenario. "You have performed your part so well," she said, "we are willing to entrust it all to you." The captives speedily were sent to prison camps, there to await parole.

Morgan's fame, although he was still only a company commander, was fast spreading. To the Louisville *Courier*, he was "a thieving, pillaging murderer for whom hanging was none too good." Journalist Whitelaw Reid, no lover of the Rebels, would state the obvious: "In early 1862 a new name (is) growing into popular favor and fear. . . . Morgan and his men [are occupying] as much popular attention in Kentucky and along the border as [Pierre] Beauregard and [Robert E.] Lee."[2]

This unconventional cavalier came into the world on June 1, 1825, in Huntsville, Alabama, the first of ten children of Calvin Morgan, a less-than-successful businessman and colonel of militia, and Henrietta Hunt, daughter of one of the richest men in Kentucky. Within a few years Calvin moved his family to Lexington, where he managed his father-in-law's plantations and kindred enterprises. There, bolstered by Hunt connections and wealth, he set down roots.

John Hunt Morgan grew up in the front rank of the city's elite, and like most such young men, became well versed in riding, hunting, and racing. He attended Transylvania College, where he was an indifferent student but enthusiastic carouser and, it appears, a participant in a much bally-hooed duel. Neither party was hurt, but the school decided to crack down on such practices, and he was expelled for the remainder of the term. He never resumed his formal education.

Volunteering for the Mexican War in 1846 with his brother Calvin, he became a lieutenant in the 1st Kentucky Cavalry, and the next year partic-ipated in the triumph at Buena Vista, experiencing the grimness of hand-to-hand combat. He enjoyed military life, and sought to remain in the service, but despite his best efforts, he could not win a commission in the peacetime army.

Morgan returned to Lexington, and in 1848 married eighteen-year-old Rebecca "Becky" Bruce, whose even temperament balanced his own im-pulsiveness. With his brother, for the next dozen years he engaged with profitable results in hemp and wool trading and manufacturing. Like Bed-ford Forrest, he also traded in slaves, frequently renting them out as la-borers. During this period, his father and maternal grandfather died, and his mother, now wealthy in her own right, provided both guidance and capital.

With the war looming, Morgan found himself a bona fide member of the Lexington establishment: a successful businessman, the inheritor of the Hunt tradition, a role model for his numerous siblings, even a captain of militia—the so-called Lexington Rifles. His sole regret was that Re-becca's physical problems, which had increasingly made her an invalid, had left them childless. Then on July 21, 1861, the same day that First Manassas was being fought, his wife mercifully passed away, and he turned his full attention to the conflict.

Morgan had known Rebecca's death was coming, and for months before he therefore had withheld his commitment to the Confederacy. Now in September 1861, he saw that Kentucky's attempts at neutrality were com-ing to a close. Federal troops were lodged in Louisville, their sympathizers controlled Frankfort, and the legislature had opted for the Union. Senti-ment throughout the state, moreover, was at least three to one in favor of the Federal government. With Lexington on the cusp of occupation, he fled the city. His departure, with seventeen men and two wagonloads of guns, was made in dead of night—an inauspicious start. Within weeks after crossing the Green River and reaching the relative safety of Bowling Green, however, he was a captain of Rebel cavalry, with a company of some eighty troopers.

These largely were the men, in small detachments, that Morgan for the rest of 1861 and into early 1862 employed in his hit-and-run escapades. Meanwhile, the main body of Confederate troops, falling back before the enemy, was evacuating Bowling Green and Nashville and, in February, establishing its headquarters at Murfreesboro, Tennessee. It was there that Morgan met twenty-one-year-old Martha "Mattie" Ready, the flirtatious daughter of a former U.S. congressman, when her father invited Morgan to his home for dinner. "Tell Mattie that Captain Morgan is a widower and a little sad," Mr. Ready said, sending a messenger ahead. "I want her to sing for him." Before the year was out, she would be his bride.[3]

Promoted in April to colonel and now leading a squadron of some 300 troopers, Morgan, like Bedford Forrest, served at blood-soaked Shiloh. There in the midst of the carnage, when a brigade of Kentucky infantry cracked the enemy line, Morgan sounded the charge and sent his men forward in support—with mixed results. "The attack resembled a wild horse race more than a military movement," said one biographer. ". . . It was a crowded mass that converged on the Federals, who fired one volley and retreated." Basil Duke went down with a wound, a dozen others were killed and wounded, and Morgan chose not to follow up. He dismounted his men and took cover, even as the overall Southern front advanced. "Morgan was true to form," maintained the biographer. "In a regular battle the true partisan will be reluctant to expose his men to danger. . . . He will seek to avoid a decisive confrontation. . . . Morgan could not bring himself to play his cards—the odds of losing his men were too great."

Later, during the Southern retreat to Corinth, Mississippi, Morgan was more in his metier, falling on the enemy in swift and vicious sorties and delaying the pursuit. The newspapers of the day, eager for heroes, magnified these exploits. Published accounts would extol him, claiming that the Confederate ordnance and supply wagons during the withdrawal had been "saved by the gallant and indefatigable Morgan, whose very name is a terror to the enemy of the Southwest."[4]

Within weeks, back from Corinth, he initiated a series of raids behind enemy lines in middle Tennessee. Near Pulaski on May 1, he captured several hundred wounded and convalescing Federals, and then put to rout a company of cavalry. Local sympathizers plied the visitors with food and drink, and the ladies made much of Morgan's splendid mount, Black Bess—although their attempts to snip off the mare's hair for souvenirs forced him to stable her for the night.

Moving to Murfreesboro, which now had fallen to the enemy, he learned that nearby Lebanon, Tennessee, was unguarded, and he changed direction. Entering that town at dusk on the 4th, he again received a warm welcome. Around midnight, he put out pickets and bedded down. But he was entirely too sanguine. In the early hours of the morning, the 1st Kentucky Union Cavalry, 600 strong, coming out of nowhere, overwhelmed his sentries and galloped into town, scattering his half-awake men and putting them to rout.

Morgan and some 100 of his troopers fled east toward the Cumberland River, twelve miles away, with the Federals close behind. There they commandeered the sole ferry and made it across the river to safety, though the boat was not large enough to take their horses. From the far bank, as the enemy arrived, he could see Black Bess neighing and wandering along the shoreline, trying to find him.

For Morgan, the rout at Lebanon, which cost him one-third of his command and reduced him to tears of frustration, was humbling. But the war did not allow for introspection, and within days he recovered his élan. On May 11, with a patched-together force of some 150, he neared Cave City, a train station just north of Bowling Green, aiming to disrupt the Louisville & Nashville Railroad. "I rode up alone to the station [in civilian clothes], got off my horse and sat down on the rails to rest my feet," he would tell Virginia French, a friend. "The conductor came up and taking me for some old farmer who was waiting for the train, inquired the news."

"Oh, nothing much," he replied, "only they tell me that John Morgan's captured."

"Whereupon [the conductor] fell to cursing Morgan—vowing that he was never so glad of anything in his life—that Morgan ought to have been hung long ago. . . . I told him I agreed with him. Just then a party of my men rode up. . . ."

"Well, [Colonel] Morgan, what are we to do?"

The conductor hastily backed off, white-faced, and Morgan and his troopers took over the station. Commandeering the first train that pulled in, they set it afire and sent the locomotive at full throttle, together with forty-five boxcars, down the track toward Nashville.

"It was a grand sight," he said, "that burning train going at headlong speed to destruction." The subsequent explosion, when it came, was deafening.

Next arrived a passenger train from Louisville, filled with the wives of Yankee officers and a few of their husbands. When Morgan went aboard, the women crowded anxiously around him.

"One pretty girl—she had only been lately married—her husband was with her—a Federal officer in poor health—this pretty girl grasped my hand . . . sobbing, 'Oh, [Colonel] Morgan, what will you do with my husband?'

"I could not resist such a sweet face. I said, 'Madame . . . if you desire it, your husband shall accompany you home.' She kissed my hand and thanked me a thousand times—my hand . . . that had not been washed for two days."[5]

In a grand gesture calculated to enhance his legend, Morgan then sent—not just the petitioner and her husband back to Louisville—but the entire train, taking time only to confiscate $6,000 in U.S. greenbacks.

Within the next few weeks, with the approval of his superiors, Morgan began raising and training his largest force to date, a brigade he named the 2nd Kentucky Cavalry. It consisted of a 400-man regiment of Kentuckians, and a second regiment composed of Texans, Georgians, and Mississippians. Handsome and affable Basil Duke, great nephew of Chief Justice John Marshall, had recovered from his Shiloh wound and was again at Morgan's side. Others in his immediate circle included Robert A. Alston of South Carolina, his forceful adjutant; the aforementioned George Ellsworth, a telegraph expert whom Morgan had recruited; Lieutenant Gordon E. Niles, a former journalist who on and between raids would initiate the publication of a unit newspaper, *The Vidette*; and George St. Leger Grenfell, an English soldier of fortune bearing a letter of introduction from Robert E. Lee.

The 2nd Kentucky left Knoxville on July 4 and headed 100 miles directly west to Sparta, whence it turned north and galloped into Kentucky. Its purpose (similar to that of Forrest's move into middle Tennessee) was to go into Federal-held territory and disrupt General Buell's designs on Chattanooga. Quite soon, Morgan found Southern sympathizers flocking to his ranks, raising his numbers to some 1,100.

His first brush with the enemy came on July 9 at Tomkinsville, where his force came upon a 350-man battalion of the 9th Pennsylvania Cavalry. Sending the Texans and Mississippians to the right to get in the Federals' rear, Morgan with the main body, mostly dismounted, assailed the enemy position head-on. "We had to cross open fields to get at them," said Basil Duke. "They fired three or four volleys while we were closing in." Here St. Leger Grenfell "spurred his horse forward between the two opposing lines . . . leaped a low fence behind which the enemy were lying, and began lashing at them left and right with his saber." The fight ended within minutes, with the Confederates taking some 300 prisoners.

Up to this point no one had quite known what to make of Grenfell, a man in his fifties who looked twenty years younger, wore a bright red silk cap with cord and tassels, and claimed to have fought in campaigns all over the world, including the Charge of the Light Brigade in the Crimea. "If England is not at war," he had explained, "I go elsewhere to find one." But now Morgan's free-spirited troopers, who judged an officer solely on his courage, embraced him. The Englishman returned the compliment, saying he had never met such men, "who would fight like the devil, but would do as they pleased, like these damned Rebel cavalrymen."[6]

The command paused briefly in Glasgow, where Gordon Niles visited a printer to run off some recruiting posters. Then they crossed the Green River, and just below Horse Cave on the Louisville & Nashville Railroad they paused again so Ellsworth could tap into the telegraph lines, using a pocket device that would not break the circuit and warn the enemy of his presence. From these and future intercepts, Morgan learned where and when he could expect to find opposition, information that on his raids would be invaluable. Ellsworth also sent off some messages of his own. "No Rebels here," he would say. "Morgan believed withdrawing into Tennessee."

Late on the 11th the Confederates neared Lebanon, Kentucky, where a small enemy garrison guarded the covered-bridge crossing. Here two mountain howitzers—dubbed "bull pups" for their sharp bark—came into play, sending the guards fleeing into the town. "They can go over ravines, up hills, through thickets, almost anywhere," Duke enthused about the guns, ". . . in as close proximity to the enemy as two horsemen can go . . . they throw shell with accuracy 800 yards . . . they throw cannister and grape two and three hundred yards."

By nightfall the 2nd Kentucky had entered and pacified the town, 200 more prisoners had been taken, and more than $100,000 worth of supplies were being put to the torch. A correspondent for the Louisville *Journal* subsequently reported: "The destruction was immense . . . sugar, coffee, flour, guns were bent double by hard licks over rocks—powder, cartridges and caps were thrown into the creek." The Rebels "had no general uniforms, and were armed to suit their own taste. They all had Adams' patent six-shooters, many of them had shotguns, a few only had sabers." Townspeople, even those with Southern sympathies, saw the troopers confiscating their horses, "swapping" them for their own tired mounts. "The soldiers stole horses by the wholesale." In summing up, the correspondent kept his harshest criticism for Grenfell, whom he called a "degenerate Englishman" for setting fire to the depot and the courthouse.[7]

On Sunday, July 13, Morgan next moved to Harrodsburg, a town heavily sympathetic to the Southern cause, where people rushed from church to cheer and fete him. "Oh, the grand and glorious sight it seemed to us!" Lizzie Hardin wrote. "Eleven hundred Southern horsemen rushing at full speed amid the waving of caps and the glancing of steel. . . . The men and boys rushed up the road to meet them. . . . The ladies waved handker-chiefs and threw flowers, and wept."

This was the same day that Forrest took Murfreesboro, Tennessee, and the two raids fueled Federal anxieties that the Rebels, whose numbers they much overestimated, were riding at will through their lines. Morgan now was within twenty-eight miles of Lexington, and not all that far from Louisville and Cincinnati. Union General Boyle, in command at Louisville, at this juncture repeatedly and frantically wired Washington for help, say-ing, "Morgan is devastating [us] with fire and sword," and "Morgan has invaded the state with 3,000 men . . . and is murdering and stealing every-where." To tamp down the panic, Lincoln urged his then general-in-chief, Henry Halleck, to turn his attention to the matter: "They are having a stampede in Kentucky. Please look to it."[8]

Morgan had been tempted to assault Lexington, hoping to see his mother who, with five sons in the Confederate army and two daughters married to Rebel officers, was all but a prisoner in her own home. But learning that the city was garrisoned by 3,000 men, he decided to bypass it, go thirty miles further north, and assail the more lightly guarded town of Cynthiana on the Licking River.

On the way, passing through the "Secesh" village of Georgetown, he did not overlook his recruiting responsibilities, instructing Gordon Niles to set in type and distribute a bold manifesto. It read in part: "Kentuck-ians! I come to liberate you from the despotism of a tyrannical faction and to rescue my native state from the hand of your oppressors. . . . My brave army is stigmatized as a band of guerillas and marauders. Believe it not. . . . Your gallant fellow citizens are flocking to our standard."[9]

Nearing Cynthiana the afternoon of July 17, Morgan easily drove in the Federal pickets and reached the covered bridge on the river. Here, with some 800 of the enemy dug in on the far bank, he met far more resistance than expected. Richard M. Gano and his Texans, together with Company G, were sent wide across the Licking in a sweeping pincer attack, and the rest of his troopers, dismounted, were ordered forward. It soon became apparent, however, that sending the command in large numbers across the bridge would be suicidal; the Federals had trained a 12-pound howitzer on it. Morgan therefore plunged his men, holding their firearms over their heads, into the river in several sorties both above and below the structure. Many were killed and wounded in the ensuing fighting, but more made it across.

While the enemy was concentrating its fire on these assaults, St. Leger Grenfell again showed his verve, charging with a small group of horsemen hell-for-leather across the bridge and falling on the cannoneers. The main body of Rebels followed, joining with their comrades on the far bank and the flanking columns and overcoming the defenders. "I cannot too highly complement Colonel St. Leger Grenfell," said Basil Duke, "for the execution of an order which did perhaps more than anything else to gain the battle. His example gave new courage to everyone who witnessed it." Eleven bullets pierced Grenfell's clothing and bright red cap and grazed his skin, but he suffered no serious injuries. Duke, noting a bullet hole in the skullcap, would say: "[The cap] fitted so tight upon his head that I previously thought a ball could not go through it without blowing his brains out."[10]

Some 200 Federals, according to Morgan, were killed and wounded during the two-hour affair at Cynthiana, and most of the rest taken prisoner and then paroled. Three hundred horses and caches of small arms likewise were captured, and the rail depot and ordnance and supply stores demolished.

Late on July 17 his command again was under way, this time turning southward to safety, moving through such towns as Paris, Winchester, Richmond, Crab Orchard, and Somerset. Everywhere, when he found them, he set fire to enemy supply depots. "Morgan had intended to remain for some time at Richmond and recruit as large a number of new soldiers as possible," one Confederate trooper would say, "but [General Green Clay] Smith was behind him, other detachments were converging . . . and the Federal colonel, Frank Woodford, was collecting forces to intercept his march. . . . Notwithstanding all this . . . he preserved the dignities of a complacent withdrawal from scenes, though full of danger, not yet so imminent as to make him rush away."

On July 22, six miles past Somerset, Morgan crossed the Cumberland River, later culminating the raid at Livingston, Tennessee. "I left Knoxville on the 4th of this month with nine hundred men," he would say, "and returned to Livingston . . . with twelve hundred, having . . . traveled over a thousand miles, captured seventeen towns, destroyed all the government supplies and arms in them, dispersed around 1,500 Home Guards, paroled nearly 1,200 regular troops. I lost in killed and wounded . . . about ninety."[11]

One postscript should be made, in the aftermath of Morgan's 1st Kentucky raid, to underscore his abilities. On August 12 he quietly stole into Gallatin, Tennessee, where he captured Union colonel William P. Boone in his bed and the 375-man garrison without firing a shot. Then he ran a train filled with blazing hay through Gallatin's twin rail tunnels, closing them down for the rest of the year and severing the Federal rail link with the North. This feat, following a withdrawal from the town, moved Gordon Niles to put out the first issue of *The Vidette*, which understandably focused on "tremendous and overwhelmingly decisive Confederate victories," as well as "the horrors of Federal invasion."

The Gallatin success bred a series of repercussions. Hearing that vengeful Federals subsequently had descended on the town, arresting and taking away all the adult males as well as committing other brutalities, Morgan returned there on August 20, found the rumors largely true, and chased down the enemy column. "We take no prisoners today!" shouted one of his troopers. Morgan re-creates the scene: "The first Yankee I came up to had an old man nearly exhausted, driving him forward at the point of a bayonet. . . . I felt all humanity leave my heart." The soldier dropped his gun and begged for his life; Morgan shot him. He then dispersed and put to rout the Federals, who suffered heavily, and freed the captives, whom he returned forthwith to their homes. In this action, which involved few Confederate casualties, Gordon Niles lost his life.[12]

General Don Carlos Buell, seeing his advance on Chattanooga grinding to a halt because of Forrest's and Morgan's incursions, had vowed retribution. During this August period, he had ordered General Richard W. Johnson, with 800 men—the best companies of the 2nd Indiana, 4th and 5th Union Kentucky, and 7th Pennsylvania—to find and capture the Kentuckian at all costs. Johnson had welcomed the assignment, boasting he would "bring [Morgan] back in a bandbox." By happenstance then, early on the 21st the vanguard of this search party galloped toward Gallatin just as the Rebels were mounting up and preparing to leave.

Not knowing how large a force he was facing, Morgan's first impulse was to withdraw. But the opposing column was closing too fast. "We will have to whip those fellows, sure enough," he told Basil Duke. "Form your men."

The Texans, feinting a charge, blunted Johnson's advance just long enough for the main body to dismount, form battle lines, and take cover behind low fences. Most of the ensuing action now took place on open pastureland, several hundred yards in length, across which the enemy, sabers drawn, galloped at full speed. The results were predictable. "Every man had elbow room and took dead aim at an individual foe," Duke said of his dismounted troopers, who held their fire until the Federals were within 30 yards, "and, as the blaze left the guns, two-thirds of the riders and horses seemed to go down."

Though the enemy tried to rally, even using a sign of truce as a delaying tactic, they were cut down time and again. Panicking, they broke and fled, throwing down their arms and equipment and thinking of nothing but escape. Some 70 were killed and wounded, and perhaps 180 taken prisoner. Among the captives were Johnson and his staff. "General Johnson was evidently a fine officer," Duke would say of the reckless saber charge against his dug-in troopers, "but he seemed not to comprehend 'the new style of cavalry' at all."[13]

Union General Buell could only grit his teeth.

FIVE

THE EAST, AUGUST 22–23: STUART AT CATLETT'S STATION

Following his defeat of George McClellan around Richmond during the Seven Days, Robert E. Lee turned his attention northward to General John Pope, who was commanding a second Union army near Washington, in the angle formed by the confluence of the Rapidan and the Rappahannock Rivers. Prior to advancing against Pope with his main force, however, Lee ordered Stuart to cross over in the Federal rear and destroy the railroad bridge at Rappahannock Station, cutting off the enemy's primary means of retreat. Recently promoted to major general, Jeb now commanded a division comprised of three brigades, which in turn were led by Fitz Lee, Wade Hampton, and Beverly Robertson, and at this point were widely separated.

On the evening of August 17, Stuart and various aides arrived at the hamlet of Verdiersville to rendezvous with Fitz Lee's brigade, which had been chosen to carry out the plan. But Jeb's instructions to his subordinate, it seems, had been indefinite as to exactly when they should meet. Therefore Fitz, going twenty miles out of his way to replenish his supplies, would be nowhere near Verdiersville that night. Unaware of this, Stuart took off his brand-new plumed hat and cloak and settled down for a few hours of sleep in the yard of a friendly house owner. Dawn came, and still no Fitz! Concerned, Stuart sent Major Norman Fitzhugh to find him.

Then through the morning mist, a column of troopers could faintly be seen coming down the road Fitz Lee should have been taking. Wild shouts and shots ensued, and with them the realization that the newcomers were Union cavalry. "The approach of the enemy's troops . . . had attracted no special attention," said one of Jeb's aides, "until they fired on and charged the party sent with [Major] Fitzhugh. Then suddenly they were at the gate of the yard in which Stuart had slept."

The Virginian reacted instinctively, leaping onto his mount, digging in his spurs, and forcing the animal to leap the yard's fence. Heros von Borcke, at six-foot-four and 250 pounds loath to do anything so athletic, thundered with his horse through the open gate, which the woman of the house had rushed to unlatch. Bullets whizzing past them, Stuart and his aides outrode their pursuers and evaded capture. Jeb had left behind his plumed hat, cloak, and haversack filled with military maps, but it was the loss of the hat that would plague him.

For the rest of the day, with the summer sun rising hotly, he used a handkerchief to shield his head and continually endured the same biting question, "Where's your hat?" Trying to keep a straight face, von Borcke would say, was almost impossible. "We could not look at each other without laughing."

Stuart, keeping an outward calm, inside was seething. "I intend to make the Yankees pay for that hat," he promised.[1]

The Verdiersville mishap made the destruction of the bridge at Rappahannock Station moot, with Pope within the next few days falling back behind the river. But Lee soon approved Stuart's plan for a new attack in the enemy's rear, one in which he would cross the Rappahannock near Warrenton, then move east to raze the supply base and bridge at Catlett's Station and sever the Federal rail line from Washington.

Cantering across the river at Waterloo Bridge in the early afternoon of August 22, Stuart with 1,500 troopers from Fitzhugh Lee's and Beverly Robertson's brigades received a tumultuous welcome as he rode into Warrenton. Here a spirited young woman approached him, saying she had bet a bottle of wine with a Federal quartermaster, a Captain _____ , that he would not, as he maintained, "be in Richmond in thirty days." The woman knew she would lose the bet, she told him, because she was confident that Captain _____ would end up in Richmond after all, not as a conqueror but as a prisoner. She wanted Jeb to see that the Yankee got the wine as a consolation prize of sorts. Stuart laughed, said he would do what he could, and turned to an aide, William Blackford, saying, "Take [the man's] name . . . and look out for him."

The column reached Catlett's Station at dusk, and Blackford was given the task of reconnoitering. "I rode all around the outskirts of [the Federal] encampment, and found a vast assemblage of wagons and a city of tents . . . occupied by the luxuriously equipped quartermasters and commissaries, and countless hangers-on . . . but no appearance of any large organized body of troops."

Hearing his report, Stuart resolved to encroach on the camp slowly, taking down the sentries one by one and replacing them with his own men before, under cover of darkness, making an all-out assault. "The leading regiment was to go for the depot," said Blackford. "The next was to go for Pope's headquarters . . . to scatter among the tents and wagons, burn them and collect prisoners and horses and mules."[2]

Rain now was falling heavily, deepening the blackness. Guiding the Confederates to Pope's wagons, ironically, was a captured Negro, a runaway slave who had been promised lenient treatment in return for his help. Their victims still had no inkling of what was about to happen. Cooks, orderlies, and teamsters sat in front of innumerable fires, cooking their suppers, laughing and talking, relishing the end of the day. Some of the Union officers had just poured a round of toddies when one remarked, "Now this is something like comfort. I hope Jeb Stuart won't disturb us tonight."

The Confederate attack commenced. "Sound the charge, Freed!" Stuart told his chief bugler, and its peal quickly filled the air.

"There he is, by God!" shouted the Yank, downing his drink and grabbing his pistol.

Even before the bugle notes came to an end, they were drowned out by the howl of Stuart's onrushing troopers screaming the Rebel yell. "I went in with the leading regiment," said Blackford, "and the consternation among the quartermasters and commissaries as we charged down the main street, scattering pistol balls right and left among them, made the men laugh until they could hardly keep their saddles. Supper tables were kicked over and tents broken down in the rush to get out, the tents catching them sometimes in their fall like fish in a net."[3]

Just about the only infantry in the camp were the 1st Pennsylvania Rifles, the Bucktails who had clashed with Turner Ashby in the Shenandoah. They sprang to arms, trying to defend the rail depot. "Receiving one withering volley," continued Blackford, "our men dashed among them . . .

leaping their horses upon the low platform and crashing into the freight room. . . . [Soon] all was over, and no further resistance was offered to our work of destruction."

Other Rebel troopers, meanwhile, headed for Pope's tents and wagons. He was not there, but the capture of his headquarters "had given us possession of all his papers and among them the morning reports of his army . . . by which we learned as much about his force as he knew himself . . . We also secured his army treasure chest which I afterwards heard contained $500,000 in greenbacks and $20,000 in gold. From Pope's private baggage a full-dress uniform coat and hat was taken to General Stuart as a trophy, in compensation for his loss at Verdiersville."[4]

Blackford, who was Stuart's engineer officer, had been deputized to destroy the Catlett's Station bridge. But around midnight, with the rain becoming torrential, the wind fierce, and the darkness relieved only by flashes of lightning, he found it a hopeless task. "Every fire was extinguished, and we were left in utter darkness," he said. ". . . I could have cried for vexation, for I knew the importance of destroying the bridge before Pope sent troops to protect it." Henry McClellan, soon to be Jeb's adjutant, would agree: "It was impossible to set fire to the bridge because of the rain . . . and the heavy timbers defied the attack of the few axes which could be found. . . . The enemy also opened fire from a cliff on the opposite side. After exhausting all the means at his disposal, Stuart was compelled to acknowledge that [its] destruction . . . was beyond his power."

The raid, nonetheless, was not without its compensations. Well before dawn, the Confederates vacated Catlett's, taking with them 300 prisoners, a like number of horses, and all the plunder they could pilfer from the well-stocked Federal storehouses. Stuart would be his usual irrepressible self, sending Pope a note that read: "You have my hat and plume. I have your best coat. I have the honor to propose . . . a fair exchange of the prisoners." There is no record he received an answer. Pope's starched and spiffy dress coat, however, was sent to Richmond, where for weeks it was prominently displayed, to the delight of the residents, in a shop window.[5]

What of "Captain _____ ," the Federal quartermaster whose wine-bottle bet that he would soon be in Richmond so concerned the young woman in Warrenton? He was among Stuart's captives, as it turned out. "I sought out the prisoners, who were assembled under guard in a field and looked very disconsolate," said Blackford. "Riding up to them, I asked if Captain _____ was in the party. A much surprised and genteel looking man came forward who, after hearing the story[,] laughed very heartily, in which he was joined by his comrades. . . . It seemed to restore them all to good spirits, and they resumed the march talking . . . about the won wager."

Jeb was jubilant when he learned the quartermaster had been found. "[He] told me to ride on to Warrenton," said Blackford, "and let [the woman] know so she would be ready with the bottle of wine as we passed. Stuart halted the prisoners in front of the house, and the Captain stepped forward to receive the bottle of wine from [her] pretty hands . . . amid the enthusiastic cheers of his comrades."[6]

The prime result of the expedition turned out to be the confiscation of Pope's papers and dispatches. Poring over them subsequently, Lee confirmed what he already suspected. Pope was delaying any offensive action until George McClellan's troops could be transported up the Rappahannock to join him. Within days his 50,000 men would grow first to 70,000, then to 130,000. Lee, with less than half that number, could not let this happen. He determined he would go on the offense immediately, sending Stonewall Jackson around Pope's right flank through Thoroughfare Gap and initiating the success that was the Battle of Second Manassas.

SIX

* * * *

THE WEST, SEPTEMBER 4 – NOVEMBER 1: MORGAN REVISITS KENTUCKY

The work of John Morgan's and Nathan Forrest's cavalry in stopping Union General Buell's advance toward Chattanooga had encouraged the Confederates, under Edmund Kirby Smith and Braxton Bragg, to counter-attack and move north into Kentucky with a two-pronged assault. Smith, commanding the easternmost column, defeated a Federal force at Rich-mond, Kentucky, on August 30, and two days later entered Lexington, which the enemy had evacuated. There Morgan and his brigade of troop-ers joined him. Confederate General Braxton Bragg, in overall charge in the theater, soon thereafter left Chattanooga and, crossing the Tennessee into Kentucky, moved north on Smith's left, capturing Glasgow and Mun-fordsville, and proceeding toward Louisville.

Morgan's reception in Lexington on September 4, as he rode down the main street in full dress uniform at the head of his men, was tumultuous, with Southern sympathizers turning out en masse and Unionists nowhere to be seen. According to one observer, "The bells of the city pealed forth their joyous welcome—men, women, young boys and girls, with smiles, tears, shouts, and cheers rushed into the streets, waving white handker-chiefs and small Southern flags. . . . For hours the most intense interest prevailed." Marveled an admiring Mattie Wheeler, whose brother was raising a company of horsemen and enlisting in his command, "John Morgan could scarcely get to his home, the people almost carried him."

Indeed, the Kentuckian counted on such excitement to fuel his recruiting efforts. With Major Robert Alston, his adjutant, filling in for the slain Gordon Niles and finding a willing printer, he began to circulate a broadside, which read in part: "*Arouse, Kentuckians!* Let the old men of Kentucky, and our noble-hearted women, arm their sons and lovers for the fight! Better death . . . than a life of slavery!"

Morgan's mood was ebullient, much different than it had been months earlier when he learned that rabble-rousers were harassing his mother, Henrietta, the family matriarch, and other kin. Then he had sounded a blunt warning. "I understand at Lexington they threaten my Mother & Sister's, Mrs. Duke's life & to burn their property," he told a friend. "Burn it if they dare. . . . [But] so help me God if they trouble those helpless women and children whom I love so fondly I will make the name of John Morgan more terrible than in their wildest imagination [they] ever conceived it could be." Now those concerns, for the nonce at least, were pushed aside.[1]

Old friends in Lexington flocked to his headquarters, and laughed with him over the Federal soldiers that had been posted around his mother's house, hoping to snare him if he paid a clandestine visit. A horse breeder gave him a splendid mount, a gelding named Glencoe, to replace Black Bess, lost in the aftermath of the debacle at Lebanon, Tennessee. And of course, there were the ladies, a bevy of whom presented him with an ornate regimental flag for the 2nd Kentucky that they had fondly and painstakingly embroidered.

In this last regard, it must be said that the mustachioed, goateed Morgan rarely lacked an attentive female audience. "[He was] so mild & gentle in his manners," remarked one woman, "that [I] would not have taken him for a soldier but for his boots & spurs, so unwarrior-like did he seem." Confessed another, "Like all the ladies who see him, [I] fell perfectly in love . . . fascinated with his elegant and fine personal appearance." A Louisville newspaperman would decry such sentiments, sniffing that *some* women needed to "admire and idolize a 'dashing hero,' especially if he has the spice of sin and the devil in him. A bold robber chief captivates their romantic fantasies."[2]

Within days, Morgan and his troopers again were on the road. Sighed his mother, "I had not five minutes private conversation with John while he was here. There was [always) a crowd around him, or someone in pursuit of pressing business." Kirby Smith, intent on creating a diversion while Bragg was moving toward Louisville, dispatched six companies of the 2nd Kentucky under Captain John Hutchinson north to Covington, Kentucky, just across the Ohio from Cincinnati. Basil Duke with the remaining companies soon followed. The tactic set off a panic in mid-September among Federal authorities in the area. They abandoned any thoughts of going on the offensive in the short term, and huddled behind their fortifications.[3]

Morgan himself, with Richard Gano's and William Breckinridge's regiments, was sent into eastern Kentucky, with orders to cut off a Federal infantry column under General George Morgan—no relation—until reinforcements could join him. Confederate infantry support never did arrive, and John Morgan could do little but badger his opposite number by throwing up roadblocks, setting up ambushes, and picking off stragglers. The Federals eventually would escape into Ohio.

In late September, however, while he and his command were nipping at George Morgan's flank, he encountered some unwelcome visitors. Mountaineers in the eastern part of the state often were Unionists and Home Guards, and at this point a group of them with their rifles leveled approached Morgan and his aides, who were watching the action on a knoll, isolated from the main body of cavalry. Luckily he and the others, to protect themselves from a drizzling rain, were wearing oilcloths over their uniforms, concealing the fact they were Confederates.

"I'll pass for DeCourcy," Morgan told his aides, referring to Colonel John DeCourcy, 16th Ohio Infantry, whom he knew was a brigade commander in the Federal column. When the mountaineers inquired who they were, Robert Alston gestured toward his chief and said, "That's Colonel DeCourcy."

"Why, the boys told us DeCourcy's brigade was behind," said one of the locals, as he and the others put down their guns and relaxed, "and we're mighty glad to see you." *Why don't you join the Union army and fight with us?* Morgan asked, continuing the playacting.

"We can do more good at home," the man answered, "killing the damned Secesh."

"Oh, have you killed many Secesh?"

"I reckon we have. You'd have laughed if you had seen us make Bill kill his brother."

"What did you do that for?"

"Well, you see, Bill went south, and we burned his house, and he deserted," the mountaineer said with relish. "We arrested him, and said we were going to hang him as a spy. He said he'd do anything if we let him off, that his family would starve if we hung him. . . . [So] we made him kill his brother Jack."

Masking his disgust, Morgan began quizzing the visitors about Federal troop strength, local roads, and the names of Home Guardsmen. When he had gleaned all the intelligence he could, he and his aides pulled out their revolvers.

I am John Morgan, he told them, *and I'm going to have you shot.*

The mountaineers were stunned. Some fell to the ground, moaning and groaning, begging for their lives. "What will Susy do without me?" one cried plaintively.

That night, reunited with his command, Morgan conducted a swift court-martial that condemned the men to death. They were marched to an open field, and the execution squad readied itself and took aim. But the order to fire was never given. Just when the Unionists had given up all hope, Morgan let them go. Perhaps he felt they were not worth shooting. Perhaps he felt they would spread the word that preying on Southern sympathizers was a dangerous business.[4]

In northern Kentucky about this time, Basil Duke, unbeknown to his chief, was planning a daring raid. He had seen the consternation that the diversion against Covington had aroused in Cincinnati, and he was convinced that crossing the Ohio would create even greater hysteria. On September 27, therefore, he forded the river with his troopers and approached Augusta, Kentucky, which he knew was defended only by a company of Home Guards. Two Union stern-wheelers, each armed with a 12-pounder, were moored at the town pier, but these gunboats soon steamed off when the regiment's howitzers, its "bull pups," began raining shells on them.

Entering Augusta, Duke found the streets eerily empty, and realized that the enemy had taken cover inside private houses. When his advance reached the dwelling of Major Joshua Bradford, the Home Guard commander, it appeared at first there would be no fight at all. Bradford, seeing he was outmatched, waved a white handkerchief and cried out that he was surrendering. Almost simultaneously, however, other elements of Duke's command came under an assault as fierce as it was unexpected. One young lieutenant sounded a charge and led his men on horseback toward the hidden enemy, something he had been warned never to do. Not only did they encounter a deadly fusillade, but also fire from the "bull pups," whose gunners took them for foes.

The Rebel troopers in the streets were incurring severe casualties. Officers in particular were being picked off. One of John Morgan's cousins, Sam Morgan, fell mortally wounded, and his brother Wash, enraged, now led a series of assaults on the houses, kicking in doors and giving no quarter. "He was a most vicious-looking man," said one Augusta resident, "with a revolver almost as long as his arms."

Even when the defenders did try to give up, Duke's men would have none of it. White flags and handkerchiefs were meaningless, as the Rebels avenged what they felt was a sham surrender. The "bull pups" blasted gaping holes in doors and walls, houses were set to the torch, and the duplicitous enemy rooted out. "I never saw them fight with such ferocity," Duke would say of his troopers.

Before the fight ended—Kentuckians against Kentuckians—Duke's command had suffered about 40 killed and wounded, some of the best men of the original Green River squadron.

Mary Coburn, a witness to the mayhem, would say of the Home Guards, who were all but exterminated: "They tried so hard to have a fight . . . and they accomplished it to their sorrow. I don't pity them one bit for it was their own fault. They have no one to blame but their selves."[5]

In early October, Morgan and Duke were reunited in Lexington, only to learn to their chagrin that the city again was being evacuated. Bragg's column moving toward Louisville had for some time been at a standstill at Bardstown, some 35 miles south of its goal—its commander worried about his supply lines and apparently lacking the instinct to go for the jugular. Union General Buell, given this respite, had marched up from Tennessee, passed through Bowling Green, and reached Louisville before him. Now Buell had regrouped and was turning on Bragg with better than a two-to-one advantage. At this juncture, Kirby Smith on Bragg's right had no choice but to fall back from Lexington, ordering Morgan to cover his withdrawal.

Buell and Bragg fought the climactic battle of the Kentucky Campaign on October 8 at Perryville, 40 miles south of Louisville and Lexington and midway between them. Tactically the fight was a draw, with the Federals suffering 4,200 casualties and the Rebels 3,400, but it ended any faint hope of bringing Kentucky into the Confederacy. Bragg fell back toward east Tennessee, with Morgan again screening Kirby Smith's infantry. Buell, because climatic conditions muffled the sound of gunfire, did not appreciate the extent of the fighting until late in the day, and got only nine of his 24 brigades into the action. He soon would be relieved from command and replaced by William Rosecrans.

Morgan had been loud and vocal in suggesting the Kentucky Campaign, claiming that the state's citizens would eagerly embrace the Confederates, and he could not have been more wrong. While certain areas did produce volunteers for the Rebels, the populace in general took a wait-and-see approach. Bragg put it best in a letter to his wife, saying that Kentuckians had issued a calculated challenge: "We are with you, only whip these fellows out of our country, and let us see you can protect us, and we will join you."[6]

Now the two sides took up new positions in east Tennessee. The Federals centered their lines around Nashville; the Confederates, around Murfreesboro.

The Federals made little effort to pursue their foes after Perryville, and Morgan, smarting over his passive role in the retreat, persuaded Smith to let him leave the main force and make a strike in the enemy's rear. On October 18, near Lexington, he laid plans to surprise the 4th Ohio Cavalry in its camp just before dawn. Duke's regiment, dismounted, was to advance from the east; Breckinridge's men, likewise on foot, were to come in from the west; Gano's Texans were to make a mounted charge and deliver the coup de grace. Though the raid was successful, in the dim light Morgan's troopers also began shooting at one another.

Some of Breckinridge's fire went over the heads of the enemy and into Duke's troopers. The 2nd Kentucky in turn lobbed a howitzer shell into the Federal camp just as Breckinridge was sacking it. So far, remarkably, there were no casualties from this friendly fire. But then, just as the 4th Ohio was surrendering, the Texans galloped up and delivered a volley into Duke's van. This was too much for Captain Patrick Thorp, the 2nd Kentucky's adjutant, who, dim light or not, wanted to have Gano court-martialed, saying his actions had been deliberate.

"Colonel Gano may not have recognized my face," shouted the indignant Thorp, who always wore a Zouave jacket studded with bright red buttons, "but he couldn't have failed to [see] my buttons!"[7]

As the fighting was ending, Wash Morgan was mortally wounded. He was taken to Lexington, which offered no serious resistance to the Rebels, and borne to Henrietta Morgan's home. Propped up in bed, he called for a big black cigar. It was clenched between his teeth when he died.

Moving west toward Bardstown the next day, the brigade encountered and burned a 150-wagon Federal supply train; then they continued their raid to Elizabethtown, where they torched Louisville & Nashville rail assets and directed several fusillades at a passing troop train. On October 21, at Leitchfield, Morgan captured some Home Guards and, as was becoming his wont, threatened them with execution. "I want to impress these people with a wholesome fear as far as possible," he told one of his men, "to put a stop to their persecuting their neighbors." The next morning, after the guardsmen swore to reform their ways, he freed them. Some reputedly kissed his boots.[8]

Turning south, Morgan passed through Greenville, where he endured an early snowfall, and then reached Hopkinsville, where he destroyed more railroad track, and arrested and threatened more guardsmen. There he met with Confederate colonel Thomas G. Woodward, whose cavalry regiment, in one of the war's many incongruities, likewise was called the 2nd Kentucky. Though Morgan used all his charm, he could not persuade Woodward to merge the two units. On November 1, he led his brigade back into Tennessee, still not believing that Kentucky was lost.

SEVEN

THE EAST, OCTOBER 9 – 12: STUART'S CHAMBERSBURG (PA.) RAID

The battle of Antietam Creek in Maryland, fought to a standoff between Robert E. Lee and George McClellan on September 17; produced an awesome total of 22,700 casualties, the most in American history for a single day of warfare. Because the terrain was not suitable for large numbers of troopers on horseback, the exuberant Jeb Stuart had turned artilleryman on that occasion and prevailed on his incongruous friendship with the dour Stonewall Jackson to be entrusted with the latter's nineteen cannon on Nicodemus Hill. From there, aided by twenty-three-year-old Major John Pelham, his head of field artillery, Stuart had exerted a murderous crossfire on the Federal right flank and added to his luster.

Now in early October, Lee again was in need of intelligence. The Federals were encamped around Sharpsburg, Maryland, and Harpers Ferry, Virginia, just northeast of the Confederates, who were around Winchester in the Shenandoah. Lee wanted to know what McClellan might be doing and how his supply lines were organized. He ordered Stuart to move across the Potomac into Maryland and, if not intercepted, to proceed to Chambersburg, Pennsylvania, and destroy the rail bridge there, gathering information as he went. If all went well, horses could be commandeered and rounded up, prisoners taken, and additional damage inflicted.

Lee was ambiguous on the route Stuart should take on his return: "Reliance is placed upon your skill and judgment. . . . Should you be led so far east as to make it better . . . to continue around to the Potomac, you will have to cross the river in the vicinity of Leesburg." Jeb was being told, in effect, he could double back the way he had come or continue in a wide arc around the enemy—a second Ride Around McClellan.

His new assignment would tear him away from the good times at The Bower, Stephen Dandridge's estate near Charlestown, filled to overflowing with comely Dandridge daughters and nieces and female visitors. "Every afternoon," said aide William Blackford, "we all assembled at the house for riding, walking or fishing parties, and after tea . . . came music, singing, dancing and games of every description mingled with moonlight strolls along the banks of the beautiful Opequan."[1]

Stuart was as much at home in the ballroom, it seems, as on the battlefield. "Those who saw him only in his hours of recreation could form no true estimate of his character," Blackford continued, "and from such as these the impression prevailed that he was frivolous. . . . On the contrary, though he dearly loved, as any good soldier should, to kiss a pretty girl, and the pretty girls dearly loved to kiss him, he was as pure as they; and as to dissipation, he never touched wine or spirit of any kind." John Esten Cooke echoed these sentiments: "He became famous for his gaiety, activity and romantic exploits, and after fighting all day would dance nearly all night at some hospitable house. . . . [But] he was, in morals, among the [best] of men—a faithful husband . . . an earnest and exemplary Christian."[2]

On the eve of his expedition, Stuart was his usual self, mixing play and work—dancing at The Bower until 11 p.m., pausing for two hours to review his plans, and then staging, with violin, banjo, and bones, a farewell concert at which he sang four solos. On October 9, however, he was all martial business, assembling some 1,800 of his best troopers, dividing them into three "brigades," and leading them to Hedgesville about 25 miles up the Potomac from Sharpsburg. Heading the units were Brigadier Wade Hampton and Colonels Rooney Lee (filling in for Fitz Lee, who was recovering from a mule kick) and William E. "Grumble" Jones. In the column also were Pelham and four guns of the horse artillery.[3]

Let us take a closer look at these officers. Forty-four-year-old Wade Hampton III of South Carolina, born in Charleston on March 28, 1818, was perhaps the state's richest plantation owner. The grandson and son of

Revolutionary War and War of 1812 officers, he was a robust outdoorsman without formal military training who, after Fort Sumter, had organized and equipped the 600-man Hampton Brigade, composed of infantry, artillery, and cavalry, to whose ranks had flocked South Carolina's young elite. Hampton's sons Preston and Wade IV, in fact, were members of the brigade's cavalry.

Hampton arrived at First Manassas after the battle had begun, and marched to the sound of the guns. Fighting to the right of Stonewall Jackson in the thick of the action near Henry Hill, his brigade took more than 100 casualties, and he himself was wounded by shrapnel. Infantry service during the Seven Days followed, and then in July 1862 a transfer to Stuart's cavalry, which was largely composed of Virginians. Hampton would command South Carolina and other non-Virginia units. Rightly or wrongly he would feel that Stuart and his close friend Fitz Lee considered him an outsider, and it would not help that he was at least fifteen years their senior.

William Henry Fitzhugh Lee, capriciously nicknamed Rooney by his father Robert, was born on May 31, 1837, on the Lee-Custis estate at Arlington, Virginia, and by the time he was five was being described as "a large, hearty fellow [who] requires a tight rein." Turned down by West Point, he enrolled at Harvard, where his popularity in his freshman year insured his election as class president. But he was an indifferent student, drawing the pique of fellow student Henry Adams of Massachusetts, whose frail physique and snobbishness were in contrast to Rooney's burliness and open nature. "No one knew enough to know how ignorant he was; how childlike; how helpless before the relative complexity of a school," wrote Adams. ". . . Strictly the Southerner had no mind; he had temperament."

Rooney soon withdrew from Harvard, desirous of a military life. Named a second lieutenant in the army in 1857, courtesy of General Winfield Scott, he married, and subsequently, during leaves from peacetime service, showed special talent for managing the estate on the Pamunkey River he inherited from his grandfather. With the coming of war he embraced the Confederacy, never doubting his decision.[4]

The aptly named Grumble Jones, a West Pointer despite his sharp edges, was something of an anomaly in camp, at least among those devoted to Stuart. In fact, Blackford would call him "ugly" and "surly." Thirty-eight years old and a native of the Shenandoah, Jones was an able and effective trooper, particularly at scouting and hit-and-run tactics, but he was prickly, and he and Jeb were like oil and water. They simply could not get along, perhaps because Jones envied his superior's effortless charm.

Heading the horse artillery was the boyish-faced, startlingly handsome John Pelham, whose steady gaze and clean-cut features were making him irresistible to eligible Virginia women. Born in 1839 in Benton County in southeastern Alabama, the son of a prominent and wealthy doctor and his wife, he had grown up with five brothers on a 1,000-acre estate. He then had gone to West Point where he excelled in horsemanship, boxing, and fencing, and where two weeks before graduation he resigned to throw his lot with the Confederacy. Through hard drills, he had perfected the knack of closing on the enemy, firing his guns with precision, and then hitching them up and rolling them to a new position minutes before they could be targeted in return.[5]

In the early hours of October 10, Stuart's column left Hedgesville, crossing the Potomac at McCoy's Ferry, brushing aside the few Federal pickets there, and heading north through Maryland. Hampton's brigade was in the lead, and twenty-six-year-old Colonel Matthew Calbraith Butler's 2nd South Carolina in the van. Around 8 a.m., a few miles past Hagerstown, Jeb captured a small signal station and received some welcome news from locals, who told him that six regiments of General Jacob Cox's Union infantry had just vacated the area, heading west. There now seemed to be no great force separating him from Chambersburg. Nonetheless, Stuart had reason to worry. Two officers had escaped from the station, and he assumed they were sounding the alarm.

Up to this point he had been thinking of veering off a few miles to Hagerstown, where a rail terminal was crammed with Federal supplies, and razing the depot. But now, learning the town was defended, he gave up the idea. "I was satisfied," he said, ". . . that the notice the enemy had of my approach and the proximity of his forces would enable him to prevent my capturing it."

By 10 a.m. the Rebels were crossing into Pennsylvania, well behind the Union lines, and nearing Mercersburg. There William Blackford, hearing that a resident had a detailed map of the countryside and knowing that it would be invaluable, decided to appropriate it. The man of the house was not home, and the women were unfriendly, but the aide put aside his good manners. "Only the females of the family appeared," he said, "who flatly refused to let me have the map . . . so I was obliged to dismount and push past the infuriated ladies . . . into the sitting room where I found [it] hanging on the wall. Angry women do not show to advantage, and the language and looks of these were fearful, as I cut the map out of its rollers and put it in my haversack."[6]

Throughout the day the Confederates confiscated horses and foodstuffs from the bountiful Pennsylvania countryside. Parties of a half dozen or so men would dash repeatedly into wheatfields, barns, and well-filled pantries, returning with animals tied together by their halters, and roasted turkeys, hams, rolls of beef, baked bread, and crocks of cream and butter. Blackford joined several of these raids, and on at least one occasion showed his usual courtly side. "We had just taken [a] usually nice looking lot of horses out of the barn," he said, "when a genteel looking old lady . . . asked that we let her keep her old driving horse, which she assured us was in the thirty-fifth year of his age." Blackford was incredulous. The animal in question seemed a handsome specimen, but on closer inspection, when he opened the horse's mouth, he saw that "his teeth were worn off level with the gums. This was an animal whose age was as seldom reached by his kind as that of one hundred and twenty-five years would be to a human being. Bowing to the old lady I returned her faithful and noble favorite."[7]

The column arrived at Chambersburg after dark, under a steady rain, with Wade Hampton still in the lead. Unable to ascertain whether the town was garrisoned, he boldly sent a detachment from the 2nd South Carolina forward to demand its surrender. That Chambersburg was defenseless became clear when a group of citizens came forward, asking for terms. Hampton responded that the surrender must be unconditional. Private property would be respected, unless it "should be needed for the use of our army." The representatives promptly agreed, and about 8 p.m. the weary Rebels, who had ridden forty miles that day, moved into the town.

Just before the surrender, town officials had wired the news of their predicament to the governor in Harrisburg, and he in turn, clamoring for help, had urged the War Department to take action. The two Federal cavalry commanders within striking distance of Chambersburg—Alfred Pleasanton and George Stoneman—had known since noon, courtesy of the officers who had escaped the signal station, that Stuart was across the Potomac in force. Now they knew precisely where he was. But Pleasanton would dawdle in pursuit, not getting under way until early on October 11, and Stoneman would be indecisive, wondering where Jeb would go next.

The Confederates stayed the night in Chambersburg, but failed to destroy the rail bridge over Conococheague Creek, which Grumble Jones, who was assigned the task, found to be made of iron. His axes were useless, and he lacked explosives. This development did not improve his disposition. Calbraith Butler, told by Stuart to plunder the town bank, likewise was frustrated, the greenbacks having been removed earlier to safety. But he took the sight of the empty vault in good humor, so much so that the relieved cashier, who had feared unpleasant, even violent, retribution, "summoned the ladies of his family, and voluntarily brought forth food for the men who, though hungry, had made no demand on him."[8]

Jeb as usual made the best of the situation, looting an army warehouse of hundreds of overcoats and boots, as well as 5,000 rifles and many pistols and sabers, and burning the rest of the materiel, together with the Cumberland Valley Railroad's machine shops. The blue overcoats were much appreciated by the troopers, who snatched them up to ward off the nighttime chill, and the next morning, October 11, were still wearing them at reveille, confidently expecting to retrace their route.

But Stuart again would do the unexpected, instead turning the column east toward Gettysburg, Pennsylvania, preparatory to moving south toward Emmitsburg, Maryland, and the lower fords of the Potomac. While riding with the advance guard, he called Blackford to his side.

"I want to explain to you my motives for selecting this route," he said, "and if I do not survive I want you to vindicate my memory." He believed that Cox's infantry, which he had so narrowly missed on the way in, and possibly other units would now be waiting for him. "You see, the enemy will be sure to think that I will try to recross above, because it is nearer to me and further from [their main body]. They will have all the fords strongly guarded in that direction, and scouting parties will be on the lookout for our approach. . . . They will never expect me to move three times the distance and cross a ford below them and so close to . . . [Harpers Ferry].

"Now, do you understand?"

"I was much touched by this confidence," Blackford said, recalling that "both his eyes and mine filled as we closed the conversation."[9]

The Confederate column, perhaps five miles long, at this point was beginning a daunting 100-mile-plus trek, to be made without a significant stop. Two factors would make the escape feasible. The troopers would switch from their own mounts to the captured horses and back again to give the animals respite; and their progress over the roads, soaked by the rain of the previous day, would not raise the immense dust clouds that could be observed from Federal signal towers.

Sundown on October 11 found the expedition at Emmitsburg, but there would be precious little rest. Through the night the Rebels rode on. "To be sleepy and not to be allowed to sleep is exquisite torture," said

Blackford. "Many of the men went to sleep on their horses, and snores long and loud could be heard all along the column." Crossing the Monocacy, a tributary of the Potomac, Stuart bypassed Frederick, where he ascertained there were Union troops, and proceeded through such towns as Liberty and New Market until at daylight he reached Hyattstown. He was three-quarters of the way to safety. "It was this great speed," Blackford went on, "which baffled the enemy, who by this time had found out that we were moving southward, and were crowding all their available troops toward our route. . . . Stoneman and Pleasanton with their cavalry were in pursuit, infantry was strung along the [Potomac]."[10]

Barnesville was passed about 8 a.m., and directed by a guide who knew the countryside, the column headed toward White's Ford, a little known crossing on the Potomac just below its convergence with the Monocacy. More importantly, the approach was made through heavy and concealing woods, again frustrating the enemy's scouts and signal towers. Rooney Lee and Stuart were in the lead, then Grumble Jones and Hampton while Butler guarded the rear. Here a squadron of Pleasanton's cavalry suddenly appeared. "Yankees!" The word echoed through the ranks.

The Rebels were still wearing the blue overcoats they had taken from the stores at Chambersburg. The enemy hesitated, thinking they might be friends. Stuart closed at a canter, then attacked. "Charge! Charge!" he shouted, galloping down the road straight at the Federals, who were thrown into confusion and wild retreat. Jeb's impulsive assault was of the greatest importance. "By it he occupied the road up to the Little Monocacy, where a high bluff, extending nearly to the [Potomac] protected his left flank, and screened his subsequent movements," said Henry McClellan, his adjutant. ". . . He also gained a commanding position . . . in advance of the road by which [we] expected to approach White's Ford."[11]

Now Pelham with one gun of the field artillery rushed to take advantage of this elevated site. He opened up posthaste on Pleasanton's troopers on the Rebel right, keeping them at bay and creating a corridor for the crossing. Rooney Lee in the van, taking advantage of this passage, quickly moved to the ford with his brigade and two of the remaining three guns—Butler had the other—only to find a Union infantry regiment on the far bank of the Potomac blocking his passage. "It seemed a desperate undertaking to attempt to dislodge this force," McClellan continued. "But *something* must be done." The situation seemed so dire that Lee sent a messenger to Stuart, asking him to come forward and give him counsel. But Jed was busy elsewhere. He replied that the ford must be taken at all hazards.

While making his preparations for the attack, Lee decided a show of bravado could do no harm. The "temperament" that Henry Adams at Harvard had so disparaged at this point came to the fore. He sent a note to the Federal commander, via a courier with a handkerchief tied to his saber, stating that Stuart with his whole command was in his front, and calling on him to surrender to avoid a bloodbath. "Fifteen minutes were granted for compliance with this demand," said McClellan. ". . . The [time] passed, and yet there was no sign of a white flag. . . . Lee opened with his artillery and ordered his regiments to advance. In another moment he expected to receive the fire of the enemy."

Instead the Federals inexplicably began to withdraw. "They are retreating! They are retreating!" sounded throughout the Rebel ranks, amid wild cheering and gleeful backslapping.

In short order Rooney was across the Potomac, posting his guns rearward whence he had come and protecting the rest of the command as it galloped through the shallows. Pelham on the Maryland side meanwhile was keeping up his shelling in Pleasanton's front to the last, moving his single cannon from position to position, waiting for the rear guard under Butler to come into sight. "He was making his last stand . . . firing now up, now down the river, at the enemy approaching from both directions," said McClellan. ". . . Courier after courier had been sent to hasten Butler toward the ford, but no tidings of him had been received."[12]

Here Stuart rode up to Blackford, who knew nothing of the dilemma, telling him in a voice heavy with concern, "Blackford, we are going to lose our rear guard!"

"How is that, General?"

"I have sent four couriers to Butler to call him in, and he is not here, and you see the enemy is closing in upon us."

Blackford immediately volunteered to ride back and find Butler. "As I rose the bank I passed Pelham who with one gun, kept back for the purpose, was rapidly firing . . . at masses of the enemy not a quarter of a mile away. We waved our hats at each other as I passed." Three miles in the rear he found Butler, who quickly had his command with drawn sabers galloping toward the ford, prepared to cut their way through. "There was a gun with the rear guard and there was some doubt of the team being able to move fast enough. . . . [Butler] was very reluctant to abandon [it] and to our surprise . . . the horses held out and brought the gun in." Nearing the Potomac, concluded Blackford, "There stood Pelham with his piece and there the enemy, just as I had left them, with an open gap between for us to pass through. In a moment we were at the ford and Pelham's gun rumbling along after us into the water."[13]

Stuart's Chambersburg Raid clarified in Lee's mind the strength and disposition of the Army of the Potomac. But its real value lay in the surge it gave to Confederate morale, and the embarrassment it caused the Union. McClellan sought to explain Jeb's success by saying his own cavalry was badly in need of fresh horses. To this the fuming Lincoln on October 24 made the following reply: "I have just read your dispatch about sore tongued and [fatigued] horses. Will you pardon me for asking what the horses of your army have done since the battle of Antietam to fatigue anything?"

Days later, while aboard a boat on the Potomac with government officials, Lincoln again showed his anger.

"Mr. President," one politician asked, "what about McClellan?"

Lincoln picked up a stick and drew an imaginary circle on the deck. "When I was a boy," he said, "we used to play a game—three times around and out. Stuart has been around McClellan twice. If he goes around him once more, gentlemen, McClellan will be out."

We will never know if Stuart, who had taken to signing his private letters, "The Knight of the Golden Spurs," would have made a third circuit. On November 7, McClellan was relieved from command and replaced by Ambrose Burnside.[14]

EIGHT
* * * *

THE WEST, DECEMBER 11– JANUARY 3: FORREST'S SECOND TENNESSEE RAID

In December 1862, with Ulysses S. Grant advancing into Mississippi and moving on Vicksburg, the ordinarily hesitant Confederate General Braxton Bragg initiated two cavalry expeditions intended to hamstring his supply lines and deprive him of stores. One would involve sending Nathan Forrest into west Tennessee, with instructions to destroy the Mobile & Ohio Railroad tracks from Jackson, Tennessee, all the way north to the Kentucky border. (The other, which Earl Van Dorn would conduct against the forward Union supply depot at Holly Springs, Mississippi, will be discussed in the next chapter.) If successful, the joint attacks would bring Grant's progress in the West to a temporary halt, complicating the Union's logistical problems in its efforts to penetrate the Southern heartland.

Forrest did not respect Bragg, and for good reason. The cavalryman was a warrior, untutored, but a soldier who instinctively knew how to fight and how to win. Bragg, a West Pointer and confidant of Confederate President Jefferson Davis, was a military bureaucrat who, perhaps because he could not shoulder his responsibilities, was inclined to procrastinate or slough them off on others.

Certainly Forrest, given the risk-filled task of driving deep into enemy territory, was receiving little support from his superior. The troopers he had trained and led so well at Murfreesboro in July, except for a squadron of Alabamians, had been transferred by Bragg to another officer. Forrest's new brigade, which he had just raised, was raw and untested, and it was lacking in arms and ammunition. When he protested that he had almost no firing caps for his guns and pistols he was told there were none to spare, and curtly ordered to go on the march.

This with his intense sense of duty Forrest did, leaving Columbia, Tennessee, on December 11 and arriving two days later at the icy, three-quarter-mile-wide Tennessee River, near Clifton. His command totaled some 2,000 troopers and six cannon, and 400 more men soon would join him. It consisted of the 4th, 8th, and 9th Tennessee, led, respectively, by Colonels James W. Starnes, George G. Dibrell, and J. B. Biffle; the 4th Alabama under Colonel A. A. Russell; and a smattering of other units.

The Confederates crossed the river in heavy rain from December 13 to 15, effecting their passage by night on makeshift skiffs and rafts, taking care to watch for enemy gunboats. Once on the west bank, Forrest rested for a day and then received some welcome ordnance. It included 50,000 firing caps, produced by an agent—one of the war's anonymous heroes— he had sent behind the lines, with orders to get them at all costs. Whether the caps were bought, or stolen from an enemy depot, the Yankees in effect were making the Rebel raid possible.

Now began the bluffing game that Forrest often played during his expeditions. Heading toward Lexington, Tennessee, he spread the word that he was the spearhead of a larger force to come, knowing the misinformation would precede him. The boom of kettledrums, to make it sound as if infantry were supporting his cavalry, reinforced the ruse, as did the light of countless campfires. Then, six miles outside of Lexington early on December 18, he delivered the swift strike that was becoming his trademark. The 4th Alabama with Captain Frank Gurley's squadron in the lead drove in some pickets, repaired a bridge at Beech Creek that the defenders thought they had made impassable, and closed on the town. There the Rebels, during a brisk but brief encounter, put to flight some 1,000 Federals, capturing Colonel Robert G. Ingersoll of the 11th Illinois Cavalry and 150 of his men.

Two enemy guns during this action made the only real resistance, temporarily blocking the advance. But Gurley and his 200 troopers swept to their right, moved through a ravine to within 100 yards, and fell on the cannoneers without warning. "The last shot was fired just as we reached the battery," said Gurley, "and my first sergeant, J. L. P. Kelly, and his horse were blown to atoms. . . . With the taking of the guns the cavalry gave way in a stampede, and many of them were captured." A dazed Colonel Ingersoll would estimate Forrest's total strength not as 2,400, but as at least 5,000 men. "The enemy was repulsed at first," he later reported, "but, coming again in overwhelming numbers, [ultimately] was successful."[1]

Not only did the Confederates take from the victory at Lexington the two cannon, but also hundreds of firearms, mostly Sharps carbines, permitting many of them to discard their obsolescent muskets. Such weapons were mightily prized, and their capture would be oft-repeated.

The Federals continued to magnify Forrest's numbers, even as he moved west the afternoon of December 18 toward the Mobile & Ohio and the town of Jackson, which was protected by 10,000 soldiers. "My cavalry was whipped at Lexington today," wired an alarmed General Jeremiah C. Sullivan to Grant. "Colonel Ingersoll taken prisoner. The enemy reported to be *from ten to twenty thousand.*"

Forrest had no intention of assaulting Jackson. His purpose was to drive back the timorous Sullivan within the town's fortifications, leaving the railroad unprotected. That night and the next morning he conducted a series of feints, using cavalry and artillery, that achieved his aim. "The Confederate artillery—six pieces—were brought up and employed with such effect that the enemy was speedily driven to his entrenchments," wrote Forrest's campaign historians. "Nearly simultaneously . . . the Confederate cavalry, remaining mounted or not . . . were brought up and ostentatiously displayed within half a mile of the [breastworks]."[2]

While Sullivan huddled behind his works, waiting for an all-out attack, Forrest was proceeding north toward Humboldt and Trenton, wrecking the railroad as he went. The former was handily captured by Starnes's 4th Tennessee about noon on the 20th, yielding 500 firearms, 300,000 rounds of ammunition, and 200 prisoners. Trenton fell later that day after offering stiffer resistance, with Biffle's 9th Tennessee moving on the Yankees from the rear while Forrest personally directed a frontal artillery bombardment. It provided more small arms and ammunition, and about 400 prisoners.

When Colonel Jacob Fry, the commander at Trenton, offered Forrest his sword, he remarked that it had been in his family for a hundred years.

"Take back your sword, Colonel, as it is a family relic," he was told. "But I hope, sir, when it is next worn it will be in a better cause than attempting the subjugation of your countrymen."[3]

Now the prisoners, who were more than 750 and who before the expedition was over would total well over 1,000, were becoming a burden. Forrest would parole them and send them to Union headquarters in Columbus, Kentucky, but first he strove, through repeated orders in their presence to "couriers" and "generals," to preserve the fiction that he was leading a vast host. His success depended on keeping the 5,000 Federals at Columbus, like Sullivan's 10,000 at Jackson, on the defensive as long as possible. He meanwhile maintained his swift but destructive pace northward, passing through Rutherford, crossing the Obion River, and on the afternoon of the 23rd, capturing Union City without firing a shot. Lamented Captain Samuel B. Logan of the 54th Illinois, "From the time their forces first appeared in sight three minutes did not transpire before we were thus surrounded."[4]

For the next twenty-four hours, the work of razing the Mobile & Ohio's trestles, bridges, and rails continued, until by Christmas Eve the line was a disaster from Jackson to the Kentucky border. Forrest's troopers had fulfilled their assignment, and well armed with Yankee weapons and well fed from Yankee stores, they were in far better fighting shape than when they began.

Their leader soon afterward, as he turned his column homeward on December 26 and moved southeast to Dresden, received word from his scouts that General Sullivan, prodded by an angry and frustrated Grant, finally was coming northeast in pursuit, though with less than half of his command. One 1,800-man Federal infantry brigade, under Colonel Cyrus L. Dunham, was in the van; some 2,000 infantrymen under Colonel John W. Fuller were close behind, with Sullivan accompanying the latter unit. The question now was whether the Federals would catch up with the Rebels and, if so, where the blue and gray columns would converge.

The next day found Forrest still farther southeast, past the village of McKenzie and approaching Huntingdon. Here, over the Obion, the enemy had destroyed all the bridges. But one overpass was left, in such ruinous condition that the Federals had not bothered to put it to the torch. The Confederates set to work. Timber was cut and shaped, and men heaved and hammered in the freezing water and mud to slap together supports. Getting the troopers and mounts across the shallow river was no problem; getting the heavily laden wagons and cannon over would be another matter.

Late on the 28th, Forrest drove the first ammunition wagon across the bridge, but the two behind him, much to his chagrin, skidded off and into the water. Ranting against fate and swearing a blue streak, he sent 500 men with innumerable bags of captured coffee and flour along the length of the train, with orders to spill out the contents for traction. The trick worked, and the wagons soon were on the east bank. By this time, however, the bridge was so fragile that the guns had to be hauled through the riverbed. He straightaway assigned 50 men to each piece, and toiling through the night with backbreaking effort, they made the transfer.

The delay at the Obion had been costly. The Federal infantry, nearing Huntingdon themselves on the 29th, had made up much ground and were closing in fast. Forrest's choice at this juncture was to continue his withdrawal to the Tennessee River and Clifton, some forty miles away, or to stand and fight. Characteristically he decided to challenge his pursuers, confident that the odds, if he could keep the actions separate, would be in his favor. He planned first to take on Dunham's brigade, and then deal with Fuller's. Union General Sullivan meanwhile was euphoric, wiring Grant: "I have Forrest in a tight place. The gunboats are up the river as far as Clifton. . . . My troops are moving on him in [all] directions, and I hope with success."[5]

The battle of Parker's Crossroads, just south of Huntingdon, did not begin until 10 a.m. on December 31. Through a series of stealthy maneuvers, Forrest had managed to interpose himself between the two Federal infantry brigades, which were perhaps six miles apart. He intended to use his superior artillery to smash Dunham, then to turn with the full impact of his cavalry on Fuller. He had little reason to think the latter would be energetic in joining the fight, especially since the dilatory Jeremiah Sullivan was riding with him, but nonetheless he dispatched Captain W. S. McLemore with four companies of Tennesseans to his rear, to warn him if Fuller was coming.

Lieutenant Nat Baxter Jr., a Rebel cannoneer, takes up the story: "Very early in the morning . . . General Forrest . . . went ahead to the crest of a hill and selected a position for my gun. To my great surprise, as I reached the top . . . I saw the Federals in heavy line of battle not more than four hundred yards away. With the exception of two or three hundred cavalry immediately behind my gun, and one or two hundred dismounted men in front . . . there were no other Confederate[s] in sight."

The Rebel artillery, comprising eight guns with the two taken at Lexington, now opened up with round after round on Dunham, who with three cannon was badly outmatched. "I succeeded in dismounting one of the Federal guns," Baxter said, "to the great satisfaction of General Forrest, who remained with me all through the duel. . . . The fighting on our side was done almost entirely with our artillery. We drove the Federals back beyond the crossroads, and had them corralled in a wooded lot, from which they made two or three charges to capture my battery, but failed. We were at such close quarters a good deal of the time that we used two charges of canister with a single [one] of powder."

Grape and canister poured from the Confederates, relentlessly pushing back the blue line. By noon Dunham was reeling under the barrage, and Forrest ordered an overall advance and sent out Starnes's 4th Tennessee and Russell's 4th Alabama in enveloping movements. "I dismounted a portion of my cavalry to support my artillery and attack in front," he said, "while I [flanked] them on each side and [got] Col. Russell's [cavalry] in their rear." Recounted Union colonel H. J. B. Cumming, whose 39th Iowa had endured the worst salvos: "I [was] reforming when we were opened upon by a fire of dismounted men, who had advanced within fifty feet. . . . [My troops] in more confusion fell back and received, standing, the fire from the enemy artillery, and under it the confusion became worse." His regiment broke in panic.

By 3 p.m., Dunham, making his final stand, was close to capitulating. He had used up his reserves and made the last of his countercharges, lost his cannon, and seemed all but helpless in the face of the ongoing assault. "I was whipping them badly with my artillery," said Forrest, ". . . was taking it leisurely, and trying as much as possible to save my men." Indeed, Lieutenant Baxter thought the Federals *were* giving up. "The white flags appeared all along the Union line," he said. "I was under the impression that they had surrendered and had gone in front of my gun . . . to converse with one of their officers. Just at this moment a volley of small arms was heard behind the location of our batteries and in our rear. I rushed back . . . to see what had happened."

The gunfire announced the unexpected arrival of Fuller's brigade, with General Sullivan, in the Confederate rear. Forrest was astounded. "At this time . . . we had demanded [of Dunham] a surrender," he said. "Thirty minutes more would have given us the day. . . . Knowing that I had four companies . . . on the Huntingdon Road, I could not believe [the assailants] were Federals until I rode up myself into their lines. [Their] heavy fire . . . unexpected and unlooked for, caused a stampede of horses belonging to my dismounted men, who were . . . driving the enemy before them." Three hundred of these mounts, and a like number of troopers, were captured.[6]

But what of Captain McLemore and his Tennesseans, who had been en-

trusted with guarding the rear? The truth is that the instructions given
him, written secondhand by a Forrest aide, were vague—a common Civil
War failing. McLemore interpreted them to mean he was simply to reconnoiter, not to stay and observe. Finding little Federal activity on the Huntingdon Road that morning, and hearing the onset of battle at Parker's
Crossroads, he had galloped back to take part.

Forrest was a world-class swearer, but one who simultaneously cursed
and took direct action. He soon would have the rest of his dismounted
men in the saddle, galloping out of the trap and heading south for Lexington. Meanwhile Colonels Starnes and Russell, who had been flanking
Dunham, renewed their attacks and kept him from joining the fight. Regardless, Forrest was not about to abandon his cannon. Gathering up a
ragtag force, he managed to check Fuller's oncoming infantry long enough
to save six of his eight pieces. Lieutenant Baxter, running behind his gun,
remembered Forrest grabbing him and telling him to turn on the Federals.

"General," he protested, "I am entirely unarmed; have neither gun, pistol or sword." *Makes no difference,* he was told. "Get in line and advance . . . I want to make as big a show as possible."

Considering what could have happened during the debacle, Forrest's
losses were light, a tribute to his quick thinking. Besides the 300 troopers
taken in the first stages of Fuller's attack, he suffered some 100 killed and
wounded, but lost only two guns and preserved most of his wagon train
laden with munitions and stores. The Federal losses—captured, killed, and
wounded—were about 700.

General Sullivan, reverting to form, made no effort to pursue. Instead
he indulged a taste for fiction. "Forrest's army is completely broken up,"
he wired Grant. "They are scattered over the country without ammunition. We [only] need a good cavalry regiment to go through the country
and pick them up."[7]

Regrouping at Lexington, the Confederates rested for a few hours, and
then through the night accelerated their march to the Tennessee. Just after
sunrise on January 1 they encountered a regiment of enemy cavalry, the
6th Union Tennessee, but Colonel George Dibrell and his 8th Tennessee
easily brushed their Unionist neighbors aside. Not knowing how many
Federal columns besides that of Sullivan might be after him, Forrest decided to leave behind, for a brief period, one regiment as a rear guard,
along with a section of artillery under Lieutenant Edwin Douglas.

Watching the cannon unlimbering and digging in, he suddenly grew
irate, not realizing that the movement of the horses to the rear, along with

extra ammunition, was standard procedure. "Mistaking it for a cowardly runaway on the part of the drivers," said Douglas, "he rode up to the man on the lead horse and, as he struck him over the shoulders with the flat of his saber, yelled, 'Turn those horses around, or by God I'll kill you!' "

The artilleryman protested, saying he was only doing what he should.

"No, you are not!" Forrest thundered. "I know how to fight, and you can't run way with the ammunition-chest!"

Not until some time later, after producing a manual of tactics in the quiet of camp, would Douglas succeed in convincing Forrest, self-taught in the art of war, that the horses indeed should have been taken out of range. "This was accepted," said Douglas, "and he became greatly interested. In less than a week, he had mastered the manual and become an expert among experts. . . . I may also add that he was just as prompt and earnest in his apology to the soldier he had wronged."

By the afternoon of the 1st, the command, entirely unpursued, was at the river near Clifton. Here, while keeping alert for Federal gunboats, they put together the same mélange of skiffs and rafts that originally had allowed their passage. The artillery and wagons went first across the water, propelled by oars and then the current. Next the troopers, in groups as few as a half dozen or as many as several score, crowded with their saddles and guns into the makeshift vessels. The horses were made to swim, hundreds of them in the water together, all paddling for the far bank. "Two men would [launch] a canoe or skiff," wrote one of Forrest's biographers, "while a third, holding the bridle of a horse, would strike out with the animal [paddling] by the side of the boat. When this piloted horse was a short distance from the shore, the other animals . . . [were] one after another pushed into the stream. They could do nothing but swim, and struck out to follow the lead of the horse already in the river."[8]

Two days later Forrest, his men well armed and battle-tested, was back in Columbia, Tennessee. His total losses during the raid, including the 300 troopers captured at Parker's Crossroads, were some 500; total Union losses—captured, killed, and wounded—exceeded 1,500.

For Grant, the enemy expedition was crippling. "Forrest got on our line of railroad between Jackson, Mississippi, and Columbus, Kentucky, doing much damage," he admitted. ". . . It was more than two weeks before rations or forage could be issued from stores. This demonstrated the impossibility of maintaining so long a line of road over which to draw supplies. . . . I determined, therefore, to abandon my campaign into the interior with Columbus as a base."[9]

NINE

THE WEST, DECEMBER 20: VAN DORN CUTS GRANT'S SUPPLY LINE

In the aftermath of Confederate General Earl Van Dorn's failure to retake the vital rail center at Corinth, Mississippi, in early October 1862, Ulysses S. Grant advanced into the state from Grand Junction, Tennessee, some fifty miles to the west of Corinth, along the tracks of the Mississippi Central Railroad. He handily seized Holly Springs, where he established a major supply base, and moved through Abbeville and Oxford as far south as Coffeeville, preparatory to driving on the Confederate stronghold at Vicksburg by land while William Sherman, his chief lieutenant, attacked from the river. Grant's progress seemed assured, his triumph all but inevitable.

The courtly, aristocratic Van Dorn once had been, next to Confederate President Jefferson Davis, Mississippi's favorite son. Indeed, in the months just after secession, he had succeeded Davis as head of the state's militia. But the war subsequently had frustrated his ambitions. First at Pea Ridge, Arkansas, in March 1862, and then at Corinth, he had suffered crushing defeats. The outcry after Corinth, in fact, had been so loud that he had been relieved of command in the state and replaced by John Pemberton. Moreover, stories of Van Dorn's drinking and womanizing were rife, though his admirers stoutly denied them. In the midst of the brouhaha, almost as an afterthought, he was named to head Pemberton's cavalry.

Now in mid-December, even as Forrest was moving against Grant's extended supply lines in Tennessee, Van Dorn was being told to deliver a second blow, this one in Mississippi. Having gone within ten weeks from commanding an army to being something of a scapegoat, he must have felt that this was his chance for vindication. His orders were to flank the enemy lines at Coffeeville, move north and level the depot at Holly Springs, and complete the cutoff of Grant's supplies. If successful, he would regain his reputation.

Earl Van Dorn was born September 20, 1820, at The Hill, the family estate near Port Gibson, Mississippi, the fourth of six surviving children and the first son. Sophie, his genteel mother, died when he was nine, and Peter, his father, an influential and monied magistrate and planter, when he was sixteen. Through most of his formative years Earl was raised by Olivia, his oldest sister, who tended to give him free rein—perhaps too much so. His was the privileged young Southerner's life. He hunted and rode with his friends, had few responsibilities, and fewer cares.

Imbued with a swashbuckling image of the military, he enrolled in West Point in 1838, courtesy of an appointment from President Andrew Jackson, his great-uncle. There he chafed under the academy's strict discipline but showed considerable skill as a horseman. He graduated fifty-second in a class of fifty-six. Impetuous, charming, headstrong—these are the terms used to describe him. "I never could be happy out of the army," he later would say. "I have no other home."

In 1843, posted to the 7th Infantry at Mount Vernon Arsenal, Alabama—his low marks at West Point had precluded a cavalry assignment—he met sixteen-year-old Caroline "Carrie" Godbold, daughter of a local plantation owner. Despite her family's protests, they soon married. Theirs would be an odd union in the years to come, with long periods of separation, relieved only by correspondence, that did not seem to trouble either husband or wife. Though they would have two children, Olivia and Earl Jr., they essentially would lead disconnected lives.

Van Dorn embraced the Mexican War during 1846 to 1848, several times engaging in hand-to-hand combat and receiving one wound and two brevet, or temporary, promotions for gallantry. "He [rode] a beautiful bay Andalusian," Dabney Maury, a fellow officer, would say, "and as he came galloping along the lines, with his yellow hair waving in the wind . . . we all loved to see him. His figure was lithe and graceful, his stature did not exceed five feet six inches, but his clear blue eyes, his firm set mouth, with white strong teeth . . . gave assurance of a man [we] could trust and follow."[1]

Tours of peacetime, humdrum duty followed, interrupted only by brief service against the Seminoles in Florida. For the most part Van Dorn's assignments were in Mississippi, and the separations from his wife became more and more frequent. When they were together, their meetings could be painful. "Carrie and myself now sit down to our meals opposite each other and alone and present a perfect picture of domestic felicity," he would write Emily, his favorite sister. ". . . Everything is so silent. I feel too much the passing of time."

Then in 1855 an elated Captain Van Dorn again found himself in action, transferred to the 2nd U.S. Cavalry and confronting the Comanches in Texas. (The 1st and 2nd Cavalry, both newly formed, included such future Rebel stalwarts as Robert and Fitzhugh Lee, Joseph and Albert Sidney Johnston, John Bell Hood, and Jeb Stuart.) "On the frontier Earl Van Dorn came into his own," wrote one biographer. "Not only was he popular among the soldiers but his striking personality made him a great favorite among the citizens. . . . His dashing exploits both on and off the field provided topics of conversation around many a dinner table or campfire. He was still impulsive, shortsighted, and a bit arrogant. But definite leadership qualities were emerging, and his courage was the pride of the regiment."[2]

In Texas, Van Dorn's most notable sortie occurred in 1858, when he and his 100-man squadron trailed some 200 Comanche horse thieves across the border into Indian Territory (now Oklahoma). Stealing up on their camp while they slept, he sounded the charge, and in the ensuing two-hour melee his command killed and wounded about half the Comanches and put the rest to flight.

His superior horsemanship, however, brought him grief. Chasing the survivors in advance of his troopers, he took two arrows in the body and fell from the saddle. Only the arrival of his men kept the Comanches from finishing him off. "My first wound was in the left arm," he wrote Carrie with great pride and precision. "The arrow . . . passed between the two bones and stopped near the elbow. The second . . . entered opposite the ninth rib on the right side, passed through the upper portion of the stomach . . . and passed out on the left side between the sixth and seventh rib."

Here he turned reflective. "When I pulled the arrows from me the blood followed as if weary of service, and impatient to cheat me of life. . . . The contemplation was awful. . . . I gasped in dreadful agony for several hours."[3]

Following Mississippi's secession in January 1861, then Major Van Dorn resigned from the U.S. Army and, with Jefferson Davis backing him, went from heading the Mississippi militia to being named a Confederate major general—in charge of the Trans-Mississippi Department. Now for the first time he was directing large bodies of troops, numbering in the thousands. That he was cool and resolute, and a passionate fighter, was a given. But did he have the skills to lead a vast army? The answer unfortunately would be no. His instincts were aggressive enough, but he would give little attention to proper planning.

This was demonstrated in his two major battles in 1862—at Pea Ridge and at Corinth. Van Dorn boldly went on the attack in both two-day affairs, enjoyed initial success, and then ultimately succumbed to problems of his own making.

In March, for instance, soon after the Federals had seized control of Missouri, he pushed forward with some 17,000 men toward the Pea Ridge range in northwest Arkansas, just across the Missouri border, looking every inch the confident commander. "He was of medium height, slender, free in his address and movements . . . sitting his horse in an easy style," recalled one Rebel. "His features were regular, forehead rather high, eyes black and fiery; lips thin and compressed; the chin was large and the jawbone prominent." His purpose was clear: to throw back the Unionists. "We Missourians were delighted," said a Confederate officer, "for he was known to be a fighting man, and we felt sure he would help us regain our state."[4]

Van Dorn arrived in the immediate area the night of March 6, following a debilitating fifty-five-mile march through an ice storm to get to the rear of the enemy, who were entrenched in front of Pea Ridge with their faces to the south. His force consisted of Missourians under Sterling Price, and Arkansans and Texans under Benjamin McCulloch. But his opponents, 11,000 Federals under the competent General Samuel Curtis, soon detected Van Dorn's movement, and in the predawn hours, hurriedly left their works and marched to the north to take him on.

About 10 a.m. on the 7th, Van Dorn belatedly learned that Curtis was awaiting his flanking attack. He had already divided his weary army, sending Price's column around Pea Ridge against the enemy right at Elkhorn Tavern, and McCulloch's against their left at Leetown. His tactics called for falling on the Federals with a quick one-two punch, disconcerting them, and driving them from the field. Diluting one's own strength while allowing the foe to remain concentrated was dangerous, and Van Dorn knew this. But he had counted on the element of surprise.

That first day, nonetheless, it appeared in the early going that the Confederates just might prevail. Price's men on the Confederate left, accompanied by Van Dorn, repeatedly drove back the enemy and by midafternoon captured Elkhorn Tavern. But meanwhile the troops on the right at Leetown were being bloodied. McCulloch was killed by a sniper's bullet; his senior officer, Brigadier James McIntosh, died while directing a charge; and their leaderless men appeared to lose heart. Soon Curtis, with his shorter interior lines, would have all the better of the fighting, moving reinforcements here and there as he saw fit. Van Dorn, with his widely separated columns, would not have that luxury.

Darkness shut down the combat, but it offered him little solace. His men were exhausted, there was little or no food, and he had allowed his ammunition wagons to go astray. During the night McCulloch's depleted force passed behind Pea Ridge and straggled into the Confederate camp at Elkhorn Tavern, but their bedraggled look did little to cheer him.

The next day was anticlimactic. Though Van Dorn drew up his army in a defensive V formation, his men had neither the will nor the shells and bullets to stand fast. Curtis, resupplied through the night, was the aggressor. "The roar of cannon and small arms was continuous," he said, "and no force could then have withstood the converging line and concentrated cross fire." Wrote one Confederate: "We [were] like trees in the forest [who stand] still till they are cut down." By noon Van Dorn was in retreat. "I so disposed of my remaining forces," he said, "as best to deceive the enemy as to my intention, and to hold him in check."

He moved southeast, circumventing his pursuers and, despite his defeat, accomplishing a skillful withdrawal. "There was nothing left for Van Dorn but to get his [wagon] train on the road," said Dabney Maury, ". . . and his army off by the same route, and to fight enough to secure them. This he did."[5]

Van Dorn's assault at Corinth would follow a similar pattern. Early on October 3, Van Dorn with 22,000 troops, including those of Sterling Price, advanced from the northwest on the rail center, where Union General William Rosecrans waited with some 23,000 men. With his usual fervor, but not enough forethought, he hurled his men against the town's outer defenses, taking heavy casualties but by midafternoon surging through the works and pushing the Federals back to their inner ring of fortifications. "The Rebs soon closed about us and came on with countless numbers," said Sergeant Cyrus Boyd of the 15th Iowa. "They swarmed around . . . and fired from behind trees and logs and kept pressing forward." There in the inner ring the bluecoats rallied. "The fighting was of unparalleled fierceness," Van Dorn would report.

He had hoped to take Corinth in a single day, thinking that an all-out frontal assault would rock Rosecrans back on his heels and keep him from maneuvering. But about 5 p.m., with dusk coming on, he realized this was not to be. Once again, as at Pea Ridge, the enemy, benefiting from shorter lines, had been too resistant; his own men were too fatigued; his ammunition was running too low. For a while he considered fighting on in the gathering gloom, but then thought better of it. "I saw with regret the sun sink below the horizon. . . . One hour more of daylight, and victory would have soothed our grief," he mourned.[6]

The next morning at 10 a.m., Van Dorn sent Sterling Price against the Federal right, the troops traversing open ground with battle flags flying and drums sounding. Price's closely packed columns, said the correspondent for the Cincinnati *Commercial*, formed a "monstrous wedge" which "drove forward impetuously toward the heart of Corinth." The reporter, noting the casualties the Rebels were taking, wrote that it was "terrible and beautiful to see the [enemy] advance, in spite of a perfect storm of grape and cannister . . . On they marched and fired, though the ranks were thinned at every step." For a brief time, Price's troops were not to be denied. Crashing through the Federal lines, they scattered the enemy, captured an artillery position, and entered the north side of town, where they fought house to house.

This would be the Confederate high-water mark. Timely reinforcements thrust Price's men back, and soon they were in general retreat, taking even more punishment in their flight. Elsewhere, on the Federal left, a series of charges and countercharges produced nothing but stalemate and a like number of casualties. By noon the fighting was, for the most part, finished all along the front, and Van Dorn again was pulling back. He had lost 4,800 men; Rosecrans, 2,350.

The Confederate commander the following month would face a court of inquiry, charged with neglect of duty and drunkenness, rumors that even the Federals had come to hear. "When the smoke cleared away we learned that the enemy had fled in confusion," Cyrus Boyd said. "They had been *cut to pieces*. . . . The prisoners tell us that Van Dorn commanded and that he was *drunk* and ordered his men to drink whiskey and . . . then ordered them to take the works at any cost *however great*."

That Van Dorn was devastated by the defeat is clear. "Do not blush that I have lost a battle," he wrote Carrie, "for the enemy themselves say that we fought as valiantly as men ever fought before. . . . Many falsehoods are told about me by the cowards who fled from the field . . . Do not believe them."[7]

The three-man court of inquiry, perhaps weighed in his favor by the presence of his close friend Dabney Maury and subordinates like Price and Lloyd Tilghman, found him innocent on all counts.

Relieved of overall command in the Trans-Mississippi following Corinth, the crestfallen Van Dorn had been placed in charge of the Rebel cavalry, with his superiors not expecting much from him. But on December 18, ordered out of the blue to sever Grant's supply line in Mississippi, this born horse soldier was in his element, galloping east from Grenada with 3,500 men toward Pontotoc just before swinging north in a half circle to assail the Union depot at Holly Springs. Perhaps he was thinking of the Texas frontier, intent that his current expedition would be just as successful as his forays against the Comanches. Certainly his three brigades, consisting of Texans, Tennesseans, and a mixed unit of Missourians and Mississipians, believed in his leadership. "Give us Major General Earl Van Dorn, than whom no braver man lives," one of his officers had pleaded, "[and] we will penetrate to the rear of the enemy, capture Holly Springs . . . [and] force him to retreat."

Leaving Pontotoc that afternoon, Van Dorn learned from a courier that his rear guard had encountered a much smaller Federal force. Here he showed newfound restraint. Instead of taking the time to rout them and slowing his progress, he brushed the news aside.

"Are they still in the rear?" he asked.

"Yes, sir."

"Well," he said, "you go back and tell Col. _____ that the Yanks are just where I want them."

By noon on the 19th, Van Dorn was within fourteen miles of Holly Springs. "As it was important to avoid coming in contact with any reconnoitering parties the enemy might have out," said Colonel Albert F. Brown, a staff officer, "we were now halted until night. A careful inspection of arms and ammunition was made, the horses were fed, and at dark we were ordered to move forward in perfect silence; at midnight, the head of the column being within a mile of the enemy's pickets, the men were ordered to dismount and rest. . . . Even our horses seemed to comprehend the situation, for they quietly nodded in their places."

The garrison at Holly Springs consisted of Illinois infantry and cavalry, some 1,500 men in all, under the command of Colonel Robert C. Murphy. Half the infantry was at the railroad depot and the rest in the town beyond, occupying the courthouse; the cavalry were in the fairgrounds, north of the town. Because the three camps were at least a half mile apart, a simultaneous attack on three fronts was impractical—moving troops in the darkness would have alerted the sentries.

Instead Van Dorn decided to strike on the 20th with a hammer blow up the road leading into the rail depot. "By hurling his whole force straight at the enemy and entering his lines at one point," said Colonel Brown, "he would come in contact with only one picket post and diminish the chances of alarming the garrison." Thereafter each of the three Rebel brigades was to fan out. "The first . . . was to dash into and capture the infantry camped in front of us; the second . . . was to sweep by the encampment, move straight into the town until it reached the street leading to the fairgrounds, then wheel . . . and charge the cavalry camp; the third . . . was to dash through the town, disregarding everything until it struck the enemy guarding the public square."[8]

The Confederates need not have worried that the Federals would be unduly alert. Some of Murphy's officers, getting a head start on Christmas celebrating, had been drinking heavily, and discipline was lax. Murphy himself had been warned by a runaway slave (a so-called contraband) that the Rebels were in the area, but he had been slack in alerting his lieutenants. Moreover, his wire asking for help, sent just before the attack to Grant's headquarters at Oxford some twenty miles away, would be so late as to be inconsequential.

Van Dorn's column, with its leader in the van, advanced on Holly Springs just before dawn. "We moved forward at a trot, soon increased to a gallop, and when a turn in the road brought the pickets in view," said Brown, "they were standing looking at us . . . unable to decide whether we were friend or foe. . . . We passed them like the wind. Another turn in the road, and the white tents of the camp were in full view." Here Van Dorn pointed toward the enemy with his sword, eliciting a spontaneous cheer. "The effect of the silent order was electrical. The charge was instantly turned into a steeplechase, and in another moment we struck the camp."

Thus awoken, the bleary-eyed and confused Yankees—members of the 101st Illinois Infantry—stumbled from their tents straight into an avalanche of horseflesh. "The scene of a regiment, with night garments fluttering in the breeze . . . was truly laughable," Brown continued. "There was no thought of resistance, and in a few moments the comedy ended. . . . The attack on the center of the town was also a complete success. . . . [Meanwhile] the [2nd Illinois] cavalry at the fairgrounds made a spirited defense. . . . They were booted and spurred preparatory to starting on a scout when the alarm was given. . . . They met [us] with a counter-charge, and a sharp fight ensued at close quarters. . . . It was a gallant but hopeless effort."

Traveling with Van Dorn was a correspondent for the Mobile (Ala.) *Register and Advertiser*, who previously had hailed his transfer to the mounted service: "[He] is undoubtedly the right man in the right place, and if he be permitted to retain command of our cavalry he will make what so far has been one of the poorest arms . . . one of the most efficient and famous." Now the reporter took special pride in reporting Van Dorn's triumph. "The scene was wild, exciting, tumultuous, Yankees running, tents burning, torches flaming, Confederates shouting, guns popping, sabers clanking; Abolitionists begging for mercy, Rebels shouting exultingly, women *en dishabille* clapping their hands, frantic with joy, crying 'kill them, kill them.' "[9]

The fighting was over by 8 a.m., with no more than a hundred or so of the enemy escaping, and the rest surrendering. Now, amid general pandemonium, the looting began. Grant had amassed at Holly Springs an immense quantity of stores—everything he would need for the advance on Vicksburg. Commissary, quartermaster and ordnance supplies, filling every available building, proved irresistible to the perennially needy Rebels. "Boots and hats seemed to be the most popular articles in the way of clothing," said Colonel Brown. ". . . Sugar, coffee, crackers, cheese, sardines, canned oysters &c. were not neglected; sacks were filled with these articles and tied behind saddles. . . . Among the ordnance there was a large quantity of arms and equipment . . . manufactured especially for cavalry, which [we] did not fail to appropriate."

Brown did not mention the large amount of liquor "liberated," which flowed freely and in some instances too much so. "We had stepped from privation to plenty," said one trooper, "and many were disposed to inaugurate a jubilee, inspired by the spirit of John Barleycorn, Esq."

Within hours, however, Van Dorn had restored order, and was turning his men to the serious business of burning and leveling the depot. That said, he also took great care in seeing to the well-being of a distinguished resident. Mrs. Julia Grant, it seems, had established herself in the town, the better to be near her husband, a common practice among the wives of senior officers during the war.

By sundown, with the ruin of stores valued at $1.5 million complete and the prisoners paroled, Van Dorn was vacating Holly Springs, knowing the incensed Federals would be in pursuit, and heading north—not south—to see what further mischief he could cause. "[He] had destroyed an accumulation of military supplies which it had taken months to collect," said Brown. ". . . It was a terrible disaster to General Grant."[10]

Galloping up to the 250-man Union garrison at Davis's Mill on December 21, Van Dorn confronted a far more able adversary than Colonel Murphy, whom an enraged Grant soon would cashier. He was Colonel H. Morgan, and with the aid of railroad ties and cotton bales, he had created a formidable barricade for his small force. Three charges failed, and Van Dorn, who had no field artillery, was obliged to withdraw. For the next 48 hours he continued north, contenting himself with pulling up track and severing telegraph lines. Then on the 24th he attacked an even smaller, but just as well fortified, Union garrison at Middleton, Tennessee, and was similarly repulsed.

He had accomplished all he could. Finally turning south, he and his men made their escape.

The raid on Holly Springs not only stopped Grant's advance toward Vicksburg cold, but thwarted Sherman's Mississippi-borne assault on the fortress. The Federal commander had no way of alerting his lieutenant to his predicament, with the result that Sherman, dutifully attacking Vicksburg at Chickasaw Bluffs on the 29th, suffered an embarrassing defeat. "I had no opportunity of communication with him after the destruction of the road and telegraph to my rear," Grant lamented. ". . . He did not know but that I (myself) was in the rear of the enemy and depending on him."[11]

Van Dorn's future at this point seemed bright, and Confederates in the West were comparing him to Forrest and Morgan. But through the winter of 1863 and into the spring, his reputation as a rake persisted. Newspapers, without proof, continued to call him a drunk and a fornicator, and there was little he could do about it. In May 1963, a wealthy fifty-one-year-old doctor, who long had thought that his twenty-five-year-old wife was taking lovers, became incensed. He stole up on Van Dorn in his Spring Hill, Tennessee, headquarters, shot him in the back of the head, and then sought refuge in the Federal lines. It was murder, pure and simple. The South had lost a gallant, if flawed, cavalier.

TEN

THE WEST, DECEMBER 21–
JANUARY 1: MORGAN'S THIRD
KENTUCKY RAID

The widower John Morgan married Mattie Ready, his beauteous and spirited fiancée, in her family home in Murfreesboro, Tennessee, on December 14, even as Union General William Rosecrans, at Nashville some forty miles to the north, was massing his troops for an assault on the town. Morgan was thirty-seven, sixteen years older than the bride, but the two were so clearly in love that the age difference seemed inconsequential. Just the day before, his brigadier's commission had become official, adding to his happiness. Serving as groomsmen were Mattie's brother, Horace, a Rebel staff officer, and Colonel St. Leger Grenfell, the inimitable English soldier of fortune. The ceremony itself was performed by General Leonidas Polk, an Episcopal bishop, and the affair was attended by the military grandees of the West: Generals Braxton Bragg, John Breckinridge, William Hardee, and Benjamin Cheatham.

Food was plentiful, with "all the delicacies and good dishes of a Southern kitchen," and Colonel Ready's cellars still had a sufficient stock of wine for the drinking of many toasts. Two regimental bands serenaded the couple and their guests, and after supper there was dancing until the hour grew late.

Not all the revelers, however, favored the marriage. Both Basil Duke, the brother of Morgan's first wife, and St. Leger Grenfell worried that Mattie's influence would make the cavalryman less of a risk taker. The latter went so far as to tell Colonel James Fremantle, a British observer on leave from the Coldstream Guards, that Morgan would be "enervated" by marriage and "would never be the same man as he was." But his reservations did not keep Grenfell from offering many toasts, as well as singing "Moorish songs with a French accent to English airs."[1]

That Morgan's marriage would affect his celebrated élan seemed dubious. After conferring with Bragg, he would be off within days on his so-called Christmas raid into Kentucky, again trying to sever the Louisville & Nashville Railroad (L&N) and deprive Rosecrans of supplies. By now the Federals had constructed a series of protective blockhouses on the line from Nashville up north to Bowling Green, with weak points—such as the tunnels at Gallatin that the Rebels had destroyed in August—heavily guarded. Morgan nonetheless concluded that a pair of trestleworks near Elizabethtown, Kentucky, where the L&N traversed Muldraugh's Hill, might be vulnerable. Each was about 500 feet long and 100 feet high, and their destruction would cripple the line for months. His problem was that Muldraugh's Hill was some 200 miles deep into Kentucky, only 50 miles below Louisville. Getting there, routing the garrison, and burning the trestleworks would be a challenge; getting out, with thousands of the enemy converging on him, would be a miracle.

Morgan left the Murfreesboro area during December 21 to 22 with some 4,000 men, the largest force he would ever lead. His original 2nd Kentucky had grown into one massive command, which he decided to divide in two to give him greater tactical control. One brigade, under Colonel Basil Duke, consisted of the 2nd, 3rd, 8th, and 9th Kentucky, plus a 4-gun battery; the other, under Colonel William Breckinridge, was comprised of the 10th and 11th Kentucky and the 14th Tennessee, with three cannon.

Not with the column was Colonel Grenfell, who had fallen out with Morgan, perhaps because he thought he should have had Breckinridge's brigade, perhaps because he disagreed with his easygoing disciplinary ways. Though they would reconcile later, he would not ride with him again.

Two hours out, spontaneous cheers erupted in the column's rear. The men far in front knew what was happening. Morgan had taken leave of his wife and was coming to join them. "Magnificently mounted, superbly dressed, riding like a centaur, bare-headed, with a plumed hat in his right hand, waving salutations, the general came galloping by," said a young trooper. "Pride and happiness radiated from every feature of his joyous face. . . . He had with him four thousand Kentucky boys, well armed."[2]

By the night of December 24, the Confederates were well into their journey, moving past Tomkinsville, Kentucky, and nearing Glasgow. During the march they had fortuitously come upon a Union supply wagon laden with food and drink for the enemy garrison, which they had commandeered. "Tis Christmas Eve," said Lieutenant James McCreary, who later became a Kentucky governor. "I am sitting with many friends—around a glorious campfire. Shouting, singing and speechifying make the welkin ring, for the boys have a superabundance of whisky. . . . We have not yet seen an enemy."

While McCreary and the main body were making camp, Captain Tom Quirk and his company of some fifty scouts were as usual in the van, advancing into Glasgow to reconnoiter. A free spirit and ferocious fighter, Quirk had been with Morgan since the command's inception, and no one observing his bellicose ways or hearing his Irish brogue would have guessed that he once owned an upscale confectionery in Lexington. It being Christmas Eve, he decided a drink was in order, and he and his men approached a Glasgow saloon to slake their thirst. A handful of Michigan troopers had the same idea, and the adversaries met head-on. "A collision was the result," said one of his men, "then a skirmish, then—a stampede."

No one was hurt in the fracas, and the two sides, perhaps tacitly acknowledging the need that night for peace on earth, quickly parted, but the scouts did not immediately return to camp. Instead they tarried at a couple of Glasgow Christmas parties, "long enough to enjoy a dance with some [Kentucky] girls—very much to their surprise. . . . They had not the remotest idea that Morgan was near. . . . We danced our set, though the whole country was alive with the enemy."

Still leading the column the next day, Quirk left Glasgow behind and approached Munfordville, where about 2 p.m. he learned that the road ahead was full of Yankees. Seventeen-year-old John Wyeth, who later would ride with Forrest's veterans and be his biographer, tells the story: "Quirk drew his six-shooter and, yelling to his company . . . to draw theirs, he dashed down the road. . . . Right ahead of us, as we swung around a turn . . . was a formidable line of Federal cavalry. The number in sight checked the enthusiasm of our plucky captain, for, as they opened fire on us . . . he told us to dismount and fight on foot, which we promptly did."

Here a second enemy detachment, concealed behind a rail fence, delivered enfilading fire on the scouts and forced them to scatter. "Our one chance," said Wyeth, "was to [clamber] over the fence on the other side of the lane." He and Quirk jumped the barricade together, with the enemy shooting at them from less than forty feet away, and took refuge in a thicket.

Now blood was spurting down Quirk's face. "The damn Yankees've shot me twice in the head," he vowed, "but I'll get even before the sun sets."

Wrapping the wounds in a makeshift bandage, he dispatched Wyeth with a message. "Tell my men if they don't come back here and help me clean these fellows out, I'll shoot the last damn one of them myself."

There would be no need for such drastic measures. The lead elements of Morgan's cavalry, coming up within minutes, soon surrounded the Federal patrol and insured its surrender. Quirk would refuse a doctor's attention. Gathering together his scouts, he again took the point.[3]

Wasting no time in Munfordville and continuing north along the tracks of the L&N, the column on December 26 burned the bridges over Bacon Creek and Nolin Creek, and the next day reached Elizabethtown, which was garrisoned with some 650 men of the 91st Illinois Infantry. Rather than sweep around the Federals to the nearby trestleworks and leave the foe in his rear, Morgan called on the Union commander, Colonel H.S. Smith, to surrender. This he refused to do. "As nothing but a fight would satisfy Colonel Smith, said one Rebel, "General Morgan prepared to give him what he wanted. . . . Skirmishers were thrown forward and . . . the enemy enveloped. He had taken positions in brick houses . . . and resolved to have a street fight. The Federals had no artillery, and the Confederates had seven pieces. . . . A few well-directed shells convinced the Federals of the folly of resistance."

In the aftermath of the fighting, while the prisoners were being paroled and hundreds of rifles and thousands of rounds of ammunition were being confiscated, Lieutenant McCreary visited one of the heavily damaged buildings. "I dismounted and went in. Saw that a shell had entered the window, exploded and killed three Yankees, who were then weltering in their blood on the floor." The young women of the household calmly offered him refreshments. "With hair disheveled . . . these ladies like proud Spartans walked contemptuously through the blood of those who had insulted them, and invited me into a room where there were many quarts of wine, cakes, etc. I did justice to Christmas and an empty stomach. . . . These so dear Kentucky ladies have a charm which no others possess."[4]

Other Rebels spent the rest of the day shopping, paying for clothing, boots, and other items with Confederate currency. Such money, of course, was worthless in the Union-controlled state, and its use was a polite pretext for looting. Many of Elizabethtown's shopkeepers, Southern sympathizers though they might be, would be less than pleased with the business. Morgan himself, we are told, "spent" some $1,200, buying garments for Mattie and shipping them back to Murfreesboro.

"You should not have married," Miss Belle McDowell, a Rebel stalwart, reputedly told him as they walked through the town's streets, "for there are a thousand hearts that beat at the sound of your name."

"I wish that I had a thousand hearts," was the reply, "and I would give them all to my wife."[5]

On the 28th the column pushed forward six miles to the two looming trestles on Muldraugh's Hill, which were jointly defended by 700 Union soldiers. Morgan's advance had been rapid, but it remains puzzling that his route had not been anticipated, and that reinforcements had not been rushed to such critical points. Certainly the Union cavalry was still lacking in training and leadership. Certainly the infantry, far more formidable, could not march with anything near the speed of a mounted command. But Rosecrans seems to have been obsessed with preventing Morgan's escape, not forestalling the damage he would cause.

Once more Morgan's cannon made short work of resistance. "On this expedition Captains Palmer and Corbett handled the artillery with consummate skill," said an admiring trooper. "Their well-directed shots in a brief while brought both garrisons to terms. The flames ascending high in the air told the story. . . . The columns of smoke . . . proclaimed to the pursuers that the dreaded calamity had overtaken the all-important trestles. . . . General Morgan had wrecked the road now for fifty miles. Nothing inflammable had escaped the touch of his destructive torch."

One of the enemy units on the trestles, the 71st Indiana Infantry, had at some point earlier in the war surrendered and then been paroled. This was the second time they had been captured, and Morgan could not resist making light of their plight. He forthwith instructed George Ellsworth, his telegrapher, to tap the lines and wire Indiana governor Oliver P. Morton his thanks for Indiana's much appreciated contributions to the Southern cause, adding: "Next time just send the quartermaster stores and the ordnance—don't bother sending the men."[6]

Within hours Morgan turned east for Bardstown, knowing that the Federals were closing upon him and that his first challenge, on the way to the town, would be fording the swollen Rolling Fork. On the morning of December 29, with most of his command across the stream, it appeared he would be entirely successful. Then some 3,000 men under Union colonel John Harlan, mostly infantry who had marched through the night, drew near enough to shell Morgan's troopers still on the west bank. "Lay your wires to kill him," Rosecrans had told Harlan, a Louisville lawyer who would become a U.S. Supreme Court justice. "Don't credit the big stories he sends abroad."

The Confederate rear guard made its escape, but just barely, and here Basil Duke, its leader, again was wounded. Struck in the head by a shell fragment, he fell unconscious from his horse. But Tom Quirk picked him up, threw him over his own mount, and dashed across the stream. "One of the enemy's batteries was proving especially destructive," said one Rebel of what happened next, "and Captain Virgil Pendleton of the 8th Kentucky was ordered to charge [it]. He killed the cannoneers or drove them from their guns, and this silenced [them] for a quarter of an hour."

Fifteen minutes made all the difference. Soon Morgan's entire command was safely on the east bank and streaming into Bardstown. There Colonel Duke was taken to a private home, laid on a thick bed, and attended by a surgeon. "The wound was on the right side of the head," said one witness, "and when the doctor had washed the blood from it, I was invited to examine a cannon's work . . . a piece of skin and bone behind the ear was gone."

Duke at this point regained consciousness and opened his eyes. "That was a close call," he said, smiling despite a pounding headache.

Elsewhere in the town, some of Morgan's men were behaving more like freebooters than soldiers, and though he did not encourage their behavior, he did not curtail it. Prisoners claiming to be Southern sympathizers were freed from the jail; money was stolen from the post office; the general store, when its owner refused to accept Confederate currency, was ransacked. "I was amused by one trooper," said John Wyeth, "who induced others to let him out of the building by holding an ax in front of him, cutting edge forward, one arm clasping a bundle of a dozen pairs of shoes . . . while on his head was a pyramid of eight or ten soft hats, one on top of the other."

The next day the column plunged on, heading south toward Springfield and Lebanon. Morgan was in the van, eclectically dressed in a black slouch hat, double-breasted jacket, and green pants. "A splendid-looking man," commented one onlooker. Farther back, the still-impaired Duke was ensconced in a carriage, its interior well padded and its driver, one of Quirk's scouts, "handling the reins like a proud coachman."[7]

By midafternoon the expedition was in Springfield, where Morgan learned that several thousand Federals were already in Lebanon, with at least 10,000 more on the way. Here he made another fateful decision. "He saw that the best way of escape was the longest way," said Bennett Young, one of his troopers. "He determined to make a detour to the right of Lebanon, pass the Federal Army there, then swing back on the road which led from Lebanon to Campbellsville, and rush to the latter place with all possible speed. He calculated that . . . by a forced march he would reach Campbellsville before his escape would be discovered and before the [enemy] could get in his front."

Everyone in Morgan's command would agree that the fifteen-mile march around Lebanon was the worst they had thus far experienced. It began at 11 p.m. on December 30, in pitch-black darkness and freezing rain, and continued through the night and into the next day. "The cold was so intense that it partially stupefied the [horses]," said Young. "The men were compelled to dismount to keep themselves from being frost bitten." Icicles gathered on the horses' manes, covered their bridles and halters, and dangled from their nostrils. Ice coated the beards and moustaches of the men. "Half the time they walked by their steeds, stamping their feet, swinging their hands and beating their bodies to drive away the stupor which extreme cold imposes on flesh and blood." There was no loud word spoken. "Commands, if given, were uttered in soft tones, and all were directed to ride, walk or march in absolute silence."

By dawn on the 31st, the Confederates had covered only eight miles, but luck was with them. The Federals in Lebanon, heeding the weather, had chosen to stay in their works, believing Morgan would come to them. They would not discover his detour till the late afternoon, when his van was safely in Campbellsville.[8]

During these daylight hours, however, a singular event took place, one that underscored the bitterness existing in a divided Kentucky. Colonel Dennis Halisey, leading the 6th Kentucky Union Cavalry, was scouting far in advance of his command when he and an aide were confronted by two officers of Morgan's 2nd Kentucky. They were Captain Alexander Tribble and Lieutenant George Eastin, and they had been lagging behind the rear guard, looking for a fight. "We had never heard of Halisey until the day before," said Eastin, "and then through the prayers of the women sympathizers of the South . . . who had besought us that we kill [him] before we left the State."

Halisey's ill-timed reconnaissance would lead to his undoing. The two Rebels surprised their foes at a turn in the road, and took shots at them but missed. Then Tribble and the aide grappled at close quarters. Both lost their pistols in the struggle and fell from their saddles into a roadside creek. There Tribble, a powerful man, pushed the Yank's head under the water until he surrendered. Meanwhile Eastin, moving to within ten feet of Halisey, leveled his revolver at him and was about to fire when the latter threw up one of his hands.

"I am your prisoner, sir! I am your prisoner!" he shouted.

The Confederate closed on Halisey's right and demanded his pistols. "Instead, however, of giving them up," Eastin would report, "he dropped his bridle rein and, reaching over with his left hand, grabbed me in the collar and, at the same time . . . fired at me again. The discharge burned and blackened my face, and the flash for an instant blinded me, but almost instinctively . . . I [grabbed] him, and putting my pistol firmly against his temple, I fired again."

Halisey was killed instantly. Eastin barely had time to catch his breath before a third Yankee galloped upon the scene. "Tribble was completely disarmed," he said. "The pistol that I had been using and still held in my hand was empty, and while I had [another] under my overcoat . . . there was no time to make the exchange—so I leveled the empty one at [him]."

The bluff worked. "Seeing the fate of his companions, [he] rode up and handed me his carbine and a pair of pistols."[9]

Morgan spent New Year's Eve in Campbellsville, still a jump ahead of the Federals, and twenty-four hours later crossed the Cumberland River and withdrew into Tennessee. Summed up a well-satisfied John Wyeth: "This was Morgan's most successful expedition. The Louisville & Nashville Railroad was a wreck from Bacon Creek to Shepherdsville. . . . We had captured about nineteen hundred prisoners, destroyed a vast amount of Government property, with a loss of only two men killed, twenty-four wounded, and sixty-four missing. The command returned well armed and better mounted than when we set out."[10]

Despite these setbacks, the Federals in east Tennessee would not be denied. Rosecrans previously had amassed large quantities of stores in Nashville, so the shutting down of the L&N, in the immediate term, did not prevent his going on the offensive. On January 2, he assailed and defeated Braxton Bragg at Stones River, forcing the Rebels to evacuate Murfreesboro and withdraw farther south to Tullahoma, Tennessee.

Earlier, during the first days of the raid, the love-smitten Morgan had bought a silk party gown for Mattie and sent it to her in Murfreesboro. It arrived just in time for a gala Christmas celebration. "I wore it to the ball last Friday night," she later wrote her sister, "given in honor of 'the bandit and his bride.' It was magnificent and very much admired. I had a splendid time and of course was something of a belle. . . . My life is all a joyous dream now, for I know my liege lord is devoted to me."

Replied the sister, "Dear Mattie: You think the honeymoon will never pass, don't you?"

The comment seems more than a trifle arch. Thus far, Morgan was proving himself more than capable of juggling martial and marital responsibilities.[11]

ELEVEN

THE EAST, DECEMBER 26–31: STUART AND HAMPTON ON THE RAPPAHANNOCK

On December 13, in his first test as commander of the Army of the Potomac, the hapless General Ambrose Burnside had sent his troops across the Rappahannock River at Fredericksburg, midway between Washington and Richmond, with cruel results. He lost some 13,000 men in futile head-on assaults against the entrenched Confederates, and under cover of night had little choice but to pull back the Union forces to the north bank in humiliation and confusion.

Jeb Stuart and his cavalry, mostly stationed with Stonewall Jackson on the right of the Rebel works, saw little action in the engagement. But twenty-three-year-old Major John Pelham, head of the horse artillery, had added to his luster, persuading Jeb to let him take a single 12-pound Napoleon a mile outside the defensive lines. There he riddled the oncoming enemy, at a right angle, with enfilading fire. Though four Federal batteries targeted him, he had gotten off his rounds so quickly, and moved his piece so expertly, that they failed to silence him. Three times, a concerned Stuart suggested Pelham withdraw, but only on the last occasion, with his ammunition all but gone, did he comply.

Taking in the scene from a hilltop, Robert E. Lee was exhilarated. "It is glorious to see such courage in one so young!" he told his aides.[1]

In the days before the battle was joined, Stuart had been keeping his men busy with traditional cavalry duties, sending Wade Hampton up the Rappahannock, far west of the main lines, to raid in the open country between Fredericksburg and Washington. During the first of two such forays, Hampton crossed the river at Kelly's Ford with some 150 Carolina and Georgia troopers and, on November 28 near Warrenton, bagged some 90 men and 100 horses of the 3rd Pennsylvania Cavalry. In the second instance, he left Brandy Station on December 10 with some 520 men, and two days later near Dumfries and the Potomac River, captured 50 more Federals and 24 wagons laden with supplies. In neither action did he suffer a single casualty.

"[We found] almost every variety of goods," said one Confederate of the Dumfries raid, "eatables, drinkables, confectionaries, buckskin gauntlets, boots, shoes, hats, [the] choicest underwear, etc." Colonel Calbraith Butler appropriated a four-horse team and a covered wagon. "Tired of the saddle and having a . . . fancy to drive," he wrote his wife, "I mounted the seat just at dusk, and got on swimmingly until it got very dark, when I struck a stump and over went the wagon, driver, passengers, plunder and all. My foot caught in the reins and dragged me . . . in the reddest sort of Culpeper mud. . . . I never laughed so [much] in my life when I found nobody was hurt."[2]

Following Burnside's defeat, while the Federals were settling in along the Rappahannock for the winter, Stuart ordered Hampton across the river on a third expedition—not entirely to the latter's pleasure. No horse soldier was braver than the pragmatic South Carolinian, but he continued to chafe under the flamboyant Jeb's authority, believing he favored Virginians. "General Stuart . . . has always given us the hardest work to perform and the worst places to camp," he wrote a family member. "My numbers are already reduced by our hard service, and I fear there will be no chance to restore our horses to condition."[3]

Hampton nonetheless complied with the order, and on December 17 with some 300 troopers, mostly Carolinians, crossed the Rappahannock on his way to the town of Occoquan. Near there the next day, he came upon an immense 100-wagon supply train on the north bank of the Occoquan River. Capturing it and taking 150 prisoners was no problem; overcoming the shortage of rafts and getting the wagons back across the stream was a formidable task. Hampton solved the problem, at least partially, by posting up his best marksmen and having them pick off pursuing infantrymen. Even so, he got only 20 of the wagons across the Occoquan before hightailing it for the Rappahannock.

"General Hampton has again made a brilliant dash into enemy [territory]," Stuart reported, "and I cordially commend his conduct."[4]

Jeb spent a lively and festive Christmas Day as one of Jackson's dinner guests, along with Robert E. Lee and General William Pendleton, at Moss Neck, an estate owned by Richard Corbin, who was serving in the infantry as a private. The party was held in an outbuilding, comfortably furnished and decorated with sporting scenes, that Corbin had used as an office and that Stonewall had made his headquarters. Stuart and the reserved Jackson, both devout Christians and firm teetotalers, were fast friends despite the difference in their personalities, and Jeb used the occasion to indulge in some good-natured joshing.

Seated at a table laden with oysters, ham, turkey, bread, pickles, and even a bottle of wine, he feigned shock at how Jackson was living. "He pointed to the racing and sporting pictures . . . ," wrote one historian, "and he called on his fellow guests to say what would be the judgment of the admiring old ladies of the South if they had this exhibition of the real tastes of their idol." Then Jeb picked up a crock of butter, stamped with the outline of a rooster. "Observe its adornment. . . . Any man with two eyes could see for himself—it was a rooster, doubtless a gamecock. Jackson might protest that the print had been made by the person who gave him the butter, but who could believe that? [He] had carried his sporting taste so far that he had to have a gamecock on the very butter he used at his table!" Gesturing toward the bottle of wine . . . well, here Stuart could only shake his head in mock disapproval.

Jackson, as was his wont during Jeb's flights of fancy, for the most part kept his silence, but reportedly "blushed like a girl."[5]

Early on December 26, Stuart was back in the saddle, leading 1,800 men under Hampton, Fitz Lee, and Rooney Lee, and four guns under Pelham, in his most ambitious Rappahannock raid to date. Once more, the target would be the Occoquan-Dumfries area. Hampton was to move on the former; Stuart with the two Lees on the warehouses near the latter.

Neither operation would be entirely successful. Fitz Lee did capture a few wagons and pickets on the way to Dumfries, but Jeb, even as he was planning an assault on the town the next day, found he had to revise his plans. "Before [the attack] became serious," said his aide Henry McClellan, "Stuart discovered that the statements of prisoners . . . were correct, and that the town was held by a force of infantry and cavalry whose numbers exceeded his own." Rather than risk an all-out assault, he contented himself with a demonstration, and then under cover of darkness moved west to bivouac for the night at Cole's Store.

Hampton, who had the longer march, did not arrive at Occoquan until near sunset on the 27th. He forthwith divided his force, directing Calbraith Butler to make a frontal attack while he swept to the rear of the town and cut off the enemy's escape. But Butler moved forward before Hampton could set up his blockade, and the Federals for the most part got away, yielding few wagons and prisoners.

The next morning, the reunited expedition moved east from Cole's Store back toward the Occoquan River, still looking for a proper fight. "At a short distance from Greenwood Church," said McClellan, "the advance of Fitz Lee's brigade encountered the enemy's cavalry." The 1st Virginia promptly charged, putting to flight the 2nd and 17th Pennsylvania, and pursuing them for some two miles to Selectman's Ford. "[There] the enemy was tempted by the narrow and difficult nature of the ford to make a stand. . . . The long chase from Greenwood Church had now brought the 5th Virginia to the front." Without hesitation, Colonel Thomas Rosser thrust his regiment across the stream. "The charge was of necessity made by file; but it was executed with such spirit that Rosser suffered no loss."[6]

Once across the Occoquan the Rebels overran some hastily evacuated Federal cavalry camps, including that of the 3rd Pennsylvania, burning what they could not carry away. Stuart at this juncture, having met and thrashed the enemy's horsemen, doubtless was permitting himself a smile.

Now what to do? To withdraw, or to press one's luck? For Jeb, the answer was clear: he would push northward to the Orange & Alexandria Railroad at Burke's Station, confident that he could inflict further damage but still escape without harm. Like John Hunt Morgan, he had with him a telegrapher who could tap the lines and keep him informed of the enemy's thinking. "It was ludicrous," said one Rebel officer of the foe's consternation, "as [the Federals] were in great alarm, and orders were telegraphed to destroy everything in case of our attacking them."[7]

Sometime after dark on the 28th, Stuart arrived at Burke's Station, taking over the telegraph office before the operator could sound a warning. There through the night he monitored the frantic messages describing efforts to find him. Then, before moving out, he dispatched a wire of his own. It was addressed to M. C. Meigs, quartermaster general in Washington, and it straightfacedly took the officer to task for "the bad quality of the mules lately furnished [by the Federals], which interfered seriously with our moving the captured wagons."

December 29 found Stuart at Fairfax Court House, a scant ten miles from the main Washington defenses. "[He] conceived that it might be possible to surprise and capture the post . . ." said Major McClellan. "He therefore marched direct to that point; but within about a mile of the town his advance was stopped by a volley from infantry and artillery, which showed that the enemy . . . was on the alert."[8]

Jeb took no more chances, withdrawing first to Vienna, and then by easy stages to Middleburg and Warrenton. Recrossing the Rappahannock, he arrived in Culpeper on New Year's Eve. He had lost fourteen killed and wounded, but taken some 200 prisoners and captured twenty wagons. Just as importantly, he again had embarrassed the Yankee cavalry. Even those foes he had not fought and routed had worn out their horses pursuing his fast-moving columns.

To Stuart's disappointment, his latest foray into the enemy's rear did not bring him the press attention given his earlier feats. The Southern newspapers wrote up the raid, but made it sound no more than expected; the Northern ones downplayed the excursion or, in the case of *The New York Times*, even labeled it a "failure." That January 1, President Abraham Lincoln was drawing all the headlines, as he issued the long-awaited Emancipation Proclamation.[9]

1 8 6 3

ONE
* * * *

THE EAST, JANUARY–JUNE:
MOSBY'S RANGERS

In January 1863, a hitherto unknown lieutenant and scout named John Singleton Mosby, who had accompanied Jeb Stuart on the First Ride Around McClellan and become a trusted friend, received permission to organize a group of partisan rangers in northern Virginia and conduct guerrilla warfare in the Federal rear. Though he would roam through Fauquier, Loudoun, Fairfax, and Prince William counties, his base of operations would be east of the Blue Ridge—from Snicker's Gap in the north to Manassas Gap in the south—and west of the Bull Run Mountains. The area contained some 125 square miles of verdant farmland, and included such towns as Snickersville, Piedmont, The Plains, Middleburg, and Aldie.

Mosby's initiative had been strongly backed by Stuart, but many Southerners—and certainly their Yankee opponents—frowned on partisans, claiming they were undisciplined and more interested in looting than fighting. General Henry Heth, a confidant of Lee's, described such irregulars as "notorious thieves and murderers, more ready to plunder friends than foes. . . . They do as they please, go where they please." Indeed, Stuart's instructions to Mosby took note of this disdain. "By all means ignore the term 'Partisan Ranger,'" he told him. "It is in bad repute." Instead he suggested calling the unit Mosby's Regulars, which would be "a name of pride with friends and respectful trepidation with enemies." To emphasize the point, he added, "You ought to be very fastidious in choosing your men."[1]

There is no doubt that the Rangers, as Mosby nonetheless called them, were unusual horse soldiers. "[We] had no camps nor fixed quarters, and never slept in tents," said John Munson, one of their number. ". . . The idea of making coffee, frying bacon, or soaking hardtack was never entertained. When we wanted to eat we stopped at a friendly farmhouse. . . . Every man had some special [place] he could call his own. . . . The people in that part of the state . . . were glad to have [us] among them."

Unlike most partisan leaders, Mosby kept his men under tight rein. "[He] would not permit anyone to commit a crime, or even a misdemeanor, in his domain. One of our men, in a spirit of deviltry, once turned over an old Quaker farmer's milk cans, and when Mosby heard of it he ordered me to take [him] over to the army, which was then near Winchester, and turn him over to General [Jubal] Early, with the message that such a man was not fit to be a guerilla." If discipline was tight, drill was nonexistent. "[We] could not have formed in a straight line had there ever been any need for our doing so," continued Munson. "We did not know the bugle-calls, and very rarely had roll-call. Our dress was not uniform in make or color; we did not address our officers, except Mosby, by their titles."

Two rules, however, were inflexible: obey orders instantly, and fight like hellions. "Each of [us] was armed with two muzzle-loading Colt's army revolvers of forty-four caliber. They were worn in belt holsters. Some few who could afford it . . . wore an extra pair in their saddle-holsters or stuck into their boot legs. These weapons were extremely deadly and effective in hand-to-hand engagements. . . . Long and frequent practice had made every man in the command a good shot. . . . As a general thing our fights were fast and furious and quickly over, one or the other side retiring at a dead run when the pistols were empty."[2]

No one knows how many troopers Mosby actually led. Beginning with a handful of men, he soon attracted hundreds of young bucks—perhaps over the course of the war as many as a thousand—from all over Virginia and Maryland. But he kept his numbers as low as possible on any given raid—sometimes several score, rarely more than one or two hundred—so as to move all the faster and escape notice until he struck. His men saw themselves as an elite fighting group, riding into danger and smiting the enemy with devil-may-care indifference. "Usually a young fellow who joined [his] command," said Munson, who himself walked ten days from

Richmond to do just that, "came to him with romantic ideas. . . . It was
something vague in his mind."

That Mosby was a charismatic figure is a given, and he could be a vain
one as well, but he was modest about the reasons troopers flocked to his
standard. "The true secret," he said, "[is] that it was a fascinating life, and
its attractions far more than counterbalanced its hardships." There was
none of the drudgery of camp, only the rush of adrenaline that came in
moments of peril. It was warfare especially suitable for the young, and
most of his men were teenagers. "Why, they are the best soldiers I have,"
he said, with charming but chilling candor. "They haven't sense enough to
know danger when they see it, and will fight anything I tell them to."[3]

John Singleton Mosby was born on December 6, 1833, in Powhatan
County, Virginia, one of eleven children of Alfred D. and Virginia McLau-
rine Mosby, both of whom were members of the landed Piedmont gentry.
When John was seven, the family moved to Albemarle County, where his
father bought a 400-acre farm near Charlottesville. The boy grew up
sickly and frail, and was often bullied in grade school, but he was much
praised at home, giving him inordinate self-confidence. "His mother loved
him intensely; she was right, and the outsiders were wrong," wrote one biographer. ". . . Some victims of bullying turn inward and become shy and
withdrawn, but, with his tremendous inner strength, he always counterattacked. . . . He came to identify with the underdog struggling against a
stronger opponent."

When Mosby was sixteen he enrolled in the University of Virginia,
where he concentrated and did well in Greek language and literature but
largely ignored his other courses. There he became involved in several un-
dergraduate scrapes, revealing a hair-trigger temper under his mannerly
exterior. The worst of these by far occurred in March 1853, when he was
nineteen. Learning that George Turpin, a burly fellow student with a well-
deserved reputation for violence, had been making rude and disparaging
remarks about him, Mosby, following the traditions of the day, sent off a
note via a friend asking for an explanation.

Turpin, who already had used a knife to slash one opponent's face and
a rock to smash another's skull, exploded with rage when he read the letter, belittling the weak-looking Mosby all the more and vowing, "I will
see the damn rascal and eat him up, blood raw, *on sight.*"

Within hours he showed up at Mosby's boardinghouse, eager to fulfil
his threat. "I understand you have been making some assertions," the os-
tensible victim told him. Turpin growled something inaudible and rushed

forward, but before he took two steps, Mosby pulled a small pistol from his pocket and fired, the bullet going through the assailant's mouth and into his neck, and knocking him to the ground.

Turpin would survive, and he hardly was well liked, but the indisputable fact is that Mosby had shot an unarmed man. The ensuing trial in Charlottesville revolved around Mosby's contention that he had acted in self-defense. After due deliberation the jury acquitted him of "malicious shooting," but found him guilty on the lesser charge of "unlawful shooting," sentencing him to one year in prison.

Mosby would spend seven months in jail and then, in December, be pardoned by the governor. Ironically, during his time in prison, he would embark on his future career, borrowing a copy of Blackstone's *Commentaries* from William Robertson, the town prosecutor, and beginning the study of law. He continued his training after his release and soon was admitted to the Virginia bar, opening an office in Howardsville. It was there he met Pauline Clarke, the pretty, intelligent daughter of a former U.S. congressman, whose quiet assurance mirrored his own.

Following his marriage in 1857 in a Roman Catholic ceremony, Mosby transferred his practice to Bristol, where the couple settled and, before the outbreak of the war, had two children. Pauline was a devout Catholic, and the children were raised in her faith, but Mosby seems to have had little interest in religion. "I rarely go to any," he answered a relative who asked what church he attended. "Occasionally to the Catholic, because my wife [is] a Catholic."[4]

In early 1861, just after secession, Mosby enlisted as a private in a cavalry unit led by William E. "Grumble" Jones that was soon absorbed into the 1st Virginia, then headed by Jeb Stuart, and in July fought at First Manassas. "When we were first brought upon the field we served as a reserve just in rear of our artillery," he wrote Pauline. ". . . For two hours we sat there on our horses, exposed to a perfect storm of grapeshot, balls, bombs, etc. . . . Yet nobody was hurt." Later he was ordered to reconnoiter. "I rode my horse nearly to death . . . going backward and forward, watching the enemy's movements to prevent their flanking our command." Then the Federals suddenly gave way. "They fled like a flock of panic-stricken sheep. We took enough arms, accoutrements, etc. to equip the whole army. . . . I have provided myself very well."

In the weeks after the battle, Stuart, noting Mosby's verve and energy, began to see him as a potential leader, and in 1862 made him a lieutenant, adding him to his staff as an aide and scout. In that capacity, Mosby participated in the First Ride Around McClellan and the Seven Days, was briefly captured, and then upon his exchange, served at Second Manassas, Antietam, and Fredericksburg. More and more, however, he was becoming an advocate of guerrilla warfare—so much so that Stuart, in the final days of the year, would yield to his entreaties and send him off on his own. "It looked as though I was leading a forlorn hope," Mosby would say, "but I was never discouraged. In general my purpose was to threaten and harass the enemy on the border and . . . compel him to withdraw troops from his front to guard the line of the Potomac and Washington."

He still was scrawny and whippet-thin, but his daring and intensity more than made up for his physical shortcomings. John Munson would remember the first time he saw his commander: "The shock was something considerable. I beheld a small, plainly attired man, fair of complexion, slight but wiry, talking quietly to one of his [troopers]. . . . The total absence of visible might, the lack of swagger . . . all contributed to my astonishment. . . . He did not even strut."[5]

Now in late January 1863, with fifteen troopers loaned to him by Stuart from the 1st Virginia, Mosby began the raids in northern Virginia that would make him famous. The odds seemed ludicrous—the Yankee cavalry in the area numbered some 3,300. But they were spread out in a half dozen camps, their pickets were bored, and their commanders indolent. "In a day or so after I arrived in Loudoun," he explained, "we began operations on the outposts of Fairfax. . . . Up to that time the pickets had passed a quiet life in their camps . . . but now they were kept under arms or awake all night by a foe who assailed them where he was least expected."

The first of the forays occurred on January 26. Guided by John Underwood, a local man who knew every inch of Fairfax County, Mosby's men emerged from the darkness at Chantilly Church and surprised the Federal pickets, capturing eleven men and horses. The following night, when 200 of the 5th New Jersey under Colonel Percy Wyndham trotted into nearby Middleburg looking for the assailants, the Rebels struck again, falling on the rear of the column and in the confusion killing one Yankee and capturing three more. Wyndham, the British soldier of fortune who had been taken prisoner by Turner Ashby, had been paroled and exchanged, and was once more in the saddle.

Mosby's raids continued unabated through February—he seemed to own the night. "Have had a gay time with the Yankees," he told Pauline. Meanwhile his ranks were doubling, and then doubling again, as recruits came to his side.[6]

On the 26th, his force was strong enough to attack forty-four men of the 18th Pennsylvania while they slept in a schoolhouse near Chantilly, taking shelter from sleet and rain. "As only a raccoon would travel on such a night," he said, "I knew the pickets would feel safe and be sound asleep, so that a single shot would create a panic." That is precisely what happened, with half-awake Yankees fleeing the schoolhouse and taking cover in the woods, even as the Rebels were making off with their horses.

Mosby, soon to earn the sobriquet "Gray Ghost," had little regard for Wyndham, who was lodged at Fairfax Court House. "He was familiar with the old rules but . . . they were out of date, and his experience in war had not taught him to counteract the forays and surprises that kept his men in the saddle. . . . The loss of sleep is irritating to anyone and, in his vexation at being struck by an invisible foe, he sent me a message calling me a horse thief. I did not deny it, but retorted that all the horses I had stolen had riders, and that the riders had sabers, carbines and pistols."[7]

Early in March, Mosby learned that the Federals inadvertently had left a gap—between Chantilly and Centreville—in the lines protecting Fairfax Court House. This lapse, combined with inside information he was receiving from James Ames, a Union deserter, intrigued him. Both Wyndham and General Edwin Stoughton, commander of the 2nd Brigade, were, according to Ames, sleeping in comfortable houses in the town apart from their troops. A quick, slashing raid just might bag the two of them before the hundreds of Federals in the immediate area knew what was happening.

Mosby could not resist. On the night of March 8, with twenty-nine rangers, he moved east from the Bull Run Mountains in mist and drizzling rain, passed through the gap north of Centreville, and in the wee hours approached Fairfax Court House. "We entered the village from the direction of the railroad station. There were a few sentinels about . . . but it was so dark they could not distinguish us from their own people. As our great desire was to capture Wyndham, [the deserter] Ames was sent with a party to the house in which he knew [he] had his quarters." But fortune was in the Englishman's favor. He had left earlier for Washington, and the raiding party had to settle for the capture of two staff officers, some horses, and Wyndham's full-dress uniform.

The foray continued in several directions, with sentries being surprised and disarmed as necessary. Mosby himself headed the group of six or seven men who rode up before the two-story brick house where Stoughton was staying.

"We dismounted and knocked loudly on the door," he said. "Soon a window above was opened and someone asked who was there. I answered, 'Fifth New York Cavalry, with a dispatch for General Stoughton.' The door was open and a staff officer . . . was before me. I took hold of his nightshirt, whispered my name in his ear, and told him to take me to Stoughton's room."

Resistance was useless. The Rebels soon were in the general's bedchamber, where they found him fast asleep.

"There was no time for ceremony," said Mosby, "so I drew up the bedclothes, pulled up the general's shirt, and gave him a spank on his bare back[side]."

Stoughton, twenty-four, the youngest general in the Union army and a member of a prominent Vermont family, was not used to such treatment.

"What the hell is this?" he blurted out, as he rolled over and faced men with drawn pistols.

"I am Mosby!" was the reply. "Stuart's cavalry has possession of the courthouse! Be quick and dress!"

While he was putting on his clothes, Stoughton asked whether Fitz Lee, a classmate at West Point, was in the raiding party. Mosby replied in the affirmative. "My motive in trying to deceive Stoughton was to deprive him of all hope of escape and induce him to dress [faster]. We were in a critical situation, surrounded by the camps of thousands of troops, with several hundred in the town."

The Rebels had been in Fairfax for almost an hour, without a shot being fired. "When we reached the rendezvous, I found all the squads waiting us with their prisoners and horses. There were three times as many prisoners as my men."

Now Stoughton saw how few troopers Mosby was leading. "This is a bold thing you have done. But you will certainly be caught. Our cavalry will soon be after you."

"Perhaps so," was the quiet reply.

The return, however, would be without incident, though some of the prisoners, taking advantage of the fact there were so many of them and so few guards, managed to escape. "We were now half a mile from Centreville," Mosby said, "and the dawn was just breaking. . . . The [Federal] camps were quiet; there was no sign of alarm; the telegraph lines had been cut, and no news had come about our exploit. . . . We could see the cannon bristling through the redoubts and hear the sentinel on the parapet call us to halt. But no attention was paid to him, and he did no fire. . . . No doubt he thought we were a body of their own cavalry going on a scout."[8]

Two days later, on the 10th, in the midst of a pouring rain, Mosby brought Stoughton and his staff to Fitzhugh Lee's headquarters at Culpeper. He knew that Fitz disapproved of partisans, but he was completely unprepared for his reception. Everyone was dripping wet, a fire was blazing in the office, and the ranger leader must have been looking forward to sitting down and drying out. "General Lee," he announced, "here is your friend General Stoughton, whom I have just captured."

Fitz rose from his desk and greeted Stoughton warmly, providing him with a chair and seat at the hearth, deliberately ignoring Mosby. "If I had been an orderly who brought him a morning report," the latter would say, "he could not have treated me with more indifference." Previously, the two men had been well acquainted. "He was very polite to his old classmate and to the officers, but . . . he did not ask me to take a seat by the fire, nor seem impressed by what I had done."

Seeing he was not welcome, a visibly angry Mosby ignored Lee in turn, shook hands with the prisoners, and left. That evening Major General Stuart, as it happened, arrived in Culpeper from Fredericksburg. "I can never forget the joy his generous heart showed when he met me," said Mosby. "That was a sufficient reward."

For good measure, however, Stuart promptly promoted his protégé and issued a general order praising him. "Captain John S. Mosby," it read in part, "has for a long time attracted the attention of his generals by his boldness, skill and success. . . . His last brilliant exploit—the capture of Brigadier Stoughton, two captains, and thirty other prisoners . . . and fifty-eight horses, justifies this recognition. . . . This feat, unparalleled in the war, was performed . . . without loss or injury."

Fitz Lee nonetheless continued his vendetta, soon afterward ordering Mosby to return the original fifteen men who had been detailed to him from the 1st Virginia. "This attempt to deprive me of a command met with no favor from Stuart. . . . He issued an order for them to stay until *he* recalled them."

The luckless General Stoughton, who was soon paroled, found that his military career was over. He would not receive another command, and indeed his capture would give rise to many jokes. "I do not mind so much the loss of a general," Lincoln reputedly said, "for I can create another in five minutes—but I hate to lose the horses."[9]

Throughout March the quick-witted Mosby continued his harassing activities, sometimes in daylight and often against great odds. On the 17th, for instance, leading some 50 men near the Little River Turnpike, he encountered 200 Federal horsemen. "At a point where the enemy had blockaded the road with fallen trees," he said, "I formed to receive them, for . . . I knew they would imagine themselves fallen into an ambuscade. When they [came] within 100 yards of me I [instead] ordered a charge." The Yankees, not expecting the onslaught, broke and fled, with Mosby's pursuit lasting for miles. "We killed five, wounded a considerable number, and brought off one lieutenant and 35 men [as] prisoners."

Such constant riding induced carelessness. On March 31, after reconnoitering with sixty-nine men near Dranesville and covering some forty miles in snow and mud, he and his exhausted troopers bedded down about 10 p.m. at a farm owned by Thomas and Lydia Miskel, neglecting to post outlying videttes. "I confess that on this occasion," Mosby would say, "I had not taken sufficient precautions to guard against surprise."

At dawn some 150 troopers from the 1st Vermont Cavalry, headed by Captain Henry C. Flint, learned of Mosby's whereabouts and galloped toward the farm to take him unawares. "One of my men, whom I had left on the Leesburg Pike, came dashing in. . . . But he had scarcely given us the [alarm] when the enemy appeared a few hundred yards off. . . . At this time our horses were eating; all had their bridles off, and some even their saddles."

Since both the house and barn were enclosed by a high plank fence, as was the long, narrow lane leading up to the property, the Federals appeared to have the Rebels trapped in a cul-de-sac. But here Captain Flint made a crucial mistake. Mosby's troopers, we will remember, used revolvers; they had few weapons effective at long range. Instead of laying back and having his men dismount and use their carbines to pick off the Rebels at a distance, the reckless Flint charged down the lane toward the barn and closed on them, compounding his mistake by closing the gate behind him, thinking to prevent the foe from escaping.

Mosby and a dozen men took up the challenge, waiting coolly with their revolvers behind cover while their comrades saddled up, ignoring the glinting sabers and thundering noise of the charge. "Shoot the brave men and the cowards will run" was a Stonewall Jackson maxim, and the ranger leader endorsed it. He and his troopers, each firing two pistols, laid down a fusillade at thirty yards in the narrow lane that killed Flint instantly, and leveled some dozen other bluecoats, stopping the attack cold. Riderless horses—rearing, snorting, and milling about—added to the confusion.

By now a score of his rangers were mounted, and Mosby, still on foot, led them down the lane toward the dazed enemy in a counterattack. "Fol-

low me! Charge 'em! Charge 'em! Go through 'em," he screamed. Someone brought him a horse and he mounted. Once more the Colt revolvers
blasted away, making the Yankees' sabers useless. Each Rebel was dis-
patching or capturing two, three, or four opponents.

The panicked Federals, especially those in the second rank, at this juncture had no other thought than to get away. But before they could reopen
the gate they suffered even more harm, and when they succeeded they became clogged in the opening, each man trying to get through at once.
"The Yankees," said Mosby, "terrified at the yells of [our] men . . . broke
and fled in every direction. . . . We left on the field nine of them killed—
among them a captain and lieutenant—and about fifteen too badly
wounded for removal; in this lot two lieutenants. We brought off 82 prisoners . . . and about 100 horses and equipments."[10]

The Union contingent suffered seventy-five percent casualties. His own
losses consisted of one trooper killed and three wounded. Within days he
would be promoted to the rank of major.

Through May and June, in the aftermath of Lee's triumph at Chancellorsville, Mosby remained a constant irritant in the Federal rear. His adversaries, meanwhile, resorted to what can best be called dissembling.
Reported General Julius Stahel, then in overall charge of the cavalry in the
area, on May 5: "Had our horses been in better condition . . . [Mosby]
and nor a single one of his men would have escaped." Again from the
delusional Stahel on May 30: "We whipped him like the devil. . . . My
forces are still pursuing him."

During this period the Gray Ghost further enhanced his reputation, on
one occasion using an artillery piece. "Last Saturday evening," he told
Stuart, "I captured a train of twelve cars on the Virginia & Alexandria
Railroad loaded with supplies. . . . Having destroyed the train, I proceeded some distance back when I recognized the enemy in a strong force
in my front. One shell which exploded in their ranks served to put them to
flight. After going about a mile further, the enemy [was] reported pursuing. Their advance was again checked by a shot from the howitzer. . . .
Twice again did they rally and as often were sent reeling back. At last our
ammunition became exhausted and we were forced to abandon the gun."

On June 11, he even crossed over the Potomac to the Maryland shore
with 100 troopers, falling on elements of the 6th Michigan Cavalry. "Had
I succeeded in crossing the river at night, as I expected, I would have had
no difficulty in capturing them; but unfortunately my guide mistook the
road and . . . I did not get over until daylight." The result, nonetheless,

was predictable. "The enemy (between 80 and 100) formed to receive me. A charge was ordered; the shock of which [they] could not resist . . . with the loss of seven killed, and 17 prisoners; also 20 odd horses or more."[11]

Mosby, whose men had been formally mustered in mid-June into Confederate service as the 43rd Battalion of Virginia Cavalry, was proving invaluable to Stuart, providing him with vital information on the disposition of the Federal forces west of the Shenandoah. How the headstrong Jeb, on the eve of Gettysburg, interpreted these accounts is another matter, a story that dramatically affected the outcome of that battle, and one which we will recount in a future chapter.

TWO

* * * *

THE EAST, MARCH 17: FITZ LEE
V. AVERELL AT KELLY'S FORD

Up to this point in the war, the Federal cavalry in the East—and the West as well—clearly had been outclassed by its opponents, but Joseph "Fighting Joe" Hooker, who had replaced Ambrose Burnside as head of the Army of the Potomac, was determined to change all that. About 5 a.m. on March 17, he sent Brigadier William Averell with 2,100 troopers and six guns across the Rappahannock at Kelly's Ford, with strict orders "to attack and rout or destroy" Fitz Lee's command, which was at Culpeper. Averell knew his own neck was on the line. The Confederates under Fitz had been particularly active in recent weeks, despite Fitz's personal feud with John Mosby, and the incensed Hooker wanted him taught a lesson.

Defending the ford were a dozen or so pickets under the able Captain James Breckinridge of the 2nd Virginia, whose deadly fire somehow managed for two hours to delay the assault's progress. "Averell dismounted two squadrons and endeavored to cross his advance guard under their [covering] fire, but failed," said Major Henry McClellan. "Two similar attempts made by his pioneers met with the same result. An effort was made to find a crossing below the ford; but the swollen stream, four feet deep at the ford, was impassable elsewhere."

Lieutenant Simeon A. Brown of the 1st Rhode Island now was dispatched with sixteen men on what amounted to a suicide mission. He and two of his troopers miraculously reached the opposite bank; the rest did not. But they opened up the way for their comrades to splash across in their wake. Brown's horse was wounded in two places, and he himself, though unhurt, received three bullets through his clothing. Two to three more hours were consumed, once the resistance at the ford was quashed, in moving the whole of the Union command over the stream. "The river was deep and swift, and the caissons and limbers of the guns were submerged," said McClellan. "It was necessary that the cavalrymen should carry across the artillery ammunition in the nose-bags of their horses."[1]

Shortly after 10 a.m., when the Federals were a half mile inland, Lee with 800 troopers met them head-on. Averell, who had known Fitz at West Point, was not surprised. "From what I had learned of Lee's position," he said, "and from what I knew personally of his character, I expected him to meet me on the road to his camp."

The fight opened on the C. T. Wheatley farm, where Averell's van had dismounted and taken cover. "From this point General Lee ordered the 3rd [Virginia] to charge," said McClellan. ". . . The regiment swept down the line of the stone fence which separated them from the enemy in the woods beyond, delivering the fire of their pistols. The utmost exertions of the Federal officers were required to keep their men from flight. . . . But no outlet could be found through the fence." Now more and more of Averell's troopers came up and made their numbers felt. Though the 5th Virginia galloped forward to stem the onslaught, it could not resist the pressure, and all along the front the Rebels slowly began to yield. In the series of clamorous saber-clashing charges and countercharges that followed, said McClellan, "General Lee found himself largely outnumbered and was compelled to withdraw; but he retired in such manner that Averell was able to gain no advantage over him." Now the front stabilized again, perhaps one mile further from the river.[2]

The engagement would last through the afternoon, with men on both sides fighting with great intensity. Surely no soldier was more heroic than Sergeant W. J. Kimbrough of the 4th Virginia. "Wounded early in the day, he refused to leave the field," said Fitz Lee in his official report. "In the last charge he was the first to spring to the ground to open the fence; then dashing in at the head of the column, he was twice sabered over the head, his arm shattered by a bullet, captured and carried across the river, when he escaped, and walked back twelve miles to his camp."[3]

With Lee in the cavalry clash that morning were Major John Pelham and Stuart, both of whom were in Culpeper by happenstance. Days earlier the blond, handsome Pelham, "as grand a flirt as ever lived," had received permission from Jeb to inspect some artillery at Orange Court House and, of course, visit some pretty young women in the vicinity. No sooner was he gone than Stuart, who had a habit of keeping his favorite artillerist close at hand, regretted his decision and sent a courier after him. The man did not catch up with Pelham until late on March 15, when he was already in Orange, so he decided to stay there for the night.[4]

The next morning, learning that the Federals might be crossing the Rappahannock at Kelly's Ford, Pelham took a train to Culpeper, eager to join the action. Besides, he knew that Stuart would be there, participating in a court-martial. That evening they met and briefly conferred, leaving Pelham plenty of time to call on a local beauty, Miss Bessie Shackleford.

When the news came the next day that Averell was advancing, the two men borrowed horses and rushed to the front. Though Fitz Lee remained in general charge of the battle, Stuart at one juncture could not resist taking the lead. When elements of the 3rd Virginia were breaking, he personally rallied them, waving his plumed hat and yelling, "Confound it, men, come back! Don't leave me here alone!"

Pelham meanwhile worked with Captain James Breathed in bringing up and sighting the horse artillery's guns, which until then had been left behind in the cavalry's rush toward the ford. "Do not let your fire cease! Drive them from their position!" Pelham shouted. Later, while he was galloping forward to rejoin Stuart, a shell burst overhead, and he fell wordlessly from his horse. He lay on the ground, in the words of Captain Harry Gilmor, "on his back, his eyes open, and looking very natural." Gilmor saw that the wound, which was caused by a tiny shell splinter and bleeding profusely, was in back of Pelham's head, and he assumed it was mortal.

He and others lifted him onto a horse and enlisted the help of two troopers.

"Take this officer to the nearest ambulance! Call a surgeon! Hurry!"

Gilmor next found Stuart, who saw the blood on Gilmor's hands and thought he was hurt.

"No, General," said Gilmor. "It's not my blood. It's Pelham's. He's dead. They killed him a few minutes ago."

Stuart mumbled a few words, dropped his head, and sobbed.[5]

With the two sides at stalemate, the fighting ended about 5:30 p.m., and the bluecoats returned whence they had come. Averell, an overly cautious man, had held back much of his command and not gone all-out to rout Fitz Lee, despite Hooker's admonitions, evidently fearing that Rebel infantry was drawing near. But he had shown that the Union cavalry in the East was improving, and could no longer be dismissed.

For the Confederates, the greatest concern in the aftermath of the battle was the wounding and subsequent death of the twenty-four-year-old Pelham, who was beloved throughout the army for his courage. Toward dusk Captain Gilmor came upon the two men he had ordered to take Pelham to a surgeon. They were trudging toward Culpeper, the body draped over the horse, the arms and legs hanging on either side—thinking he was dead. When Gilmor stretched Pelham out on the grass, so as to clean the blood from his face, he discovered he was still breathing. "Imagine my . . . vented wrath," he said, "when I learned that, instead of looking for an ambulance, they had moved toward Culpeper, a distance of eight miles. . . . I firmly believe that, had surgical aid been called . . . his life might have been saved."

No one will ever know. Pelham was taken to Judge Shackleford's house, where investigation showed, as Bessie and other women scurried about with hot water and blankets, that the shell splinter had entered and exited the back of the skull two inches apart, not touching the brain but inflicting neural damage. Regardless, Pelham had lost so much blood that he died at 1 p.m. the next afternoon.[6]

The sorrow was intense. "During the winter Pelham and I had become more intimate than we ever had before," said William Blackford, the Stuart aide. "Our tents were next [to] each other and we had built our stable together. . . . [He] and I had been reading aloud to each other [Sir Charles] Napier's 'Peninsula War,' and the day he left us . . . I marked the place we stopped and I have never had the heart to read more in it since." Wrote Robert E. Lee: "I mourn the loss of Major Pelham. I had hoped that a long career of usefulness and honor was still before him. He has been stricken down in the midst of both." Not bothering to restrain his tears, Stuart told the cavalry, "The noble, the chivalric, the gallant Pelham is no more." Just months earlier, he had lost his five-year-old daughter, Flora, to illness. Soon he would name his next child Virginia Pelham Stuart.[7]

By slow trains the body was taken back to Alabama, escorted by Heros von Borcke, who had a small window placed in the coffin lid so friends and admirers could take a last look at the smooth handsome face. It was as a posthumous lieutenant colonel that Pelham returned home. "I was [there] the night the body was brought in his casket," said a relative. "He had been dead two weeks, and the news of his death had gone all over [Benton] county, and they came, old men (the young ones were all at the front) and women, young ladies and children . . . to meet and honor the remains of one so loved and admired. It was a beautiful moonlit night the last of March and as the casket, covered with white flowers . . . [was] borne by white-haired old men . . . it seemed a company 'all in white.' . . . And I heard a voice near me say, 'made white in the blood of the Lamb' and I knew it to be the voice of his Mother. The Father and Sister were crushed and in sorrow kept to their rooms, but that Spartan Mother met her beloved dead on the threshold as she would have done had he been living, and led the way into the parlor and directed that he . . . be laid where the light would fall on his face."[8]

THREE

* * * *

THE WEST, APRIL 7 – MAY 3:
FORREST V. STREIGHT

In early April, Union General William Rosecrans was stalled at Murfrees-boro, Tennessee, blocked by Braxton Bragg at Tullahoma from advancing on Chattanooga, and desperate for a way to gain the upper hand. Coming to him with a proposal to do just that was Colonel Abel D. Streight of the 51st Indiana Infantry. His idea was to move west with a mounted com-mand up the Cumberland and down the Tennessee Rivers, debark in the northeastern corner of Mississippi, and then come back east through Al-abama and Georgia. The object of this roundabout raid would be the Western & Atlantic Railroad south of Chattanooga. Cutting it for any lengthy period would deprive Bragg of supplies and perhaps insure a withdrawal from the city.

Rosecrans thought the proposal had great merit. What intrigued him all the more was that Colonel Streight would be mounting his infantry on mules. Not only were horses in short supply, but mules could better cope with the rugged countryside of northern Alabama and Georgia, and re-quired far less forage.

On April 7, Streight, a stocky, muscular man, with deep-set eyes and a square jaw, was sent to Nashville with instructions to form his command with all haste. Besides his own regiment, he would be taking the 73rd Indiana, the 3rd Ohio, the 18th Illinois, and two companies of Alabama (Union) cavalry—the latter, troopers who knew the terrain he would be traversing during the critical part of the journey. Two days later, he proudly informed Rosecrans, "We can start within three hours." Noted one Federal officer, "Colonel Streight was . . . particularly fitted for such a raid. He was active, clear-headed, determined, and of excellent judgment."

With some 2,000 men and 800 mules—Streight was told to secure more animals as best he could—he boarded steamboats on the 10th and the next day debarked at Palmyra on the Cumberland. From there he proceeded overland, confiscating additional mules and giving his troops, who "were at first very easily dismounted, frequently in a most undignified and unceremonious manner," some painful riding lessons. On the 16th he made his rendezvous with the same boats at Fort Henry on the Tennessee, and three days later was in Eastport, Mississippi.[1]

There he met with General Grenville Dodge, who with some 7,500 infantrymen had the assignment of screening his raid. Dodge's instructions were to drive on to Tuscumbia, Alabama, and push the Rebels in the vicinity back toward Decatur—both of which were on the Tennessee River—giving Streight a head start in racing through Alabama and entering Georgia. "Dodge, with the marine brigade and the gunboats," said Rosecrans, "can occupy or whip the [Confederates at] Tuscumbia . . . and let my force go directly to its main object, the destruction of the railroads. The enterprise, fraught with great consequences, is commended to [his] care, enjoining on him to dispatch Streight by every means to his destination."[2]

Dodge was cooperative but concerned. On April 17, while waiting for the raiding party to arrive, he had been severely bloodied by a much smaller force of Rebel cavalry under Colonel Philip D. Roddey, and had lost a cannon, a score of artillerists, and a company of infantry, compelling him to send for reinforcements. His would be a prudent advance in front of the expedition, one that did not risk his own command.

Streight here suffered a setback of his own. In the dead of night, even as he and Dodge were conferring, Roddey's troopers crept up on the corrals at Eastport into which the mules had been herded and, with hooting, yelling, and the firing of pistols, stampeded them into a wild breakout. "Daylight revealed to me," said Streight, "that nearly four hundred of our best animals were gone. All that day and part of the next were spent scouring the country . . . but only about two hundred were recovered. . . . The loss of these animals was a heavy blow . . . for besides detaining us nearly two days at Eastport . . . it caused further delay at Tuscumbia to supply their places."[3]

He did not leave Eastport until April 21, marching eastward behind Dodge as he pushed Roddey back toward Tuscumbia. So deliberate was the former's progress, despite outnumbering his opponent four to one, that he did not reach the town, some twenty miles away, until late on the 24th.

From there two days later, Streight left Dodge's protection, moving south and then east. He had with him some 1,500 men—the rest having been judged unfit—and not enough mules, but he had added some wagons, and the unmounted troopers would ride in them until more animals were procured. "We were in the saddle at 1 a.m., and started on the Russellville [Alabama] road, but made only five miles by daylight, on account of the badness of the roads and the depth of the streams," said Sergeant H. Briedenthal of the 3rd Ohio. ". . . We reached Russellville at 10 a.m . . . At sunset reached Mount Hope, a small village thirty-six miles from Tuscumbia, where we went into camp."[4]

Back in Tuscumbia that same day, the 27th, Dodge was in the process of overpowering Colonel Roddey's troopers, driving them back by nightfall to the east bank of Town Creek. The next morning, however, he found the Rebels had been reinforced. *Mirabile dictu*, the implacable Nathan Bedford Forrest and a brigade of his tough Tennessee cavalry were on the scene. That worthy's military biographers, Thomas Jordan and J. P. Pryor, describe the action: "Posting [James] Starnes and [J. B.] Biffle's regiments out of range of the Federal artillery, with his right resting on the Tuscumbia road, [Forrest] assigned Roddey's force to position on the left, to watch the upper crossing . . . the 11th Tennessee [under James Edmonson] was held concealed in a woods north of the railway."

Swollen by recent rains, Town Creek was nearly unfordable. "All was quiet in the encampment opposite, as the Confederate commander ordered Captain [John] Morton to throw a shell from one of his steel guns through the Federal headquarters. The aim was skillful; in another instant the inmates of the building swarmed forth." Dodge had eighteen guns to Forrest's eight, but it did not seem to make a difference. "The cannonade soon waxed violent. Open fields intervened on both sides, unobstructed by [trees], except the few that fringed the banks of the creek, behind which sharpshooters kept up a warm, incessant fire."

The barrage went on for five hours. The 11th Tennessee at one juncture opened up a premature fusillade, giving away its position. "A fierce, pelting storm of mini[é]-balls, of grape and exploding shells was quickly poured into the woods, so that the limbs of trees flew in great profusion, and caused many casualties." James Moon, a local resident, now informed

Forrest that a considerable but unusual Union cavalry force had detached itself from Dodge and was heading east to Mount Hope and Moulton. The Rebel leader, like his superiors, had no inkling of Streight's threat to the railroads; he had been rushed from Tennessee to Alabama by Bragg to bolster Colonel Roddey and help check the Federal advance.

Dealing with the mystery column would have to wait, Forrest decided. Seemingly undisturbed by the news that Streight was on his left, "as if he had no flank to be turned," he continued the fight along Town Creek. Simultaneously he ordered George Dibrell with the 8th Tennessee to demonstrate on the Rebel right as if he intended to cross the Tennessee River in boats, backing up the feint with a fearsome cannonade. "This barrage, and other intimations of the threatening presence of a large Confederate force in his rear . . . reached General Dodge, whereupon that officer . . . having now detained the Confederates long enough [for Streight] to get well on his way . . . began a hurried retrograde movement."[5]

What this meant, of course, was that Dodge was making an early and circumspect withdrawal. Forrest at this point determined he would pursue and capture Streight, whose intent he already was beginning to fathom. Leaving three of his five regiments with Roddey, to keep up the pressure on the main Federal force and at the same time guard his flank, he took two regiments and some cannon and went after the mule column. Thus began a memorable chase.

By dusk on April 29, Streight had long passed Moulton and was almost halfway through Alabama, camped at the entrance of Day's Gap, a narrow passageway through Sand Mountain. Much to his satisfaction, he had along the way confiscated enough mules and even horses to outfit his entire brigade. "Every man now was mounted," he said, "and although many of the animals were very poor . . . we had strong hopes we could secure all future demands."

Shortly after dawn that day, however, the hard-riding Forrest was himself at Moulton, where he confirmed Streight's identity and purpose, and hours later he was joined by part of the force he temporarily had detached, swelling his numbers to some 2,000 troopers. By 2 a.m. on the 30th, he was within four miles of the raiding party's camp. Now he too paused for rest.

The Rebels fell on Streight's rear guard the next morning, while the bulk of the Federal column was strung out the length of the gap. A lesser commander might have panicked, especially since he knew that it was Forrest who was on his trail, but instead he sent word for his men to turn and fight, and delay the attackers as long as possible. Meanwhile he dismounted his column, taking the mules out of harm's way, and concentrated and concealed his force on one side or the other of the defile. Then he trained his two howitzers on the path he knew the oncoming enemy would be taking.

Rarely during the war would Forrest fall victim to ambush, but this was one of those occasions. "Shoot everything in blue and keep up the scare," he had been urging his troopers, with the result they rushed into a hail of minié balls and grapeshot all the more deadly for being unexpected. The Union charge that followed proved irresistible, sending their adversaries reeling down the gap. "The enemy, after a short but stubborn resistance," Streight said, "fled in confusion, leaving two pieces of artillery, two caissons, and about forty prisoners, representing seven different regiments, a larger number of wounded, and about thirty dead on the field." Among the wounded was Captain William Forrest, a younger brother of Nathan, down with a fractured thigh.[6]

The Rebel commander did not take defeat lightly. First he took out his rage on Lieutenant A. Willis Gould, the officer who had lost the cannon, with consequences we will describe in a later chapter. Then he rode among his demoralized men, in the words of John Wyeth, his biographer, "with his saber drawn and accompanied his deft employment of this weapon with a series of remarks well calculated to increase the temperature of the mountain atmosphere. He told every man to get down and hitch his horse to a sapling. There would be no horse-holders in this fight; men were too scarce. Those guns had to be retaken if every man dies in the attempt, and if they did not succeed they would never need their horses again."

Forrest's hell-for-leather pursuit had left a string of broken-down horses and exhausted troopers behind him. Now he weakened his command all the more, detaching some units back west to observe Dodge and others north to insure that the Federals did not escape across the Tennessee. His numbers were down to some 900 effectives, much less than the opposition, but he nonetheless ignored the odds.

Just before the countercharge up Day's Gap, Captain Henry Pointer, a Forrest aide, turned to a fellow officer and offered him some sliced ham and bread. "We had better eat this now, I reckon," he said, "for from the way the old man is preparing to get his guns back it might spoil before we get another chance at it." His pessimism was justified. When the Rebels gained the crest of Sand Mountain, they found that Streight had fled and again was moving east. It was just about noon. With Forrest at this point were Biffle's 9th and Starnes 4th Tennessee (Starnes being ill, the latter regiment was under Major W. S. McLemore), plus elements of several batteries.

Recounted John Wyeth: "The running fight had opened. The tactics of both leaders were now in evidence. With Colonel Streight it was to move with celerity, until his rear was too hard pressed, and then . . . to ambuscade his adversary. . . . Forrest would thus be compelled to attempt to ride around him and head him off." For the next four or five hours, the skirmishing was constant. Remembered Lieutenant R. Y. Jones, a Rebel cannoneer: "Streight made a stand at every creek or stream on the way, and burnt all the bridges. The battery was ordered up on most of these occasions, and after giving them a few rounds of shell or shrapnel . . . the cavalry would charge and carry the position, and so it would go to the next creek."[7]

Toward dusk, nine miles beyond Day's Gap, all-out fighting resumed. "Finally the enemy pressed upon our rear so closely that I was compelled to prepare for battle," said Streight. "I selected a strong position on a ridge called Hog Mountain. The whole force became engaged one hour before dark. The enemy strove first to carry our right, then charged the left, but with the help of the two pieces captured in the morning and the two mountain howitzers we were able to repulse them."

The meeting, sometimes hand-to-hand, was bloody but inconclusive. Forrest, in the thick of it as usual, had one horse killed and two wounded under him. The action continued until 10 p.m. and then Streight, who imagined himself badly outnumbered, once more withdrew east, leaving his dead and wounded behind. " 'Forward!' was the order," said Lieutenant Jones, "and forward we went. In passing through the Yankee camp, the men hastily grabbed up . . . scattered hard tack, little wallets of ground coffee, etc. I did not leave the road, and only found a clothes brush." In his hurry Streight left behind the Rebel cannon, but not before spiking them. Though Forrest had regained his guns, it was a hollow triumph.[8]

Skirmishing continued until 2 a.m. on May 1. Then the Rebel commander, to give his column badly needed respite, called a temporary halt to the pursuit. The civilian populace all along the line of march, which had been thrown into panic by the fighting, must have welcomed the lull. "Both Federals and Confederates had come upon the people of this isolated region unexpectedly," wrote Jordan and Pryor, "and the outburst and tumult of the battle-storm was their first warning of such fearful presence. . . . They were filled with wild terror; the poor women with their little children fled frantically from their homes, and were found seeking shelter, they scarcely knew from what dire peril, in grotesque hiding-places, such as ash-hoppers, horse-troughs, and in recesses behind chimneys."

Streight meantime marched through the night, and at 10 a.m. reached Blountsville, some forty miles beyond Day's Gap. There he found badly needed corn for his mules and horses. Two hours' rest were all he could give his men, however, before he was warned that Forrest, who had gotten his troopers moving at dawn, was drawing near. "We resumed our march in the direction of Gadsden [Alabama]," said Streight. "The column had not got fairly in motion before our pickets were driven in. . . . The enemy followed closely for several miles, continually skirmishing with the rear guard, but were badly handled by small parties of our men stopping in the bushes by the side of the road, and firing at them at short range."

Forrest could be just as hard on his own troopers as on his foes. Just before reaching Blountsville, a scout who had been getting his horse shod at a nearby blacksmith's shop rode up to him in great excitement, mistakenly claiming that a heavy force of Union cavalry was moving to Streight's support.

"Did you see the Yankees?" Forrest demanded.

"No, I did not," the scout admitted, ". . . but while I was at the blacksmith's a citizen came galloping up . . . and told me he had seen them."

Forrest, who did not suffer fools gladly, pulled the man from his horse, grabbed him with both hands around the throat, and smashed his head three or four times against a tree.

"Damn you!" he snarled. "If you ever come to me again with a pack of lies, you won't get off so easily!"[9]

About 3 p.m. on May 1, at the Black Warrior River, the two sides once more clashed, with the Confederates prevailing two hours later and advancing to the east bank, suffering no casualties other than two mules loaded with boxes of hard bread. Here Forrest gave his command a three-hour break. One hungry trooper used the time to clamber back in the water and relieve the dead mules of the hard tack. "Boys, it's wet and full of mule hair," he said, handing out the rations, "but it is a damn sight better than anything the old man's a-givin' us now."

By 9 a.m. the next day, the resourceful Streight, still unbending under the Rebel pressure, had succeeded in getting his men across Black Creek, just outside of Gadsden, and burning the only bridge behind them. Here it appeared that Forrest's pursuit would be stymied. Black Creek was crooked and deep, with steep clay banks, and it was thought unfordable. But fate, in the person of a sixteen-year-old girl named Emma Sanson, would have it otherwise.

"We were at home the morning of May 2," she remembered, "when . . . a company of men wearing blue uniforms"—they were Streight's—"and riding mules and horses galloped past the house and went on towards the bridge." Some asked for water. "Sister and I each took a bucket and gave it to them. . . . One of them asked me where my father was. I said he was dead. He asked if I had any brothers. I told him I had six. He asked where they were, and I said in the Confederate Army.

"Do they think the South will whip?" the soldier asked.

"They do," Emma replied.

"What do you think about it?"

"I think God is on our side and we will win."

"You do? Well, if you had seen us whip Colonel Roddey the other day . . . you would have thought God was on the side of the best artillery."

The Yankees soon galloped off to torch the bridge, and on their heels, as the flames rose skyward, came a sweating, swearing Forrest, riding in the van of the pursuit. Approaching Emma, her sister, and her mother, he doffed his hat, stopped his cursing, and asked whether there was another way of crossing the stream.

"I told him," said Emma, ". . . that I knew of a trail about two hundred yards above the bridge on our farm, where our cows used to cross . . . and that if he would have my saddle put on a horse, I would show him the way."

"There is no time to saddle a horse," Forrest replied. "Get up here behind me."

Just as they were about to start off, her mother came up, gasping for breath.

"Emma, what do you mean?" she said, worried about the proprieties.

"She is going to show me a ford. . . . Don't be uneasy. I will bring her back safe."

Nearing the creek, he and Emma dismounted and crept through the thick undergrowth on the bank. "When we were right at the ford," she said, "I happened to be in front. He stepped quickly between me and the Yankees, saying: 'I am glad to have you for a pilot, but I am not going to make breastworks of you.' The cannon and the other guns were firing fast . . . as I pointed out to him where to go into the water and out on the other bank, and then we went back toward the house. He asked me my name, and asked me to give him a lock of my hair."[10]

Soon the Rebels were across Emma Sanson's ford, compelling Streight, after the briefest of rests, to keep his troopers moving. "I halted at Gadsden sufficiently long to destroy a quantity of arms and stores found there, and proceeded," he said. "Many of our animals and men were entirely worn out. . . . Our only hope was crossing the river at Rome [Georgia] and destroying the bridge, which would delay Forrest a day or two and allow . . . a little time to sleep."

The skirmishing went on until dark, ending twelve miles beyond Gadsden at the Blount plantation. Here Streight's principal lieutenant, Colonel Gilbert Hathaway of Indiana, was struck dead by a sniper's bullet. "His loss to me was irreparable. His men almost worshipped him, and when he fell it cast a deep gloom of despondency over his regiment. . . . We remained in ambush but a short time. . . . I then decided to withdraw as silently as possible."[11]

If conditions were bad for the Yankees on the 2nd, consider the plight of their pursuers. Each time they moved into a position previously occupied by Streight, they found the countryside stripped of livestock and stores. Needing both mounts and food, Forrest now was down to less than 600 troopers. The Federal force, meanwhile, though bedraggled, was largely intact, composed of more than twice as many men. Streight nonetheless continued to believe he was outnumbered—testimony to Forrest's continual harassment.

May 3 would bring the chase to an end. The Union commander had sent ahead 200 of his best troopers under Captain Milton Russell to the outskirts of Rome, with orders to capture and hold the bridge over the Oostanaula River until the main force could come up and cross. There Streight hoped to burn the span, buy himself time, and set about the destruction of the Western & Atlantic Railroad. But John H. Wisdom, a rural mail carrier in Gadsden, had the previous day begun a dash for Rome to warn the populace that the blueclad mule column was fast approaching. "It was then three-thirty in the afternoon," said one Rebel sympathizer. "Mr. Wisdom, still in his buggy, grabbed up the reins, urged his horse forward, and set out with the most important message he would ever carry."

He reached his destination at midnight, wearing out six horses and covering sixty-seven miles in the process.

"The Yankees are coming! The Yankees are coming!" Wisdom cried again and again, galloping through the dark streets and rousing sleeping men and women. Well before daylight, through his efforts, armed civilians were dug in behind the bridge, barricaded behind bales of cotton and determined to deny the Federals passage or, if all else failed, to destroy the span themselves.

By 9 a.m., Streight was between a rock and a hard place. While pausing briefly at the Lawrence plantation, less than twenty miles from Rome, he learned from Captain Russell that the bridge was being denied him. From pickets, he learned that Forrest "was moving on our left, on a route parallel with the one we were marching on, and was nearer Rome than we were." Quite soon the two sides became engaged. "Every effort was made to rally the men for action," Streight continued, "but nature was exhausted and a large portion of my troops actually went to sleep while lying in line of battle under severe skirmish fire."[12]

Here Forrest, with his customary brusqueness, sent Captain Pointer forward to demand a surrender to prevent "the further effusion of blood." Knowing his inferior numbers, however, he took care not to antagonize his foe by threatening his usual "or I will put every man to the sword." Later the two commanders met, with Streight asking for terms. "Your men to be treated as prisoners of war," was the reply. ". . . The officers to retain their side-arms and personal property."

The Union leader hesitated. He had come so far that he found it hard to concede he had failed. Belatedly, he was starting to wonder, knowing his own travails, just how many men and guns Forrest still had with him. Now he wanted assurances he was not surrendering to a lesser force.

During these moments, one of the two Rebel cannon that had survived the pace of the pursuit menacingly came into view. Streight demanded it be pulled back, and Forrest agreed, sending Pointer to see that this was done. While giving the order, he did so with a wink and a nod, and the aide immediately caught his drift. Soon both cannon were rolling in and out of distant woods, giving Streight the impression he was facing more than a dozen pieces.

"Name of God! How many guns have you got?" he blurted. "There's fifteen I counted already!"

"I reckon that's all that has kept up," Forrest replied.

Prompted by Pointer, groups of Rebel troopers now began marching in and out of sight, likewise magnifying their numbers. Streight still did not buy the charade.

"I won't surrender until you tell me how many men you have!"

"I've got enough to whip you out of your boots," Forrest said. He then turned to his bugler and ordered, "Sound to mount!"

Streight finally capitulated. By noon his men were stacking their weapons.[13]

Forrest reveled in his hard-earned triumph. "I ordered my men to come forward and take possession of the arms," he said. "When Streight saw they were barely [six] hundred, he did rear! Demanded to have his arms back and that we should fight it out. I just laughed at him and patted him on the shoulder. . . . 'Ah, Colonel, all is fair in love and war, you know.' "[14]

The outcome indeed was sweet. Forrest had outraced and outbluffed an able and dedicated opponent, and in so doing preserved the Confederate supply lines to Chattanooga. The chase had solidified his reputation, moreover, as an officer who could respond swiftly to all contingencies. His skills would be much needed in the months to come.

FOUR

* * * *

THE WEST, APRIL 17-MAY 2: GRIERSON'S RIDE

Ulysses S. Grant's efforts to take Vicksburg, the Rebel fortress looming over the upper Mississippi River, had been stalled since December, when, as we have seen, Nathan Forrest in west Tennessee and Earl Van Dorn at Holly Springs combined to cut his supply lines. Now in April he advanced his army along the Louisiana bank of the waterway as far south as Hard Times Landing, intent on turning the city's left flank. On April 16 and 22, the navy succeeded in running Vicksburg's guns with the transports that would take the troops across the river, and on the 30th, Grant loaded his men onto them and landed unopposed at Bruinsburg, Mississippi.

Earlier, to confuse General John Pemberton about his plans and keep him from concentrating his forces on the waterway, Grant had conceived the idea of a diversionary cavalry raid down the Mississippi heartland, some 100 miles to the east.

Leading the 1,700-man expedition would be thirty-six-year-old Colonel Benjamin H. Grierson, an enthusiastic music teacher and failed storekeeper from Jacksonville, Illinois. Though he hated horses—he bore a scar from chin to ear where he had been kicked by one as a youngster—the army in its wisdom had put him in the cavalry. His command would consist of the 6th and 7th Illinois and the 2nd Iowa, and his mission would be clear: to create havoc throughout east Mississippi and, if possible, to sever the Vicksburg & Jackson Railroad.

Grierson was born on July 8, 1826, in Pittsburgh, Pennsylvania, and grew up in Youngstown, Ohio. The horse-kicking incident, which occurred when he was eight, not only scarred the boy but also blinded him for two months. His passion was music, and by the time he was thirteen he was conducting and composing for Youngstown concert bands, as well as playing a half dozen instruments. His only military training, it seems, was some drilling with the Ohio militia, after which, he said, "the men worked systematically to get the officers drunk," and then pushed them into a canal.

In 1851 Grierson moved to Jacksonville, where he eked out a living as a music teacher. Three years later he married Alice Kirk, whom he had known since childhood, and to support her and a growing family, opened a general store in the river town of Meredosia, Illinois. There he became a staunch member of the Republican party. Lincoln, in fact, stayed at Grierson's home after a political debate, and during the 1860 presidential election, he composed a campaign song for the candidate. During this time Grierson's business failed, throwing him deeply into debt.

When war broke out, he was back in Jacksonville. There, despite his concerns about money, he enlisted as a private in the infantry. But his political activities soon marked him for promotion. He attracted the attention of the Illinois authorities and then of General Henry Halleck, commanding in the area, who appointed him—over his protests—a major in the 6th Illinois Cavalry. The quirky Halleck, Grierson would lament, would not be denied, insisting that he "looked active and wiry enough to make a good cavalryman."

In this instance, Halleck was right. "[Grierson] was by nature an intelligent and resourceful leader," said one military historian, "and was qualified to command in any branch of service. He learned the subtleties of mounted warfare so quickly and so well as to become one of the best volunteer horse soldiers in the West."

The mild-mannered Grierson, who was of Scots-Irish heritage, would prove an instinctive fighter. He was loose-limbed, swarthy, with jet-black hair and a flowing beard, and ironically, he seemed born to the saddle. In April 1862, he was made the colonel of the 6th Illinois. For the rest of the year, riding in west Tennessee and Mississippi, he served under Ulysses Grant and William Tecumseh Sherman in numerous engagements, earning increasing respect.

Now, leading a brigade, he was being tapped for semi-independent command. "It seems to me," said Grant ruminatively, "that Grierson . . . might succeed in making his way south, and cut the railroad east of Jackson, Miss. The undertaking would be a hazardous one, but it would pay well if carried out." Seconded Sherman, "Grierson has been with me all summer. He is the best cavalry officer I have yet had."[1]

The three regiments of raiders left La Grange, Tennessee, on April 17. Sergeant Richard Surby of the 7th Illinois used the occasion to wax poetic. "The morning . . . was a beautiful one, with a gentle breeze from the south," he said. "The fruit trees were in full bloom, the gardens were fragrant with the perfume of spring flowers, the birds sang gaily." Sergeant Stephen Forbes, his comrade, was more laconic. "A cavalry raid at its best," he said, "is essentially a *game* of strategy and speed. . . . [It is] not inconsistent . . . with the players killing each other if the game cannot be won in any other way, but it is commonly a strenuous game, rather than a bloody one."[2]

For the first three days Grierson and his 1,700 men headed south, sending out patrols on the flanks while scattering various Rebel detachments and leaving a trail of devastation. When one enemy squadron crossed their path, its officer unwisely sounded a charge, urging his troopers to "make 'em holler." Badly outnumbered, the squadron was routed.

"Well, captain, we made one [Yank] holler," one of the fleeing Rebels later commented.

"What did he say?" the officer asked.

"He said, 'Forward, skirmishers!' "

On April 20 in Pontotoc, Mississippi, Grierson made a series of moves to disrupt pursuit. Selecting some 175 of his men, who either were injured or whose mounts were lame—the so-called Quinine Brigade—he sent them back north in the column's tracks with the prisoners thus far taken, hoping to give the impression he was ending the raid. "All is well, and everything looks favorable," he wrote his wife. "We have had considerable skirmishing with the Rebels; killed and wounded a number, and captured about 25. No loss on our side. . . . Do not be uneasy. I still have faith and hope that all will be well."[3]

The next day, below Houston, he enlarged on the deception, sending Colonel Edward Hatch and an entire regiment, the 2nd Iowa, eastward toward Columbus, Mississippi, with orders to damage the Mobile & Ohio Railroad and, in so doing, make it appear the main column was ending its southward penetration. Hatch took with him one of the expedition's guns.

"The cannon was turned in the road in four different places, thus making its tracks correspond with the four pieces of artillery which Grierson had. . . ." said Sergeant Lyman Pierce of the 2nd Iowa. "The object was to deceive the Rebels . . . into the belief the entire column had taken the Columbus Road."

Both ruses proved effective. The Quinine Brigade drew pursuit, but made it safely back to La Grange. Hatch's movement was equally telling. Though some 800 Confederates caught up with him near the railroad, he used his superior weaponry—he had repeating rifles, the enemy only single-shot—to stop them cold and inflict many casualties. "Our boys kept the cover of the trees until they were in short range," said Pierce, "when they opened upon them such a fire from their trusty revolving rifles, that they were not only repulsed, but stampeded." During the night, Hatch disengaged. He later survived a second firefight, and then returned to Tennessee.[4]

With his remaining 950 men, meanwhile, Grierson pushed south through such Mississippi towns as Starkville, Louisville, and Philadelphia—the enemy not quite knowing where he was or where he was going. "We moved through a dismal swamp nearly belly-deep in mud," he said of the trek through the soggy bottomlands, ". . . sometimes swimming our horses to cross streams. . . . The inhabitants generally did not know of our coming, and would not believe us anything but Confederates."[5]

One reason for the locals' incredulity was the so-called Butternut Guerrillas, a small group of scouts who fanned out in advance of Grierson's column and pretended to be Rebels. Wearing captured gray or butternut uniforms, and affecting drawls, they easily gained the Southerners' confidence. Their leader, Sergeant Surby, remembered three pretty sisters—"Secesh Gals"—who with beaming faces told him how their father and brothers were off helping General Pemberton keep that "madman" Grant out of Vicksburg.

Had any other Confederate troops been in the vicinity recently? Surby asked.

"Lawd, it's been two months, hasn't it, sisters?" the oldest replied.

Hearing Surby and his men were hungry, the women ran into their house "and soon returned, with two black servants following, loaded down with eatables . . . half a ham, biscuits, sweet cakes, fried sausage, and peach pie, all in abundance . . . while one of the young ladies plucked some roses . . . presenting one to each as they bade us adieu, with many blessings and much success in our 'holy cause.' "

The comparatively few Confederates the Butternut Guerrillas met likewise were fooled. "It proved to be the simplest of matters . . . to encounter
a Rebel soldier and chat him up about which bridges were burned or the
whereabouts of Confederate forces," wrote one historian. "Then came a
request to admire the soldier's fine weapon, his willingness to hand it over
for inspection, and a pistol-point denouement: 'You, sir, are my
prisoner.' "[6]

When necessary, however, the scouts offered the opposition a simple
choice: give way or die. Reconnoitering the only bridge over the Pearl
River, Surby's men reined up before an elderly plantation owner. Courte-
ously, they inquired whether there were any Rebels in the area. Indeed
there were, he replied. His own son was one of a handful of militia guarding the bridge, with orders to burn it at the first sign of Federal cavalry.
Surby drew his pistol and dropped his drawl. "It lies in your power," he
told the Southerner, "to save your buildings from the torch, to save your
own life, and probably that of your son, by saving the bridge." With that,
he sent the man packing, to deliver the message to the guards. Minutes
later, he saw the Rebels mounting up, leaving the structure untouched.[7]

On April 24, some 300 miles deep into enemy territory, lead elements of
Grierson's cavalry, including the scouts, rode into Newton Station on the
Vicksburg & Jackson Railroad—their prime objective—intent on disrupting that vital east-west connection. "Lieutenant Colonel (William) Blackburn dashed into the town," Grierson said, "took possession of the
railroad and telegraph, and succeeded in capturing two trains in less than
half an hour after his arrival. One of these, twenty-five cars, was loaded
with ties and machinery, and the other thirteen cars were loaded with
commissary stores and ammunition."

In the taking of the second train, which carried both passengers and
freight, the inimitable Sergeant Surby played a key role. "On she came
rounding the curve," he said, "her passengers unconscious of the surprise
that awaited them. The engineer decreased her speed. She was now nearly
opposite the depot. Springing upon the steps of the locomotive, and presenting my revolver at the engineer, I told him if he reversed the engine I
would put a ball through him. He . . . obeyed orders. It would have done
anyone good to have seen the men rush from their hiding places amid the
shouts and cheers which rent the air."[8]

The Federals dynamited the locomotives and cars, tore up track, and
took seventy-five prisoners, all of whom they paroled. Following a brief
rest, the column moved south to Garlandville. "At this point we found the

citizens, many of them venerable with age, armed with shotguns and organized to resist our approach," said Grierson. "As the advance entered the town, these citizens fired upon them and wounded one of our men. We charged . . . and captured several. After disarming them, we showed them the folly of their actions, and released them."

Here he made the decision to swerve west toward the Mississippi. "From information received through my scouts and other sources, I found that Jackson and the stations east . . . had been reinforced by infantry and artillery; and hearing that a fight was momentarily expected at Grand Gulf . . . I decided to strike the New Orleans & Jackson Railroad at Hazelhurst and, after destroying as much of the road as possible, endeavor to get on the flank of the enemy and cooperate with our forces."[9]

Reaching Hazelhurst on April 27, the Federals found rail cars loaded with artillery shells and stores destined for the Rebel defenses at Grand Gulf and Port Gibson. These they promptly put to the torch. When the flames were at their height, however, a sudden windstorm blew up, endangering the homes of the townspeople and producing one of the many incongruities of the war. The bluecoats—even those wearing butternut—pitched right in to help, forming bucket brigades with the citizens and dousing errant blazes with pail after pail of water.

Pemberton at this juncture was frantic. Grant was about to cross the Mississippi in his front, and Grierson was cutting the railroad supply lines in his rear. Much of his cavalry had been transferred to Bragg in east Tennessee, and his entreaties for their return to Joseph Johnston, the overall Rebel commander in the West, were unavailing. "These raids endanger my position," he wired Johnston. ". . . The enemy are today at Hazelhurst, on the New Orleans & Jackson Railroad. *I cannot defend every station on the road with infantry.*"[10]

Grierson meanwhile on April 28 was growing concerned. Grant to the west had not yet crossed the river at Bruinsburg—he would not do so until the 30th—and Confederate detachments were closing in on the raiders from the north and east. Pondering how long he could wait in place, Grierson advanced a few miles further west to Union Church, halting about 2 p.m. to eat. "While feeding," he said, "our pickets were fired upon by a considerable force. I immediately moved out upon them."

The assault was the first serious opposition the 6th and 7th Illinois had faced during the entire ride. It served to underscore the fact that they were draining some 3,500 Rebel troops from the Vicksburg defenses, but this was small comfort with minié balls whistling past them. One Union

trooper re-created the scene: "The camp was all in confusion, men running as fast as they could in every direction, carrying saddles, leading
horses on the gallop, gathering up carbines and sabers and buckling on
belts, while the air was filled with cries and oaths and quick impulsive ex-
clamations and sharp stern orders and shouts of 'Fall in here, men
quick!' "

Grierson's troopers soon recovered, driving the attackers, who proved
to be the van of the 1st Mississippi Cavalry, through the town. But their
chief now realized he could wait near the river no longer. By April 29 he
was backtracking to the New Orleans & Jackson line and Brookhaven,
twenty-two miles away. "We moved directly south along the railroad," he
said, "destroying all bridges and trestlework. . . . Hearing nothing more
of our forces at Grand Gulf, I concluded to make for Baton Rouge
[Louisiana]."[11]

With the enemy closing in, the column wended its way toward the
promised haven of that Union-occupied city, first passing through
Brookhaven, and then Bogue Chitto and Summit. By the morning of May
1, it appeared the Illinois regiments would escape virtually unharmed.
Here Sergeant Surby, the Butternut leader, again allowed his lyrical im-
pulses full sway: "A gentle breeze flashed through the trees. . . . Perched
among the branches was the mocking bird, singing a variety of notes, the
whole impressing the beholder with a sense of the Creator of all this
beauty."

Reality set in at Wall's Bridge over the Tickfaw River, just a few miles
from the Louisiana border. There the column's lead elements drew the fire
of the 1st Louisiana Partisan Rangers. Three men were killed and several
wounded, Colonel Blackburn and Surby among the latter, when Blackburn, not waiting for support, ordered the charge. "The passage of the
Tickfaw might have been accomplished without loss," said Grierson, "but
for the incident of firing the alarm. . . . Colonel Blackburn, calling on the
scouts to follow him, dashed forward to the bridge without waiting."[12]

With the main force's arrival, the Rebels broke and ran. Blackburn's
and Surby's injuries were so severe, however, that they had to be left behind. To keep Surby from being shot for being in Confederate gray, his
comrades took care to uniform him in Union blue.

Next the column rode for Williams' Bridge over the Amite. "The enemy
were now on our tracks in earnest," said Grierson. "We were in the vicinity of their stronghold [Port Hudson], and from couriers and dispatches
which we captured, it was evident they were sending troops from all di-

rections to intercept us. The Amite River, a wide and rapid stream, was to be crossed, and there was but one bridge. . . . This I determined upon securing before I halted."

He crossed the 200-hundred-yard-long span about midnight, and afterward destroyed it. The Union leader could do so, reputedly, only because a 2,300-man Rebel infantry force, dispatched from Port Hudson to intercept him, had been grossly negligent. Underestimating Grierson's progress, the enemy officers had stopped off at Clinton, Louisiana, where the townspeople, anticipating the capture of the raiders, feted them at a dinner dance. "While, therefore, we were stretching our legs for the bridge," said Captain Henry Forbes of the 7th Illinois, "these gentlemen were stretching theirs in the cotillion." Whatever the truth, the Confederates did not arrive at the smoldering span until 2 a.m., two hours too late.[13]

Grierson's troopers rode through the night and into the morning and then, four miles from the Federal lines at Baton Rouge, halted at a large plantation. "So tired they were," he said of his men, "they scarcely waited for food, before every man save two or three was in a profound slumber." Invited by the owners into the main house, he entered a parlor and saw a piano. "I astonished the occupants by sitting down and playing . . . and in that manner I managed to keep awake. . . . I felt that we had nobly accomplished the work assigned to us and no wonder that I felt musical; who would not under like circumstances?"

While Grierson was still playing, a scout brought him the news that a large mounted force with field artillery was fast closing in. Luckily it turned out to be, not the enemy, but the Louisiana Union Cavalry, on patrol from Baton Rouge. "I rode out to meet them, and found it difficult to approach," said Grierson, "so cautious were they, with their skirmishers creeping along behind the fences." He tied a white handkerchief on his saber and continued on, calling out his name and that of his command. "The captain then climbed on the fence while I kept towards him, and soon he jumped to the ground, and when we met and shook hands his soldiers sprang up . . . and gave a shout."[14]

The raiders cantered into Baton Rouge the afternoon of May 2, their mission complete. "For half a mile before entering the city, the road was lined with spectators," said Grierson. ". . . Amidst cries and cheers and waving of banners, heralded by music, the tired troops marched around the public square, [then] down to the river to water their horses."

During the expedition, he would report, "We killed or wounded 100 of the enemy, captured and paroled about 500 prisoners . . . destroyed between 50 and 60 miles of railroad and telegraph, captured and destroyed over 3,000 stand of arms and other army stores ... to an immense amount; we also captured 1,000 horses and mules. Our loss during the entire journey was 3 killed, 7 wounded, 5 left on the route sick [Lieutenant Colonel Blackburn would die of his wounds, Seregeant Surby would survive], and nine men missing, supposed to have straggled."

Largely with the help of the Butternut Guerrillas, he would add, "We were always able by rapid marches to evade the enemy when they were too strong and whip them when not too large."[15]

Sergeant Stephen Forbes had been prescient. Cavalry raids indeed were "games" of strategy and speed, and Grierson's 1,600-mile gambit had been all but faultless. For sixteen dramatic days, the former music teacher turned reluctant horse soldier had kept Pemberton from fully addressing the Federal turning movement south of Vicksburg. Writing to General Halleck, Grant would call the raid "the most successful thing of its kind since the breaking out of the Rebellion." For the Union in the West, it was the first significant cavalry triumph.[16]

FIVE

THE EAST, APRIL 29 – MAY 8: STONEMAN AT CHANCELLORSVILLE

In the spring of 1863, Joseph Hooker, who had replaced Ambrose Burnside as head of the Army of the Potomac, was spoiling for action. He had reorganized his 115,000 troops, who were still facing Lee's Army of Northern Virginia along the Rappahannock at Fredericksburg, paying particular attention to the cavalry. Now the Federal horse soldiers were concentrated in a separate corps, under the command of Major General George Stoneman, a forty-one-year-old West Pointer. This measure was long overdue, and all concerned felt it would make the mounted service far more potent.

Hooker's overall plan was to move half his army thirty miles up the river to Kelly's Ford, and then cross over and march southeast, taking Lee with his less than 60,000 men in the rear. Meanwhile the rest of the Union force, left behind at Fredericksburg, would hold their ground and enable him to catch the Confederates in a vise.

Central to Hooker's thinking was the role of the cavalry, 10,000 of which he sent up the Rappahannock in advance of the infantry on April 13, with orders to traverse the river as quickly as possible and head farther south to cut Lee's lines of supply and communications with Richmond. "Let your watchword be fight, fight, fight, bearing in mind that time is as valuable as Rebel carcasses," he told Stoneman. "It devolves upon you . . . to take the initiative in the forward movement."[1]

But on the 14th, after meeting minor resistance from Rooney Lee's pickets, the methodical Stoneman hesitated. He would regroup, he decided, and make the crossing the next morning. It was a bad decision, for that night the skies opened and the rain fell in buckets, raising the Rappahannock seven feet within hours. For two weeks the rain came down, with the result that the cavalry did not advance until the 29th—the same day as the infantry.

Once across the river, pursuant to orders, Stoneman left some 2,000 of his troopers with Hooker and divided the rest of his command in half. One column consisted of William Averell's division, Benjamin "Grimes" Davis's brigade, and a battery of horse artillery. It was to move to Brandy Station and Culpeper Court House on the Orange & Alexandria Railroad, cross over the Rapidan, and proceed to Gordonsville. The second column, on Averell's left, was composed of General David McMurtrie Gregg's division, John Buford's brigade, and a battery of cannon. It was to cross the Rapidan at Raccoon Ford and advance to Louisa Court House on the Virginia Central, and then move east to the Richmond, Fredericksburg & Potomac Railroad—the Confederate lifeline.

Opposing this formidable mounted force was a greatly outnumbered Rooney Lee with elements of two brigades—no more than 1,300 men. Jeb Stuart and Fitz Lee were with Robert E. Lee at Fredericksburg, doing what they could to harass Hooker's infantry. The third Rebel cavalry division, Wade Hampton's, was recruiting and refurbishing in the Carolinas.

By the night of April 30, both Federal columns were behind schedule. Though Averell reached the Rapidan, he made no real effort to ford the stream, wildly exaggerating Rooney Lee's numbers. "Averell had the opportunity to run over Lee and possibly destroy most of his command," said one historian. "But he lacked the drive and fortitude to do so and made only half-hearted attacks against what he called 'strong and skillfully constructed' defenses with rifle pits full of sharpshooters and guns sweeping the entire area. Lee, by contrast, was prepared to fight against great odds."

Gregg, who was accompanied by Stoneman, did cross the Rapidan, but not until late. Even then, worried that Rooney might attack, the two generals kept the column on alert. "Hungry, wet and fatigued, we were illy prepared to spend a night in standing to horse," said the chaplain of the 6th Pennsylvania, "but such were our orders; and without unsaddling . . . the men dismounted and [stood] at their horses' heads all night. No fires could be kindled; and it became very cold, and our clothing being wet, we suffered greatly before morning."[2]

The cautious Averell tarried at the Rapidan for the next day and a half, for the most part unwilling to risk a frontal assault on Rooney's dug-in troopers, but also believing his passivity was justified by Stoneman's ambiguous instructions. An irate Hooker at this juncture called him back to headquarters on the Rappahannock. By the time he got there, May 3, the entire tactical situation had changed. Lee and Stonewall Jackson had boldly advanced northwest from Fredericksburg; Hooker in effect had lost his nerve and adopted a defensive posture at Chancellorsville; and Jackson just before dusk on the 2nd had led the flanking march that collapsed the Federal right.

It was understandable, therefore, that the Union commander was in no mood for excuses. "It was [Averell's] duty to do *something*," Hooker would say, ignoring his own offensive shortcomings. "If the enemy did not come to him, he should have gone to the enemy."[3]

Once at Chancellorsville, with the battle still raging, Averell and his men were given the task of scouting the enemy's right flank. When he returned within an all-too-brief time to state the obvious—that the dense, tangled underbrush around Chancellorsville was unsuited for cavalry—Hooker's reaction was predictable. He promptly and profanely relieved him of command.

Stoneman's and Gregg's column, meanwhile, reached Orange Springs on May 1 and Louisa Court House the next day, only to find that Confederate resistance was nonexistent. There the troopers set about destroying track on the Virginia Central for some five miles, wrecking railroad structures and municipal buildings as well. They also tapped the telegraph. "For nearly an hour, we received Rebel intelligence," said one man. "When the discovery was made in Richmond that the 'Yankees' held the line, some very decided remarks of disapprobation came over the wires . . . [whereupon] they ceased to communicate."

Louisa's inhabitants were shocked to find the enemy so suddenly among them. "No doubt some thought we came from the clouds and looked for our wings, horns and forked tails," wrote a former seminarian named Nathan Webb. The Federals spared private homes, but Southern pantries were, of course, another matter. "A huge slice of ham in one hand, a fritter . . . in the other," one soldier would observe of his comrades' antics, "the utter abjuration of knives and spoon[s], faces all grease or wiped off with their jacket sleeves . . . all laughing and jolly as kings in their palaces."[4]

The Federals continued south on May 2, bivouacking that night at Thompson's Crossroads near the South Anna River. There Stoneman called his officers together and told them, despite the recall of Averell's troops, that he was confident the expedition would succeed. "I gave them to understand," he said, "that we had dropped in that region of the country like a shell, and that I intended to burst in every direction, expecting each piece or fragment to do as much harm . . . as would result from sending the whole shell, and thus magnify our small force into overwhelming numbers."[5]

Here, on the eve of Stoneman's major thrust against the Confederate infrastructure, a digression is in order. Some believe that his absence from Chancellorsville permitted Jackson to make his march, in the sense that most of the Federal cavalry was not there to read his movements. After all, Fitz Lee's reconnaissance had led to the discovery that the Union flank was in the air. But Jackson's progress *had* been observed, by the infantry, and ignored because Hooker chose to believe it meant the enemy was falling back. Stoneman's raid, therefore, hardly explains the eventual Rebel triumph back at the Rappahannock.[6]

Now on the morning of May 3, knowing little if anything of Hooker's reverses at Chancellorsville, the Federal cavalry leader pursued his mission. But instead of moving east in strength on Hanover Court House and the vital Richmond, Fredericksburg & Potomac, Stoneman took liberties with his orders. Intent on inflicting the most damage he could, he separated his regiments into seven groups—the so-called fragments he had described at his council of war—sending six of them in various directions across the Virginia countryside.

Soldier of fortune Percy Wyndham took his 1st New Jersey, together with most of the 1st Maryland, southwest to Columbia, with orders to destroy a canal and aqueduct over the Rivanna River. The headstrong Judson Kilpatrick soon would head southeast with the 2nd New York to Richmond and the railroad bridges over the Chickahominy. Lieutenant Colonel Hasbrouck Davis, a Unitarian minister, moved east with the 12th Illinois to Ashland Station on the Richmond, Fredericksburg & Potomac and thence to Hanover Station on the Virginia Central.

General David Gregg, with the fourth and largest group, the 1st Maine and the 10th New York, advanced eastward along the South Anna, told to sever the trestles and footbridges. Moving out a few hours before him, with similar instructions, was Captain Thomas Drummond with the 5th U.S. Cavalry. Lastly Captain Wesley Merritt, a Stoneman aide, likewise proceeded along the South Anna, leading the rest of the 1st Maryland and looking for a fight.

Stoneman himself, ailing with severe hemorrhoids—no joking matter for a cavalryman—and unable to take the saddle that day, remained at Thompson's Crossroads, making the intersection his headquarters and fortifying it with 500 men from John Buford's brigade.[7]

Colonel Wyndham, whose eighteen-inch moustache indicated an equally outsized ego, initially on May 3 met little resistance. Following a fifteen-mile march, his troopers burned a bridge across Byrd Creek just outside Columbia, and then galloped through the town, hooting and shooting and quickly scattering a handful of defenders. There he had no trouble destroying the four bridges over the canal, some locks and boats, and numerous warehouses, one of which contained valuable medical supplies.

The aqueduct spanning the canal was another matter. It was made of solid concrete, and smashing it would require blasting powder. Since he had none, Wyndham mounted up his men and left the town to spread havoc elsewhere. Not giving up so easily, however, was Major Myron Beaumont of the 1st New Jersey, who received permission to return to Columbia with fifty men, bringing with him a huge sack of cartridges that he hoped could be detonated. While he was planting them on the aqueduct, he serendipitously came upon several barrels of gunpowder and some waterproof fuses, and for a time it appeared the structure would be blown to smithereens.

Then came the urgent word from Wyndham: Rooney Lee with some 800 troopers, freed from the need to defend the Rapidan and Gordonsville from Averell, was moving on Columbia! *Evacuate at once!* This Beaumont did, leaving the aqueduct intact, and by nightfall both he and the whole of Wyndham's command were back at Thompson's Crossroads.

Judson Kilpatrick, whom fellow officers regarded either as "a frothy braggart without brains," or someone whose "busy form [is] always in the thickest of the fight," did not move out on the 3rd, choosing to ride through the darkness and reach Hungary Station on the RF&P at dawn the next day. There he tore up miles of track, burned buildings, and cut the telegraph before galloping on toward Richmond.

Just north of the city he encountered Lieutenant R. W. Brown, an aide to Richmond's provost marshal, who with a dozen men was reconnoitering.

"What regiment?" Brown asked, thinking Kilpatrick's troopers were friends.

"The 2nd New York Cavalry," was the response, ". . . and you, sir, are my prisoner."

Brown swallowed hard. "You're a mighty daring sort of fellow," he finally said, "but you will certainly be captured before sundown."

"I'll do some mischief first!" Kilpatrick answered.

He was as good as his word, skirting the heavily fortified city but promptly putting the bridges over the Chickahominy to the torch. Later he captured a supply train, setting it afire and sending it into one of the smoldering spans to plunge into the river, where "the whole thing well-nigh disappeared in the deep mud and water."

Confederate columns from Richmond at this point were fast advancing on Kilpatrick's position, which was now some thirty miles from Thompson's Crossroads, and he decided to withdraw. Concerned he might be intercepted before rejoining Stoneman, however, he turned northeast, aiming for the Pamunkey and the distant safety of the Federal lines at Gloucester Point. Crossing the river in a single flatboat, twenty men at a time, he made the north bank by the narrowest of margins, and then destroyed the ferry. The Rebel pursuers watched in silent rage.

"Cheer after cheer now rent the air," said one of Kilpatrick's men, "[for] the skillful manner in which their leader conducted the hazardous enterprise." The detachment would not reach Gloucester Point until May 7, capturing and burning more than 100 supply wagons along the way.[8]

Hasbrouck Davis, who like Kilpatrick had the task of cutting the railroads north of Richmond, rode with the 12th Illinois for twenty miles through the predawn hours of May 3 and arrived at Ashland Station on the RF&P in the early morning. "Words cannot describe," he would say, "the astonishment of the inhabitants at our presence." There again the familiar tableau of destruction was repeated, interrupted only by the arrival of a train from the Chancellorsville battlefield, which was quickly seized. On it, in one of the ironies of war, was Lieutenant Joseph Morrison, aide and brother-in-law to the mortally wounded Stonewall Jackson, who had been dispatched to Richmond to escort his sister to Jackson's side. Somehow Morrison eluded capture, and thereafter completed his assignment.

Next Davis pushed on farther east to Hanover Station on the Virginia Central, reaching the place at nightfall. There, unopposed, he ripped up the rail lines and burned scores of supply wagons. May 4 found him at

Tunstall's Station on still a third rail line, the Richmond & York River, where he almost came to grief, challenging a train carrying Rebel infantry and three cannon, and suffering two men killed and several wounded before breaking off the engagement. Then he, again like Kilpatrick, thinking himself too extended to return to Stoneman, raced north across the Pamunkey, using a flatboat in much the same manner, and eventually arriving at Gloucester Point.[9]

The quietly competent General David Gregg, with the 1st Maine and the 10th New York, preceded by Captain Merritt's Maryland squadron, moved east on May 3 along the South Anna to Rocky Mills, burning bridges and other installations and confiscating horses and foodstuffs. Hearing that the span carrying the RF&P over the river was lightly guarded, Gregg that afternoon sent a 150-man squadron to Ashland Station. The Federals under Lieutenant Colonel Charles Ferguson Smith got there at nightfall and enlarged on the ruin that Hasbrouck Davis earlier had inflicted, focusing on rail culverts, track, and outlying buildings. But they failed to sever the bridge, which was stubbornly defended by a small infantry force and several cannon.

Smith withdrew in frustration and returned to Rocky Mills, only to find that Gregg already had departed for Thompson's Crossroads. The two commands eventually merged, marching most of the night and wearing out both horses and men. "We started back with our plunder, which consisted of horses, mules . . . [and] what flour, bacon, grain and tobacco we could well carry," said William Baker of the 1st Maine. "On the whole we had a big time, though suffered much through want of sleep."[10]

Gregg's and Merritt's "fragments" did not get back to Stoneman's headquarters until noon on May 4. There they were reunited with Captain Drummond and his 5th U.S. Cavalry, who also had rampaged along the South Anna, and Colonel Percy Wyndham.

Earlier that day, as dawn was breaking, Rooney Lee with his 800 troopers galloped toward Shannon Hill, about midway between the Crossroads and Columbia. There Stoneman, with his penchant for dividing his command, had stationed Captain William Harrison with some 100 men. The ensuing hand-to-hand struggle was no contest. The Rebels charged eight abreast with hair-raising yells, leading Harrison to report that the shock "was so great that my foremost horses were completely knocked over." He soon sounded the retreat, leaving a half dozen killed and wounded, and another thirty captured.

Rooney later talked to one of the prisoners, Captain Wesley Owen, a friend from the Old Army, and learned that the bulk of the Federal cavalry was at the Crossroads. With his own men too worn out to fight further, he retired to Gordonsville.[11]

Consider Stoneman's situation at this juncture. Six days had passed since he splashed across the Rappahannock, and he still had no definite word as to what was happening at Chancellorsville. There were rumors of Hooker's setback, of course. If they were true, he imagined that fresh Confederate troops would soon be on his trail. With rations and forage running low, he now turned his column north.

Leading the way, in a sweeping diversionary effort, were General John Buford's regulars. On May 5 they headed across the South Anna to Louisa Court House, then late in the day veered west toward Gordonsville. There at nightfall they met and evaded a strong contingent of Rebel infantry and cannon, although briefly, admitted one trooper, "it looked . . . as if our time had come."

Feeling he had done his duty, Buford at this point turned back east, aiming to rejoin the main column. "The night was very dark, and much of the way led through dense woods," said one soldier, ". . . and for several hours it was utterly impossible for one to see the person riding immediately in advance." The troopers crossed the North Anna about 2 a.m. on the 6th, and later that morning made camp at Orange Springs.

Stoneman, Gregg, Wyndham, and the rest followed the trail of Buford across the South Anna, but made straight for the North Anna, subsequently encountering the same blackness. "It was a dismal ride," said one man in the 1st Maine, "made more so by the sound of an occasional shot from a guerilla, and the doleful note of a single whippoorwill that followed the column all night long." By noon on May 6, Stoneman was in Orange Springs himself, sharing some coffee with Buford.[12]

Thereafter the column's path was unimpeded. Robert E. Lee, elated by victory but chagrined that Hooker had saved his army by withdrawing across the Rappahannock, had no interest in chasing Stoneman's tired cavalry. His troopers returned without incident the way they had come— except for Kilpatrick and Davis, who had opted for Gloucester Point—the last of them reaching safety on May 8.

In the immediate aftermath of the raid, the Northern press was ecstatic. *The New York Herald*, for instance, hailed the incursion in glowing terms, citing the destruction of twenty-two bridges, seven rail intersections, five canal boats, three rail depots, and four supply trains, as well as the capture of 300 horses and mules and the downing of five telegraph lines. The numbers, however, were misleading. Because Stoneman had not concentrated on key targets with sufficient force, for significant periods of time, the damage to the Confederate rail system was minimal. Service was resumed on the RF&P late on May 5, and on the Virginia Central three days afterward.[13]

Overlooked too was that the mission had taken a deadly toll on horses. At least a thousand of them had to be abandoned and shot during the trek, victims of back trouble incurred by long marches, and many more later succumbed to various diseases. Toward the end of the month, mounts would be available for no more than half the available riders.

What cannot be overstated, regardless, is the growing sense of confidence that the expedition engendered in the Federal cavalry. Captain Merritt of the 1st Maine called it "one of the most remarkable achievements in the history of modern warfare . . . teaching the deluded white people of ten counties . . . that Yankee soldiers are men, and are to be respected." Enthused one of his troopers, "It was ever a matter of pride with the boys that they were on 'Stoneman's Raid.' " Summed up the historian of the 1st New Jersey: "For the first time the cavalry made themselves found useful . . . and treated as something better than military watchmen for the army. They saw that the long desired time had come when they would be permitted to gain honor and reputation."[14]

Hooker needed a scapegoat for his defeat at Chancellorsville, however, and in Stoneman he found a vulnerable officer. By May 10 he was already telling Secretary of War Stanton: "The bridges of importance appear to have remained untouched. With the exception of Kilpatrick's operations . . . my instructions appear to have been completely disregarded." Much later he would elaborate, saying, "Neither [Stoneman] nor Averell were of any account. I sent them to cut off Lee's communications and the devils went so far around that they never accomplished anything."

Even Stoneman's hemorrhoid problems and the Southern sympathies of his wife, a vivacious Baltimore belle half his age, became factors in the attacks, with Hooker behind a furtive whispering campaign. Not until long afterward would he reveal the extent of his animosity. "Stoneman had married just before [the war] a Rebel wife and at the same time was terribly afflicted with piles, and between the two he became completely emasculated."[15]

The handwriting was on the wall. The Federal cavalry leader was placed on medical leave, and on May 22, he was succeeded by Alfred Pleasanton.

Despite his machinations, Hooker would not long outlast Stoneman. On June 28 he was relieved of command of the Army of the Potomac and replaced by George Gordon Meade.

SIX

* * * *

THE EAST, JUNE 9: BRANDY STATION

Jeb Stuart on June 5 was his usual ebullient self, staging a grand review of his command on the level plains near Brandy Station on the Orange & Alexandria Railroad, some five miles west of the Rappahannock. Invitations had been issued far and wide, nearly 10,000 cavalrymen took part, and throngs of visitors were there to cheer the spectacle. Stuart and his aides galloped down the front of the lines and came back by the rear, the general officers and their staffs joining them as they passed, until nearly a hundred horsemen reined up at the reviewing stand. Then the cavalry broke into a column of squadrons and marched by at a walk. Finally it came around at a trot, at the last moment breaking into a gallop and thundering past the dignitaries on the stand with Rebel yells and brandished sabers.

"The effect was thrilling, even to us," said the aide William Blackford, "while the ladies clasped their hands and sank into the arms, sometimes, of their escorts in a swoon if the escorts were handy, but if not they did not. While the charging was going on, [Robert] Beckham with the Horse Artillery"—he had replaced the fallen Pelham—"was firing rapidly and this heightened the effect. It would make your hair stand on end to see them."[1]

That night there was even a ball, with moonlight and huge bonfires illuminating the fete, while hundreds of couples danced on the grass. One would never have thought the Yankees were just across the river.

Three days later, Stuart held a second review for General Lee's benefit. This one was more restrained, with the commanding general, ever mindful of not taxing his men unnecessarily, not allowing the cavalry to gallop or the artillery to fire. Subsequently, toward evening, the brigades went their separate ways: Fitz Lee's troop—under Colonel Tom Munford, as Lee was ailing—rode toward the upper Rappahannock; Rooney Lee moved toward Welford's Ford; Grumble Jones blocked Beverly Ford; Beverly Robertson moved toward Kelly's Ford, four miles down the river; and Wade Hampton bivouacked between Brandy Station and Stevensburg. Stuart himself bedded down on Fleetwood Hill, near Brandy Station.

Now in the predawn hours of June 9, while the Confederates were sleeping, they suddenly came under attack. Some 8,000 Federal horsemen under Major General Alfred Pleasanton, newly remounted in the aftermath of Stoneman's Raid—together with 3,000 supporting infantry—pushed across the Rappahannock, looking into reports Lee was consolidating his command to move into Pennsylvania. The largest cavalry battle of the war was about to begin.

The thirty-nine-year-old Pleasanton was far more of a military bureaucrat than a field commander, and somewhat of a poseur as well. Moreover, there were those who questioned his courage. Whatever the truth, there is no doubt that the short, slight West Pointer was adept at furthering his career, cultivating helpful politicians and journalists. "He does nothing save with a view to a newspaper paragraph," sniffed a captain in the 1st Massachusetts. Simultaneously the cavalry leader fostered a dapper, devil-may-care image, affecting a straw hat, white gloves, and a riding crop, and indulging a fondness for oysters and champagne.

Pleasanton's three division heads were the estimable generals John Buford and David Gregg, both West Pointers with more taste and talent for combat, and the French-born, Saint-Cyr-educated Colonel Alfred Duffie.

One fellow officer would describe Buford, thirty-seven, as "straightforward, honest, conscientious, full of good common sense, and always to be relied on in any emergency." He was expert at reconnaissance, and also at training his troopers to dismount and fight as infantry. Gregg, thirty, was so unruffled under fire that he gave reassurance to all around him. "Be calm, gentlemen—no occasion for haste!" he would counsel his men in the wake of all-too-close cannon blasts. "I was more or less in awe of him," admitted one aide. ". . . One could not have been under a . . . finer commander." Duffie, twenty-eight, had seen cavalry action in Algeria and the Crimea. He knew how to organize troopers and whip them into fighting shape, but was rigid in his tactics—an Old World officer in a New World setting.[2]

The Federal raid was carefully planned. One column under Buford dashed across the river upstream at Beverly Ford just before 5 a.m., heading for the main Rebel lines in front of Fleetwood Hill. A second column under Gregg, with Duffie leading the way, crossed downstream an hour later, ordered to move inland and then turn north to take the enemy in flank.

Stuart's men clearly were unprepared for the assault, some of them forced to leap onto horses without putting on uniform coats or saddling up. In the van of Buford's column at Beverly Ford, the 8th New York and Colonel Benjamin "Grimes" Davis brushed aside the Rebel pickets and made straight for some horse artillery, whose crews were frantically trying to limber up and pull the guns to the rear. "When Colonel Davis found the Rebels he did not stop at anything, but went for them heavy," said one of his troopers. For a moment, it appeared the horse artillery would be captured—the first such cannon Stuart would lose.

Then 150 troopers of the 6th Virginia, hurriedly scraped together by Major Cabell Flournoy, burst out of the nearby woods, bringing the Federals up short. Davis held his ground in the midst of the maelstrom, emptying his Colt revolver at the newcomers and slashing at them with his saber. Here Lieutenant R. O. Allen galloped forward and engaged him, evading a wicked saber cut and firing a revolver in his face. The bullet knocked Davis from his horse and killed him instantly, temporarily leaving the confused Federals without leadership.

Grumble Jones now brought up the 7th Virginia and other units, desperately trying to form a defensive line. "A charge was instantly made to support Flournoy, but it was repulsed by the enemy," said one Rebel officer, "and in the recoil the 7th was carried back past the guns stationed on the road. These gallant cannoneers . . . proved that they were able to take care of themselves. Although exposed to the enemy, they covered their own retreat with cannister, and safely retired to the line at St. James Church [to the right and in front of Fleetwood Hill], where they found efficient support."[3]

So went the initial confrontation between Buford's and Jones's troopers—with each side making wild and often chaotic charges. Sometimes amidst the gunfire the horses could not be controlled. Remembered

Private John Opie of the 6th Virginia, whose mount took him straight toward the Federals: "I hallooed, 'Whoa! Whoa! Whoa!' but to no purpose. . . . I thought of killing her, but I had nothing but a saber. . . . I thought of jumping off, but that would not have done."

Union Captain George Custer, at the time still an aide to Pleasanton, had the opposite problem. Panicked by the shot and shell, his horse huddled next to a fence and refused to budge. Swearing a blue streak, Custer dismounted and pulled the animal from his imagined shelter by sheer force. He was barely back in the saddle before the horse bolted, racing *away* from the action.[4]

Now about 10 a.m. there occurred a lull in the fighting. Buford used the time to regroup. Major William McClure, taking over for the slain Davis, was on the left of the Federal line, near St. James Church. Pugnacious Colonel Thomas C. Devin, a New York City businessman, moved his brigade to McClure's right. Major Charles J. Whiting, commanding the reserve, positioned his troopers still farther right.

The Confederate line in front of Fleetwood Hill, under Stuart's guidance, likewise stabilized. Rooney Lee came up on Jones's left and Wade Hampton on his right—the South Carolinian's position being closest to the church—and there Beckham lodged his horse artillery.

Subsequently some of Buford's men, the 6th Pennsylvania and the 6th U.S. Cavalry, charged again. This onslaught, over a plateau some 800 yards wide and aimed at the Beckham's cannon, proved heroic but futile. The Federals, said Captain James F. Hart, "dashed up to the very muzzles, then through and beyond our guns, passing between Hampton's left and Jones' right. Here they were attacked from both flanks, and the survivors driven back."[5]

Undoubtedly Stuart was congratulating himself on his cavalry's spirited reaction to the assault at Beverly Ford when, about 11 a.m., a courier from Grumble Jones brought an unwelcome message. Jones was reporting that a second Federal column, later found to be David Gregg's, was coming up from the south and threatening to engulf the Rebel right flank.

The incredulous Stuart could not believe the news. Hadn't he placed Beverly Robertson's brigade to block an attack from Kelly's Ford? Jeb's long-standing distaste for Jones clouded his judgment. Grumble, besides being an irritant, must be an alarmist. "Tell General Jones," he said brusquely, "to attend to the Yankees in his front, and I'll watch the flanks."

Mused Jones aloud when he heard the reply, "So he thinks they ain't coming, does he? Well, let him alone; he'll damn soon see for himself."[6]

In short order Stuart did see his peril, as other couriers confirmed the report: Gregg's column was galloping toward Brandy Station, endangering the Confederate right and rear. Coming up from Kelly's Ford, the Federals had made no effort to engage Robertson, but simply swept around him. That officer, perhaps reluctant to divide his command, had sent no troopers in pursuit to engage them, but simply held his position. His was a terrible lapse in judgment.

Stuart reacted instinctively. "The tiger was aroused in him," John Esten Cooke, an aide, would write. "His face flushed; his eyes darted flame; his voice grew harsh and strident." Ordering Jones and Hampton out of the St. James Church line, he raced with the former to Fleetwood Hill, two miles distant and, because of its elevation, the key to the whole battlefield. Staying behind alone to hold back Buford was Rooney Lee; Tom Munford would not arrive until hours later. Now the all-important question was: Who would seize control of Fleetwood first, Stuart or Gregg?

Here occurred a fortuitous circumstance. When Stuart earlier had rushed forward to direct operations against Buford, his adjutant Henry B. McClellan had remained on the hill with a handful of men and one 6-pound howitzer.

Seeing Gregg's column approaching, McClellan took immediate action. He ordered Lieutenant John Carter to push the gun forward to the crest, found a few shells and some round shot in the limber chest, and began a slow fire on the oncoming foe. "The enemy was deceived by appearances," he said. "That the head of his column should have been greeted by the fire of artillery . . . must have indicated to General Gregg the presence of a considerable force on the hill; and the fact that his advance had been entirely unopposed, together with his ignorance of what has transpired with Buford, must have strengthened the thought that his enemy, in force, here waited an attack."[7]

Though their ammunition soon was exhausted, McClellan and Carter succeeded in slowing Gregg's progress. Nonetheless the Federals were only fifty yards distant when Jones's troopers arrived, touching off a contest that lasted all afternoon.

In the Confederate van were Colonel Asher Harman's 12th Virginia and Lieutenant Colonel Elijah "Lige" White's 35th Battalion, who recklessly charged up the north slope of the hill and down the other side. But with no time to form proper line of battle they quickly were cut up and scattered by Percy Wyndham's 1st New Jersey. "It was a trying position . . . to be put into action in such manner," said McClellan. ". . . I have, however, always believed that the circumstances justified the sacrifice . . . for, had Colonel Wyndham obtained undisputed possession of the summit . . . the subsequent fighting would probably have had a different result."

Cabell Flournoy's 6th Virginia at this point came up, along with some cannon under Captain Hart, reaching the crest and, under Stuart's direction, restoring some equilibrium to the affair. Once more the two sides exchanged charges and countercharges. Harman went down with a severe wound, as did Wyndham. "Not a man fought dismounted," said Stuart aide William Blackford of the saber-to-saber fighting, "and there was heard but an occasional pistol shot and but little artillery, for soon after the opening . . . the dust was so thick that it was impossible to use either without risk to friends."

Then sheer numbers began to prevail. The Federals attained the summit, sending their adversaries pell-mell down the slope. "As the enemy poured an incessant fire at my back," said Private Opie of the 6th Virginia, "I felt as if lizards and snakes were crawling up my spine, and expected to be perforated every moment."[8]

Wade Hampton, leading his South Carolinians, Georgians, and Mississippians, now thundered onto the battlefield, passing through the fleeing Rebels and taking on their pursuers. "This charge was as gallantly made and gallantly met as any . . . I witnessed during four years of active service," said Captain Hart. "Taking into estimation the number of men who closed sabers (nearly a brigade on each side), it was by far the most important hand-to-hand combat between the cavalry."

The patrician Hampton did not glory in war, as the much younger Stuart did, but once involved he was equally merciless. His attack took Wyndham's men in flank on the Fleetwood crest, where they had been joined by Judson Kilpatrick's brigade, giving the Virginians time to rally and rejoin the fight. The blue and the gray riders hacked and thrust, with the battle in the balance. "[Hampton] was everywhere seen, amid the clouds of smoke," said John Esten Cooke, ". . . fighting like a private soldier, his long sword doing hard work in the melee, and carving its way as did the trenchant weapons of the ancient knights."

Lieutenant R. B. Porter, one of Kilpatrick's officers, vividly remembered Hampton's charge: "There followed an indescribable clashing, banging and yelling. . . . We were now so mixed up with the Rebels that every man was fighting desperately to maintain his position. . . . A big Reb bore down on me with his saber raised. I parried the blow . . . which, however, was delivered with such force as to partially break the parry and leave its mark across my back." Lieutenant Henry C. Meyer of Gregg's staff likewise found himself outmatched. "Having only one [bullet] left in my revolver," he said, "I had to allow the [Rebel] to ride up to and strike me, so as to be sure of my aim." When his piece misfired, Meyer for a moment thought he was a dead man. "The point of his saber cut into my collar-bone."

Both officers survived, but they and the rest of Gregg's troopers inexorably were pushed back—down the south slope, toward Brandy Station, and then beyond. By 4:30 p.m. the Federal threat to Fleetwood was over, and Jones and Hampton were fortifying the crest.[9]

Back at the St. James Church line during these crucial hours, the resourceful Buford was launching another assault. Hitherto he had been constrained from coming to Gregg's aid, fearful that Rooney Lee would have taken him in flank had he done so. Now he moved to envelop the Rebel left, sending forth the 6th Pennsylvania and the 2nd U.S. Cavalry.

Taking up the challenge was the 9th Virginia, which had been Rooney's old regiment before being promoted to brigadier. About 4 p.m., he placed himself at its front, and proceeded to engage the 6th Pennsylvania head-on. "There, some 200 yards away, stood a long line of blue-coated cavalry," said one of his troopers. "Lee did not hesitate an instant but dashed at the center . . . with his column of fours. "The Yankees were of course cut in two at once, but each of their flanks closed in on our column, and then a most terrible affray with sabers and pistols took place."

The 2nd U.S. came up in the Pennsylvanians' support, and the hand-to-hand fighting became all the more chaotic. Union Captain Wesley Merritt closed with a "prominent Rebel officer" and shouted, somewhat unwisely, "Colonel, you are my prisoner!" The officer's response was a saber blow that took off Merritt's hat and narrowly missed his head. A second blow slashed his leg, and then, with "the dusk and smoke and steam from the heated horses making the air dark," Merritt in the continuing melee lost sight of his opponent. Only later did he surmise the officer was Rooney Lee, who had not yet bothered to replace a colonel's three stars with a general's laurel leaf.

Here the 10th and 13th Virginia entered the fray, tipping the balance and forcing a Federal withdrawal. "General Lee directed in person the counter charge," said the Rebel trooper, "and as his mounted men swept

over the hill . . . a bullet passed through his leg." The twenty-six-year-old
Rooney was carried from the field. Weeks later he would be captured by
Union raiders while recuperating at a relative's home near Richmond, and
not exchanged until March 1864.[10]

Both Buford's and Gregg's columns at this point had been decisively repelled. But what of Colonel Duffie, whose 1,900 troopers had moved
across Kelly's Ford in advance of Gregg that morning and then marched
inland? By 11 a.m., Duffie's progress, slowed as much by excessive wari-
ness as unfamiliar roads, was just nearing Stevensburg, five miles south of
Brandy Station. There he was met by Colonel Matthew Calbraith Butler's
2nd South Carolina, which had been alerted to his flanking movement.
"There was nothing left for me to do," said the handsome, graceful Butler,
"but to move without orders as rapidly as our horses would carry us
and . . . check the advance."

Butler's 225 men were badly outnumbered, but they were resolute, and
their position was particularly well chosen. Lieutenant Colonel Frank
Hampton, Wade's younger brother, was posted on horseback with some
troopers on the road leading into Stevensburg; the rest of the regiment was
on foot in the bramble and trees. "The woods concealed the smallness of
[Butler's] numbers," said Major McClellan, "and even on the road the
sloping ground prevented the enemy from discovering any but the leading
files of Hampton's detachment. The enemy's advance was cautious, even
timid. As Butler had anticipated, the first attempt was to break the line of
his dismounted men, on his left, and two such attacks were made; but
both were repulsed by the close fire of his Enfield rifles."[11]

Now Duffie turned his attention to Hampton on the Confederate right,
who, seeing the 1st Massachusetts approaching, met the charge with one
of his own. He and his men never had a chance. The weight of the Yankee
onslaught overwhelmed them, scattering the command and sending
Hampton to the ground with a mortal wound.

Duffie followed up this success with slashing attacks by the 1st Rhode
Island and the 6th Ohio on Butler's main body, pushing it back through
Stevensburg. "The enemy having gained possession of the road . . . to
Culpeper," said Major Thomas Lipscomb of the 2nd South Carolina,
". . . the right of our line fell back obliquely to the road leading from
Stevensburg to Brandy Station. They were rallied and formed by Colonel
Butler . . . but the columns of the enemy pouring on the woods on his left,
and threatening to gain his rear, compelled him [again] to fall back."

Williams Wickham's 4th Virginia was moving up in support on Butler's right about this time, doubling the number of defenders. Instead of stabilizing the situation, however, the newcomers, constrained by the terrain from forming a battle line, would become sacrificial lambs. "[Wickham's] regiment was in a position where it was impossible for it to act, enclosed as it was in a thick pine copse, on a narrow by-road," said McClellan "where even a column of fours could scarcely move. It was therefore necessary to turn the head of his column westward, toward Stevensburg."

Riding into the full fury of the Federal advance, without cover, the Virginians endured a hail of fire, then broke and ran. "There was not a finer body of men in the service," continued McClellan. ". . . But on this day a panic possessed them. They did not respond to the efforts of their officers, and the enemy's pursuit was continued through Stevensburg and beyond . . . where Colonel Wickham and a few of his men threw themselves into a field by the road-side and by the fire of their pistols checked further pursuit."[12]

It was now about 1:30 p.m. The South Carolinians, bloodied but still intact, were digging in behind Mountain Run, blocking the Brandy Station road. Butler and Captain Will Farley, Stuart's chief scout, were conferring side by side on horseback when an enemy shell struck the ground near them and ricocheted, cutting off Butler's right foot, passing through both mounts, and severing Farley's leg. A staff officer and a civilian observer rushed to tend to Butler who, despite the severity of his own injury, waved them off and urged them to help the scout.

The observer, James T. Rhett, describes the scene: "We went to Captain Farley . . . and placed him in an old flat trough. . . . Just as we were about to send him away, he called me to him, and pointing to the leg that had been cut off by the ball . . . he asked me to bring it to him."

"It is an old friend . . . and I do not wish to part from it," he said.

Farley would die within a few hours, and be buried with his severed limb. Butler would survive, and three months later be named a brigadier. His lost foot, embalmed, would become a family keepsake.[13]

By midafternoon, meanwhile, just as Duffie was about to renew his assault on the South Carolinians, he received orders to report to Brandy Station in all haste. Choosing not to cut his way through the defenders, he moved east the way he had come, and then turned north, arriving just as the fight on Fleetwood Hill was ending. His brigade, which might have insured a Union victory, had been wasted on a fool's errand, compounded by its leader's foot-dragging.

Confederate losses on June 9 totaled some 525 men; Federal losses, 485. For Stuart, fifteen regiments did almost all the fighting: five of Hampton's, five of Jones's, four of Rooney Lee's, one of Fitz Lee's. Beverly Robertson's brigade, as we have seen, was not engaged.

The Federal reconnaissance in force learned nothing about Lee's intentions to move into Pennsylvania. But it marked a milestone for the Army of the Potomac's horsemen, far more so than Stoneman's controversial expedition. "It *made* the Federal cavalry," said the admiring McClellan. ". . . They gained on this day the confidence in themselves and in their commanders that enabled them to contest us so fiercely on subsequent battlefields."

Stuart refused to admit he had been lax in anticipating the attack, but newspaper commentaries and the opinions of fellow officers were almost all negative. "Vigilance, vigilance, more vigilance, is the lesson taught us by the Brandy surprise," editorialized the *Richmond Sentinel* in one of the milder rebukes, "and which must not be forgotten by the victory that was wrested from defeat. Let us all learn from it, from the Major General down to the picket." Wrote one Rebel officer to his wife, "I suppose it is all right that Stuart should get all the blame, for when anything handsome is done he gets all the credit."[14]

Used to basking in praise, or at least receiving the mildest of criticism, Stuart must have chafed under these sentiments. In the Gettysburg Campaign to come, seeking to burnish his reputation, he would embellish on his orders with fateful results.

SEVEN
* * * *

THE EAST, JUNE 25–JULY 2:
STUART'S GAMBLE

Robert E. Lee's Army of Northern Virginia, with General Richard Ewell's corps in the van, began to cross the Potomac in mid-June, stealthily moving down the Shenandoah Valley west of the Blue Ridge Mountains, with Jeb Stuart's cavalry shielding its progress. The Confederates subsequently would march into Maryland and Pennsylvania, intent on bringing the war to the Union. The Federals under Joseph Hooker, when they learned of the advance, soon would cross the Potomac themselves and push north on a parallel path, precipitating the three-day Battle of Gettysburg.

Before it was known what the enemy would do, however, Stuart on June 22 and 23 received two messages from Lee. "If you find that [Hooker] is moving northward, and that two brigades can guard the Blue Ridge and take care of your rear," the first one said, "you can move with the other three into Maryland, and take position on General Ewell's right . . . guard his flank, keep him informed of the enemy's movements." Read the June 23 message: "If General Hooker's army remains inactive . . . I think you had better withdraw this side of the mountains tomorrow night, [and] cross at Shepherdstown the next day. . . . You will, however, be able to judge whether you can pass around their army without hindrance . . . and cross the [Potomac] east of the mountains. In either case . . . you must move on and feel the right of Ewell's troops."[1]

Stuart was being given discretion by Lee, or so he chose to interpret his orders, as to whether he should ford the Potomac *west* or *east* of the Blue Ridge. This point is crucial. If he crossed west of the mountains at Shepherdstown, he would be tying himself to the main army; if he crossed east of them, he would have far more freedom. For Stuart the choice was obvious. He would ride east to ford the river between the Federals and Washington, make another triumphant ride around the Army of the Potomac, and then take up his duties on Ewell's right.

Leaving Grumble Jones and Beverly Robertson with some 3,000 men to guard the passes, Stuart at 1 a.m. on June 25 rode east out of Salem, Virginia, with 6,000 troopers—the brigades of Wade Hampton, Fitz Lee, and the wounded Rooney Lee under its senior colonel, John R. Chambliss—together with six guns.

From the start the expedition met obstacles. Lee had stressed the need for speed, but this was not to be. Some hours later, at Haymarket, where Stuart intended to turn north to the Potomac, he encountered Union General Winfield Scott Hancock's corps, headed north on the same road he expected to take. "A brisk artillery fire was opened upon the marching column," said Major McClellan, "and was continued until the enemy moved a force of infantry against the guns. Not wishing [unduly] to disclose his force, Stuart withdrew from Hancock's vicinity after capturing some prisoners and satisfying himself concerning the movement. . . . This information was at once [sent] to General Lee by courier."

Whether Lee received this dispatch from Stuart is doubtful. If he did, it would be the last communication between the two men until the night of July 1, when the first day of the Battle of Gettysburg would end.

Toward dark, Stuart bedded down in nearby Buckland. There he pondered his next move. Retracing his footsteps and crossing west of the mountains at Shepherdstown would mean a march of sixty miles. Far better, he reasoned, to keep heading east in a wide detour. This he did the next day, going through Bristoe Station, Brentsville, and Wolf Trap Shoals on the Occoquan River, and arriving on June 27 at Fairfax Court House. His progress was deplorable. He had covered but thirty-five miles in some fifty hours, and was still twenty miles from the Potomac.

Much of Jeb's tardiness was due to the problems the Rebels were experiencing in feeding their mounts. "It had been necessary to halt the command several times . . . to graze the horses, for the country was destitute of provisions," acknowledged McClellan. "Nowhere was any forage found," wrote one historian. "The country had been swept bare. Horses that had endured hard service . . . now gave signs of approaching exhaustion. Halts had to be called to graze the weakened animals."[2]

Late that night Stuart neared Rowser's Ford on the Potomac. "The ford was wide and deep and might well have daunted a less determined man than our indomitable General, for the water swept over the pommels of our saddles," said William Blackford, the engineering officer. "To pass the artillery without wetting the ammunition in the chests was impossible . . . but Stuart had the cartridges distributed among the horsemen and it was thus taken over in safety. The guns and caissons went clean out of sight beneath the surface . . . but all came out without the loss of a piece or a man."

By 3 a.m. on June 28, continued Blackford, "We all stood wet and dripping on the Maryland shore." There the need to feed the horses again held up the march for several hours. "It was absolutely necessary, though time was so precious, to allow the horses some rest and a chance to eat the fine grass around us after their hard night's work; so it was nearly the middle of the day before we reached Rockville, a pretty village on the main road from Washington."[3]

Near Rockville the Confederates came upon a huge wagon train of 150 wagons, laden with food, fodder, and equipment. "Galloping full tilt into the head of the train," said Blackford, "we captured . . . over half the wagons before they could turn round; but then those beyond took the alarm, turned and fled as fast as their splendid mule teams would go. After them we flew, popping away with our pistols at such drivers as did not pull up. . . . Finally, coming to a sharp turn in the road, one upset and a dozen or two others piled up on top of it. . . . It was as exciting as a fox chase . . . and when the last was taken, I found myself on a hill in full view of Washington. One hundred and twenty-five uninjured wagons were . . . safely brought into our lines."[4]

By the time Stuart reorganized the train—which he chose to commandeer rather than burn, a decision that would further slow him down—and paroled more than 400 prisoners, it was nightfall.

Lee in Pennsylvania at this juncture did not know where his cavalry was, and Stuart was just as ignorant of the commanding general's whereabouts. What Lee belatedly did know, informed by scouts other than Jeb's, was that the Federal army pursuing him—now led by George Meade, replacing Hooker—was at Frederick, Maryland, and racing north toward Pennsylvania. Much alarmed, he alerted his own columns, which were as far apart as Chambersburg and Carlisle, and ordered them to converge west of Gettysburg.

Meanwhile, Stuart at Rockville soon would realize that he was separated from Lee by tens of thousands of fast-moving Federals on his left, half of whom were ahead of him and half in his rear. His days of riding around the enemy were in the past.

The morning of June 29 found Jeb in the Cooksville area, routing a small Union force—whose paroles again necessitated delay—and then severing the Baltimore & Ohio Railroad. "Much time was necessarily consumed in tearing up the track at Hood's Mill, in burning the bridge at Sykesville, and in [downing] the telegraph line," said McClellan. "But this work was effectually accomplished, and the last means of communication between General Meade's army and Washington was destroyed."

Entering Westminster, Maryland, about 5 p.m., Stuart met brief but stubborn resistance from troopers of the 1st Delaware Cavalry. Their commander, Major Napoleon B. Knight, had deserted them after spending a few hours boozing in a local tavern, but his men, despite the enormous disparity in numbers, chose to stay and fight. Twice they threw back the Rebel van, losing sixty-seven out of ninety-five men in the process, before falling back and fleeing. "By now the close proximity of the enemy," Major McClellan would admit, ". . . and the separation of the brigades by the wide interval which the [wagon] train occupied was a disadvantage. . . . But it was not in Stuart's nature to abandon an attempt until it had been proven to be beyond his powers; and he determined to hold onto his prize. . . . This was unfortunate."[5]

The next day, crossing into Pennsylvania at last, the Confederates again encountered the enemy. The 2nd North Carolina, Chambliss's brigade, galloped into Hanover and came upon Union General Judson Kilpatrick's division, whose rear guard was vacating the town. The Rebels quickly scattered the trailing regiment, the 18th Pennsylvania Cavalry, but then found the tables turned.

The 2nd North Carolina's charge, McClellan would maintain, "if it had been properly supported, would have resulted in the rout of Kilpatrick's command. But Hampton was separated from [Chambliss's small] brigade by the whole train of captured wagons, and Fitz Lee was marching on the left flank to protect the column from an attack. . . . Before anything could be brought to the assistance of the 2nd North Carolina . . . [the Federals] rallied . . . and drove the Carolinians from the town."[6]

Stuart and Blackford were still several miles from Hanover when the

sounds of fighting broke out. They immediately spurred their mounts forward, arriving in the midst of the Carolinians' flight. "We tried to rally
them," said Blackford, "but the long charge *in* and the repulse *out* and the
hot skirmish fire opened upon them by citizens from the windows on the
street had thrown them into utter confusion, and in spite of all we could
do they got by us, and before we were aware of it we found ourselves at
the head of the enemy's charging column."

The road was walled on each side by towering hedges, but at some in-
tervals, fortunately, there were lower growths. Stuart pulled up, waved his
saber, theatrically shouted, "Rally them, Blackford!" and then jumped his
mare, Virginia, over the hedge and into an open field. "I know that he only
said what he did to let me know that he was off," said the aide, "so I followed him. I had [recently] . . . mounted Magic, having had her led previously, and Stuart had done the same with Virginia, so they were fresh."

Once over the hedges, the two men faced a new challenge. Two dozen
Yankees, making a flanking movement, closed upon them in the field and
called for their surrender. "We let our two thoroughbreds out," said
Blackford, "[and] they followed . . . firing as fast as they could cock their
pistols. The field was in tall timothy grass and we did not see, nor did our
horses until close to it, a gully fifteen feet wide and as many deep stretched
across our path."

Their mounts had no more than a few seconds to gather themselves for
the jump. "Stuart and myself were riding side by side," said the aide, "and
as soon as Magic rose I turned my head to see how Virginia [was react-
ing], and I shall never forget the glimpse I saw of this beautiful animal up
in mid-air over the chasm, and Stuart's fine figure sitting erect and firm in
the saddle." Both horses and their riders landed safely on the far bank,
even as the bluecoats, now alerted to the obstacle, reined in their horses
and reluctantly gave up the chase.[7]

Backed up by the horse artillery, Stuart now restored order to the 2nd
North Carolina and the rest of Chambliss's troopers, forming a battle line
south of Hanover. Soon he was joined by Hampton, coming up on the
right, and Fitz Lee on the left. The ordinarily reckless Judson Kilpatrick,
for his part, contented himself during the rest of the day with maintaining
a defensive posture. "Store boxes, wagons, hay ladders, fence rails, barrels, bar iron," an observer remarked, "[were stacked] to prevent the enemy from dashing through the town."[8]

Not until night had fallen did Jeb think it prudent to disengage, circling
Hanover and moving northeast to Dover, a route that distanced him all the

more from Lee's growing concentration at Gettysburg. Hunger was setting in, and the march through the darkness was enervating in the extreme. "Nearly four hundred prisoners had accumulated since the parole at Cooksville," said McClellan. "Many of these were loaded in the wagons; some of them acted as drivers. The mules were starving for food and water, and often became unmanageable. Not infrequently a large part of the train would halt in the road because a driver toward the front had fallen asleep. . . . The train guard became careless through excessive fatigue."

During a four-hour rest at Dover the morning of July 1—the first day of the fighting at Gettysburg—Stuart learned from locals that Lee was preparing for battle, but he still did not know when or where. He dispatched aides to the west to gather intelligence, and then veered his column northwest toward Carlisle, "hoping there," said McClellan, "to obtain provisions for his troops, and definite information concerning the army." This march, too, was exhausting. "It is impossible for me to give you a correct idea of the fatigue . . . of the men and beasts at this time," Lieutenant George W. Beale of the 9th Virginia wrote his mother. "From great exertion, constant mental excitement, want of sleep and food, the men were overcome, and so tired and stupid as almost to be ignorant of what was transpiring around them."

Lee meanwhile was beside himself as to Stuart's whereabouts. "Have you heard anything about my cavalry?" he would ask his aides. "I hope no disaster had overtaken my cavalry."[9]

The Confederates, arriving at Carlisle in late afternoon, found the town garrisoned by two brigades of militia—some 2,000 men—under General William F. "Baldy" Smith, a veteran officer who had fallen in disfavor with the War Department for his outspoken criticism of Union tactics at Fredericksburg. Stuart promptly demanded that he surrender, or else suffer the effects of a cannonade. "Shell away!" the crusty Smith replied.

Though the ensuing bombardment did little to weaken Smith's resolve, it torched the town and terrified its citizens. "Now began a general flight of the inhabitants into the country and cellars and behind anything strong enough to afford hope of protection," said one witness, "a stream of women and children and infirm people on foot, with outcries and terrified countenances." There was a letup in the firing, during which a second order to surrender was rejected, and then the shelling resumed, setting ablaze private homes as well as the county courthouse and government warehouses. "In the middle of the night there was another pause in the firing, and another call for surrender, to which a rather uncourteous reply was made by General Smith, and the shelling proceeded, though with diminishing power and frequency. It is supposed that ammunition had become precious in the hostile camp."

Lack of shells was not responsible for the respite, but the return of Stuart's aides, with instructions from Lee, who was thirty miles to the south, to join him posthaste. "The whereabouts of our army," Jeb said, "[had been] a mystery, but during the night I received a dispatch from General Lee that [he] was at Gettysburg and had been engaged." The cavalry leader promptly broke off his cannonading and left Carlisle about 1:30 a.m., taking his weary troopers on another all-night march—this time toward the fighting. Chambliss and Fitz Lee were in the van; Hampton followed with the wagons and prisoners.[10]

Stuart would not report to Lee until the early afternoon of July 2, just before the Rebels launched their fruitless assaults on the Union left at Cemetery Ridge. Their meeting, as might be expected, was a painful one.

"General Stuart, where have you been?" Lee asked, reddening with anger and raising his voice.

Jeb tried to explain his movements, and how the Federal columns had kept him from rejoining the army, or even communicating with it.

Lee interrupted him. "I have not heard a word from you for days, and you [my] eyes and ears."

"I have brought you 125 wagons and their teams, General," said Stuart.

"They are an impediment to me," was Lee's brusque answer. Then, to a degree, he relented. "We will not discuss this matter longer. Help me fight these people."[11]

Stuart's cavalry would assemble on the Confederate left that day, but other than a brief but spirited clash between Kilpatrick and Hampton, it would see little action. During this period, however, Wade Hampton would have a singular experience, and a narrow escape. He was dozing on his horse when a sniper's bullet whizzed by his head. Judging that it came from his left front, perhaps 300 yards distant in a clump of trees, he quickly spurred the animal forward—all alone. Within 100 yards of the bramble, he quickly spotted the shooter, nineteen-year-old Frank Pearson, a Michigan trooper who was naively standing atop a tree stump instead of hiding behind it, and lifting his carbine for another try. Hampton whipped out his pistol, and the two men fired almost at the same instant.

The Yank's bullet splintered the rail fence near the Carolinian, while Wade's bullet tore bark from the stump. Two more shots were exchanged, and a bullet passed through Hampton's cavalry cape. Pearson's gun then jammed. He raised his right hand, palm out, as if asking for a moment's forbearance. The bemused Hampton, a superb marksman, obliged, pointing his pistol straight up. Minutes passed before Pearson succeeded in reloading his rifle, and then the opponents fired again. This time Hampton's bullet shattered his adversary's wrist. The young trooper dropped his carbine, jumped from the stump, and fled into the brush.

Just at this moment Hampton heard hoofbeats behind him. Before he could turn, however, he took a saber blow on the back of his head. His attacker, it would turn out, was an officer of the 6th Michigan cavalry, out reconnoitering. "Hampton, a tall man on a tall horse, rode inches higher than his assailant," wrote a biographer, "and the blow lacked full force. . . . Even so, his scalp was opened by a cut four inches long, and a weaker man or one less surely seated might have been unhorsed."

The Carolinian, in a blood-red rage, wheeled his horse and fired at his attacker at point-blank range. The pistol "that had just struck one enemy at a phenomenal range now failed. The charging was faulty. Only a dull snap sounded as the hammer fell." Doubtless counting his blessings, the Yank now turned and raced away, pursued by Hampton, who ultimately reined up, hurling both his useless pistol and a strong oath at the man's back.[12]

The denouement to this tale did not come until ten years later, when the self-same Michigan officer sought out and met Colonel Frank Hampton, Wade's younger brother. "Seeing a solitary Confederate firing into our lines," he explained, "I determined to capture him. There was nothing about him to indicate his rank. . . . The bend in the [rail] fence prevented him from noticing my approach. . . . I would have run him through . . . but I was incapable of stabbing any man in the back. I saw that he was of formidable stature, and as his pistol was in his hand, I was sure that if I ordered him to surrender he would instantly turn and fire on me.

"He was mounted on a horse of light chestnut color, which I thought the finest animal I had ever seen. . . . I at once changed my plan and decided to unhorse the rider and capture his splendid mount. As I struck the blow he turned upon me. . . . [Thereafter] it was a three-mile race for [my] life. I heard his pistol snap three times at my back, and also his parting curse, as I went through a gap in the fence."

This information was passed on to Wade Hampton, who later wrote the officer that he regarded his pistol's failure to fire "with a deep sense of gratitude to Him in whose hands are the balance of life and death." Later still, Hampton received a letter from the sniper, who said that he was glad that he had missed; the Carolinian, in turn, responded that he was sorry he had injured the young man.[13]

That Stuart's 6,000-man attempted Ride Around Meade on the eve of Gettysburg was a failure is a given. Whether his absence from the Army of Northern Virginia for seven days substantially affected the outcome of the battle is endlessly debated. Lee always intended to fight in Pennsylvania; at best, Stuart's scouting might have resulted in better terrain and timing. The real question is *why*, once the cavalry leader came to see his predicament, did he not take remedial action? Couriers and aides could have dispatched in all directions, sooner than July 1, to determine Lee's position. Skirmishes and engagements, which sapped the column's strength, could have been avoided. The wagon train, whose food and fodder Stuart so studiously protected despite his troopers' needs, could have been pillaged and abandoned.

The best answer may be that Jeb had been in the saddle, almost without respite, for a solid month. His iron physique was unimpaired, but fatigue was clouding his judgment. Decisions he normally would have made within minutes were put off, alternatives were never considered.

Lee would have no patience with such conjecturing. In his official report after the battle, the mild-mannered commanding general's rebuke to Stuart could not have been more pointed. "The movements of the army preceding the Battle of Gettysburg," he wrote, "had been much embarrassed by the absence of cavalry."[14]

EIGHT
* * * *

THE WEST, JULY 2−26:
MORGAN'S INDIANA-OHIO RAID

Hoping to relieve the growing Federal threat to East Tennessee and Chattanooga by disrupting the enemy's supply lines, Confederate general Braxton Bragg in early June authorized John Hunt Morgan to lead still another raid deep into Kentucky, but instructed him not to go any farther. The cavalryman, however, had bigger plans. He intended to do all the damage to the railroads in Kentucky that he could, but then to move north across the Ohio River and proceed through Indiana and Ohio, spreading fear and consternation as he went.

In truth, the timorous Bragg and his mercurial lieutenant were polar opposites. Morgan, the commanding general allowed, "had few superiors, none perhaps in his line," but, he continued, the raider was "a *dangerous man*, on account of his intense desire to act independently." Basil Duke, who was Morgan's ranking officer, nonetheless saw his chief's risk taking as a strength: "So positive were [his] convictions that . . . his raid should be extended to Northern territory, [that] he deliberately resolved to disobey the order restricting his operations. . . . He did not disguise from himself the great dangers he [would encounter], but was sanguine of success."[1]

Though he was sidetracked for several weeks by Bragg's insistence that he chase an imaginary Union column, Morgan on July 2 with some 2,500 horsemen, two Parrott guns, and two howitzers left Burkesville, Kentucky, just across the border from Tennessee, and headed for the nearby Cumberland River. His 1st Brigade, led by Duke, was comprised of the 2nd Kentucky—his original regiment—plus the 5th and 6th Kentucky and the 9th Tennessee. His 2nd Brigade, under Adam R. Johnson, included the 7th, 8th, 10th, 11th, and 14th Kentucky. The ranks of the Kentuckians and Tennesseans also contained recruits from Alabama, Georgia, Mississippi, and Texas—troopers attracted by Morgan's reputation. In their number, too, were four of his five brothers: Richard, leading the 14th Kentucky; Charlton; Calvin; and Thomas.

Certainly the commander's appearance inspired confidence. "He was tall and broad-shouldered," said one historian, "with a flowing mustache and elegant goatee, and an intelligent, kindly face." Photographs show a steady, discerning gaze, and a mouth that seems ever ready to break into a smile. "Six feet in height, his form was perfect," said an impressed Private George D. Mosgrove, "a rare combination of grace, activity and strength. . . . [He was] easily approached, all men were his friends."[2]

Married just six months, Morgan's thoughts as he rode must have been, in part, on Mattie, his pregnant wife. Not long before, he had sent her by rail to the safety of Augusta, Georgia, and thereafter had written her as often as possible. "It was a long ride for you[,] My Darling," he said in one such letter. "How much I regretted not being able to accompany you—I should have anticipated all your wants. . . . Enclosed find a sprig of geranium." Later he wrote: "Shall read two chapters in [the] Prayer Book you gave me . . . and in bidding you goodnight send you a heart full of love. . . . You will present me with a beautiful present this winter."[3]

The Kentuckian had prepared well for his latest expedition. Tom Hines and Samuel Taylor, troopers who had been with him from the start, had been sent into Indiana and Ohio to scout his route. They returned with valuable information, confirming that there would be especial danger points. The first, just ahead, was the crossing of the Cumberland River; the second, the traverse of the mighty Ohio below Louisville; the third, the long march past the well-fortified ramparts at Cincinnatti; and the last, the perilous recrossing of the Ohio.

Morgan had shared his intentions with his officers, but not the rank and file. No matter. The men had total faith in his judgment, and were eager to begin another raid—wherever he led. "His rapidly formed plans, promptly and brilliantly executed, surprised his friends and confounded his foes," Private Mosgrove would say. ". . . He marched swiftly and continuously. . . . When advancing he rarely declined to fight, believing that a concentration of superior forces against him was more difficult—the vigor of his enemy being paralyzed by the celerity of his movements and the mystery that involved them. When retreating, however, he would resort to every stratagem to avoid battle, fearing that while fighting one enemy another might overtake and assail him."

Cantering toward the Cumberland that morning, Morgan's troopers could not have been in higher spirits. "We were ready and willing to go," said one. Soon they were raising their voices in song, and the heartfelt words of "My Old Kentucky Home" were resonating up and down the length of the column.[4]

The Confederates found the Cumberland rain-swollen and more than half a mile in width, but were not deterred. They hurriedly fashioned rafts from derelict flatboats and canoes to transport their guns, ammunition, and saddles, and then horses and most of the men, many of whom left their clothing on the rafts, plunged into the water. "The horses with their bridles and halters were driven into the stream and forced to take their chances," said Bennett Young, one of Tom Quirk's scouts, "not only with the rapid current, but with the driftwood, which was abundant and large. . . . Many of the men clung to the [rafts] and thus swam across . . . while others swam with their horses, holding to their manes or tails."

The Federal pickets, who belonged to Colonel Frank "Old Meat Axe" Wolford's 1st Kentucky Union Cavalry, were few in number, their commanders thinking that the river at this stage was unfordable. They were soon dispersed and driven back. "Those [of us] who had clothing on rushed ashore and into line," said Young, "[others] . . . unwilling to be laggard, not halting to dress, seized their cartridge boxes and guns and dashed upon the enemy. The strange sight of naked men engaging in combat amazed [them]. They had never seen soldiers before clad only in nature's garb."[5]

With Tom Quirk's scouts in the van, and the crack 2nd Kentucky close behind, Morgan's men moved inland toward Marrowbone Creek. There in midafternoon Quirk was severely wounded, and over his vehement objections sent back to Burkesville for treatment. "Only one man received a wound," said Kelion Peddicord, another of his scouts, "Captain Tom, whose rein arm was broken." This was a bad sign, many troopers felt. On all the previous raids, Quirk had been the regiment's, and Morgan's, most trusted outrider and guide.[6]

By July 3, the Rebels were in Columbia, where again they met little resistance. "We drove the enemy in great haste through the town," said Robert Alston, Morgan's chief of staff. But, he admitted, "Our men behaved badly . . . breaking open a store and plundering it. I ordered the men to return the goods, and made all the reparation in my power. These outrages are very disgraceful." That Morgan was not a disciplinarian we already know; he liked his men, regarded them as friends, and wanted them to like him. The result would be that many of his troopers, especially when there was little fighting to be done, felt free to loot. They knew he could be unbending in dealing with the enemy, but easygoing with them.

The next day the column was at Tebb's Bend, preparatory to crossing the Green River. There it encountered Colonel Orlando H. Moore with 200 men of the 25th Michigan Infantry, ensconced on high ground in an improvised timber-and-dirt fortification that was largely impervious to cannon fire and protected on three sides by water and woods. "General Morgan sent in a flag of truce and demanded the surrender," said Lieutenant Colonel Alston, "but [Moore] quietly remarked, 'If it was any other day I might consider the matter, but the Fourth of July is a bad day to talk about surrender, and I must therefore decline.' "

Perhaps annoyed by Moore's flippancy, Morgan sent forward Colonel David W. Chenault's 11th Kentucky, dismounted, in an unwise frontal attack. The troopers were decimated, and Chenault was killed just as he reached the fortification. Two more attacks also failed. "Many of our best men were killed and wounded," wrote Major James McCreary, who succeeded Chenault in command. "It was a sad, sorrowful day, and more tears of grief rolled over my weatherbeaten cheeks on this mournful occasion than have before for years. *The commencement of this raid is ominous*. Total loss in killed and wounded—71."[7]

Morgan now did what he should have done from the start. He bypassed Tebb's Bend, crossed the river farther down, and headed north to Lebanon, Kentucky. What he did not know, of course, was that the Confederacy elsewhere on July 4 was suffering two far more momentous setbacks. In Mississippi, Vicksburg and its 29,000-man garrison were surrendering to Grant, and in Pennsylvania, Lee was retreating from the three-day purgatory of Gettysburg after incurring 20,000 casualties.

Nearing Lebanon early on the 5th, Morgan again tried to force a surrender. In the town were 500 Kentucky Union infantry under Lieutenant Colonel Charles Hanson, men whom he and many of his troopers knew from before the war. The Rebel cavalryman lined up his 2,500-man column to make a show of force, and sent forward Colonel Alston. "I went in with a flag of truce," said the chief of staff. "It was fired on five times. Officer apologized, saying he thought it a man with a white coat on. Very dangerous mistake, at least for me."

Colonel Hanson refused to surrender. "I then ordered him," said Alston, "to send out the non-combatants, as we would be compelled to shell the town. He posted his regiments in the [railroad] depot and in various houses, by which he was enabled to make a desperate resistance."

In point of fact, the fight lasted more than six hours. Morgan's cannon again were ineffective, because they could not be brought to bear on the various defensive positions, clustered around the depot. Colonel Roy Cluke's 8th Kentucky, in the van, soon found itself pinned down by heavy fire, unable to move forward or rearward. Meanwhile the scorching sun and 100-degree heat were taking their toll. Finally Morgan, after setting several buildings ablaze and watching the flames spread to the rail station, sent in the 2nd Kentucky, troopers who had never failed him. Kelion Peddicord and the scouts were in the fore, weaving through the streets and dashing up to the depot, then firing blindly through any opening they could find. "A street fight," he acknowledged, "is one of the most desperate modes of warfare known to a soldier. The advantage is strongly against the storming party."

The charge carried the day, and Hanson soon gave up. But the fighting resulted in fifty more Rebel casualties, among them Lieutenant Tom Morgan, the commander's youngest brother. "Poor Tommy Morgan, who was always in the lead, ran forward and cheered the men with all the enthusiasm of his bright nature," said Alston. "Almost at the first volley he fell back, pierced through the heart. His only words were, 'Brother [Calvin], they have killed me.' "[8]

Tom Morgan's death put his siblings into a near-deranged state. When two Federal officers emerged from the burning depot, their hands in the air, Charlton Morgan threatened to kill them. Colonel Hanson tried to intercede, but the grieving brother would have none of it. He grabbed Hanson by the beard, twisted his neck, and shouted, "I will blow your brains out, you damned rascal!" The two were pulled apart, but Tom's death later stirred up the Rebel troopers. Besides tearing up track, they burned much of Lebanon and plundered the rest, including private homes. Previously Morgan had to some extent respected the rights of civilians—the main exception being the confiscation of their horses. Hereafter he made little or no attempt to stop looting.[9]

The Confederate van rode through the night and reached Bardstown early on July 6. There George "Lightning" Ellsworth, the column's telegrapher, quickly moved on a few miles to the railroad wire station and captured the operator. He found the man wearing a uniform of sorts, newly issued to telegraphers, which consisted of a dark blue shirt and silver striped trousers, a dapper brown vest, and a blue forage cap. "Hello, sonny," said Ellsworth, showing him a cocked pistol, "move an inch except as I tell you, and you'll be buried in that fancy rig." Then he tapped into the lines, learning that the Federals finally were bestirring themselves, organizing a pursuit that was no more than twenty-four hours in the rear of the raiding column.

Colonel Alston, who had been left behind with a small detachment just outside of Lebanon to parole prisoners, that morning learned firsthand just how close the enemy was, and in an embarrassing manner. Finishing his task, he had no sooner started out to rejoin Morgan than he ran into a squadron of the 9th Michigan, which promptly made him a prisoner himself. "My God! How I hated it," he would say of his arrest, "no one can understand."

Back in Bardstown about 5 a.m., the Rebels corralled Union Lieutenant Thomas W. Sullivan and his tiny 25-man garrison in a livery stable and demanded their surrender. Not once but twice did Sullivan refuse, despite the cannon being leveled on his position. Then, at the last moment, he walked from the stable, waving a white flag.

"What do you want?" shouted Richard Morgan, incensed that the column's march had been delayed.

"I accept your terms of surrender," was the reply.

"Go back! You refused twice. . . . You have no right to demand them now!"

Dick Morgan, still smarting over Tom's death, would have shot Sullivan then and there, but John Morgan overruled him and accepted the surrender. Subsequently, before moving on, the Confederates destroyed several locomotives and considerable track on the nearby Louisville & Nashville.[10]

Heretofore Morgan had been advancing through central Kentucky. Now he veered some thirty-five miles west, heading for Brandenburg, where he had determined he would cross the Ohio into Indiana. Simultaneously, as a diversion, he dispatched Captain William Davis and a company of the

2nd Kentucky toward Louisville, with orders to burn railroad bridges and track east of the city.

One reason, up to this point, for the lack of a stronger Federal response to his advance had been the enemy's uncertainty as to where the Confederates were going. Now that problem was being resolved. Union territory was being invaded! A second reason had been the hand-wringing of General Henry M. Judah, a slow-moving officer who was in overall charge of the area. But at this juncture several of his subordinates, Kentuckians all, were being unloosed, and the chase would begin in earnest. Each man was tenacious and battle-tested: Brigadier Edward Hobson, leading the 9th and 12th Kentucky Cavalry; Brigadier James Shackelford, commanding the 1st, 3rd and 8th Kentucky Cavalry, as well as the 2nd E. Tennessee Mounted Infantry; and reporting to Shackelford, the aforementioned Colonel Frank Wolford, heading the 1st Kentucky. Altogether, the force totaled some 4,000 bluecoats.

Eventually Judah and still more regiments would join in the pursuit, all intent on bringing the Rebels to bay and making them pay for their brashness.

About 10 a.m. on the 7th, captains Samuel Taylor and H. Clay Meriwether of Morgan's 10th Kentucky led their companies into Brandenburg, a small ungarrisoned town on a hill above the river, and began looking for transport to take the column across the broad and imposing Ohio. The pickings at first seemed slim. But they soon learned that the steamboat *John B. McCombs* would be arriving that afternoon, and made their plans accordingly. When the steamer came alongside the wharf, Rebel cavalrymen left their hiding places and leaped aboard, taking control of the vessel. When another boat, the *Alice Dean,* made an appearance, she was likewise commandeered.

The main force arrived early the next morning, with Morgan and Basil Duke in the van, and the troopers now realized they were raiding into the Union. Not all were happy with the decision. Private Patton Troutt, a Tennessean as religious as he was patriotic, declared, "I have no quarrel with those people. I am perfectly willing to fight for my home land and my rights, but making war on civilians in the North, I cannot do so." He returned to Tennessee.

Most men, however, were eager to bring the war to the enemy. Captain Tom Hines, who had replaced Quirk as head of the 2nd Kentucky's scouts, minced no words: "We are going where there will be a great deal of fighting and a great deal of hard riding," he told his command. "If there are any of you who do not wish to go, who feel they will dread the long and tiresome march . . . now is the time for them to ride out."

No one stirred.

"We were all anxious to ride with our captain," said Private John Conrad.[11]

With the 2nd Kentucky aboard the *Alice Dean* and the 9th Tennessee on the *McCombs*, the nearly three-quarter-mile crossing began about 10 a.m. Horses were temporarily left behind; the advance guard would have to fight on foot. Some militiamen on the far bank opened up with rifle fire and a single, antiquated field piece, but Morgan's Parrott guns and howitzers soon sent them into retreat.

Just as the first troopers were landing on Indiana soil, the *Springfield*, a small Federal gunboat carrying six 24-pound howitzers, came downriver and happened upon the operation. Basil Duke described her sudden appearance: "She tossed her snub nose defiantly like an angry beauty of the coal pits . . . and commenced to scold. A bluish-white, funnel-shaped cloud spouted out from her left hand bow and a shot flew at the town, and then changing front forward, she snapped a shell at the men on the other side."

Captain E. P. Byrne, commanding Morgan's artillery, returned fire on the *Springfield* from his elevated position at Brandenburg. The ensuing duel lasted about an hour, with the troop transfer suspended and the crossing threatened. Some fifty enemy shells rained down on the town and the ferries, but miraculously no critical damage was done and no one was killed. Finally, its ammunition exhausted, the gunboat backed away, steaming upriver to spread the alarm.

The ferrying resumed, but by late afternoon only half of Morgan's men were across the river; the rest would not complete their passage until 1 a.m. To insure that the pilots of the boats did not delay or frustrate the movement, guards were posted in the wheelhouses.

"I'm here to see you act right," six-foot-six Tom Boss of C Company—a rifle across the crook of his arm, a pistol in his belt—told the *Alice Dean* pilot. "I don't want no nonsense."

Soon he and the helmsman, a man named Smith, were making small talk.

"You got anything on this boat stronger'n water?" Boss asked. "I'm beginning to feel powerful dry."

"Of course, I'll get you a toddy," Smith answered, eager not to antagonize the giant. Besides, he needed a drink himself to calm his nerves. He lashed the wheel in place, went down to the ship's bar, and returned within minutes bearing two stiff toddies. Boss grabbed both of them and tossed them down without blinking.

"Don't bring no more, Mr. Smith," he said, "until just before I'm relieved. I don't like to drink too much when I'm on duty."[12]

Bugle calls roused Morgan's command from slumber on July 9, even as the Federals under General Hobson were arriving on the Kentucky bank. But the *Alice Dean* had been put ablaze, and the captain of the *McCombs,* which was mercifully spared, had long since fled the scene. The enemy could only watch and wait for transport.

Now the long march through Indiana and Ohio began for the Confederates. Sergeant Henry Stone, who was a Hoosier from Greencastle, the day before had written his father a note: "We intend to live off the Yanks hereafter. . . . Horses we expect to take whenever needed, forage and provisions also. . . . I hope I'll get close enough to pay you a visit. This will be the first opportunity for the Northern people seeing Morgan and they'll see enough."

The column proceeded straight north to Corydon, Colonel Adam Johnson's 2nd Brigade in the van. Just on the outskirts of the town, about 12:30 p.m., the troopers encountered some split-rail barricades and several hundred militia. To minimize casualties, Morgan halted Johnson, ordered an artillery salvo, and then sent Duke's 1st Brigade regiments around the defenders. The militiamen broke and ran. "The enemy opened upon our forces with three pieces of artillery," said one, "making the shells sing the ugly kind of music over our heads. . . . In the meantime [they] had completely flanked the town. . . . The fighting was very sharp for a space of 20 minutes, [but] seeing the contest was hopeless, Col. [Lewis] Jordan wisely hoisted the white flag."

Here Morgan learned for the first time of Lee's defeat at Gettysburg; if the news gave him second thoughts about his Northern incursion, he did not betray them. His men suffered some 40 casualties, and in the skirmish's aftermath they continued their pattern of looting, seizing food, clothes, even horse and buggies. Two storekeepers were robbed of $300 each, and two mill owners of $700.

The next day, just as General Hobson was traversing the Ohio in his rear, Morgan entered Salem, where he met some 150 defenders. Lieutenant A. S. Welch of Company L, the 2nd Kentucky, was in the forefront of the ensuing attack, which scattered the Home Guard and sent them scurrying. By noon all the Rebels were safely in the town square, watering horses, burning the rail depot, and of course, taking whatever they wished from helpless merchants.

One hamlet after another heard of Morgan's advance, largely through the incessant pealing of bells. From church, municipal building, firehouse, and school steeples, against a backdrop of railroad and factory whistles, the urgent message rang out: Morgan is coming! Morgan is coming! His exploits for months had been celebrated in rhyme, and now the doggerel was recited anew:

> I'm sent to warn the neighbors, he's only a mile behind.
> He's sweeping up the horses, every horse that he can find.
> Morgan, Morgan, the raider, and Morgan's terrible men,
> With Bowie knives and pistols are galloping up the glen.[13]

For the rest of July 10, and then on the 11th and 12th, the remaining Indiana towns on Morgan's route for the most part offered little resistance. Vienna, Lexington, Vernon, Dupont, Versailles—all were passed through or around without undue incident—even as the destruction of the railroads continued. Governor Oliver P. Morton, helped by the bell ringing, had quickly mustered thousands of citizens under arms, but most contented themselves with ineffective bushwhacking.

We should not overstate, meanwhile, the damage Morgan's men were inflicting on the populace. Fresh mounts continually were seized, it was true, but only to replace the exhausted horses they left behind. Likewise, while the Rebels' taking of private property from shopkeepers and civilians was wrong, the confiscation of U.S. greenbacks from municipal treasures, according to its rules of war, was quite legal. Commented one historian of the raid: "Robbing stores, stealing food, clothes, weapons and valuables pales when compared to some of the harsher actions Union soldiers demonstrated in Southern towns. Morgan's [troopers] rarely harmed a man unless he showed armed resistance, and women were never abused or threatened."

In Vienna late on the 10th, Sergeant Peddicord would say, "The women were soon crying, begging and imploring us to spare their children. The boys heard this with amazement, and asked the women if they thought we were barbarians. . . . The men assured them that not a hair of their heads would be injured."

Morgan and his column galloped on, sleeping for a few hours in Lexington, then on the afternoon of the 11th advancing to Vernon. There several hundred militiamen behind barricades blocked his way. He boldly asked for the town's surrender, but during the negotiations Union general John Love arrived by rail with reinforcements, swelling the defenders to some 2,000. Well aware of the Federal hoofbeats behind him, Morgan wisely stole away, leaving Vernon's garrison none the wiser.

By nightfall he was in Dupont, where his men quickly set about burning the depot, the rail bridge, and a locomotive and twelve cars. Riding past the home of a young schoolteacher named Sally Trousdale, the raiders saw two American flags on her front porch. When they stopped to take them down, Miss Trousdale came out with a broom to drive them off. Morgan promptly intervened, doffing his hat and assuring her that the flags would go untouched.

About 2 p.m., on July 12, the Confederates entered Versailles, where they rushed to the county courthouse and demanded the contents of the safe. They found that most of the currency had been removed and secreted elsewhere, but $5,000 had been left behind. Deputy B. F. Spenser dutifully handed over the money to Richard Morgan, hoping it would placate him.

"What are those?" Morgan asked, pointing to some bags on a shelf in the safe.

"They are purses of money placed by several widowed ladies for safe-keeping," Spenser hesitatingly replied.

"Keep them," said Dick Morgan. "I never robbed a widow yet."[14]

July 13 was the Rebels' last day in Indiana. From Sunmansville at day-break that morning, fifteen miles from the Ohio line, they proceeded to New Alsace, where Southern sympathizers gave them hearty breakfasts, and thence through the hamlets of Dover, Logan, and Bright. Near Logan, the expedition happened upon a hearse drawn by six powerful steeds. Within minutes the undertaker's horses were wearing saddles and carrying Confederate riders; six tired horses were left behind to convey the deceased. In Bright, Indiana, civilians at a second funeral were more fortunate. When the troopers began to appropriate the mourners' horses, one of them approached John Morgan.

"Sir, I too am a Southerner," he said. "But where I come from, we have respect for the dead."

"Leave those horses alone!" Morgan ordered, and with that the column passed on.[15]

About 11 a.m., the tired raiders, who had been riding an average of twenty hours a day, crossed the Whitewater River, burned the bridge behind them, and advanced into Ohio. Severing the traverse would force the

Federal pursuit—whose dust cloud clearly could be seen by Colonel Cluke's 8th Kentucky rear guard—to fall behind some six to eight hours while it searched for a navigable ford.

Galloping shortly thereafter into Harrison, Ohio, Morgan's men used the respite to continue their high-spirited, if unconscionable, looting. They helped themselves to all manner of storekeepers' merchandise, including women's finery, and extorted $1,000 apiece from the owners of several mills and a distillery, who feared their buildings otherwise might be set ablaze. Several of them at this point loaded their booty into a horse and buggy driven by twenty-two-year-old Emeline Roudebush, a prosperous farmer's wife who had come to town to see her sister. They meant her no harm, they told her; they needed the buggy, temporarily, to carry the goods for a few miles to spare their mounts the added weight.

Mrs. Roudebush was up to the challenge. Her horse was the fleetest in the county, and when her captors, riding beside her, let down their guard, she whipped the animal into a several-mile, all-out dash, careening down the road and leaving them far behind.

"The ride was worse than the raiders," she later told her husband. "They were perfect gentlemen."[16]

Now the Confederates on July 13 were perhaps fifteen miles northwest of Cincinnati. To neutralize the strong Federal garrison there, and keep it from leaving the city and falling on his column, which through attrition was down to 2,000 men, Morgan once more employed "Lightning" Ellsworth's talents. The telegrapher tapped into the lines and made a convincing case that Nathan Forrest and several thousand Tennesseans would soon be supporting the incursion. Meanwhile Morgan sent some detachments south toward the city's suburbs, making it appear he intended to attack; he made a similar feint north toward Hamilton, where another enemy garrison was located. He was hoping to keep the bluecoats contained within their lines, thereby creating a corridor through which he could safely pass.

Both ruses worked, confusing the Federals and permitting Morgan's column, beginning that afternoon, to move through the opening. Soon the troopers were in the middle of a grueling night march. "The many suburban roads [around Cincinnati] were confusing," said Private George Mosgrove, "especially as the night was extremely dark. Small bonfires of paper . . . were used to light the way. The danger of taking the wrong road was always imminent, the rear battalions often being at a loss to ascertain which one . . . had been taken by those in advance. . . . The direction in which the dust 'settled or floated' was the most reliable guide, as when the night is calm, as on this occasion, the dust stirred up by cavalry will remain suspended in air for a time."

Fatigue took its toll. "Strong men fell from their saddles," remembered Mosgrove, "and at every halt the officers, themselves exhausted, were compelled to use heroic measures to rouse the men who, having fallen from their horses, were sleeping in the road. Not a few crept off into the fields and slept until they awoke to find themselves in the hands of the enemy."

But most Confederates persevered. By 3 a.m. the next day, they had left Cincinnati behind and were passing through Glendale, and by dawn they were skirting Camp Denison, a place for convalescent Union soldiers. Late in the afternoon, they finally arrived at Williamsburg, thirty miles past Cincinnati. There they dropped from their saddles, fed their mounts, and enjoyed their first lengthy sleep since dawn the day before. Though they did not know it, their ride was already being celebrated in a South starved for victory. Wrote the Richmond *Enquirer*: "This bold raid is the only real movement we are making toward a restoration of peace, for peace must be conquered on the enemy's ground, or it will not come at all."[17]

Early on July 15, Morgan dispatched foragers along the column's flanks to search for food and fresh horses and then resumed the march, heading due east to Buffington Island, a ford on the Ohio some 100 miles away, where he intended to cross the river and seek refuge in western Virginia. There, his scouts had told him, the Ohio would be no more than a couple of feet deep, too shallow for Federal gunboats to be a threat.

In his diary, Major James McCreary summed up the raiders' experiences as they rode.

> *July 15* ... Traveled through several unimportant towns, destroyed one bridge, and bivouacked at Walnut Grove.
> *July 16* ... We find the first obstruction in our way, consisting of felled trees. The enemy are now pressing us on all sides, and the woods swarm with militia. We capture hundreds of prisoners, but, a parole being null, we can only sweep them as chaff out of our way. Toady we crossed the Scioto to Piketon, and as usual destroyed the bridge. Thence we moved to Jackson.

In Jackson there was still more looting of shops. Morgan, who had taken to riding in a barouche, helped himself to a pair of ladies' kid boots, obviously thinking they would make a fine gift for Mattie, and dangled them by their silk laces from one of the posts supporting the carriage top.

July 17 . . . We find our way badly blockaded and "axes to the front" is now the common command. We have today passed through many little Dutch towns with which this country abounds. Tonight we halt near Pomeroy. The enemy are in considerable force in our front. We attacked them and drove them [back] and then moved rapidly in the direction of Buffington.[18]

The skirmishes near Pomeroy, which carried over to July 18, involved Union regulars: Indiana and Illinois cavalry under the bureaucratic General Henry Judah, who in recent days had finally bestirred himself. These troops and several thousand more had been brought upriver from Cincinnati on steamboats, and thence to Portsmouth, Ohio, to overtake and intercept the Confederates. Now they were coming up from the south, on the right flank of the 4,000 men under generals Hobson and Shackelford, Morgan's principal pursuers. Meanwhile, on Hobson's left, a 2,000-man militia force under Colonel Benjamin P. Runkle likewise was advancing.

Despite the vast net that was closing about him, Morgan on the 18th projected his usual air of confidence. He was convinced that he and his raiders would stay a jump ahead of the enemy, and ford the Ohio at Buffington without incident. Colonel Adam Johnson would remember meeting him that morning: "I found him sitting on the gallery of a crossroads store, where there was a fine well; the boys were filling their canteens from the pump. The General greeted me with his bright smile . . . remarking: 'All our troubles are now over, the river is only twenty-five miles away, and tomorrow we will be on Southern soil.' "[19]

Not until sundown did the Confederates reach the river town of Portland, less than a mile from Buffington. There in the darkness they saw the outline of a barricade, hastily thrown together to prevent a crossing, and soon learned it was garrisoned by several hundred Federals and some cannon. "Should they attack and try for the river?" wrote one historian. "Or should they wait until morning? It was a difficult decision for Morgan and his officers to make. After some discussion they finally agreed that even if they could capture the earthwork without severe losses, the dark river would claim many lives. The Ohio was running much higher than normal."

The upper Ohio's unusual depth that year was due to the fact that the so-called June rise, produced by the melting of snow in the mountains, had been delayed, causing instead a July rise—a once in twenty-year occurrence—in what should have been shallow water. Whether Morgan that night fully realized the implications of this event is a matter of debate. The next morning, however, the delay would have drastic consequences.

When dawn came and the mist lifted on July 19, some 500 Rebels stormed the barricade, only to discover it had been evacuated. Just about this time, two Union gunboats led by Lieutenant Commander Leroy Fitch steamed into sight, opening up with their 24-pound bow pieces and emphatically shutting down what Morgan's scouts had assured him would be an easy crossing. Here Judah came onto the scene, with Hobson arriving soon thereafter, catching Morgan in a pincers.

Their access to the river denied, the Confederates wheeled to face the land threat from Judah. "Our effective strength was now little more than eighteen hundred," said Basil Duke. "The men were almost without ammunition. . . . Nonetheless they formed with alacrity, and prepared for a resistance which should secure a safe retreat. . . . It would have been successfully done had not Hobson arrived just at this crisis with [four] thousand men and attacked our right flank."

Belatedly the Rebels realized they were in a deadly trap. Duke recounts: "If the reader will picture in his mind a long valley, which may be roughly described as . . . an enormous V, one side of which is a wooded, ridgy hill, and the other the river; if he will imagine this angle crowded with Confederates, while Judah pressed into the opening, Hobson aligned his command upon the ridge, and . . . gunboats steamed up the river and took position at short range on the left, he will have formed an accurate idea of the situation."[20]

Now the only means of retreat was at the apex of the V—to the north. Morgan and Johnson with some 1,100 men managed to squeeze through the narrow opening, but Duke, forming the rear guard, was not so fortunate. "We were subjected," he said, "to a tremendous direct and crossfire from [thousands of] small arms and fifteen pieces of artillery. The screams of the shells downed the hiss of the bullets; coming from three different directions . . . the air seemed filled with metal, and the ground was torn and ploughed into furrows. . . . The odds were too overwhelming."

When Duke's own battalions came to the point of exit, it was too late. "[Discovering] that only two narrow roads afforded avenues of escape," he continued, "they broke ranks and [bolted] for them. Both were instantly blocked. . . . The gunboats raked the roads with grape, and the Seventh and Eighth Michigan Cavalry dashed into the mass of fugitives. In a moment the panic was complete, and the disaster irretrievable." Duke, Dick Morgan, and some 700 troopers were captured.[21]

In the battle's aftermath, a *Cincinnati Gazette* reporter described the Rebels and the scattered remnants of their pillaging: "[They] were dressed in every possible manner peculiar to civilized man. . . . They wore large slouch hats peculiar to the slave States, and had their pantaloons stuck in their boots. A dirty gray-colored coat was most prevalent, although white dusters were to be seen. . . . On the battlefield . . . one could pick up almost any article in the drygoods, hardware, house furnishing or ladies' or gentlemen's furnishing—linen, hats, boots, gloves, knives, forks, spoons, calico, ribbons, drinking cups, carriages, market wagons, circus wagons."

Captain Theodore Allen of the 7th Ohio, who accepted Duke's surrender, moved his prisoners to a tree-shaded glade near the river. "First one man and then another asked permission to go to the water's edge to wash his face," he said, "till pretty soon about one-half the men, both Union and Confederate, were at the river's edge . . . digging the dust out of their ears, eyes and nostrils."

Minutes later the troops were asking to swim. Allen agreed, letting half the prisoners and half the guards, so recently bitter foes, shed their clothes and go into the water, while the rest watched and waited their turn. Soon the two sides were splashing and frolicking. "It's difficult to tell one from the other when they're like that," Allen remarked to one of Duke's officers, who smilingly agreed.[22]

Fifteen miles upstream, opposite Belleville in western Virginia, Morgan was making another attempt to traverse the Ohio. Colonel Adam Johnson was leading part of his command across when one of Commander Fitch's gunboats appeared downstream and began firing at them. "Looking back across the river," said Johnson, "I saw a number of hats floating on the surface, and knew that each represented a brave and gallant Confederate who had found a watery grave. . . . We reached the woods . . . a little over three hundred." Some 330 actually crossed safely; besides Johnson, they included Colonel Warren Grigsby, head of the 6th Kentucky, and Lightning Ellsworth, the indefatigable telegrapher.

Morgan, halfway across the river when the shelling began, immediately returned to the Ohio shore. "He could easily have escaped," said one steadfast admirer, "but . . . he returned against some of the urgent protest of some of his officers and men, to share their fate."[23]

Over the next seven days, Morgan and his remaining 800 troopers, 200 of whom were members of the tough 2nd Kentucky, were constantly on the move, galloping west, north and east in a series of zigzag routes, frantically trying to outpace and evade their pursuers. On July 22 after passing through Chester and McArthur, they entered Nelsonville, Ohio, where they confiscated food and horses before leaving, with Shackelford perhaps six hours behind. Exhausted though they were, they seemed able to live in the saddle, proceeding through Eagleport—where the persistent Colonel Frank Wolford captured 100 of their number—and later Zanesville, Senecaville, Old Washington, and Moorefield. Home Guards were everywhere, and the bushwhacking was constant.

On the 25th, riding into Smithfield, the troopers again demanded food and drink, and took some prisoners as well. One captive, a landowner named Finley, asked Morgan if he had any hope of escaping.

"I intend to surrender at the first opportunity," was the surprising reply. "It seems like every fence corner turns into a man."

Finley offered to accept the cavalryman's sword.

Morgan quickly recovered his savoir-faire. "I may surrender to a soldier," he laughed, "but I will be damned if I will ever surrender to a farmer!"

Learning of a ford over the Ohio near Steubenville, Morgan later that day neared the town and got within five miles of the water. But there a strong militia and the pursuing Union cavalry again interposed themselves, forcing him away from the river.

The Confederates barely had left the area when Wolford's cavalry approached the town from the southwest. Thinking they were Morgan's men, the militia opened up with an old 6-pounder loaded with scrap iron. The bluecoats dived for cover, and General Shackelford, riding to the front, was forced to send a courier forward under a white flag.

"What are you fools shooting at?" the messenger demanded, mixing a few well-earned profanities into his remarks.[24]

By the time the confusion was resolved, Morgan was miles away.

The end for the expedition came on Sunday, July 26. Two fresh Michigan regiments under Major George W. Rue—some 800 men who had been transported to the vicinity from Cincinnati—that morning fell on the Rebels near Salineville, inflicting seventy-five casualties and taking 200 prisoners. Morgan, who was riding in his barouche, escaped with less than 400 men by leaping onto a horse tethered behind the carriage.

Midday found the survivors near West Point, Ohio, where they encountered and captured some militia. Knowing the situation was hopeless, and looking to gain the best possible terms, Morgan resorted to a shameless ploy, offering to surrender to one of them, Captain James Burdick, in exchange for immediate paroles for himself and his men.

"I don't understand the nature of a surrender," said Burdick. "I am not a regular officer."

"I have a right to surrender to anyone," Morgan insisted. "I want an answer right off, yes or no?"

"Yes," Burdick naively replied.

When Major Rue arrived, Morgan informed him he already had been given his parole. The bluff did not work. Rue largely ignored him, ordered the Rebels to give up their arms, and declared them Federal prisoners.

Now Shackelford and Colonel Wolford rode up, precipitating an all-Kentucky meeting. Old Meat Axe alighted from his horse and gave Morgan his hand. "I'm glad to see you," he said.

"You and the Colonel have met before?" Shackelford asked.

"Not as friends," answered Morgan.

When Shackelford heard the raider's claim that he and his men had been paroled, he began yelling and cursing. Wolford, who despite his threatening appearance had a soft heart, tried to intervene. "It is wrong to speak harshly to one whose hands are figuratively confined," he said. "Morgan's terms should be honored."

"No way I will accept these terms!" declared Shackelford.

"Then put us back on the battlefield and let us fight it out," said Morgan angrily.

Shackelford would not be persuaded. "Your demand will not be considered for a moment. You have surrendered, and the terms are unconditional."

With that, the debate concluded. Morgan and his staff soon would be taken to Cincinnati, and thereafter placed in the Ohio State Penitentiary at Columbus. For them, there would be no parole.

Wolford that night tried to make amends. He invited Morgan and his officers to a chicken and dumpling dinner at a local inn. "Everything is at my expense," he told his guests. "Just do not [leave] the square in front of the hotel."[25]

Morgan would be condemned for initiating the Great Indiana-Ohio Raid, with critics claiming that his roleplaying and penchant for risk taking had developed into megalomania and carelessness. (Others, it should be remembered, had clucked their tongues over his marriage to Mattie, saying that domesticity would *lessen* his risk-taking.) The condemnation seems misplaced. Morgan was a gambler, admittedly, but one who scrutinized the odds before placing his bets. In this instance, even though he ultimately lost, he came within a hair's breadth of winning.

Consider what he achieved: during July he diverted perhaps 12,000 Union soldiers from the East Tennessee front either full-time or part-time, arguably setting the stage for the Confederate triumph in September at

Chickamauga. He also captured and paroled some 6,000 prisoners, mostly militia, and inflicted millions of dollars' worth of damage on the railroads and on Federal and municipal property. Lastly, he panicked the Northern heartland, contributing to antiwar sentiment.

True, in so doing, Morgan decimated his magnificent Kentucky cavalry. But in one more tantalizing what-if of the war, we must ask a question: What if the depth of the Ohio at Buffington had been the expected two feet, and what if, therefore, Lieutenant Commander Fitch's gunboats had not been able to steam onto the scene and block the river? Is it not probable that Morgan and his men would have escaped into western Virginia? We think so.

The Kentuckian's capture does not bring the story to a close. Once in the penitentiary at Columbus, a maximum-security prison, he and his officers, some seventy in number, were treated as common felons. First came a scrubbing-down by trustees with stiff brushes in brackish water, which remained unchanged as man after man immersed himself; then a convict's close haircut and the shaving of beards and moustaches. All the Southerners felt degraded, but the loudest objections emanated from Colonel D. Howard Smith, who had the longest beard in Morgan's command. "This morning," he wrote in his diary, ". . . we were marched out of our cells . . . our persons stripped and washed by a convict, and our heads shorn, and our beards taken entirely off!"

Basil Duke, who had lost his moustache, tried to cheer his friend by remarking that he had never realized how handsome Smith was. The latter would not be consoled. "It is no jesting matter, Sir," he said indignantly. Later, seeing Morgan without his beard and goatee for the first time, Duke initially failed to distinguish his brother-in-law. "He was so shaven and shorn that his voice alone was recognizable."

The Confederates were housed in a five-tier wing of the prison, each in a cell less than seven by four feet. While the doors to these cubicles were left open during the day, permitting the men to mingle in a small corridor, they were locked at night, from 4:45 p.m. to 7:30 a.m. The food was vile, reading material forbidden, and the slightest infractions brought punishment in dark, dungeonlike "black holes" that made the cells seem luxurious. Morgan, taking prison life hard, focused his thoughts on the pregnant Mattie. "My love and adulation of you almost replaces thought," he wrote her in Georgia, "it is a forgetfulness of all else." Letters were precious. "If I can hear from you each week & that you are still blessed with health, then I can be . . . as happy as any, but if a week elapses without a letter then the little clouds begin to appear & I imagine ten thousand things."[26]

The months slowly passed—August, September, October. Henrietta Morgan, the matriarch of the family, now with four of her sons in prison, used all her influence to win their freedom, but to no avail. Parole for all Rebels, it seems, had been temporarily suspended by the Union authorities; parole for the dangerous Morgan was unthinkable. When Henrietta visited the penitentiary, the warden would not even let her meet with her sons.

By late October, however, Morgan was starting to hatch escape plans. Captain Tom Hines had discovered an airshaft beneath the floor of his cell, which was in the ground-level tier; it ran under a row of six other cubicles and led to the building's foundation. "Work began on November 4," reported one historian. ". . . Starting with dinner knives, they began chipping away at the six-inch-thick concrete floor." Some two weeks later, once down in the air chamber, "a better digging tool was needed. [Captain] Jake Bennett spied a rusty garden spade. . . . He secreted it into his greatcoat and smuggled it into the tunnel. Concrete beneath the other six cells was chipped away, leaving only a thin veneer to poke through at the last minute."

Concealing the digging from the guards was the most difficult problem. Their visits during the night were every two hours, when they made bed checks, but there was no telling when they would come by during the day. Morgan and his officers, most of whom knew of the plan though only seven of them would be breaking out, served as lookouts during this time, distracting the guards as best they could.

"Where is Hockersmith?" the sentinel asked one morning, when Captain Lorenzo Hockersmith was down under the floor boring away.

"He is in my room, sick," quickly replied Morgan, whose own cell was on an upper tier. Then he pulled some legal papers asking for his release out of his pocket. "Here is a memorial I have drawn up to forward to the Government at Washington; what do you think of it?"

The guard, flattered by Morgan's query, spent the next several minutes reading the document, forgetting all about Hockersmith.

By November 27, after twenty-three days of labor in the airshaft, the Rebels had burrowed under the building's foundation and were ready to emerge into the courtyard. Midnight, just after the customary bed check, would be the escape time. Since two walls would have to be scaled, each twenty feet or higher, a scaling hook and rope ladder had been fashioned—the former from a bent poker, the latter from twisted strips of bed ticking. Nothing remained but for Richard Morgan, who was on the lower tier, to selflessly switch cells with John. "The hour approached for them to be locked up," explained one contemporary. "They changed coats, and each stood at the other's cell-door with his back exposed, and pretended to be engaged in making up their beds. . . . They 'turned in,' and pulled their doors shut."[27]

The hours until midnight dragged on. Then, minutes after the bed check, John Morgan and his six comrades rose, stuffed clothing into makeshift dummies in their beds, and descended through the floor into the air chamber.

Soon they were breaking through the soil into the yard. "Fortunately—yes, providentially—the night had suddenly grown dark and rainy, the dogs had retired to their kennels, and the sentinels had taken refuge under shelter," continued the contemporary. "The inner-wall, by the aid of the rope ladder, was scaled, and now the outer one had to be attempted. . . . When the top was gained, they found [an alarm] rope extending all around, which [Morgan] immediately cut, as he suspected it might lead into the warden's room. This turned out to be correct."[28]

Pausing in a vacant sentry box only to change clothes, the men in short order scampered down the outside wall. There they separated, Morgan and Hines staying together and proceeding to the rail station.

Previously Morgan, who had been allowed to keep some of his personal assets, had obtained a railroad timetable in exchange for fifteen dollars in gold, so he knew that he and Hines could just catch the 1:25 a.m. to Cincinnati. This they did, and once the train moved out, he was his usual debonair self, acting as if he had not a care in the world. Seeing a Union officer he walked up and took a seat beside him, remarking that "as the night was damp and chilly, perhaps [the officer] would join him in a drink." The man allowed that he would, and soon the conversation became quite convivial.

The train, crossing the Scioto River, passed by the Ohio Penitentiary. "There's the hotel where Morgan and his officers are spending their leisure," said the officer.

"Yes," blandly replied the Kentuckian, "and I sincerely hope he will make up his mind to board there during the balance of the war, for he is a great nuisance."

Because of delays at Xenia and Dayton, the train was late, and it would not be pulling into Cincinnati until nearly 8 a.m.; meanwhile, guards already had discovered their empty cells and were sounding the alarm. "If we go to the depot we are dead men," Morgan told Hines. "Now or never." With that they went to the rear and manually applied the brakes, slowing the train enough for them to jump.

Federal soldiers spotted them. "What in the hell do you mean by jumping off the cars here?" one demanded.

"What in the devil is the use of my going into town when I live here; and besides, what business is it of yours?" Morgan answered, staring down his inquisitor.

Through pathways and back streets he and Hines strode, until they reached the Ohio River, just across from Newport, Kentucky. There they eventually found a youngster with a battered skiff.

"How much to take us across?"

"Fifty cents a passenger," was the reply.

Morgan gave the boy a dollar, but he did not start rowing.

"What are you waiting for?" said Hines.

"I have room for two more," said the boy. Morgan smiled, gave him another dollar, and at last left Ohio.

In Newport, he and Hines headed straight for the home of a Mrs. Ludlow, whom he knew to be a Southern sympathizer. She greeted them warmly, gave them horses and sixty dollars in gold, and provided her son as a guide for the first leg of their trip back to their lines. "Now go, General, and ride for your life!" she counseled.[29]

Morgan and Mattie would not be reunited until December 25, when he joined her in Danville, Virginia. There he learned that their child, a daughter, had died weeks before, within twenty-four hours of her birth. His sorrow was intense. Danville Mayor Thomas P. Atkinson gave him little time for reflection, staging a military parade and artillery salute in his honor, which he dutifully attended. Subsequently he found that Colonel Adam Johnson, with 300 surviving Kentucky troopers, was in Decatur, Georgia, reforming his old command. On New Year's Day, when Morgan issued a proclamation asking for 1,000 additional recruits, his fame was such that he received thousands of applications.

Meanwhile his efforts to parole the rest of his officers were being stonewalled by Union authorities, and the experience was embittering him. Though Morgan the Raider soon would be back in the saddle, he would never again surrender.

NINE

* * * *

THE EAST, JULY 1: BUFORD HOLDS THE LINE

On June 30, the eve of the three-day Battle of Gettysburg, both the Army of Northern Virginia and the Army of the Potomac were blundering into combat—each with only its advance elements on the field, each not quite aware of the other's strength. Robert E. Lee's intent had been to avoid a general engagement until his divided force, which was north and west of the Pennsylvania city, could be brought together, but events were taking on their own momentum. George Meade had replaced Joe Hooker, and though his troops were even more spread out than Lee's, he was racing up toward the Rebels from the east and south with unforeseen speed. How the enemies would meet, it was becoming apparent, would be up to chance.

Gettysburg then was a bustling county seat where a number of roads converged, including turnpikes to Chambersburg, Baltimore, and York. Surrounded by lush open meadows and pastures, it was bordered on the west by a series of low, relatively flat hills. The farthest away of these was Herr Ridge, two and one-quarter miles from the town; next came McPherson's Ridge, one and one-quarter miles away; nearest to Gettysburg was Seminary Ridge, just three-quarters of a mile distant.

Early on July 1, the battle would begin along these hills. The Confederates touched off the fighting, with Henry Heth's division of Ambrose Powell Hill's corps marching down the Chambersburg Pike toward Herr Ridge from the west, hoping to find badly needed shoes in the town. "The only force at Gettysburg is cavalry," Hill blithely had told his subordinate, "probably a detachment of observation. I am just from General Lee, and the information he has from his scouts corroborates that I have received from mine—the enemy are still at Middleburg [some thirty miles south], and have not yet struck their tents."

"If there is no objection," said Heth, "I will take my division . . . and get those shoes."

"None in the world," was the reply.[1]

Confronting the Rebels on the 1st, however, was no mere detachment. The defenders were John Buford's 2,900-man 1st Cavalry Division, the vanguard of Meade's army. Though facing many times their numbers, they were armed with breech-loading carbines that gave them a rapid and deadly rate of fire. Their orders were clear: hold up the enemy until Meade's infantry could come up in support.

John Buford was born on March 4, 1826, in the lush countryside of the Kentucky bluegrass region near Versailles, where his father owned a large farm and ran a stage line on the side. Hunting and riding filled the boy's earliest years, and he grew up an expert horseman. When he was twelve, the family moved to Stephenson, Illinois. There his father opened a general store and raised horses, which John helped train. One neighbor would recall the youngster "scampering through the streets and over the bluffs of the town on a bareback horse that no other boy . . . could ride."[2]

In 1844, he won an appointment to West Point, where his half-brother had preceded him. During his four years at the academy he was a better than average but not exceptional student who, despite his quiet and methodical nature, amassed a surprising number of demerits. Upon graduation, he was assigned as a second lieutenant to the 1st U.S. Dragoons in Missouri. Through the rest of the 1840s and the early 1850s he served with both the 1st and the 2nd Dragoons in New Mexico and Texas, primarily in staff assignments that, to his chagrin, kept him from field duty.

While on leave in 1851, he began courting a 21-year-old Kentucky belle named Martha "Pattie" Duke, cousin of the future Rebel general Basil Duke. Three years later they would wed.

In 1855 quartermaster Buford got his first taste of combat, delivering supplies to Kansas for the 2nd Dragoons in their campaign against the Sioux. Here he saw firsthand how deadly the breech-loading firepower of the dismounted troopers was against the Indians, and how it demoralized the enemy for the saber-waving charge that inevitably followed. It was a lesson he would remember.

Two years later, again as a supply officer, he accompanied the dragoons in their march against Governor Brigham Young of the Utah Territory, who, critics maintained, was establishing a theocracy in the West. Because of this show of force, the so-called Mormon War was peacefully resolved.

In 1859 Captain Buford took extended leave in Kentucky, spending weeks with Pattie, and their son and infant daughter. Then he returned to Utah and the dragoons, resuming his quartermaster chores.

With the coming of the Civil War, he continued to be pigeonholed in staff work—a testimony to his analytical abilities—serving as an inspector general in Indiana and Kentucky. There he gave his superiors honest, clear-eyed appraisals of Union recruits. Troopers in a Kentucky cavalry regiment were "hardy, fine horsemen, and gallant men," but a nearby infantry regiment was "under no restraint, much like a herd of wild animals." Officers likewise were evaluated, some being "zealous and able," others "deficient in every respect."[3]

Not until June 1862, when Buford was passing through Washington, did his prospects improve. At that time he met General John Pope, who had been plucked from the West by Lincoln to head the 50,000-strong Army of Virginia. The bombastic Pope somehow took a liking to the unassuming Buford, still only a major, and asked him "what objections he could have . . . to being placed in command in the field." Buford must have winced. He told me, Pope would later say, that "he had tried to get a command, but was without influence enough to accomplish it."

The army leader remembered the conversation, and subsequently, after one of his cavalry brigadiers botched an assignment, he replaced him with Buford, whom he raised to the same rank and put in charge of 2,000 troopers. Though the Union defeat at Second Manassas precipitated Pope's dismissal and the folding of his command into the Army of the Potomac, Buford's own conduct during the battle drew much notice and praise. Posted with his brigade behind the Federal left on August 30, he launched a fierce counterattack when the Rebels broke through the lines, harassing the enemy onslaught with his small force long enough for the Federal main body to make its escape across Bull Run Creek.

For the rest of the year, Buford served as nominal chief of cavalry of the Army of the Potomac, first under George McClellan and then under Ambrose Burnside. But this title was deceiving; the divided command structure of the Union cavalry at this point meant he again was a staff officer, for the most part channeling instructions from McClellan and Burnside to subordinates in the field.

With Joe Hooker's reorganization of the horse soldiers in 1863 as a separate corps, however, the situation changed. Though Buford lost out to George Stoneman in the competition to head the new cavalry corps, he once more became a line officer, serving under Stoneman and, as we have seen, accompanying him in May of that year on the ill-advised raid south of Chancellorsville.[4]

Now on June 30, the diligent Buford—leading the 1st Cavalry Division in advance of John Reynolds's 1st Infantry Corps—was painstakingly scouting the terrain west of Gettysburg. The area had to be held as long as possible, he soon realized, if the scattered Federal army was to be united. "Even at a glance," said one historian, "[he] could see that a dozen or more roads entered the town from as many directions. . . . Those roads would draw together Meade's far-flung forces like no other town in that corner of Pennsylvania."

Dark-complexioned, steady-eyed, wearing a walrus moustache, Buford gave the impression, in the words of a contemporary journalist, that he possessed "a good-natured disposition, but [was] not to be trifled with." Simultaneously he projected a nonpretentious side that his troopers welcomed, affecting a nondescript blue blouse without rank and puffing on a large, ever-present pipe.

By nightfall he had dismounted and positioned his command. One of his brigades, headed by Colonel Thomas Devin, was to the right of the Chambersburg Pike; the other, commanded by Colonel William Gamble, was athwart and to the left of the road; both were spaced out along McPherson's and Seminary Ridges. Meanwhile pickets had been sent farther west along Herr Ridge. The reserve unit, led by now Brigadier Wesley Merritt, was escorting the supply wagons and not yet up.

Tom Devin, full of Irish fight, was adamant that he could hold off anything the Confederates could throw at him, at least for twenty-four hours. "No, you won't," Buford told him. "They will attack you in the morning and they will come booming—skirmishers three deep. You will have to fight like the devil to hold your own until supports arrive. The enemy must know the importance of this position and will strain every nerve to secure it."

Dawn found Buford ready. "I had gained positive information of the enemy's movements," he said, "and my arrangements were made for entertaining him until General Reynolds could [arrive]."[5]

The Buford-Reynolds relationship, it seems, was a strong one. Both men were competent and uncomplaining professionals, mutually respectful of each other. "Reynolds knew Buford thoroughly," said one Union officer, "and knowing him and the value of cavalry under such a leader, sent them through the mountain passes beyond Gettysburg to find and feel the enemy. The old rule would have been to keep them back near the infantry, but . . . Buford went on, knowing that wherever Reynolds sent him, he was sure to be supported."

The cavalryman would need his chief's backing. Down the Chambersburg Pike about 8 a.m. on the 1st came the van of Henry Heth's infantry division, driving in the Federal pickets on Herr Ridge. James Archer's Alabamians were in the lead, followed by Joseph R. Davis's Mississippians. Buford's troopers, hunkered down along McPherson's and Seminary Ridges and firing as fast as their carbines would allow, now slowed the advance, but only delayed the inevitable. Far outnumbering the defenders, the Rebels began to fan out left and right, slowly turning their flanks.

By 9 a.m., with his lines crumbling, Buford was considering a withdrawal. Not only was he in danger of being enveloped from the west, but scouts were telling him that a second Confederate division was approaching Gettysburg from the north. Here John Reynolds, whom many thought the best general in the Union army, galloped up to his headquarters.

"What's the situation, John?" he asked Buford.

"The devil's to pay!"

"Can you give me one more hour? Wadsworth is just behind me!"

Not for a moment did Buford hesitate. "I reckon I can," was his laconic reply.[6]

That answer reassured Reynolds, but also gave him pause. He hurriedly gave an aide a message to take back to Meade. "Tell him the enemy are advancing in strong force, and that I fear they will get to the heights beyond the town before I can. I will fight them inch by inch and, if driven into the town, I will barricade the streets and hold them back as long as possible."

But Buford *did* hold McPherson's and Seminary Ridges, using John Calef's horse artillery with reckless precision and refusing to retreat, and within the allotted hour the lead two brigades of Union General James S. Wadsworth's infantry, under Lysander Cutler and Solomon Meredith, came to his rescue. Reynolds quickly sent them forward, the New Yorkers under Cutler taking on the Mississipians and the Midwesterners under Meredith falling on the Alabamians.

"Forward, men, forward, for God's sake!" shouted Reynolds. Then he fell dead, instantly killed by a sniper's bullet that struck him in the head. "His death affected us much," one young officer later would say, "for he was one of the *soldier* generals of the army."

In the ensuing melee, Archer and scores of his men were captured, and his brigade pushed back to Herr Ridge. Davis, trapped in a railroad cut, was similarly routed, losing several hundred men before extricating himself. Buford and his tired troopers had more than done their duty, and the sight of the fleeing enemy reinvigorated them.

Soon the frustrated Archer encountered General Abner Doubleday, whom he had known in the Old Army and who had replaced Reynolds.

"Good morning, Archer," said Doubleday. "How are you? I am glad to see you."

"Well, I am not glad to see you by a damn sight." was the answer.

"Take him to the rear," retorted Doubleday. "Take him to the rear."[7]

The triumph along the ridges was short-lived. Heth's division would regroup, more Confederate forces would be committed, and after a lull, the fighting would resume. Up to this point, the action had been in the west, and before the arrival of Reynolds's and Doubleday's 1st Corps, it was Gamble's cavalry brigade that had borne the brunt of the enemy's assault. Now, in the early afternoon, a second Rebel force moved on Gettysburg, this time from the north, where Devin's cavalry, newly backed up by Oliver Otis Howard's 11th Corps, was positioned. Devin fought bravely, but he and the infantry could not resist the pressure. He retired in as good order as possible, making the enemy pay for every foot of ground.

The relentless two-pronged onslaught carried the day. "Even with the infantry on the field," said one historian, "it was inevitable that the Union line would collapse. The combined [Confederate] forces outweighed Doubleday's and Howard's men handily, and Federal reinforcements were hours away. John Buford had foreseen this possibility. . . . Therefore, the cavalry leader was not surprised when, about 2:30 p.m., the 11th Corps, overwhelmed on the right despite Devin's best efforts, gave way. Within minutes, foot troops and remounted troopers were retreating through Gettysburg to the higher terrain below."

Here a word is in order about this "higher terrain." It was still a fourth series of hills, the aptly named Cemetery Ridge, much higher than the others and three miles long, that curled like a fishhook directly south of the town. On this soon-to-be-storied site around 4 p.m., Devin and Howard dug in, even as Gamble and Doubleday were withdrawing from Seminary Ridge and seeking refuge there themselves.

During this crucial time Buford, to facilitate the retreat, sent Gamble's bloodied but unbowed brigade, with the 8th Illinois in the van, on a feint against the oncoming Confederates. Backed up by supporting fire from dismounted comrades behind a stone fence, Gamble's troopers came on "as steady as if on parade," indicating an attack. The enemy hurriedly formed hollow squares, anticipating a mounted charge that never came. Instead the riders melted away while the troopers behind the fence poured fire into the Rebels' congested ranks, throwing them into panic. "We went to popping at them," said one trooper. ". . . They fell like rain. The ground soon [was] covered with them. The front column broke and started to run."[8]

So the first day of the battle passed. Because Jeb Stuart had gone off on his ill-fated expedition around the Army of the Potomac and was still not on the field, Lee lacked proper reconnaissance and did not press his advantage. Buford, meanwhile, had executed his own orders to perfection, fighting an aggressive holding action and keeping his superiors informed of developments. Now with each passing hour Meade's army was coming together, and reinforcements were streaming into the defensive lines atop Cemetery Ridge.

Many were the reasons for the subsequent Federal victory at Gettysburg, but none was more important than John Buford's determined stand against the supposedly invincible Army of Northern Virginia. Within months thereafter, racked by chills and fever brought on by exhaustion, he would be on his deathbed, where belatedly he learned that he had been promoted to major general. His eulogy, here quoted in part, summed up the man: "Modest, yet brave; retiring, yet efficient; quiet, but vigilant; careful of the lives of his men with an almost parental solicitude, yet never shirking from action."[9]

TEN
* * * *

THE EAST, JULY 3: STUART V. GREGG

Doubtless hoping to atone for his tardy arrival at Gettysburg, Jeb Stuart during the late morning of July 3, the last day of the battle, circled the Federal right on the northern end of Cemetery Ridge, attempting to get in Meade's rear. His purpose was to cut the enemy's lines of communication along the Baltimore Pike, even as Lee was launching his climactic attack against the Union center. With Stuart were his usual stalwarts, the experienced brigades of Wade Hampton, Fitz Lee, and John Chambliss—the last-named officer filling in for the wounded and captured Rooney Lee. Completing the expedition was a brigade of West Virginians under Colonel Milton Ferguson. In all, the command totaled some 8,000 men.

The Union cavalry corps, newly confident with every passing week, was led by the smooth and personable Alfred Pleasanton. His division heads were John Buford, David McMurtrie Gregg, and Hugh Judson Kilpatrick. Only Gregg, an officer much in the mold of Buford, would be challenging Stuart this day. Buford's tired troopers were resting after their heroics on the 1st, and Kilpatrick's were posted on the Federal left, south of Cemetery Ridge and the Round Tops.

Gregg's command, some 5,000 men, consisted of two of his three brigades, led by Colonels John McIntosh and John Irvin Gregg, and

George Armstrong Custer's Michigan brigade, on loan from Kilpatrick's division.

McIntosh was replacing Percy Wyndham, who had been wounded at Brandy Station. The great-nephew and son of Revolutionary and War of 1812 heroes and a man with Southern ties—his brother was a Confederate general who was killed at Pea Ridge—McIntosh had made his name during the Peninsula Campaign and enhanced his reputation at Antietam and Kelly's Ford. Irvin Gregg, a dogged leader who was David Gregg's older cousin and a former iron merchant, had served in the Mexican War and then in the Old Army for ten years before reentering the service just before the outbreak of hostilities.

George Custer—we last saw him as a captain whose panicked horse was refusing to budge at Brandy Station—now was a brigadier though not yet twenty-four years old. He was called "Curly" for the blond mass of shoulder-length locks that framed a pensive gaze, blond moustache, and freckled face, and no one ever yearned more for fame. His self-designed uniform—black velvet jacket and pants generously striped in gold, with gilt buttons and gold braid galore, topped by a scarlet cravat and a rakish black, wide-brimmed hat—inspired both awe and admiration. "His aspect, though highly amusing, is also pleasing," said a brother officer, "as he has a very merry blue eye, and a devil-may-care style."[1]

Though Custer had graduated last in his class at West Point (as had George Pickett, the man who this day was leading Lee's assault on Cemetery Ridge) and was on the verge of expulsion before getting his diploma, the Michigan native, self-centered though he could be, seemed born for war. "The modest man is not always the best soldier," one of his comrades remarked. "Some of the best . . . while shamelessly sounding their own praises, were brave, dashing and enterprising to an unusual degree."[2]

Sometime before 1 p.m., Stuart arrived on Cress Ridge, three miles east of Gettysburg, only to find Gregg's troopers blocking his way toward the Baltimore Pike. The brigades of Ferguson and Chambliss were in the van, those of Hampton and Fitz Lee were still coming up. Opposing them were the Federal brigades of Custer and McIntosh. Irvin Gregg's men were in the rear.

Stuart opened up with his horse artillery, and then sent Ferguson's dismounted troopers forward as skirmishers around and below John Rummel's farm, with most of the fire directed against Custer, who responded in kind. Meanwhile all could hear, to the west, the start of Lee's deafening barrage against Cemetery Ridge, preparatory to Pickett's Charge. "Had the enemy's main body been dislodged," Stuart would say, "as was confidently hoped and expected . . . I was in precisely the right position to discover it and improve the opportunity."[3]

Here Custer received a bizarre order from Pleasanton, who had no idea of the Rebel threat, telling him to fall back from Gregg's lines and rejoin Kilpatrick. While the Michigander was in the process of doing so, McIntosh, nothing deterred by the odds, decided to take the fight to the enemy, sending forward a strong picket line toward the Rummel farm. "The First New Jersey, which had reached a stone and rail fence parallel with that occupied by the enemy," said Lieutenant William Brooke-Rawle of the 3rd Pennsylvania, "was dismounted and reinforced from the woods, and immediately became hotly engaged. Two squadrons of the Third Pennsylvania . . . were deployed, dismounted, to the left in the open fields. . . . To meet this movement the Confederate skirmish line was reinforced."

Stuart's cannon now stepped up the pressure, prompting McIntosh to inform Gregg that he was outgunned and ask that Irvin Gregg be sent up on the double-quick to his support. "That brigade was yet some distance off," said Brooke-Rawle, "and Gregg, meeting Custer in the march in the opposite direction, ordered him to return. . . . Custer, ever ready for a fight, was not loath to do so."

The joint McIntosh-Custer effort, aided by Union horse artillery, about 2 p.m. produced results. "The enemy having filled the large barn at Rummel's with sharpshooters, who, while picking off our men, were completely protected from our fire," continued Brooke-Rawle, "Captain [Alanson] Randol . . . placed a section of his battery . . . well to the front . . . and opened upon it." Shell after shell struck the barn, compelling the Rebels to withdraw. "As they did so, the centre of our line advanced. . . . Having thus pierced their line, a force was sent out to take the enemy in flank, driving back the portions of [Ferguson's] brigade that had occupied it. . . . This movement caused the left of the enemy's line . . . to give way."

Key to the Federal success at the Rummel farm was their use of repeating carbines, which the Rebs did not have.

"Now for them before they can reload!" Confederate officers would urge their men. But instantly a second volley, and then a third and a fourth, would tear the gray-clad ranks.

"One tall, lean, lank Johnny," a Union trooper would remark of a captive, "asked to see our guns, saying, 'You'ns load in the morning and fire all day.'"[4]

Stuart at this juncture counterattacked, sending forward Chambliss's and Fitz Lee's troopers, both mounted and on foot. The 5th Michigan, thus far triumphant, now was in danger of being overrun. "Repeating rifles are not only effective but wasteful weapons as well," said Union Captain James Harvey Kidd, "and at last, Colonel [Russell] Alger, finding that his ammunition had given out, felt compelled to retire his regiment and seek his horses. Seeing this, the enemy's line sprang forward with a yell . . . From field to field, the line of gray followed in exultant pursuit."

Just then a column of mounted men advanced from the Federal rear. "It was the 7th Michigan, commanded by Colonel [William] Mann," said Kidd. "Gregg, seeing the necessity for prompt action, had ordered it to charge. As it moved forward, Custer drew his saber, placing himself in front, and shouted, 'Come on, you Wolverines!'" The surge was unrestrained. "Every man yelled at the top of his voice until the regiment had gone, probably 1,000 yards, straight toward the Confederate batteries, when, by some error . . . the head of column was deflected to the left . . . and the regiment was hurled against a rail fence that ran obliquely in front of the Rummel barn."

The barrier for the moment proved impassable. "The squadrons, coming up successively . . . rushed pell mell upon each other, and were thrown into a state of indescribable confusion; though the rear companies . . . formed left or right front into line along the fence and pluckily began firing across it into the faces of the Confederates who, when they saw the impetuous onset of the Seventh checked, rallied and began to collect in swarms upon the opposite side."

Bluecoats leaped from their saddles and rushed to tear down the rails, all the while enduring a searing fire. Somehow a passageway was made, and the Federals charged again, ousting the Rebels from the Rummel farm and coming within 200 yards of their batteries. "Then, as it seemed," said Kidd, "the two belligerents paused to get their second breath. Up to this time the battle had raged with varying fortune. Victory . . . held aloof, as if disdaining to favor either. The odds, indeed, had been rather with the Confederates than against them, for Stuart [outnumbered] his adversary at every point, though Gregg forced the fighting, putting Stuart on the defense."[5]

The lull ended at 4 p.m. "There appeared in the distance . . . a brigade of cavalry," said Lieutenant Brooke-Rawle. "It was Stuart's last reserve and his last resource, for, if the Baltimore Pike was to be reached, and havoc created in our rear, the critical moment had arrived, as Pickett even then was moving up to the assault on Cemetery Ridge."[6]

The mounted troopers were Wade Hampton's men, and soon they would be followed by elements of Fitz Lee's command. An untrammeled cavalry assault was about to begin. "[The Rebels] marched with well-aligned fronts and steady reins, said Captain William Miller of the 3rd Pennsylvania, McIntosh's command. "Their polished saber-blades dazzled in the sun. All eyes turned upon them. . . . [Our artillery] opened fire with well-directed aim. Shell and shrapnel met the Confederates and tore through their ranks. Closing the gaps as though nothing had happened, on they came."

Gregg now put into play the 1st Michigan, sending the Wolverine regiment head-on against Hampton. "Custer, who was near, placed himself at its head, and off they dashed," continued Miller. "As the two columns approached each other the pace of each increased, when suddenly a crash, like the falling of timber, betokened the crisis. So sudden and violent was the collision that many of the horses were turned end over end, and crushed their riders beneath them. The clashing of sabers, the firing of pistols . . . now filled the air."

With the battle in the balance, McIntosh struck the Rebels in flank. "[He] gathered up what loose men he could, joined them to his headquarters party and charged," said Miller. "My squadron was still deployed along the edge of Lott's Woods. Standing in company with Lieutenant Brooke-Rawle . . . and seeing that the situation was becoming critical I turned to him and said, 'I have been ordered to hold this position, but if you will back me up in case I am court-martialed . . . I will order a charge. The lieutenant . . . with an energetic reply convinced me I would not be deserted. . . . My command passed through the Confederate column, cut off the rear portion and drove it back. . . . These flank attacks demoralized the [enemy]."[7]

Here Hampton was severely wounded, saber blows reopening the head wound of July 2 and inflicting further injuries. All but blinded by blood, he turned his mount and withdrew to Cress Ridge, soon to be followed by his disheartened troopers.

So the action ended, with both sides occupying the same ground they had held that morning. Though not beaten, the Rebels clearly had been repulsed. "There is no probability that Stuart could successfully have carried out his intention of attacking the rear of the Federal right flank," admitted Major McClellan, his adjutant. "As soon as General Gregg was aware of [his] presence he wisely assumed the aggressive, and forced upon Stuart a battle in which he had nothing to gain but the glory of the fighting. . . . At the close Gregg had a reserve of one strong brigade which had hardly been engaged at all. . . . Stuart had no fresh troops with which to renew the fight."[8]

If David Gregg on the Union right this day led his cavalry division with skill and prudence, the same cannot be said of Judson Kilpatrick, his counterpart on the left. Sometime after 5 p.m., with both sides at Cemetery Ridge regrouping in the bloody aftermath of Pickett's Charge, the latter ordered a cavalry assault on dug-in Confederate infantry. "Guarding the Confederate right and facing Kilpatrick," wrote a historian, "was a skirmish line of Texas and [Alabama] infantry, stretching from Emmitsburg Road to the base of Round Top, partially protected by a stake-and-rail fence. . . . That end of the valley [was] unsuitable for cavalry maneuvers, strewn with boulders and chopped up with fences, walls, and ditches."

Kilpatrick nonetheless sent the 1st West Virginia, one of Elon Farnsworth's regiments, dashing down the valley toward the enemy's barricade. (One of the cavalry's young comers, Farnsworth, like George Custer and Wesley Merritt, had been jumped from captain to brigadier.) "A thin line shot forward and attempted to throw the rails," said Captain Henry C. Parsons of the 1st Vermont, "tugging at the stakes, cutting with their sabers, and falling in the vain effort. The regiment came on in magnificent style, received a deadly volley, before which it recoiled, rallied, charged a second time, and fell back with great loss."

Parsons was present when Kilpatrick told Farnsworth to take the 1st Vermont and make still another charge. "General, do you mean it?" the latter replied. "Shall I throw my handful of men over rough ground . . . against a brigade of infantry?"

"Do you refuse . . . ? If you are afraid to lead this charge, I will lead it."

"Take that back!" Farnsworth shouted, and it seemed as if both officers would come to blows.

"I did not mean it; forget it," Kilpatrick said.

"If you order the charge," said Farnsworth, breaking the ensuing silence, "I will lead it, but you must take the responsibility."

"I will take the responsibility," Kilpatrick replied.[9]

Farnsworth set out with two battalions of the 1st Vermont: the Third under Major William Wells, which he accompanied, and the First under Parsons. "As the First Battalion rode through the line of our dismounted skirmishers, who were falling back, they cried to us to halt," said Parsons. "As we passed out from the cover of the woods, the 1st West Virginia was retiring in disorder on our left. A frantic horse with one leg torn off by a cannonball rushed toward us as if for protection."

The Third Battalion, to the left of the First, now galloped into action. "It was a swift charge over rocks, through timber, under close enfilading fire. . . . The direction was toward Devil's Den. At the foot of the declivity the column turned left and passed a battery . . . then divided into three parties. One swept . . . upon the rear of the Texas skirmish line, carrying in a part of this line as prisoners, and one rode through into the Union lines." The enemy fought back, raining minié balls on the intruders, and Farnsworth, with the third group, had his horse shot from under him. "A trooper sprang from the saddle, gave the general his [mount] and escaped on foot."

Parsons's battalion likewise was enduring a storm of lead. "We were immediately upon the enemy, within thirty paces, and a deadly volley . . . was fired, but it passed over our heads; the next, a random volley, was [far more] effective," he said. "We cleared the wall [coming down from Round Top] and formed under cover of the hill. . . . The enemy's sharpshooters appeared in the rocks above us. . . . We rode obliquely up the hill in the direction of [Major] Wells. . . . Farnsworth, seeing our horsemen, raised his saber and charged as if with an army; at the same moment his followers, together with what remained of the First, cut their way through the 15th Alabama."[10]

For the Federals, this thrust would be a last hurrah. Farnsworth and dozens of others during the fight went down with mortal wounds, and Parsons, though injured, narrowly escaped death himself. "Sergeant Duncan . . . standing in his stirrups, flew past me with his saber, shouted, 'I'm with you!' threw up his left arm and fell. My horse recoiled over his dead body . . . and for a moment I was alone on the field. The enemy ran up crying 'Surrender!' . . . But as I raised my saber a gun was planted against my breast and fired; my horse [also] was struck . . . and broke frantically through the men, over the wall, and down the hill."

Perhaps 300 Union troopers participated in this affair, and almost one-quarter were killed and wounded, sacrificed by Kilpatrick after Pickett's Charge had, to all intents and purposes, ended the Battle of Gettysburg. The cavalryman would claim, of course, that he had been on the verge of a great victory, only to be unsupported by others. "Had the infantry on my right advanced at once," he huffed, ". . . a total rout would have ensued."

Of Brigadier Farnsworth, who died weeks shy of his 26th birthday, he would eulogize: "Good soldier, faithful friend, great heart, hail and farewell." Seldom has hypocrisy been more blatantly displayed.[11]

ELEVEN
* * * *

THE WEST, JUNE–DECEMBER: FORREST BEFORE AND AFTER CHICKAMAUGA

Following his pursuit and capture of Streight's Raiders, Nathan Forrest returned to east Tennessee. There with the brigades of Frank Armstrong and James Starnes he devoted himself, during late May and early June, to shielding the left of Bragg's lines in the standoff against Rosecrans north of Chattanooga. Then on June 13 a subordinate's resentment turned into rage, all but costing Forrest his life.

The wayward officer was Lieutenant A. Willis Gould, whom he had castigated for losing two cannon during Streight's counterattack at Sand Mountain, and whom he was transferring to another command. Gould regarded the ouster as a reflection upon his courage, and asked for a meeting. The two men confronted each other in a quartermaster's office and then walked outside into a corridor. Forrest was twirling a penknife in his fingers.

"Why are you transferring me?" Gould asked.

"I need give you no reason," was the answer, "and you need not expect again to serve in my command."

The lieutenant's temper erupted. "No man can accuse me of being a coward!" He drew a pistol and fired, sending a bullet into Forrest's left side, where it passed near the intestines and then exited. Badly wounded, Forrest somehow grabbed Gould's gun hand with his left hand and turned the barrel away. With his right he brought the penknife to his teeth, opened the blade, and then plunged the weapon into his assailant's stomach, opening a gaping wound.

Gould now backed off, trying to close the gash with his hands. He staggered out into the street, with blood spurting from his belly, and encountered two civilian surgeons, James Wilkes and Luke Ridley. "My God, it's Willis Gould!" exclaimed one of them. Seeing that an artery had been cut, they led him into the first building handy, a tailor shop, and laid him on a table. Then while Wilkes tried to stem the flow of blood, Ridley went in search of surgical tools and dressings.

Forrest meantime, after Gould had gone, went to the office of still a third doctor and, after a quick examination, was advised his own wound was likely fatal. Characteristically, the cavalry leader thought only of evening the score. He quickly grabbed two pistols and went looking for Gould.

Colonel J. Lee Bullock saw Forrest coming down the street. "You need not pursue Gould. He is fatally wounded. . . ."

"Get out of my way! He's mortally wounded me, and I aim to kill him before I die!" Forrest replied, heading for the tailor shop, where a crowd had gathered.

"Look out! Look out!" he cried, pushing through the onlookers and aiming one of his weapons at the prostrate man. The crowd scattered, Dr. Wilkes jumped aside, and Gould found the strength to jump through an open window. Forrest fired but missed, and the bullet ricocheted, hitting the leg of a nearby trooper.

Here one story has Forrest finding Gould's inert body in the weeds outside, callously nudging him with his boot, and then calling for medical treatment—for himself. After being reexamined, and told the bullet had missed all the vital organs and lodged itself in the hip muscles, his mood abruptly changed. "Forget about cutting it out! It's nothing but a damned little pistol ball! Let it be!"

As for Gould, who was still breathing: "Take him to the best room in the hotel! Give him every comfort! I'll pay for everything! By God, Ridley, when I give such an order I mean it!"

Gould would last a few more days before succumbing to peritonitis, and Forrest reputedly would be carried on a litter to his deathbed, where the lieutenant asked for forgiveness, saying, "How thankful I am that I am the one who is to die and you are spared to the country. . . . What I did, I did in a moment of rashness."

"Forrest wept like a child," said one observer. "It was the saddest of all the sad incidents of the long and bitter war I witnessed."[1]

By June 25, just twelve days later, the cavalryman was healed and once more able to take the field. From that date on, through the summer and into September, he and his men skirmished incessantly in east Tennessee with the oncoming Federals, to little or no avail. Rosecrans rolled through Shelbyville, Tullahoma, and Cowan; Bragg fell back through the state all the way to Chattanooga; and Forrest fumed, convinced that the latter's leadership was both timorous and wrongheaded.

There were, however, moments of dark humor. Exiting from the Cumberland Gap near Cowan with the last of the rear guard one day, he noticed a farm woman shaking her fist and berating his troopers for not turning on the Yankees. Suddenly she directed her anger at him. "You great big cowardly rascal!" she screamed. "Why don't you fight like a man, instead of running like a cur. I wish old Forrest was here. He'd make you fight!"

He would retell this anecdote many times, laughing and admitting, "I would rather face a battery than that fiery dame."[2]

Forrest's contempt for Bragg's generalship was now so great that he tried desperately to escape his command. On August 9 he wrote to Samuel Cooper, the adjutant general at the Richmond War Office, asking that he be allowed to strike out on his own, with a eye toward turning the tide in the West. Remember that Vicksburg had fallen on July 4, just one day after the Gettysburg disaster, and Southern spirits were at low ebb. One copy of the letter went through Bragg for forwarding; another, in the event the original was *not* sent on, went directly to Jefferson Davis.

In the letter Forrest asked to be put in charge of "all the forces that I may collect together and organize . . . in northern Mississippi, west Tennessee, and those that may join me from Arkansas, Missouri and southern Kentucky." He went on to say that though he believed "the general commanding is unwilling for me to leave his department, still I hope to be permitted to go where (as I believe) I can serve my country best." He reminded Cooper and Davis that he had lived in the Mississippi area "for over twenty years," knew "the country perfectly from Memphis to Vicksburg," and was "well acquainted with all the prominent planters."

He would take no more than 460 of his troopers from the army as a cadre, he continued, and within sixty days raise a cavalry force of between 5,000 and 10,000 men in northern Mississippi and west Tennessee. This

partisan command could "seriously if not [entirely] obstruct the navigation of the Mississippi River" and severely disrupt Federal supply lines
both on water and land.

He was making this proposal, he added, "for the good of the service. . . . I have never asked for position . . . [and have] performed the duties assigned me. . . . I shall leave this department with many regrets, as I
am well pleased with the officers in my command." He would "especially
regret parting from my old brigade"—that crack unit of Tennessee horse
soldiers. "[But] there are thousands of men where I propose to go that I
am satisfied will join me . . . until all the country bordering on the Mississippi from Cairo [Illinois] down is taken."

Bragg, to his credit, passed on Forrest's letter, but with a self-serving
caveat. "I know of no officer to whom I would sooner assign the duty proposed . . . but it would deprive the army of one of its greatest elements of
strength."[3]

Davis, a close friend of Bragg, weeks later would concur. Forrest for the
nonce would stay in east Tennessee.

During September the Federals continued to push south, forcing the
Rebels to evacuate Chattanooga on the 8th and withdraw into north
Georgia. Within days, however, an overconfident Rosecrans committed
the sin of scattering his command, encouraging Bragg, at long last, to
make a stand. The ensuing battle would be fought along the winding
banks of Chickamauga Creek, which roughly ran in a north-south direction below Chattanooga. The front would be some five miles long, in
heavily wooded terrain, with visibility 150 yards at best.

Forrest's cavalry at this stage had grown to two divisions, one led by
Brigadier Frank Armstrong, the other by Brigadier John Pegram (the latter
replacing James Starnes, who had been killed in a skirmish). One of Armstrong's brigades was led by Colonel J. T. Wheeler (the 3rd Arkansas, 1st
Tennessee, and 18th Tennessee Battalion); the other (Forrest's old brigade)
by Colonel George Dibrell (the 4th, 8th, 9th, 10th, and 11th Tennessee).
Pegram's brigades were headed by Brigadier H. B. Davidson (the 1st and
6th Georgia, 6th North Carolina); and Colonel J. S. Scott (the 10th Confederate, a surviving detachment of John Morgan's command, the 1st
Louisiana, 2nd and 5th Tennessee, and 12th and 16th Tennessee Battalions). The total was some 3,500 men, and they would for the most part
fight dismounted.

The battle began on September 19, with the Federals coming straight at
Forrest's troopers on the far right, where they anchored Leonidas Polk's

Right Wing. (Bragg had divided his army into two wings; the one on the left was commanded by James Longstreet, just arrived from the Army of Northern Virginia with two rugged divisions.)

"It was now ten o'clock a.m., when the Federals threw forward a lavish line of skirmishers, and it may be said that the overture . . . began," wrote Forrest's campaign historians. "The conflict speedily became warm. . . . Dibrell's Brigade, Armstrong's Division, coming up about twelve o'clock, was placed in line on the left of Pegram's troops, dismounted. . . . No sooner had this disposition been made than a heavy body of the enemy bore down upon Dibrell with pressure that forced him back to a rocky ridge. . . . Just at this moment [A. L.] Huggins and [John Morton's] batteries—eight guns—came up so as to be brought to bear with salutary effect."[4]

Forrest at this point, without orders, took charge of all the troops on the extreme right, integrating several brigades of infantry into his own command. But the Rebels were greatly outnumbered, and the pressure was unremitting. C. B. Kilgore, adjutant to the leader of one of those infantry units, remembers the scene: "The fighting soon became fierce for us, and we were barely able to hold our ground. General [Matthew] Ector became uneasy in regard to the protection for his right flank and asked me to go to General Forrest and urge him to be vigilant. . . . I galloped up to where one of his batteries was engaged."

"Tell General Ector he need not bother about his right flank," Forrest told the aide. "I'll take care of it."

One hour later Ector began to fret about his left flank, and sent Kilgore to Forrest again. "I found him in the same spot, right in the thickest part of the fight," the aide said. "This time he got furious. He turned around on me and shouted, loud enough to be heard above the terrible din . . . , 'Tell General Ector that, by God, I am here, and I will take care of his left flank as well as his right!' "

During this hectic time, amid charge and countercharge, one of Forrest's men broke and ran to the rear, passing close to the general and Major Charles Anderson, his chief of staff. Uttering an oath, Forrest pulled his revolver and took aim.

"Oh, General, think!" exhorted Anderson, and Forrest relented, letting the man flee.

"I knew him and his moods so well," Anderson later said, "that I had learned how to [deal with] him. . . . In the excitement of the moment, knowing the supreme disregard he felt for life—even his own, when the fate of the battle [was problematic]—had I said, 'General, don't do that!' he would have killed the man without a doubt, and I might well have gotten a turn too."[5]

Now in midafternoon, with Bragg at last awakening to the threat against his Right Wing and committing greater numbers of infantry in support, albeit in piecemeal fashion, the fighting eased and the danger passed. Forrest's quick decisions and inspiring presence had prevented a devastating rout. Where Bragg was that day, no one in the front lines knew. "But Forrest had been there, on every part of [the field]," said an admiring historian, "rallying the infantry as well as the cavalry. They all saw him, wrapped in a linen duster, his pistol and sword buckled on the outside . . . galloping up and down or standing beside a battery peering through the powder like a hawk."[6]

On September 20 the action shifted to the Confederate Left Wing, where about 11:30 a.m. Longstreet found a gap in the Federal lines and sent his men crashing through the opening, panicking the enemy and causing them to flee toward Chattanooga. Only Union general George Thomas made a stand, rallying four divisions and digging in on Snodgrass Hill, some ten miles south of the city. There through the long afternoon he not only blocked the Rebel advance but launched a series of counterattacks, buying time until Rosecrans could regroup his command.

Bragg, meanwhile, for reasons disputed to this day, did not get Polk's Right Wing moving forward against the beleaguered Thomas until 4 p.m. Here once more Forrest's troops, fighting dismounted with regular infantry, conducted themselves with conspicuous courage. "Forrest, pressing forward westwardly toward the highway to Chattanooga," say his military chroniclers, "found a strong Federal force drawn up behind a fence, supporting a battery of six guns. . . . Halting only long enough to reconnoiter, he deployed a skirmish line in front of the field and established the rifled section of Huggins' Battery in the same position . . . [just] as Armstrong's Division charged with impetuosity, and the enemy gave back to another line."

Moving into the road abandoned by the bluecoats, Forrest continued the assault "under an angry fire from Federal musketry and field-pieces that thinned his ranks to a fearful extent. Nevertheless there was no faltering from these doughty Tennesseans. . . . Dibrell, adjoining the infantry on his left, gained a position with seventy-five yards of the Federal battery, and Huggins was westward of the road, when the former noticed that the

Confederates on his left had been repulsed . . . uncovering his flank. . . . Dibrell was soon enfiladed . . . and Forrest, too, had now to recede to shelter."

His own artillery promptly opened up, first producing stalemate and later a successful countercharge. "In this part of the combat the Fourth and the Ninth [Colonel J. B. Biffle] Tennessee suffered more than the other regiments . . . while the Fourth Tennessee, under [Colonel W. S.] McLemore, and the Eighth, under Captain [Hamilton] McGinnis, maintained their stand after the infantry on their left gave way. . . . The entire Federal army was now to be seen by the last rays of daylight rapidly escaping in swarms . . . but no pursuit was organized or ordered."[7]

Outspoken General Daniel Harvey Hill, who had fought in the East with the Army of Northern Virginia through the Peninsula Campaign, the Seven Days, and Antietam, and who now was serving under Bragg, was so impressed with the performance of Forrest's troopers that he sought out Major Anderson.

"What infantry is that?" he asked.

"That is Forrest's cavalry," was the reply.

Hill expressed incredulity, and asked to be taken to the cavalry leader. "General Forrest, I wish to congratulate you and those brave men moving across the field like veteran infantry," he said, touching his hat brim in a respectful gesture. "In Virginia I made myself extremely unpopular with the cavalry because I said that so far I had not seen a dead man with spurs on. No one can speak disparagingly of such troops as yours."

Hill's disdain for the mounted service was well known, and Forrest must have been elated, but he showed no emotion. Contenting himself with a thank-you, he tipped his hat in return and galloped back to his men.[8]

Bragg, almost certainly despite himself, had just won his biggest battle. But the next morning, September 21, possibly believing his troops were too exhausted, he refused to advance on Chattanooga and renew the fight. His generals were indignant. "Move instantly against Rosecrans' rear to destroy him," Longstreet told him. Polk and Hill gave similar advice.

Forrest, who was early in the saddle and scouting in advance of the lines, more than anyone realized the enemy's vulnerability. "Can see Chattanooga and everything around," he said in a dispatch. "The enemy's trains are leaving, going around the point of Lookout Mountain. . . . I think they are evacuating as hard as they can go. They are cutting down timber to obstruct our passage. I think we ought to push forward as rapidly as possible." In a second note he was even more forceful. "Every hour [is] worth a thousand men," he informed Bragg.

That night he rode to headquarters, making his case in person.

The men are tired, he was told. *Besides, we need to wait for supplies.*

General Bragg, he importuned, *we can get all the supplies we want in Chattanooga.*

His pleas went unheeded, giving the Federals an opportunity to regroup. "Rosecrans gave orders for all our troops to prepare for an attack," said Charles Dana, who was with the Army of the Cumberland as an observer for the War Department. "No attack was made that day, however, nor the next, and by the morning of September 24 the herculean efforts of the army had so fortified the place that it was certain it could only be taken by a regular siege."[9]

The South had lost a priceless opportunity. Given this respite, the Federals, with Thomas replacing Rosecrans, would hunker down in Chattanooga until late November, when Ulysses S. Grant, then in overall command in the West, would relieve the siege and deal Bragg a humiliating defeat.

Now on September 28, while Forrest and the rest of the Confederates were sealing off the city, he received a dispatch from Bragg, instructing him to turn over the bulk of his command to Joseph Wheeler, the army's chief of cavalry, and thereafter take orders from him. Forrest was incensed. Though Wheeler was a skillful general and a considerate man, he and Nathan had clashed earlier in the year, and—as was known throughout the army—the Tennessean had vowed never to serve under him. Besides, Forrest had demonstrated time and again his genius for semi-independent command. The order was like a slap in the face.

With Major Anderson taking down his words, he immediately dictated a letter to Bragg, bluntly accusing the commander of the Army of Tennessee of duplicity and faulty leadership. He would visit his headquarters in a few days, he continued, to tell him that to his face. "Bragg never had such a letter as *that* from a brigadier," he remarked to Anderson, as a courier galloped off with the note.

True to his word, Forrest subsequently rode up to Bragg's position on Missionary Ridge, overlooking Chattanooga. With him was Dr. J.B. Cowan, his chief surgeon, who knew nothing of the letter, but sensed that a storm was brewing. "I observed as we rode along that the general was silent, which was unusual with him when we were alone. Knowing him so well, I was convinced that something that displeased him greatly had transpired. . . . As we were passing the guard in front of Bragg's tent . . . General Forrest did not acknowledge the salute of the sentry, which was so contrary to his custom. . . . When we entered the tent, where General Bragg was alone, this officer rose . . . and, advancing, offered him his hand."

Forrest ignored the proffered hand. "I am not here to pass civilities. . . ." he said. "You commenced your cowardly and contemptible persecution of me after the battle of Shiloh, and you have kept it up ever since. You did it because I reported to Richmond facts, while you reported damned lies. You robbed me of my command in [Tennessee], and gave it to one of your favorites, men that I armed and equipped. In a spirit of revenge . . . because I would not fawn upon you, you drove me into west Tennessee in the winter of 1862, with a second brigade I had organized, with improper arms and without sufficient ammunition. . . . You did it to ruin me. . . . When in spite of all this I returned . . . well equipped with captures, you again began your work of persecution. . . . now this second brigade, organized without thanks to you . . . a brigade that has won a reputation for successful fighting second to none . . . you have taken these brave men from me."

Bragg was awestruck. He stepped back and sat down on a stool, even as Forrest moved forward, shaking an index finger in his face. "I have stood your meanness as long as I intend to. You have played the part of a damned scoundrel . . . and if you were any part of a man I would slap your jaw. . . . You may as well not issue any more orders to me, for I will not obey them . . . .You have threatened to arrest me. . . . I dare you to do it, and I say to you that if you ever again try to interfere with me . . . it will be at the peril of your life."

During the entire tirade Bragg did not say anything or change his expression. Forrest then turned on his heels and strode from the tent, followed by Dr. Cowan.

"Well, you are in for it now," said the physician.

"He'll never say a word about it," Forrest replied with total assurance. "He'll be the last man to mention it; and, mark my word, he'll take no action in the matter. I will ask to be relieved and transferred to a different field, and he will not oppose it."[10]

In October Forrest took a leave of absence, traveling to La Grange, Georgia, to meet his wife, Mary Ann, for the first time in eighteen months.

While there he got a second order from Bragg, reiterating that he was under Wheeler's command. He promptly submitted his resignation, which Bragg received outside Chattanooga in the midst of a visit from Jefferson Davis, who was trying to make peace between Bragg and his officers. Polk, Hill, and Longstreet all regarded the commanding general as an incompetent and were asking for change.

Davis's solution was to temporize about Bragg, resulting in eventual defeat at Chattanooga, and to give Forrest what he earlier had asked for, a transfer to Union-occupied west Tennessee and northern Mississippi. There, taking only his personal escort, Major Charles McDonald's Battalion and Morton's Battery—some 280 men—he was to recruit a new force of Southern sympathizers and outfit them, at least to some degree, by taking weapons from the enemy.

On this occasion, Bragg voiced no objection to the transfer. Forrest's only regret was his parting from his storied old brigade, Tennesseans with whom he had forged a lasting bond.

Forrest spent November establishing relationships with Joseph Johnston, the overall Confederate commander in his new theater of operations, and Stephen D. Lee, the chief of cavalry there, as well as preparing for a quick foray behind Federal lines into west Tennessee.

On December 1 he headed his small band north toward Bolivar and the Memphis & Charleston Railroad, even as Lee was helping him by making a diversion to distract the enemy. Less than a week later he advised Johnston that all was proceeding as planned. He had "arrived safely at Jackson [Tennessee] and was highly pleased . . . that a healthy spirit manifested itself among the people." He added, exaggerating a bit, that "he had already gathered together about five thousand men, and thought it likely, if unmolested until the 1st of January, he should be able to put about eight thousand effective troops in the field."[11]

To achieve these numbers, Forrest set up enlistment posts in woodland clearings, in a score or more secluded areas, where he processed 50 to 100 recruits a day. "Some were men who had never served in any military force," said a historian. "Others were deserters from the infantry who had a predilection for the cavalry. Still others were Tennesseans or Kentuckians who had been enlisted into the Federal army and then decamped at the first opportunity."

Lack of weapons and money, however, soon forced Forrest to scale back his activities. "I have had to advance to my quartermaster . . .

$20,000 of my private funds to subsist the command thus far," he complained to Johnston. "I am exceedingly anxious to get the arms promised me by the President," he wrote Johnston in a second note, "and earnestly ask that General Lee . . . be brought up to west Tennessee at this juncture, bringing with him the arms and ammunition needed for the new troops." But no such support was forthcoming. Subsequently he sent Major M. C. Gallaway all the way to Richmond, begging the War Department "to send rapidly forward all the arms, &c., that can be spared me"—again to no avail.[12]

Around December 18, learning that Union infantry and cavalry were being mobilized to close on him but still hoping for weapons, Forrest prudently sent some 1,200 of his recruits, all unarmed, southward out of Jackson under the command of Colonel A. A. Russell. Traveling by night and taking a tortuous, zigzag path, they found safety in Pontotoc, Mississippi.

By the 23rd, with enemy columns of between 10,000 and 15,000 men converging on him in earnest, Forrest realized he could tarry in the area no longer. Giving up his ambitions to create havoc in west Tennessee, he divided the rest of his raw troops—more than half of them lacking arms—into several detachments, and on Christmas Eve moved them south on parallel paths across the Hatchie River toward refuge in Mississippi. Despite the need for speed, he selflessly burdened himself with forty supply wagons, 200 cattle, and 300 hogs, food he knew Johnston badly needed.

His decision to divide his command was tactical. Each detachment, when elements of the enemy were encountered, was instructed to attack with abandon, as if it were the van of a much larger force.

In a series of ensuing firefights, the bluff worked again and again. One such clash occurred just after Forrest's sixty-man personal escort under Lieutenant Nathan Boone crossed the Hatchie at Estenaula and drove in some pickets. "Taken by surprise," said one Rebel, "and evidently thinking we were more numerous than we really were, they . . . broke and ran toward their main camp." Boone at this point stretched out his line, ten paces between each man, and told each trooper to give orders as if he were leading a company. Then he sounded the charge. "We swept across the corn-field, making a tremendous racket. . . . The Federals (600 in number) . . . ran in great disorder. . . . It must have been at least two miles beyond the camp before the pursuit was stopped."[13]

Forrest, newly named a major general, would not stop his march until the 29th, when he, the recruits, and the wagon train arrived triumphantly in Holly Springs, Mississippi. Soon thereafter, a Union reporter writing for the *Cincinnati Commercial,* waxed indignant about the whole affair:

"Forrest, with less than 4,000 men, has moved right through the Sixteenth Army Corps, has passed within nine miles of Memphis, carried off . . . wagons, beef cattle, 3,000 conscripts . . . run over pickets with a single Derringer pistol . . . and all too in the face of 10,000 men."[14]

TWELVE
* * * *

THE WEST, OCTOBER 1-9:
WHEELER AT CHATTANOOGA

The rise of the youthful Joseph Wheeler—he was only twenty-six years old in late 1862 when named by Braxton Bragg to command the Army of Tennessee's cavalry—is something of an enigma. Short, slight in build, he certainly was not physically imposing. Fanatical about following orders, even when circumstances dictated flexibility, Wheeler stands in sharp juxtaposition to such instinctual Southern horse soldiers in the West as Nathan Forrest and John Morgan, both of whom he came to outrank despite their status as semi-independent commanders. But Bragg warmed to Wheeler, who almost alone of all his generals never criticized him, and this may explain Wheeler's ascent. Both men, moreover, were West Pointers— as opposed to Forrest and Morgan, self-taught in the art of war—and both were composed and self-contained, with little of the Tennessean's volatility or the Kentuckian's flamboyance.

Not that Wheeler lacked strong leadership qualities. He already had been through countless actions and skirmishes, always at the forefront of his men. But his forte seems to have been in moving on the flanks and working closely with the main army, not in going off raiding and reconnoitering and making the rapid-fire judgments demanded by semi-independent command.

Indeed, it had been an error in judgment, at least in Forrest's opinion, that led in February 1863 to the break between the two men. Bragg had sent Wheeler, with John Wharton's troopers and elements of Forrest's, into central Tennessee to attack the Federal works in the Fort Donelson–Dover area and disrupt navigation on the Cumberland. Wharton had some 2,000 men; Forrest, 800.

Conferring with Wheeler on the eve of the assault, Nathan urged that Bragg's orders be reconsidered. The troopers were suffering in the bitterly cold weather, rations and cooking gear were in short supply, and a lack of ammunition, both for small arms and the horse artillery, would not permit a protracted engagement. Even if the works could be taken, he added, the loss of life could not be justified, as Federal gunboats would force an evacuation and restore the status quo. Wheeler would disagree, and the attack would proceed. "I intend to do my whole duty," Forrest would tell Major Anderson, his aide, ". . . but if I am killed in this fight, you will see that justice is done me by officially stating that I protested . . . and that I am not willing to be held responsible for any disaster that may result."[1]

Wheeler envisioned a simultaneous movement against the Federal garrison, some 800 men of the 83rd Illinois Infantry, with Wharton going in on the left and Forrest on the right. About 2:30 p.m., the latter led his troopers in a charge, only to find his column was making the assault on its own. Whether Nathan's advance was premature, or Wharton's was delayed, is open to debate. The upshot was that Forrest's horse was shot from under him, he barely avoided crippling injury, and his men, thinking he had been killed, took heavy casualties before falling back in confusion.

The Confederates regrouped, and Wheeler ordered a second charge. In his sector, say his military historians, Forrest overran the enemy's outer defenses and neared the main works, "though swept by a well-sustained rifle fire and by the [cannon] in the redoubt. . . . It was at this time that . . . several valuable officers and a number of the best fighting men of [his] command were killed or wounded. The General, with Major Anderson and ten or twelve of his escort, rode up within thirty yards [of the works], however, and here another horse was slain under him. His ammunition was now exhausted, and the men were forced . . . to cease the conflict."[2]

Wharton on the left also took the enemy's first line of resistance, capturing a rifled cannon in the process, but likewise expending his ammunition. He too now had little choice but to withdraw.

With darkness descending, the battle ended just as Forrest had feared. The spirited Federal defense had dragged out the action until Rebel cartridge boxes were empty; enemy gunboats were steaming along the river

and bombarding the shore in support; and his troopers had been decimated, losing one-quarter, or 200, of their number. (Wharton, with his
much larger force, had been far less active in the fighting and had taken
but sixty casualties.)

Later that night, in a commandeered house, the ranking officers met
again to hash over events. "When the signal was given, my men moved
forward," Wharton would say of the second charge, "but were met with
such a severe fire that . . . they gave way. As we fell back, I noticed the garrison on our side of the fort rush across to the other side to take part
against General Forrest's attack. . . . He must have suffered severely."

Nathan was in no mood for sympathy. "I have no fault to find with my
men," he said angrily. "In both charges they did their duty as they have always done."

Wheeler attempted to placate him. "General Forrest, my report does
ample justice to you and to your men."

The Tennessean's emotions were palpable. "General Wheeler, I advised
against this attack, and said all a subordinate officer should have said
against it, and nothing you can now say or do will bring back my brave
men lying dead or wounded and freezing around that fort tonight. I mean
no disrespect to you. You know my feelings of personal friendship for you.
You can have my sword if you demand it, but there is one thing I do want
you to put in your report to General Bragg—tell him that I will be in my
coffin before I will fight again under your command."

Wheeler, an officer of great courage and equally great patience, swallowed hard. But he held Nathan in high esteem, and here he conducted
himself with commendable forbearance. "Forrest," he said, "I cannot take
your saber. I regret exceedingly your determination. As the commanding
officer, I take all the blame . . . for this failure." And so the confrontation
passed.[3]

Born on September 10, 1836, in Augusta, Georgia, Joseph Wheeler was
the youngest of four children of Joseph Wheeler and Julia Hull, trans-
planted New Englanders who had moved South to better themselves financially. His father prospered at first in business and banking, but then lost
everything as a result of imprudent decisions, and, in 1842, after the death
of his wife, he moved back to Connecticut. Joseph and his siblings were
parceled out to relatives, and the youngster thereafter was raised by two
aunts. He attended the Episcopal Academy at Cheshire, Connecticut, and
then briefly lived in New York City with a married sister and her husband,

a prominent merchant whose connections would have set Joseph up in business.

Wheeler, however, opted for the military life, and in 1854 he entered West Point, securing his appointment through a relative in the House of Representatives. He graduated five years later near the bottom of his class, his worst grades coming in cavalry tactics. Thereafter, just before the coming of the war, he served in New Mexico, seeing action against Apaches and Kiowas.

Once Georgia seceded, there would be no question where his loyalties lay. "Much as I love the Union, and as much as I am attached to my profession," he wrote his brother William in Augusta, "all will be given up when my state, by its action, shows that such a course is necessary." By April 1861 he had resigned from the Federal army and was serving as a Confederate lieutenant under Braxton Bragg, who at the time was commanding at Pensacola on the Gulf Coast. There some politicians took up Wheeler's cause—the first in a number of serendipitous events—seeing to it that he was jumped within weeks, over older and more experienced officers, to the rank of colonel.[4]

By April 6 of the next year, Colonel Wheeler and his 19th Alabama Infantry Regiment were at Shiloh, where they participated in the fierce assault on Union General Benjamin Prentiss in the Hornet's Nest, and subsequently helped cover the Rebel retreat. He then served under Bragg during the summer and early fall in the ultimately unsuccessful Kentucky Campaign, where he led a cavalry brigade with distinction. Soon afterward, in November, the commanding general named the twenty-six-year-old his chief of cavalry, and later a brigadier, raising a good many eyebrows in the process.

The year 1863 found Wheeler a major general, for the most part remaining at Bragg's side and, from June to September, covering the Army of Tennessee's frustrating series of withdrawals from the state, culminating in the loss of Chattanooga. (Forrest, meanwhile, following his Fort Donelson clash with Wheeler in February and his pursuit of Abel Streight in April, was reporting directly to the commanding general.)

Wheeler's close relationship with Bragg, it seems, was both a blessing and a curse. It brought about his promotions, of course, but also stunted his growth. Though he was a fighter, he was being thrust by his superior into a defensive mold, one that reinforced his innate conservatism. "From an early date Wheeler seemed earmarked for lasting renown," said a historian. "It seemed shameful that in the end his shortcomings as a field commander—critically magnified by the denseness of his superior officer, who failed to make maximum use of his talents—combined to tarnish much of [his] glory."[5]

In the aftermath of Chickamauga, where he had commanded the Confederate cavalry on the left, distant from Forrest on the right, Wheeler was given instructions by Bragg on September 29 to push across the Tennessee River above Chattanooga and cut the Federal supply lines into the city. (Forrest would have his altercation with Bragg about this time, and then take leave of absence.)

Though less than ten days had passed since the enemy had fled into Chattanooga, the entrenched bluecoats, with the Tennessee at their backs, already were feeling hunger pains. Supplies had to be brought in from the north, from the Federal base at Nashville, but the railroad was under Union control only up to Bridgeport, Tennessee. Bragg, holding Lookout and Raccoon Mountains west of Chattanooga, commanded the rest of the line, as well as the shortest and best wagon routes between Bridgeport and the city. What this meant was that all food and ordnance from Bridgeport on had to be hauled, perilously and with considerable delay, over a circuitous and mountainous sixty-mile route north of the river.

Taking with him John Wharton's and William T. Martin's divisions, Wheeler cantered upriver on September 30 to Cottonport, Tennessee, some thirty-five miles above the city, and rendezvoused with Forrest's now leaderless command, the brigades of General H. B. Davidson and Colonels John Scott and George Hodge. There he saw that Forrest's troopers and their mounts were in sorry shape, having constantly been on patrol for three days without removing saddles, and were badly in need of rest. More than a few of the men, moreover, remembered the earlier affair at Fort Donelson, and shared Nathan's reservations about him.

Nothing deterred, Wheeler weeded out the most impaired of Forrest's command, and formed the rest into three small brigades, perhaps some 1,000 men. Together with his own force, he now led 4,000 troopers, augmented with six cannon.

On October 1, under cover of darkness, he crossed the river. "I can never forget the beauty and picturesqueness of the scene that was presented that moonlit night," said one of Forrest's men. ". . . It happened that the Fourth Tennessee Regiment was in front; and, headed by a single guide, we descended the banks . . . and then the line swung down the stream across the silvery surface of the broad waters, like the windings of a huge, dark serpent. . . . No creation of art could have been more imposing."[6]

The next day was spent in climbing 1,500-foot-high Walden's Ridge and then descending into the Sequatchie Valley at Anderson's Crossroads. Wheeler at this juncture divided his force. He would accompany Martin's 1,500 men and look for wagon trains proceeding through the valley toward Chattanooga; Wharton with the rest, including Forrest's troopers under Davidson, were to advance to McMinnville, Tennessee, where reportedly there was a large Union supply depot.

Early on the morning of October 3, Wheeler figuratively struck gold, coming upon and easily capturing thirty-two wagons, each pulled by six mules, and each crammed with food, winter clothing, and ammunition. These proved to be the rear segment of an even richer bonanza—hundreds of wagons and thousands of mules, similarly laden—that he caught up with an hour later. Taking this main train, however, would be more difficult, as it was guarded, front and rear, by strong detachments of cavalry and infantry. "Parts of two regiments under Colonel John T. Morgan [51st Alabama Mounted Infantry] were ordered to charge the escort," said John Wyeth, the former Morgan scout now serving with the 4th Alabama, "which they did, but were repulsed, and came back in disorder."

Wheeler next sent Colonel A. A. Russell and the 4th Alabama into the melee. "As soon as our line could be formed," said Wyeth, "we rode forward at full speed, and receiving a volley at close quarters, were successful in rising over and capturing the entire escort. . . . Such a scene of panic and confusion I had never witnessed. Our appearance . . . was wholly unexpected."[7]

Contributing to the chaos was the flight of the teamsters. "When the fighting with the escort began," said Wyeth, "the teamsters had turned about in the hope of escape in the direction of Bridgeport. As we came nearer . . . they took to their heels for safety, leaving their uncontrolled teams to run wild. Some of the wagons were overturned, blocking the road in places with anywhere from ten to fifty teams, some of the mules still standing, some fallen and tangled in the harness. . . . For six or eight miles we followed this line of wagons, with every half mile or so a repetition of this scene."

Some 1,200 Federals surrendered, nearly as many as the Rebels in the attacking column, and then the work of destruction began. "Men were detailed to set fire to the wagons and to kill the mules, since it was impossible to escape with the livestock." At one point Wyeth, like many of his comrades, could not resist the urge to plunder, filling his haversack with a wedge of cheese and some hardtack. An incensed Wheeler caught him in the act.

"Get out of that wagon and go after the enemy!" the general roared.

Wyeth quickly obeyed, and rode on with Wheeler for some distance, while the burning of the wagons and the shooting of the mules proceeded. To this day no one knows the exact extent of the damage, but one informed estimate puts the numbers at 800 wagons and 4,000 livestock.

By this time the smoke arising from the blazing train was visible for many miles. "Soon the explosions of fixed ammunition, with which [some] wagons were loaded, sounded along the valley road, not unlike the firing of artillery," said Wyeth. ". . . The capture and destruction of this immense train was one of the greatest achievements of General Wheeler's cavalry, and I was proud of the fact that the Fourth Alabama, unaided, did the fighting which took it. Its loss was keenly felt by the Federals, for it added to the precarious situation of the army in Chattanooga, and reduced rations to a cracker a day per man for several days in succession."[8]

Generals Davidson and Wharton with their 2,500 men, meanwhile, approached the 600-man Federal garrison at McMinnville anticipating stiff resistance. After Colonel Hodge entered the town under a flag of truce and demanded surrender, however, the Confederates found the Union commander, Major Michael Patterson, curiously receptive. He *might* be willing to capitulate, Patterson allowed, but first he wanted to count the attacking force and make sure he was outnumbered. When Davidson and Wharton curtly rejected his request, he promptly surrendered.

McMinnville did indeed contain millions of dollars worth of stores and munitions, and the Rebels set about destroying them with glee. They also, Patterson exaggerated, committed "the most brutal outrages . . . ever known to any civilized war in America or elsewhere," appropriating Yankee hats, shirts, pants and boots, as well as "watch, pocket-book, money, and even finger-rings or, in fact, anything that happened to please their fancy." On October 4, when Wheeler arrived at the town and reunited his command, Patterson renewed his protests. The cavalry leader waved them aside, saying "that he could not control his men; that they would do as they pleased, &c."—all of which was partially true, as Forrest's troopers, at least, were still pining for their long-time commander.[9]

Wheeler the next day, either overconfident that he could evade Federal pursuers or ignorant of their numbers, moved deeper into middle Tennessee. He sacked Shelbyville and demonstrated against Murfreesboro, on the way destroying railroad track and a trestle bridge. Close behind, however, were several divisions of enemy cavalry, with General George Crook in the van.

On the night of October 6, the Confederates were encamped in three separate positions along the Duck River—Davidson with Forrest's old command northernmost, then Martin, and then Wharton. Learning that Crook and other enemy forces were near, Wheeler ordered Davidson, who was most in danger, to fall back on Martin and consolidate his lines. For some reason—why, we do not know—the former did not follow instructions. Though he moved his encampment, he did not join Martin, but instead swerved toward the Farmington pike, remaining exposed.

The next morning Davidson was attacked without warning, with Colonel Scott's brigade bearing the full force of the assault and breaking under the impact. Riding up in support, Colonel Hodge nearly came to grief himself. "I encountered the whole of Scott's brigade crowded in frightful and horrible confusion, wild and frantic . . . choking the entire road and bearing down upon me with racing speed. . . . They rode over my command like madmen. . . . I was ridden over and my horse was knocked down, but succeeded in extricating myself and Captain Larmer's company, Twenty-seventh Virginia Battalion, which I threw into position behind a fence."

Though Hodge to a degree rallied his men, and Davidson and Scott tried desperately to halt and regroup the latter's brigade, the Rebels could not stem the onrushing Federals. For the next five or six hours, over a half dozen miles, they fell back time and again in a series of unequal clashes, leaving scores of their comrades on the ground. "My gallant brigade was cut to pieces and slaughtered," Hodge lamented.[10]

Not until 4 p.m. was Wheeler able to bring up Martin's division to help, temporarily checking the enemy. Even so, only the coming of darkness prevented a complete disaster, permitting the Confederates to disengage and make for the Tennessee River and safety. By prolonging the raid, Wheeler had turned a smashing success into an arguable failure. "One wonders what Forrest would have done in the presence of such a rout," ponders Wheeler's biographer, "or what his commanding personality on the field might have been worth. . . . But Wheeler seems to have lacked Forrest's dominating way with men, and also to have lacked the sense of movement and coordination which is so essential to an independent commander."[11]

Most important, of course, was Bragg's lack of judgment in dealing with his cavalry subordinates. The Rebel commander's attempt to turn a fierce, free spirit like Forrest into a military conformist, and the proper, conventional Wheeler into a semi-independent cavalier, was doomed to failure from the start. In trying to reverse the roles of the two men, he dealt the Army of Tennessee an incredible disservice.

Late on the night of October 9, with his beleaguered column at last crossing over to the south bank of the river and escaping its pursuers, Wheeler dispatched an aide to Colonel Richard Jones, a local plantation owner, asking permission to camp on his property.

"General Wheeler, did you say?" asked a young woman who was at her father's side when Jones acceded to the request. "I'd like to see him."

"Well, madam," said the aide, jokingly referring to Wheeler's diminutive stature, "you won't see much when you do."

When the general and the woman, the recently widowed Daniella Jones Sherrod, met soon afterward, she realized she had seen him five years before, while attending the theater in New York City on her wedding trip. Some stage scenery had caught fire, and Wheeler and several other West Point cadets, who were in the audience, had dashed onstage and put out the flames. His quick thinking had impressed her, and the incident had stuck in her memory.

Now they talked for hours, and before they parted, Wheeler was smitten. His and Daniella's romance would proceed apace, and in 1866, just after the end of the war, they would marry in the house where they first met. The ignominious flight from Farmington would have a happy, if belated, ending after all.[12]

THIRTEEN

THE EAST, OCTOBER 19: STUART V. KILPATRICK AT BUCKLAND

Following Gettysburg, the two armies moved back and forth for weeks in the environs of northern Virginia, each feverishly but erratically looking to gain an advantage. Then on October 10, Robert E. Lee left his defensive lines south of the Rapidan River and attempted to turn the Federal right, only to be thrown back on the 14th in a bloody encounter at Bristoe Station. While covering Lee's withdrawal, Stuart five days later inflicted a body blow of his own, ambushing Judson Kilpatrick's pursuing cavalry at Buckland, a village near Broad Run Creek on the road to Warrenton.

Stuart had two divisions under him: the 2,800-man command of Wade Hampton, which he was personally leading, while the latter's wounds at Gettysburg were keeping him from field service, and the 5,000-man command of Fitz Lee. In contrast, Kilpatrick's division numbered no more than 2,000 troopers and was comprised of George Custer's and Henry Davies' brigades.

Nearing Broad Run before noon on October 19, the Federal column with Custer in the van came upon Stuart with Hampton's division entrenched on the west shore, blocking the stone bridge that led across the stream. (Fitz Lee's division was some half dozen miles away at Auburn, on the left flank of the advancing Yankees.) Custer made several attempts to storm the bridge, but to no avail—the Rebel lines were too strong. He appealed to Kilpatrick for Davies to come up in support, only to have his request denied. "Send out some men to find a ford," he curtly was told.

This Custer did, though he was incensed by Kilpatrick's tone, and soon a few of his squadrons were across Broad Run and opening up enfilading fire on the enemy. Instead of repulsing the handful of attackers, however, the Confederates inexplicably began to fall back. "After a somewhat stubborn resistance, Stuart apparently withdrew," said James Kidd, now a major and leading the 6th Michigan, "permitting Custer to cross though he could have held the position against ten times his number."

Kilpatrick now galloped up, offering his congratulations.

"Well done, Custer! You have driven them!"

"I was aware of that," icily replied the Michigander.[1]

Stuart was laying a trap. Earlier he had received a message from Fitz Lee. "Let Kilpatrick come on, and withdraw in front of him down the Warrenton Road," his subordinate advised. "When he has passed Buckland I will come in with my command and cut him off in the rear." Stuart pounced on the plan. "[He] at once adopted the suggestion," said Major McClellan, his aide, "and notified Lee that he would turn upon Kilpatrick at the sound of the first gun."[2]

Custer, 23, and Judson Kilpatrick, 27, had little use for each other. Both cultivated reputations as fierce fighters and thirsted for fame, but there the similarity ended. The hot-blooded, flamboyant Custer was, on the whole, bold but not reckless; honorable and straightforward; and considerate of his men. The cold-eyed, monomaniacal Kilpatrick was heedless and rash, boastful to the extent of being untruthful, and devoid of feeling for his troopers.

In their private lives, the gap was just as wide. Custer was earnestly but thus far fruitlessly courting Elizabeth Bacon, perhaps the prettiest girl in his hometown of Monroe, Michigan. If she continued to say no, he lamented to a confidant, "I hope [the rejection] will find me the same soldier I now try to be—capable of meeting the reverses of life as those of war." Kilpatrick was married, but determinedly unfaithful. A womanizer devoted to "sack duty and horizontal drill," his couplings were casual, copious, and multiracial.[3]

Compounding the tensions between the two men was the fact that Kilpatrick had been forced to take sick leave after Gettysburg and the command of his division had devolved on Custer. Weeks later, when Kilpatrick returned to duty, he found his subordinate all but regarding him as a usurper.

Now, in the aftermath of the initial clash at Broad Run, Kilpatrick moved Davies into the van against the retreating Confederates, and instructed Custer to regroup and follow posthaste. This the latter declined to do. "Custer respectfully but firmly demurred to moving his men until [they] could have their breakfast—rather their dinner, for the forenoon was already spent," said Major Kidd. "Neither men nor horses had had anything to eat since the night before."

Rather than debate the matter, Kilpatrick galloped off to join Davies, realizing the Michigander would have to join him sooner or later. But Custer's concerns went beyond providing a hot meal for his men. He sensed that Jeb Stuart's withdrawal west toward Warrenton was a sham, and that he was luring on Kilpatrick, preparatory to advancing a force from Auburn, striking the column in left rear and cutting it off from the creek.

Several hours passed, with Custer becoming more and more fretful, but the Rebels still did not attack. Were his instincts wrong, he wondered? Was the enemy retreating after all? Finally, about 3 p.m., he realized he had no choice but to move forward and rejoin Kilpatrick and Davies. While he was doing so, however, he sent Major Kidd and the 6th Michigan out some 500 yards to the left, near a thick copse of woods, with orders to screen the departure.

"Everything was quiet," that officer later said. "Nothing could be heard except the tramp of the horses' feet and the rumble of the wheels of [Alexander] Pennington's gun carriages."

Kidd was about halfway to the copse when one of his men yelled, "Major, there is a mounted man in the woods yonder!"

It must be one of our scouts, replied Kidd, to whom Custer had not revealed his fears.

"That vidette is a Rebel," the trooper insisted. "He is dressed in gray."

No, no, no, Kidd said.

Just at this moment a torrent of enemy gunfire erupted from the woods. "Damn it!" shouted the trooper. "Now you know he's a Rebel, don't you?"[4]

Kidd had drawn the fire of Fitz Lee's van, which was at last moving from Auburn to cut off Kilpatrick from Broad Run and the main Federal army. Custer, quickly reversing his march, here came up in Kidd's support and turned his force, dismounted, toward the threat to his left flank. For ten minutes, twenty minutes, perhaps a half hour, he managed to hold his position on the Warrenton Road. But then the numbers began to tell—5,000 Rebels against perhaps 1,000 Federals. Now Custer, despairing of keeping the road open, began to fall back, retiring to comparative safety behind the creek.

Meanwhile, just before Fitz Lee made his assault, Stuart some miles farther west was lying in wait for Kilpatrick and Davies behind a low range of hills that concealed his presence. "As far as the eye could reach," said Stuart aide William Blackford of the Federal advance, "their column of splendidly equipped cavalry came marching on with flags fluttering and arms glittering in the bright autumn sunshine. . . . We waited with breathless impatience the boom of Fitz Lee's cannon. Not seeing us, the enemy was just ascending the little rise behind which we were, when rapid firing of cannon in Lee's direction announced his attack."

Jeb promptly sounded the charge. "Our two columns were let loose, and at them we went," said Blackford. ". . . They did not wait for us to get halfway to them before they broke, and then it was a race like a fox chase for five miles. . . . This was the most exciting sport I ever had."

Remembered Major McClellan: "The first sound of Fitz Lee's guns roused Stuart from his self-imposed inaction. Instantly Hampton's division was . . . hurled upon Davies' brigade. [James. B.] Gordon's brigade, led by the 1st North Carolina, took the road, and [Pierce] Young and [Thomas] Rosser charged on either flank. The attack was sudden and impetuous, and although the enemy made resistance, their lines were soon broken."

The ensuing action came to be called the Buckland Races, as Kilpatrick's and Davies' men fled back to the village and Broad Run Creek. "Routed in front, and admonished by the artillery firing that an enemy had gained their rear," McClellan continued, "Kilpatrick's men ran in a manner worthy of the occasion. . . . Naturally the crowd of fugitives, among whom all order was cast aside, made faster time than did the pursuing brigades. . . . The stampede of Davies' brigade placed Custer in a critical position, and necessitated his precipitate withdrawal from Fitz Lee's front. But Custer was a hard fighter even in a retreat, and he succeeded in saving his artillery."[5]

No more than 200 Federals were casualties in the engagement, which was chiefly notable, following Gettysburg, for the boost it gave Stuart's bruised ego. In his report, he unabashedly declared that "the rout of the enemy at Buckland [was] the most signal and complete that any cavalry has suffered during the war." Kilpatrick, whose horse was shot from under him in the melee, found another mount and made his escape, as did Davies. In Kilpatrick's own report, he made no mention of the fiasco. "It was a masterpiece of obfuscation," said one critic. Indeed, Kilpatrick even threw a party. "There was milk punch and music, both of very good quality," said Kidd, "but the punch, palatable as it undeniably was, did not serve to take away the bad taste left by the affair."[6]

FOURTEEN

THE EAST, JULY−FEBRUARY:
MOSBY'S CONFEDERACY

Though the Union army moved back into northern Virginia in force following Gettysburg, John Singleton Mosby and his Partisan Rangers—officially the 43rd Battalion, Virginia Cavalry—continued to operate with impunity east of the Blue Ridge. So tight was their grip on the area, in fact, that their 125-square-mile stronghold, centered in Fauquier and Loudoun Counties just forty miles west of Washington, now was called Mosby's Confederacy. There between raids, in such towns as Paris, Upperville, Piedmont, Rectortown, The Plains, and Middleburg, they boarded with families and well-wishers, hid their weapons and uniforms until needed, and pretended to be civilians. Railed one officer of the 1st Massachusetts Cavalry: "[We] can do nothing against this furtive population, soldiers today, farmers tomorrow, acquainted with every wood path, and finding friends in every house."[1]

Rangers and their sympathizers, it seems, were one big family. Elizabeth Edmonds and her daughter Amanda (nicknamed Tee), put up eight men at their home near Paris. Three of them were Elizabeth's sons; the rest might just as well have been adopted. Tee even hosted parties, bringing in Rangers from nearby houses for banjo playing, singing, and dancing. "When the men returned from a raid it was like a holiday," said one historian. "[They] wanted to talk at once as they related their adventures, teasing and laughing about humorous incidents on the expedition. And when they shared their booty it was like Christmas—sometimes every member of the household received a gift. There were shoes, hoop skirts, fruit, cans of meat, cakes, candy, and other items normally unavailable."[2]

Sutlers transporting supplies behind the Union lines were the Rangers' usual victims, as well as the Federals guarding them, though sometimes rail trains were stopped and boarded. Mosby and his men regarded the goods, money, and horses they confiscated as spoils of war, and in some cases named their forays for some of the loot carried away. Following the so-called Calico Raid, for instance, they were laden with so many rolls of cloth that a woman asked Mosby if she could buy some from him. "Madam, you have mistaken my profession," he replied. "I am a soldier."

In fact, Mosby made sure he did not personally profit from the pilfering, instead distributing the prizes to those of his men who had been most instrumental in seizing them. He used weapons and rode horses taken on the raids, of course, but did not enrich himself. Later in the war, during the Greenback Raid, he would stop a train and confiscate $173,000 from Union paymasters. The Rangers implored him to take a share, but he refused. Nothing daunted, the men took up a collection from their own shares and sent $8,000 to Pauline, his wife. She turned the money over to her husband, who promptly gave it back. "Boys," he said, "I didn't go into the Confederate service for money or plunder."[3]

The Rangers struck a compromise, buying him a splendid mount, and Mosby, since he would be using the steed in line of duty, accepted the gift.

Now in July, continuing to strike quickly and with precision behind the lines with troopers usually numbering from a score to a hundred, the Gray Ghost was giving the strung-out Federals all they could handle. "I sent you in charge of Sergeant Beattie," he wrote his mentor Stuart in one typical report, "one hundred and forty-one prisoners that we captured during their march through this county. I also sent off forty-five [prisoners] several days ago. Included in the number, one Major, one Captain and two Lieutenants. I also captured one hundred and twenty-five horses and mules, twelve wagons (only three of which I was able to destroy), fifty sets of fine harness, arms, etc., etc."[4]

On August 1, however, he suffered an embarrassing setback. Learning that twenty-eight sutler wagons—one of which contained all manner of sweets—had been left unguarded at Fairfax Court House, Mosby the night before had taken two dozen men and launched the Ice Cream Raid.

Capturing the wagons had been no problem. But then, perhaps out of carelessness, he abandoned his usual hit-and-run tactics—which involved commandeering the teams, taking all that he could carry on horseback and burning all that he could not. Instead he tried to drive the train, intact, back to his base in Middleburg.

Blocking his path at dawn were Colonel Charles Russell Lowell and elements of the 2nd Massachusetts Cavalry, outnumbering him six to one. But Mosby quickly reacted, forsaking the wagons and with his men making the narrowest of escapes. "Mosby is more keen to plunder than to murder—he always runs when he can," remarked the disappointed Lowell, a member of the distinguished Boston family. Just as vexed was John Munson, one of the Rangers, but for a different reason. "If the boys could only have got home safely with those . . . loaded wagons," he said, "we could have opened up a big department store."[5]

The Gray Ghost's wagon raids nonetheless continued apace, with the Federals not knowing where he next would strike. On August 6 he was west of Fairfax, on the 9th farther northwest at Leesburg, on the 11th back south at Annandale. "They gave us more trouble than a whole brigade of Confederates," wrote one Yank.

Robert E. Lee, oddly enough, at this juncture did not fully realize how much damage Mosby's small but persistent incursions were inflicting on the enemy. "The capture and destruction of wagon trains is advantageous," he told Stuart on the 18th, "but the [primary] supply of the Federal Army is carried by the railroad. If that should be injured, it would cause him to detach [troops] for its security, and thus weaken the main army." Here Lee was either ignoring, or forgetting, that Mosby did not have the large number of men, or the artillery, needed to disrupt the well-guarded Orange & Alexandria Railroad.

Moreover, the partisan's small band was taking significant losses. Between July 15 and August 20, a score of his Rangers were captured—almost a fifth of his operational command. Doing most of the harm was the 2nd Massachusetts and Colonel Lowell, who was intent on becoming Mosby's bête noire. "He is a very brilliant man, but is too hasty in his judgements of men & things," Lowell's second-in-command would say. "And is so very ambitious, that he sacrifices everything for advancement."[6]

Perhaps needled by Lee's implied criticism, which Stuart doubtless conveyed to him, Mosby reacted by moving with thirty men into the Alexandria area on August 24, intending to destroy three rail trestles. When he happened upon a similar detachment from the 2nd Massachusetts, however, he changed his plans. The bluecoats, who were taking some 100 replacement mounts to Centreville, were watering the horses when the Rangers attacked from two sides, closing fast upon them with horrific yells. Though the charge had the desired effect, routing the enemy and gaining the horses, it came at a cost. Two Rangers were killed in the melee and several wounded, including Mosby, who was hit in the groin and thigh.

For the next few weeks he recuperated at the family farm near Charlottesville, and then called on General Lee at Orange Court House. The meeting was cordial, with Mosby explaining the Rangers' strengths—and their limitations. "Old General Lee," he wrote Pauline, "[was] very kind to me & expressed the greatest satisfaction at the conduct of my command." During their conversation, Lee stressed the need to take some action—no matter how minor—against the Orange & Alexandria, and then brought up Mosby's abduction of General Edwin Stoughton back in March, encouraging him to capture other Federal officials and officers in like manner. The talk energized Mosby, and he resolved to pursue both initiatives.

Back with his command on September 20, he took twenty men and headed east toward Washington. Near Manassas Junction he fell on some unwary railroad guards, a cavalry detachment from the 19th New York, and took nine prisoners and a dozen horses. Subsequently he seized eight mules from a woodcutting party at Burke's Station, even as their protecting infantry, out of musket range, looked on helplessly. Finally he rode to the hills over Alexandria and studied the Union defenses, preparatory to returning later, stealing into the town and seizing Francis H. Pierpont, the governor of newly created West Virginia and a man the Rebels despised.[7]

That foray came the night of September 28 when, with four Rangers, he passed through the Federal lines and casually rode up to Alexandria's City Hotel, where Pierpont had a suite, only to find that the governor was not there. Nonplussed, Mosby left a threatening note ("I'll get you some night, mighty easy") and then went a few miles down the road to the home of Pierpont's aide, Colonel Daniel H. Dulaney, guided by the man's son, Ranger French Dulaney. Knocking on the front door and rousing the household, he announced he had dispatches from the governor. The darkness concealed the raiders' Confederate uniforms, and it was not until they were in the colonel's drawing room that Dulaney realized he was a prisoner.

"How do, Pa," said his son. "I'm very glad to see you."

"Well, sir," answered an outraged Dulaney, "I'm damned sorry to see you."

Led out of his house a captive, the colonel's anger with his son boiled over anew.

"Take some shoes with you. I reckon they're damned scarce in the Confederacy."

French Dulaney smiled and pulled up his trouser legs, revealing some handsome boots he had appropriated from a sutler.

"How do you like these boots, Pa?" the young Rebel replied.[8]

During October, Mosby concentrated on scouting and raiding in the Federal rear around Centreville and Warrenton, keeping Lee and Stuart informed of troop movements and simultaneously harassing the foe, taking perhaps 200 prisoners and 250 horses and mules. His triumphs were small ones, but in the aggregate they placed a heavy burden on George Meade's army. "The military value of the species of warfare I have waged is not measured by the number of prisoners and material of war captured," he wrote Stuart, ". . . but by the heavy detail it has already compelled him to make, and which I hope to make him increase, in order to guard his communications."

Mosby's most notable exploit during this time came on the night of October 26 near Warrenton, where with fifty Rangers he encountered a well-guarded, forty-wagon train that was bringing up supplies from Gainesville. The Federal escort, however, was in front and rear, leaving the center vulnerable. Mosby promptly dispatched Captain William H. Chapman with ten men to that point and had them halt the teamsters, pretending to be Union soldiers. Once again, as at Alexandria, the darkness concealed the color of their uniforms.

Chapman asked a driver the name of the commissary officer in charge of that section of the train, and then boldly rode up to him and announced he was under arrest—on unspecified charges. Minutes later Chapman had the teamsters unhitching their mules. He was about to fire the wagons when part of the escort, concerned over the delay, arrived on the scene, forcing him to melt away into the night. Nonetheless, before leaving, he took with him thirty prisoners and 140 horses and mules, all without even cocking a pistol.

"Hurrah for Mosby!" enthused Stuart when he saw the animals. "This is a good haul." Subsequently he told the War Department, "This is but another instance of Major Mosby's skill and daring."[9]

The Rangers, whose numbers would soon grow to three companies, or about 225 men, laid low for much of November, in large part because of Colonel Lowell's sweeps into their base of operations. Indeed, from the 20th to the 22nd, elements of the 2nd Massachusetts, striking between Aldie and Paris, surprised and rounded up some twenty Rebels. They were guided by Charles Binns, who had been dismissed by Mosby for bad conduct, and who knew the farmhouses where the Rangers were hiding. Binns's act of betrayal might have been even more damaging if Mosby, during this period, had not taken seventy-five men and departed from the area, moving toward Bealeton Station, near Warrenton. There, lacking the strength to attack the depot directly, he waited until a five-wagon supply train approached. His men then scattered the escort and looted the wagons, taking what they could and burning most of the rest.[10]

Later in the month, on the 26th, Mosby again struck the enemy, this time converging with 125 Rangers on Brandy Station, where he had been told some fifty wagons were lightly guarded. Once it became dark, he and several men, passing themselves off as a Federal patrol, quietly rode into the campsite and found the rumor was true. Their only challenge, as they were leaving to rejoin their comrades, came from a single sentinel.

"Who goes there?"

"We are a patrol," said Mosby, just before vanishing into the gloom.

"Halt!" cried the sentinel, firing a single shot after the group that did no damage.

It was after midnight when the Rangers returned to the wagon camp in force. Once more they were thought to be Union cavalry, and the few sentinels there did not question them as they began to unhitch the mules and horses. Then torches were lit, sporadic shots rang out in the semidarkness, and the teamsters, seeing their danger, threw up their hands in surrender.

"What should I do?" one panic-stricken driver asked Mosby.

"Unhitch those mules!" came the swift answer.

Before they took their leave, the Rangers destroyed most of the wagons, put some 120 captured mules and horses on tethers, and took twenty prisoners.[11]

With the coming of cold weather, the two main armies ceased their maneuvering and went into winter quarters. But Mosby and the Federal cavalry still continued their games of cat-and-mouse. In addition to Colonel Lowell's 2nd Massachusetts, Major Henry Cole's 1st Maryland now was emerging as a tenacious adversary. In an early meeting between the Rebels and the 1st Maryland on January 1, the Rangers were clear winners. Captain William "Billy" Smith of Company B with thirty men, taking advantage of the element of surprise, routed eighty of Cole's troopers near Middleburg, killing or wounding or capturing three-quarters of them.

On the morning of January 10, however, the outcome would not be so fortuitous. In freezing temperatures, Mosby with 100 men about 4:30 a.m. stealthily approached Major Cole's camp on Loudoun Heights, at the north end of the Blue Ridge across the Potomac River. Though the bluecoats numbered about 300, he again was counting on the surprise factor. He sent Benjamin Stringfellow, a scout on loan from Stuart, off to the right with ten men to take the enemy in the rear once the shooting started, and then prepared to launch a frontal assault. He thought the attack could not fail. "The camp was buried in profound sleep," he said, "there was not a sentinel awake."

But Stringfellow charged too soon, rousing Cole's troopers from their beds. Worse, when Mosby made his own charge, his Rangers mistook Stringfellow's for the enemy, exchanging fire with them for several minutes and giving the Federals the chance to snatch up their weapons and go on the attack themselves. "[The] Rebels were easy targets," said one Yank, "because no one else was on horseback."[12]

With the fight going against him, Mosby sounded the retreat, leaving behind eight dead, among them Captain Billy Smith and Lieutenant Tom Turner—the latter having been one of his original fifteen recruits—and five wounded. The fact that he had killed and wounded a score of the enemy, and taken six prisoners and some fifty-five horses, was small consolation. Later, seeing that Cole was not pursuing, Mosby sent Captain William Chapman back to the Federal camp under a flag of truce, offering to give up the prisoners he had taken for his dead and dying. The request was denied. Riding away, Chapman passed Smith's body and noted, with disgust, that it had been stripped of his watch, clothing, and shoes.

The return march was a gloomy one for the Rangers, who from Mosby on down believed they had killed some of their own men. "A sad and sullen silence pervaded our ranks," said one Rebel. ". . . Even the Major, though he usually appeared cold and unyielding, could not conceal his disappointment and keen regret." Stated another, "If Stringfellow had not blundered, Cole's Command would have been wiped from the face of the earth."[13]

On February 6, Mosby was promoted to lieutenant colonel. "His sleepless vigilance and unceasing activity have done the enemy great damage," Stuart wrote Lee approvingly. "He keeps a large force of the enemy's cavalry continually employed in Fairfax in the vain effort to suppress his inroads. . . . Unswerving devotion to duty, self-abnegation, and unflinching courage, with a great perception and appreciation of the opportunity, are the characteristics of this officer."

The promotion came despite a scathing report from Brigadier Thomas Rosser, who had been serving in the Shenandoah Valley and, though he had little contact with the Rangers, was critical of partisan commands. "They are a terror to the citizens, and an injury to the cause," he complained. "They never fight; can't be made to fight." Then he got to the root of his dissatisfaction. "It is almost impossible for one to manage the different companies of my brigade that are from Loudoun, Fauquier, Fairfax, etc., the region occupied by Mosby," he said. "They see these men living at their ease and enjoying the comforts of home, allowed to possess all that they capture . . . and it is a natural consequence in the nature of man that he should become dissatisfied."

Stuart and Lee, while agreeing with Rosser about the loose ways of partisans in general, clearly felt that Mosby, whose strict discipline kept his men in line, was in a different category. But they admitted that his troopers were not being fully used, and that the spoils system could lead to excesses. "Mosby's command is the only efficient band of Rangers I know of," said Stuart, "[but] he usually operates with only one-fourth of his nominal strength. Such organizations, as a rule, are detrimental to the best interest of the army at large." Added Lee, in a letter to the War Department: "There is much truth in the [report] of General Rosser. I recommend that the law authorizing these partisan corps be abolished. The evils resulting from their organization more than counterbalance the good they accomplish."[14]

These comments carried weight. In the near future, Secretary of War James Seddon would arrange for almost all partisan units to be folded into the regular army. One of the few exceptions would be Mosby's 43rd Battalion, Virginia Cavalry. But he would be urged to put more of his men in the field and, if anything, step up his will-o'-the-wisp raids behind the Federal lines.

Now a second traitor, like Charles Binns, would bring Mosby grief. Ranger John Cornwall in mid-February had hauled a wagon full of ammunition into Fauquier County, and then become embroiled in a argument about his expenses with Mosby and Quartermaster William Frankland. Cornwall stormed off in a rage and soon offered his services to the enemy, saying he could target the houses where many of his former comrades were staying. Union General David Gregg thought the turncoat reliable, but took no chances. "The officer in charge of the [raiding] party," he decreed, "will take with him the prisoner, and if he should lead [you] into a trap, he will be shot."

Led by Lieutenant Colonel John Kester of the 1st New Jersey, some 350 Federal cavalrymen rode out of Warrenton on February 17, and by the next day, fanning out in smaller detachments, were combing houses from Middleburg to Paris, from Rectortown to Piedmont. Cornwall himself took one group to the home of Jamieson Ashby, looking for Quartermaster Frankland, but to no avail; he and two others were hiding in a false closet. Elsewhere, at Ben Triplett's house, Rangers Albert and Jim Wrenn jumped from their beds, scurried out a window, and dove into a haystack; though they all but froze in the wintry weather, they evaded capture. In their home near Paris, Elizabeth Edmonds and her daughter Tee had their own hiding place, reached by a trapdoor. Three men crowded into it until the bluecoats left.[15]

Overall, however, Rangers in the so-called safe houses were not so fortunate. Time and again, they were dragged from crawl spaces and from under beds and forced to surrender at gunpoint. Twenty-eight of them were captured, the largest loss Mosby would suffer during the entire war.[16]

Within days Mosby would strike back. Learning that Major Henry Cole and the 1st Maryland, who had bloodied him at Loudoun Heights, were in the area and had taken some Rangers as prisoners, he went on the attack, catching up with the enemy on February 20 near Upperville. Though outnumbered at least three to one, Mosby managed to flank Cole and send him packing, though the latter did manage to keep his captives. Federal losses in the skirmish were five killed and wounded and one missing. Three Rebels were wounded.[17]

On the 22nd, Mosby hit the enemy again, inflicting greater losses. His victims were some 130 men of now Brigadier Charles Lowell's brigade—three companies of the 2nd Massachusetts and one of the 16th New York—and they were led by Captain J. Sewell Reed. The night before he had crept up on the Federal camp and determined the route they would be taking in the morning. Now with 160 men, he lay in ambush on the Leesburg-Alexandria Pike, concealed in the thickets and woods around a blacksmith shop run by a man named Anker. The majority of his troopers, mounted, were left and right of the road; the others, dismounted with carbines, were opposite the shop. Several mounted Rebels were left in plain sight to draw the enemy on.

"Who are you? What command?" shouted someone in the Reed's van when the decoys were spotted.

"Fifth New York. What command are you?" bluffed one of the Confederates.

"We believe you are Mosby's men. Advance and make yourselves known."

"You advance. We believe you are Mosby's men," came the rejoinder.

"I'll find out damn quick who you are," said one bluecoat, raising his weapon to fire.[18]

Here Mosby, hearing the threat, blew his whistle, and the fight was on. The twenty-five Federals, perhaps 300 yards in the advance of Reed's main column, were opposite the blacksmith's at this point, and had little chance. They threw up their hands against the torrent of carbine bullets that ensued, shielding themselves as if in a blizzard.

Next the mounted Rangers charged down the pike from two sides, screaming their Rebel yells, waving their revolvers, and giving the rest of the Federals no chance to form lines of resistance. "I want you to go right through them," Mosby had instructed his men. "Reserve your fire until you get close enough . . . and then let every shot tell." For some minutes the road was clogged with a swirling vortex of horses and riders. In their midst was Mosby. "I saw him weaving in and out of the fighting mass like a ferret," said Ranger John Munson, "[going] hand-to-hand with every man who would stand before him." Then, just as Mosby's horse took a bullet in the leg and was disabled, the enemy buckled and broke, fleeing for their lives. At least ten Federals were killed, including Reed, a dozen or more wounded, and seventy captured. Confederate losses were light: six killed and wounded.[19]

So the war continued to play out in Mosby's Confederacy, with the Rangers living off the enemy and plaguing the bluecoats who, no matter how hard they tried, could not fully pacify the Virginia countryside in their rear. The rest of 1864 would bring more of the same.

1864

ONE
* * * *

THE WEST, FEBRUARY: FORREST V. SOOY SMITH

Following his hasty withdrawal from west Tennessee in December, Nathan Bedford Forrest with his cadre of experienced men led his raw recruits into north Mississippi where, now reporting to Lieutenant General Leonidas Polk, he quickly began the arduous process of organizing, arming, and disciplining his troops. The force that eventually emerged consisted of four slim brigades, commanded by Brigadier Robert V. Richardson of Tennessee (at best, 1,500 troopers), Colonel Robert McCulloch of Missouri (1,200), General Tyree H. Bell of Tennessee (2,000), and Colonel Jeffrey Forrest (1,000), Nathan's youngest brother. Robert McCulloch's and Jeffrey Forrest's brigades, in turn, were formed into a division, led by Brigadier James Chalmers of Mississippi.

Shaping up the recruits, some of whom were having second thoughts about their enlistment, was no easy matter, but Forrest approached the task with his usual briskness. When twenty of them deserted in a body, he brought them back under armed guard, court-martialed them, and announced they would be shot. "They were . . . placed in wagons, each one seated upon a coffin, and in solemn fashion driven to the place of execution," wrote one contemporary historian. "Before the open graves the sentence of the court was read, and they were given a few minutes for prayer.

There was not one of them who was not now convinced that his hour had come." Then, just as the firing squad was about to form up, Forrest offered the deserters a reprieve, provided they assured him, with sufficient fervor, that thereafter they would be model soldiers.

We will be! We will be! the men chorused in one voice.[1]

The Federals, meanwhile, six months removed from their victory at Vicksburg, were making plans to drive deeper into the Mississippi interior, despite the onset of winter. Ulysses S. Grant, soon to become general-in-chief and make his headquarters in the East with the Army of the Potomac, and William Sherman, his chief lieutenant in the West, devised a two-pronged attack on Meridian, a key Rebel supply center. Sherman with 20,000 infantry would leave Vicksburg on February 3, march east through Jackson, and reach Meridian about the 14th. General William Sooy Smith, with 7,000 picked horsemen armed with repeating carbines, was to move south from Collierville, Tennessee, about the same time, cross the Tallahatchie River at New Albany and proceed through Pontotoc, Okolona, Prairie Station, and Macon to rendezvous with him.

Sherman would fulfill his part of the plan, on the 14th occupying Meridian—which the outnumbered Polk had evacuated—and for the next few days wrecking its railroads. But Smith never did arrive. Finally, on the 20th, not knowing where his subordinate was, a fuming Sherman moved back west to Canton, where he stayed until the 28th.

Ironically, by warning Smith in strong terms before the expedition began that Polk would be sending the ferocious Forrest to intercept him (he did not know the latter would be able to muster no more than 3,000 effectives), Sherman may have made his subordinate overly timid. "I explained to [Smith] personally the nature of Forrest as a man," Sherman would say, ". . . told him that in his route he was sure to encounter Forrest, who always attacked with a vehemence for which he must be prepared, and that, after he had repelled the first attack, he must in turn assume the most determined offensive."[2]

Whatever the state of Smith's mind before he started, he would not move south on schedule, instead waiting days for one small brigade delayed by bad weather to join him, and then wasting more time reorganizing his pack train. As a result, he did not leave Collierville until February 11.

Because the Confederates initially were uncertain of his route, his advance was relatively unimpeded until the 20th when he reached the vicinity of Prairie Station, where he was met by Colonel Jeffrey Forrest's brigade. A sharp and spirited fight ensued, after which about 3 p.m. the

Rebels first fell back to West Point and then to Sakatonchee Creek at Ellis'
Bridge. Here Smith, though he already was halfway to Meridian, began to
find reasons not to push on. That night, choosing to believe exaggerated
reports of the enemy's strength and that he was heading into a trap, he ignominiously made the decision to turn back.

The next morning, to cover his retreat, he launched a brief diversionary
attack against Jeffrey Forrest's troopers, who were positioned just north
of the bridge. Bedford Forrest now moved toward the sound of the guns,
galloping up to General Chalmers and asking for information. "In rather a
quick, harsh tone," said the well-mannered and lawyerly Chalmers, "he
asked me what the condition of affairs was at the front. . . . I replied that
Colonel Forrest had reported nothing to me beyond the fact that there was
some skirmishing going on."

"Is that all you know?" Forrest asked impatiently. "Then I'll go there
and find out for myself."

Chalmers dutifully followed him across the bridge and toward the action. When they were no more than 100 yards away, they met a panic-
stricken Confederate running toward them. He was dismounted and
hatless, and had thrown away his rifle. "As he approached," said
Chalmers, "General Forrest . . . checked up his horse, dismounted
quickly . . . and, rushing at the demoralized soldier, seized him by the collar, threw him down, dragged him to the side of the road and, picking up
a piece of brush that was convenient, proceeded to give him one of the
worst thrashings I have ever seen a human being get."

Bedford soon turned the man loose, booting him in the direction of the
battle. "Now, _____ damn you, go back and fight," he said. "You may as
well be killed there as here." By the time he joined his brother, it was apparent the Federals were in full retreat. "They are badly scared," Forrest
announced to one and all. "He at once ordered Captain H. A. Tyler," said
Trooper John Wyeth, ". . . to take his own company and one other company of [W. W.] Faulkner's 12th Kentucky, numbering in all one hundred
and fifty men, and to push on in [their rear.] . . . At the same time . . . he
ordered the rapid concentration of his scattered troops. . . . Dispatches
were sent to General Richardson, who was some twelve miles westward,
to move . . . in the direction of Okolona. . . . Jeffrey Forrest and Chalmers
were to follow in the wake of Captain Tyler, while General Forrest, with
his escort, would press forward to keep up with the Kentucky captain."[3]
Meanwhile, Bell's brigade to the east, temporarily under Colonel Clark R.
Barteau, likewise was told to intercept the retreating enemy at Okolona.

Tyler through the forenoon kept on Sooy Smith's heels, passing through West Point and arriving at a point six miles beyond, near Prairie Station. There the bluecoats turned on him at a straight segment of the road with 1,500 men, forcing him to dismount and take cover. Shortly thereafter he heard a bugle call. Forrest with his escort was coming up. "It is death, General, to attempt to go through that lane," Tyler told him.

"You have a pretty good lot with you, and you handle them well," Forrest answered. "I will give you another—the best soldiers on earth, my escort under Lieutenant Thomas Tate. . . . Follow up the enemy. . . . I'll hurry up Chalmers's division." He then rode off in search of that command.

Tyler looked over the 60-man escort and issued a challenge. "Let's see whether you're crowing cocks or fighting cocks!" he shouted.

Then the combined units renewed the attack. Somehow, in a series of flanking movements, they managed to dislodge the enemy only to find themselves, late in the afternoon, pinned down again.

Once more Tyler heard a bugle call behind him. Forrest again was coming up in support, waving his saber at the head of McCulloch's brigade. "Close in with your revolvers, Tyler," he yelled. In the ensuing melee, during which Forrest used his saber with deadly effect, the Federals were pushed back. Darkness brought the fight to a halt, with the Rebels and their horses soon thereafter feasting on abandoned food and fodder, and waiting eagerly for dawn.[4]

By 4 a.m. on February 22, Jeffrey Forrest's and Robert McCulloch's brigades—Chalmers's division—were resuming the chase, heading north toward Okolona. But it would be Bell's brigade under Colonel Barteau, hurriedly joined by Bedford Forrest as it approached the town from the east, that first closed with the enemy. The Federals at this juncture, still not realizing they outnumbered their tormentors better than two to one, were making another halfhearted stand, trying to give themselves some breathing room.

"Where is the enemy's whole position?" Forrest asked.

"You see it, General," said Barteau, "and they are preparing to charge."

"Then we will charge *them*!" replied Forrest with characteristic vigor.

Seeing a weakness in the Federal line, he signaled a bugle call, and before the first notes had ended, he and his troopers were galloping forward. "One of [Forrest's] many peculiarities," Barteau would say, "was that in battle he never seemed to touch his saddle, but 'stood up' in his stirrups, an attitude which gave him the appearance of being a foot taller than he really was. As he was over six feet in stature and of large proportions, and of necessity rode a large horse, it was not difficult to recognize his presence at any ordinary distance."

The Federals met the charge with a single volley, then fell back behind a second defensive line. Here Forrest dismounted his men, telling them to take cover behind a stout fence. Less than a half hour later, learning that McCulloch was on hand, he sent that officer's brigade to flank the enemy, even as he remounted and with his escort and Barteau's men led a frontal assault.

"Move up! Move up!" he exhorted, and soon the Federals were fleeing in confusion.[5]

Union Colonel George C. Waring, commanding the 1st Brigade in the lead of the withdrawal that day, describes the scene: "As we passed to the left of Okolona, one regiment, the 7th Indiana, was ordered to fall out and support the 4th Regulars, who had been stationed at the edge of the town. . . . The 3rd Brigade had the rear of the column. Before it had passed, the Regulars and the 7th Indiana were engaged, and [the 3rd] was ordered to the attack. It soon broke in disgraceful flight . . . abandoning five guns of its battery, without firing a shot."

Continues Waring: "Nothing can be said in excuse of [the 3rd Brigade's] behavior, but the explanation is not far to seek. It had taken part in the retreat of the day before, and having seen no cause for it, imagined itself in the toils of an overwhelming enemy. It had lost all confidence in [Sooy Smith], and its discipline dissolved."

Once the Federals entered wooded and elevated terrain, at a place called Ivey's Hill, Waring and his 1st Brigade, now assigned to the rear, managed to stabilize the situation. Here began the last of the clashes that day between the two adversaries. "[But] no real attempt was made to stop [the enemy] or defeat him," Waring said bitterly, "only to hold him back by maintaining temporary lines, formed by the leading brigade, until the others could pass through. In this manner we retreated nine miles between 11 a.m. and 5 p.m."[6]

It was at Ivey's Hill that Jeffrey Forrest was killed, brought down by a bullet in the throat as he led his brigade into the fight. His brother Nathan rushed to his side, cradling the body in his arms and calling his name aloud. Within moments, however, Nathan Forrest heeded his responsibilities. "Placing the dead man's hat over his face," said Captain John Morton of the horse artillery, "he called to Major [John] Strange . . . to take charge of the body, and looking around called in a ringing, passionate voice to the bugle to sound the charge once more."[7]

Forrest's emotions now were such that his aides feared he would seek death as he rushed into the face of the enemy. Recalled Dr. J. B. Cowan, his chief surgeon: "I had just reached the spot where Jeffrey Forrest was lying dead, when Major Strange said to me as I rode up, 'Doctor, hurry after the General; I am afraid he will be killed.' Putting spurs to my horse, I rode rapidly to the front, and in about a mile, as I rounded a short turn in the road, I came upon a scene that made my blood run cold."

There he witnessed Forrest and his small escort, locked in vicious hand-to-hand combat with several hundred Federals. "I turned back down the road to see if help was at hand," said Cowan, "and, as good fortune would have it, the head of McCulloch's brigade was coming in full sweep towards me."

So interlocked were the antagonists, however, that McCulloch's Missourians and Texans at first reined up, fearing their headlong charge would damage friends as well as foes. Then McCulloch, blood pouring from a wound in his hand, broke the spell by waving them forward, shouting, "My God, men, will you see them kill your General! I will go to his rescue if not a man follows me!" His brigade renewed its advance, and under the added pressure the bluecoats once more fell back, but not until Forrest, by many accounts, had slain at least three men.[8]

The last clash with Sooy Smith's rear guard took place near sunset, halfway between Okolona and Pontotoc. "They made a final effort to check pursuit; from their preparations, numbers, and advantageous position no doubt indulging the hope of success," Forrest later would report. "They had formed in three lines across a large field . . . [where] a turn in the road placed them directly in our front. . . . As the advance of my column moved up, they opened on it with artillery. My ammunition was nearly exhausted, [but] I knew that if we faltered, they in turn would become the attacking party, and disaster might follow."

Dr. Cowan, riding beside Forrest, urged him to take cover.

"General . . . it is not right unnecessarily to expose yourself."

"Doctor, if you are alarmed, you may get out of the way," was the brusque reply. "I am as safe here as there."

Just then his mount crashed to the ground, struck dead by gunfire. Undaunted, he borrowed another horse and drove his van—perhaps 300 men—toward the enemy's lines. "Many of my [troops] were broken down and exhausted with climbing the hills on foot and fighting almost constantly. . . . I determined, therefore, to rely upon the bravery and courage of the few men I had, and advance to the attack."

Seeing that the Federals were launching a charge of their own, Forrest halted his troopers and deployed them, mostly dismounted, in a gully. Once, twice, three times, the enemy horsemen assailed the Rebels, on the last occasion coming into their lines but failing to dislodge them. "I am proud to say that my men did not disappoint me. Standing firm, they repulsed one of the grandest cavalry charges I ever witnessed. The Second and Seventh Tennessee [poured] a destructive fire on each successive [wave] of the enemy, who soon fled the field in dismay and confusion."9

Before the fighting ended, Forrest engaged in one more bit of derring-do. Thomas Tate, his aide, had run out of bullets while involved in close combat with a Federal officer. Just as the man was leveling his revolver at Tate, Forrest galloped to his side, "and with a sweep of his saber, nearly severed the Federal officer's head from his shoulders. The man toppled to the ground, and as he did so, Tate, taking the revolver from his hand, swung himself into the vacated saddle."

Later, while inspecting the battlefield and regrouping his command, Forrest showed that his blood lust, deep as it could be, lasted only until hostilities ended. Coming upon a Federal soldier, moaning piteously, whose doctor had fled and left a medical saw deep in the marrow of the man's leg, he reacted with compassion. He quickly dismounted, called for chloroform, which he personally applied "to the nostrils of the sufferer," and ordered Doctor Cowan to complete the surgery. Soon it was clear the soldier would survive.10

Though Forrest now called off the pursuit, the ignominious Union withdrawal under Sooy Smith continued apace. Riding as if hellions were on their heels, the Federals reached the safety of occupied Memphis on February 26. Stated Colonel Waring: "The retreat . . . was a weary, disheartening, almost panic-stricken flight, in the greatest disorder. . . . The expedition filled every man connected with it with burning shame." Sherman was thunderstruck. "I wanted to destroy General Forrest, who, with an irregular force of cavalry, was constantly threatening Memphis and the river above, as well as our rotes of supply in Middle Tennessee," he said. "In this we failed utterly, because General W. Sooy Smith did not fulfill his orders. . . . Instead of starting at the day ordered . . . he did not leave until the 11th . . . and then, when he did start, he allowed General Forrest to head him off and defeat him with an inferior force."11

Smith tried to defend himself, of course, but his excuses fell on deaf ears. He had been cowed by Forrest's reputation, and beaten even before the battle was joined. Five months later, he would resign from the service.

The Rebel leader, meanwhile, was exultant. "Considering the disparity in numbers and equipment," he said, "I regard the defeat of this force, consisting as it did of the best cavalry of the Federal army, a victory of which all who were engaged may justly feel proud. Its effect upon the raw, undisciplined and undrilled troops in this command is of a value incalculable. It has . . . given them confidence in themselves and their commanders."[12]

Long after the war, Lieutenant William Witherspoon of Forrest's cavalry, talking to a Union veteran of that last clash on the road between Okolona and Pontotoc, would couch the outcome in more idiosyncratic terms. "You made a formidable appearance, mounted, with your chargers well-reined and sabers drawn," he allowed.

But then Forrest had gone down the ranks, looking each man in the eye. "Hold this line for me!" he said, over and over.

"So you see," Witherspoon told the Yank, "when you charged . . . it was not one Forrest you were contending with, but every man in our line was a Forrest."[13]

TWO

* * * *

THE EAST, FEBRUARY 28−MARCH 4: THE KILPATRICK-DAHLGREN RAID

Hugh Judson Kilpatrick's career was on the downgrade. The ambitious, smooth-talking Union officer early in the war had made a name for himself, becoming a brigadier at twenty-seven, but then at Gettysburg and again at Buckland had revealed himself as blustering, erratic, and, if truth be told, a man more willing to risk other men's lives than his own. Now in early 1864, however, he thought he saw a splendid opportunity to restore his reputation.

Public indignation in the North at this juncture about the woeful conditions endured by Federal prisoners in Rebel jails was at a crescendo, and President Lincoln was desperately looking for ways to help them. What better means could there be, Kilpatrick reasoned, than launching a raid on Richmond, freeing the 15,000 prisoners at the foul Belle Isle camps, and torching the city in the process? Skirting the chain of command, he talked up his plan with friendly politicians and newspapermen, and eventually, as he knew it would, word of the proposed undertaking reached Lincoln. Intrigued, the president called him into his office for a chat.

During the meeting, Kilpatrick elaborated on his scheme. He intended to cross the Rapidan River at Ely's Ford with some 4,000 troopers and a half dozen cannon, and move toward Spotsylvania. There his detachments would tear up the rail tracks, keeping Lee from shifting infantry from the Fredericksburg front and sending them south to take him in rear. Kilpatrick then would race through Beaver Dam Station and Hanover Junction, gallop down the Brooke Pike, and assail Richmond from the north. He assured Lincoln that the capital's 3,000-man garrison—composed of militia—and its artillery pieces would offer no real resistance. The only regular troops in the area—no more than 1,500 horse soldiers under Wade Hampton—were widely dispersed and would be no match for him. After freeing the prisoners, he would make his escape either back toward Fredericksburg or northeast toward West Point on the Yorktown Peninsula.

The president listened and then countered with a proposal of his own. He had recently issued a proclamation, granting amnesty to Southerners who swore allegiance to the Union. The offer thus far had found few takers, but he was certain that was because the Rebels did not know about it.

If you go to Richmond, can your men hand out leaflets and spread the word? he asked.

Of course, Mr. President, of course, answered Kilpatrick, telling Lincoln what he wanted to hear.

Before making a final decision, the president consulted with Kilpatrick's immediate superiors, both of whom were resentful that the officer had gone over their heads. Alfred Pleasanton, head of cavalry, thought the prospect of the raid idiotic, perhaps remembering the thousands of horses that George Stoneman's raid on Richmond had cost the army. "[It] is not feasible," he said. "Before Kilpatrick could do much damage, their vulnerable points would be secured. I cannot recommend it." But George Meade, commanding the Army of the Potomac, was more calculating. Knowing Lincoln was leaning toward the enterprise, and hoping the plan would be Kilpatrick's ruin, he hedged, calling it "practicable."

Though the expedition still was not formally approved, by February 18 it was apparent it would be, with Kilpatrick's representatives being encouraged to take their pick of the cavalry's horses. Ebullient, he bet Pleasanton $5,000 he would enter Richmond within days, a wager that his chief quickly accepted.[1]

About this time, the twenty-two-year-old and well-connected Colonel Ulric Dahlgren, who had learned of the upcoming raid from gossiping officers in the bar at Willard's Hotel, arranged a meeting with Kilpatrick. Ulric, the son of Rear Admiral John Dahlgren—whose fleet was then bombarding the harbor at Charleston, South Carolina, and who was a friend of Lincoln's—had not followed his father into sea duty but instead had opted for the army. He had distinguished himself in several cavalry actions; then, at Gettysburg, where he had impressed Kilpatrick with his élan, he had been badly wounded and lost his right leg. Now, his convalescence complete, he limped into Kilpatrick's presence on a wooden replacement, and all but demanded a role in the expedition.

Much taken with Dahlgren's fervor, and doubtless impressed by his contacts, the cavalry leader not only acquiesced, but revised his plans to give the petitioner a key role in the undertaking. Dahlgren with 500 troopers was to separate from the main force at Spotsylvania, head down toward and cross the James River, and then enter Richmond from the south, setting loose the Belle Isle captives even as Kilpatrick with 3,500 men was attacking from the north. Later the two forces would unite, and all concerned "would go romping back to the Union lines."[2]

Dahlgren was ecstatic. "There is a great raid to be made," he wrote his father, "and I am to have a very important command. If successful, it will be the greatest thing on record; and if it fails, many of us may 'go up.' I may be captured or I may be 'tumbled over,' but it is an [action] that if I were not in I should be ashamed to show my face again. . . . I find I can stand the service perfectly well, without my leg. I think we will be successful, although [it will be] a desperate undertaking. . . . If we do not return, there is no better place to 'give up the ghost.' "[3]

Even as Federal detachments made diversionary movements to lure the enemy away from their route, both parties crossed the Rappahannock the evening of February 28, Dahlgren in the lead. "Everybody was in excellent humor," said one man. ". . . It is easier to get a trooper or even a hundred for a raid than to get one to groom an extra horse." Dahlgren at Spotsylvania veered south toward the James, according to orders, while Kilpatrick proceeded to Beaver Dam, which he reached about 5 p.m. on the 29th, capturing the telegraph before the alarm could be given. Signal messages between the two forces now were impossible, as rain and snow combined with the darkness to prevent any semblance of visibility.

Kilpatrick remained sanguine, but he should not have been. Two Rebel scouts in captured blue uniforms had earlier joined the end of Dahlgren's column and surreptitiously noted his detour. Now another scout, Sergeant George Shadbourne, likewise divined the route Kilpatrick was taking. All three promptly reported their findings to Wade Hampton, who quickly began assembling his cavalry and alerting the Richmond garrison.[4]

By 10 a.m. the next morning, following a brief rest, Kilpatrick was crossing the South Anna. Then, after pausing to destroy rail track, he moved down the Brooke Pike toward the capital's outer defenses, five miles from the city. Thus far his advance was all but unimpeded. "[We could] look into the streets," said Major James Kidd, "and count the spires on the churches." But where was Dahlgren? He even then should have been approaching Richmond's underbelly, prior to unloosing thousands of prisoners on a terrified populace and throwing the militia into panic. Kilpatrick opened up with his horse artillery, hoping the noise would stir his subordinate into action. But no answer came from Dahlgren. Instead the Rebel guns replied in strength, forcing the Federals to dismount and take cover.

For the next five hours, until 3 p.m., Kilpatrick's men moved forward some four miles by fits and starts, making their commander, never a fire-breather when his own safety was concerned, more and more uneasy. Wrote one historian: "[He] rode to the front, and a soldier heard him complain, 'They have too many of those damn guns; they keep opening new ones on us all the time.' What had begun as the prelude to a smashing attack slipped imperceptibly into a sparring match, with everyone waiting for some indication Dahlgren had got into Richmond and would presently get out again. The Confederate trenches now lay a mile away. . . . The Rebel fire grew stronger."[5]

Colonel Dahlgren's progress on February 28 and 29 had been uneventful. He and his troopers rode at a steady but unhurried pace toward the James, pausing only, like Kilpatrick, to tear up track, take a handful of prisoners, and of course, hand out Lincoln's amnesty leaflets to puzzled citizens. By dawn on March 1, the 500-man column was at Dover Mills, near the river and within striking distance of the capital, on schedule for the assault. Noting that he was on the plantation owned by James Seddon, the Confederate secretary of war, Dahlgren, ever the gentleman, paid an early morning call on Mrs. Seddon. She received him in her parlor, gave him a glass of blackberry wine, and confided that his father had once been one of her suitors.

It was still no more than 8 or 9 a.m. Dahlgren proceeded to the river, guided by a black man named Martin Robinson who had assured him he knew a spot that would permit an easy crossing, only to receive a nasty surprise. "But, when all the arrangements had been made . . . we found that our guide had sold us out," said Lieutenant R. Bartley. "There was no ford at the place at all, but a steam ferry, with the boat at the opposite side of the river, and no ford short of twenty miles."

Whether Robinson did betray the expedition, or whether the ford had been so swollen by the winter rains as to be unrecognizable, is debatable. Unfortunately for Robinson, however, Dahlgren grew so enraged that he ordered him hung on the spot. Within minutes, a leather harness was wound around Robinson's neck, his last words were heard, and his lifeless body was swinging in the wind.[6]

Lieutenant Bartley continues the tale: "A change was now necessary, so Dahlgren then determined to go down the [north] side of the river and make the attack on the upper part of the city . . . and trusted to circumstances to get the [prisoners] off Belle Isle." Hours passed in this endeavor, and the blue column, now approaching Richmond from the west, did not reach the outskirts of the city until the afternoon. "We heard cannon on the Brooke Pike [to the north], and knew at once Kilpatrick had made his attack. . . . This seemed to be something the Colonel could not comprehend . . . as his own force was too small to uncover in daylight, and he did not think Kilpatrick could possibly gain an entrance through the fortifications before night. But soon the firing began to get farther off, and we knew it was defeat for Kilpatrick."[7]

Dahlgren paused, out of sight in a thicket, and then when dusk began to fall, he continued his advance toward the Rebel lines. "[He] reasoned," said Bartley, "that General Kilpatrick might make a stand near the city and at night renew the attack, when he would hear our guns. . . . But Kilpatrick did not . . . return at night." Dahlgren's column, meanwhile, was taking significant casualties from bushwhackers, with troopers dropping from their saddles at an alarming rate. Finally realizing he was fighting alone, Dahlgren halted his advance and, skirting the city, turned his men north, hoping to find and rejoin the main Federal force.

Freezing rain mixed with snow was falling hard, making it all but impossible for the troopers to see any distance and stay together. Sometime during the night the command separated; Dahlgren with some 100 men headed in a wide arc toward the Pamunkey, Captain John Mitchell with the rest took a more direct route toward the river.[8]

While waiting for Dahlgren during the long afternoon of March 1, Kilpatrick completely lost his nerve. Instead of sending out slashing flankers to find gaps in the thin ranks of Richmond's militia, he had contented himself with inching forward, taking few chances and losing whatever momentum he might have had. The passing of the hours increased his anxiety. Would the weather continue to worsen? Was the enemy in the city being reinforced? Had Lee's infantry somehow found the rail transport to come up on his rear? Late in the day he cracked.

Just before Dahlgren launched his attack from the west, Kilpatrick ordered a retreat to the northeast, and by nightfall his van was across the Chickahominy River and near Mechanicsville. There he went into a restless bivouac. "A more dreary, dismal night it would be difficult to imagine," said one trooper, "with rain, snow, sleet, mud, cold and wet to the skin." Commented another, "We were without shelter, not a tent . . . in the command. Everything was wet, so that it was almost impossible to build a fire, which meant no coffee."[9]

Perhaps because of the discomfiture, by 10 p.m. Kilpatrick was bestirring himself. Scouts had informed him the Rebels had concentrated on the Brooke Pike, leaving unguarded the Mechanicsville Road, a parallel route into Richmond. Quickly he decided he would use the darkness to send out two 500-man sorties, one to free Union prisoners and the other to capture, or perhaps to kill, Jefferson Davis. With his remaining 2,500 men, he would remain, as usual, away from the action, poised "to cover their [withdrawal] with the prisoners."[10]

By midnight all was in readiness. But just before the two detachments got under way, Confederate cavalry burst into the Federal camp. They were some 300 North Carolinians of Wade Hampton's command, hurriedly assembled to challenge Kilpatrick, and their onslaught was so ferocious and so unexpected that they threw many times their number into panic. "I determined to strike at the enemy near Atlee's [Station]," said Hampton, ". . . where we met the pickets of the enemy. I would not allow their fire to be returned, but dismounted one hundred men, and supporting them with the cavalry, ordered Colonel [William] Cheek to move on the camp, whilst two guns were opened [up] at very short range."

The best Kilpatrick could do was rally his men long enough to permit a hasty withdrawal. "Someone gave the command, 'Stand to horse!' soon followed by 'Mount!' 'Form ranks!' 'By fours, march!'" said a Union trooper, ". . . when Kilpatrick's voice was heard above all others, 'Forward!' but just which way was the query, as it was utterly impossible to distinguish roads, points of compass, or anything else."

Hampton, ignoring the odds, had attacked with audacity—something Kilpatrick earlier had neglected to do outside Richmond—and his courage was richly rewarded. "The enemy, a brigade strong here, with two other brigades immediately in their rear, made a stout resistance for a short time," said Hampton, "but the advance of my men was never checked, and they were soon in position of the entire camp, in which horses, arms, rations and clothing were scattered about in confusion."

Kilpatrick moved off farther north at a gallop, and did not stabilize his line until the morning of March 2. He had lost fifty men killed or captured, a hundred horses, and much ammunition. "I could not push on till daylight," said Hampton, "when I found that the enemy had retreated rapidly down the Peninsula. We followed to the vicinity of Old Church, where I was forced to discontinue the pursuit, owing to the condition of my horses."[11]

Kilpatrick waited there until 1 p.m., hoping Dahlgren would appear. The latter did not, so the main Union force, subdued and bedraggled, crossed the Pamunkey and toward dusk again made camp. That night Captain Mitchell and his equally weary troopers rode into the firelight and made their dismal report. Kilpatrick would reach the safety of the Union lines on the Peninsula on March 4. But no one at this point knew where Dahlgren was or what had befallen him.

That dedicated soldier, it turns out, had traversed the Pamunkey with his 100 men earlier, during the night of March 1 and 2, missing contact with his chief. With him was a Rebel prisoner, Lieutenant Henry Blair of the Salem Artillery, who gives us this account: "We rode the whole of the night as fast as the men and horses could stand it. A little after sunrise the next morning [March 2], we stopped awhile and took breakfast." Then the ride continued, and by midafternoon Dahlgren and his troopers were at the Mattaponi River, which they took turns crossing in a leaking boat while their mounts swam alongside. During this tedious process, they again drew heavy fire from bushwhackers. "Dahlgren [rallied] his men," said Blair, "went in front of them and made them return the fire of the Confederates, who . . . were driven off."

Once across, however, the nearly exhausted Federals endured still more enemy sniping. "All that evening," continued Blair, "the Confederates annoyed Dahlgren's command by firing into them from the woods." A little after dark, the column stopped for rest a mile or two from Stevensville. "After midnight we were called up, and Dahlgren [resumed] the march. . . . We had gone perhaps a half mile when I perceived there was some trouble at the front. [He] rode forward; I heard him challenge someone, and heard him snap his pistol, which was at once followed by a fire in return."[12]

Dahlgren's column at this juncture had been intercepted by regulars and militia under Lieutenant James Pollard of the 9th Virginia Cavalry, who had anticipated his route and were lying in ambush.

No one knows the thoughts that Dahlgren had in the last moments of his life. Clearly, riding forward, he sensed danger and sought to take the initiative. Richard Crouch, one of Pollard's troopers, remembered: "Upon the noise made by some of our men in ambush, we heard a demand of, 'Surrender, or I will shoot!' [Whoever] called out attempted to fire his revolver at us, but it failed. . . . This action drew a terrific fire. . . . He fell from his horse dead, pierced by five balls. [He] proved to be Ulric Dahlgren."

With their leader dead, the Federals milled about in confusion, many falling from their saddles under the hail of bullets, others hunkering down in the darkness. Almost all would be wounded or captured. The Kilpatrick-Dahlgren raid had come to an ignominious end.[13]

Our story does not stop here. The next morning, March 3, one of the riflemen in the ambush, a thirteen-year-old boy named William Littlepage, reported that he had searched Dahlgren's body and found some documents and a notebook. He took them to Edward Halbach, the militia leader, who happened to be his schoolmaster. Halbach, horrified by their contents, turned the papers over to Lieutenant Pollard, who, equally taken aback, rushed them to Richmond, where their publication raised an enormous hue and cry. If authentic, the so-called Dahlgren Papers showed that one purpose of the raid was the assassination of Jefferson Davis and his associates.

In the main document, an address to be distributed to the strike force on the eve of battle, Dahlgren ostensibly wrote: "We hope to release the prisoners from Bell Isle first, and, having seen them fairly started, we will cross the James River into Richmond . . . [and] destroy and burn the hateful city, and not allow the Rebel leader, Davis, and his traitorous crew to escape." A second note, a special order, was more specific: "The city must be destroyed, and *Jeff Davis and Cabinet killed.*" A third order, in the notebook, reinforced his deadly intent: "Jeff Davis and Cabinet must be killed on the spot."

Dahlgren's supporters reacted with fury to the allegations. The gentleman who had taken wine with Mrs. Seddon, although he later hung Martin Robinson, could not be such a blackguard. Though the documents were in his handwriting, they charged that the assassination references had been inserted into the papers by the Richmond authorities to bolster support for the war. "Nothing of the kind was received by the officers or privates of the command, even when Richmond was in view," said Lieutenant Bartley, "and it was highly improbable that [we] would have been uninformed of any important purpose of the expedition when [we] were on the verge of action. . . . I pronounce these papers a base forgery."

Rear Admiral Dahlgren likewise challenged the evidence: "The document alleged to have been found upon the person of Colonel Dahlgren is utterly discredited by the fact that the signature . . . cannot possibly be his own. . . . A letter is misplaced and the real name Dahlgren is spelled Dalhgren."

The Rebels had ready answers for such objections. Orders to kill Davis and his associates were so incendiary, they insisted, that they would be held in strict confidence and not issued until thousands of Federal prisoners were freed and set on a rampage through a defenseless city. Dahlgren, once he had been forced to abandon the plan of attacking Richmond from the south, had no reason to inform his men about the proposed assassinations. The transposed letters in his signature on one of the papers similarly were dismissed. Perhaps a military secretary, preparing the orders, had made the mistake. (Much later, apologists even advanced the argument that the sheet of paper in question did not misspell the name after all—it was so thin the writing on the back showed through and *appeared* to alter the spelling. "The word across the back of which Dahlgren's name is written is 'destroying' and it is the tail of the 'y' which . . . gives to the 'l' in his name the appearance of an 'h'."[14]

Even Robert E. Lee participated in the controversy. The commander of the Army of Northern Virginia sent photocopies of the documents to General George Meade, head of the Army of the Potomac, asking for an explanation. "[Did] the design . . . as set forth in these papers . . . have the sanction and approval of your authorities?" he asked. After interrogating Kilpatrick, who denied giving any such orders, Meade replied, "Neither the United States Government, myself, nor General Kilpatrick authorized, sanctioned or approved . . . any act not . . . in accordance with the usages of War."[15]

But Meade knew Kilpatrick well enough not to take his assurance at face value. Following interviews with several of his officers, he came to believe that Kilpatrick, desperate for fame, had indeed hatched such a plot. Dahlgren, honorable man though he was, had hated Secessionists so much, Meade believed, that he had gone along with it.[16]

The argument continues to this day. But it is hard to believe the Confederates were able, within a brief time span, to concoct such a complicated forgery out of whole cloth. More likely, Kilpatrick did decide to embellish his orders, playing on Dahlgren's strong feelings and making him his dupe.

In any event, the raid was a total failure, with Kilpatrick losing 340 men, almost 600 horses, and much ordnance. Of the horses that did return, 500 were unfit for further service. Soon afterward, finding himself demoted from division to brigade command, he requested a transfer to the West. It was promptly granted, and he would serve the rest of the war under William Tecumseh Sherman.

THREE
* * * *

THE WEST, APRIL 12: FORREST
AND FORT PILLOW

During early March, Forrest reorganized his command into two divisions, each roughly composed of 2,000 effectives. One was led by a newcomer, General Abraham Buford, a West Pointer and bluegrass native, and consisted of the 3rd Brigade (Kentuckians and Tennesseans under Colonel A. P. Thompson) and the 4th Brigade (Tennesseans under Colonel Tyree Bell). The other division continued to be headed by General James Chalmers, a well-born Mississippi lawyer not entirely compatible with his rough commander; it was comprised of the 1st Brigade (Tennesseans under Colonel Robert V. Richardson) and the 2nd Brigade (Missourians, Texans, and Mississipians under Colonel Robert McCulloch).

No sooner was this fine-tuning complete than Forrest on March 15 began to move his columns north from Mississippi into Union-occupied western Tennessee and Kentucky, intent on launching a series of raids and expeditions. Besides cutting enemy supply lines, he was hoping to find fresh mounts and recruits, and to give those of his men hailing from the area time to reestablish ties to friends and families. "Buford's Kentuckians were in pressing need of clothing and equipment," reported Nathan's campaign historians, "and one-third were on foot, while the horses of the rest were indifferent. . . . The Tennesseans brought out in December were also, for the most part, in great need . . . and had left their homes so suddenly as to make it important they, likewise, should be indulged in a brief visit to the region."[1]

Buford's division initially took the lead, the unmounted Kentuckians among the troopers trudging alongside their luckier comrades. By March 20 the Rebel van was in Jackson, Tennessee, where Forrest detached a battalion to warn him if the large Federal garrison at Memphis should become a threat, and two days later it reached Trenton, where he established a field headquarters and set up a recruiting station. Here he sent Colonel William Duckworth of the 7th Tennessee, Chalmers's division, with his own regiment and other units, still farther north to Union City, Tennessee, just below the Kentucky border.

Duckworth, a mild-mannered physician and Methodist minister in civilian life, arrived at the town on the 24th with some 300 men and found it protected by almost 500 bluecoats. He nonetheless demanded that Colonel Isaac Hawkins, the enemy commander, immediately surrender. His message, written in Forrest's bombastic style, stated that he "was prepared by reason of the superior force he had on the ground to take the place by storm," but "in order to prevent the loss of life" he urged Hawkins to capitulate. "Otherwise he would not be responsible for the fate of the garrison." Then for good measure, Duckworth signed Forrest's name to the ultimatum.

Hawkins, who had previously surrendered to Nathan on a raid in December 1862, had little stomach for a fight. But knowing that reinforcements were on the way, he tried to procrastinate, asking for a talk with Forrest.

Duckworth, still playing the role of his chief, replied that "he (Forrest) was not in the habit of meeting officers inferior in rank to himself under flag of truce, but would send Colonel W. L. Duckworth, an officer of equal rank, clothed with power to arrange terms."

When the two men met, the surrender was foreordained. *If you don't give up*, threatened Duckworth, *we will not spare a single member of your command*. Within minutes the garrison was disarmed, arms and ammunitions and 300 horses were rounded up and commandeered, and the triumph was complete. Union general Mason Brayman, who with 2,000 infantry was only six miles away at the time, was outraged. "I . . . learned with pain and surprise that Colonel Hawkins had surrendered, and had with his force been removed and his fortifications destroyed. . . . A considerable amount of public property was lost."[2]

Forrest, meantime, with his escort and most of Buford's division, was advancing toward Paducah, Kentucky, which he galloped into on the afternoon of March 25. There he forced some 650 Federals to flee from the town and take refuge in a nearby earthwork, protected by a deep ditch and sharp abats, near the banks of the Tennessee. Following several hours of random gunfire, during which the Rebels pinned down their adversaries both in the makeshift fort and in gunboats on the landing, he issued his usual ultimatum: "If you surrender you shall be treated as prisoners of war, but if I have to storm your works, you may expect no quarter."[3]

The enemy commander in Paducah, however, one Colonel Stephen G. Hicks of the 40th Illinois Infantry, was made of sterner stuff than his counterpart in Union City. He forthwith rejected the Rebel cavalryman's demand. No matter. Forrest had no intention of wasting his men's lives in a frontal assault. For the next few hours, while the enemy watched helplessly, he looted the town, taking some 50 prisoners, 400 horses and mules, and scores of wagons loaded with ordnance and supplies.

During this period, the most notable Confederate casualty was Colonel A. P. Thompson, a native of Paducah, who led his Kentuckians in an unauthorized charge on the works. Remembered Captain H. A. Tyler, head of Forrest's escort: "My men had been firing on the Federals running to get into the fort, and at those already firing back at us from the embankment, but we had not suffered any material loss. . . . About this time Colonel Thompson, moving at the head of his brigade, came up the street."

"I am going to take that fort," Thompson vowed.

Supposing that Forrest had ordered the charge, Captain Tyler joined in the assault. "We dashed forward in a wild rush. . . . The enemy opened up upon us with a most terrific volley. Colonel Thompson was slain and a number of troops killed or wounded. . . . The rest of us sought safety in a rapid retreat."[4]

The affair at Paducah was the first occasion that Forrest's troopers, to any real degree, had faced black troops—some 275 men of the 1st Kentucky (Colored) Heavy Artillery. "Permit me to remark that I have been one of those men who never had much confidence in colored troops fighting," Colonel Hicks later said, "but those doubts are now all removed, for they fought as bravely as any in the fort." Northern newspapers quickly picked up on the episode, inventing a series of frenzied but fruitless assaults on the fort, during which the Rebels were "ignominiously beaten back by Negro soldiers with clubbed muskets." To what degree these stories fueled Confederate anger and affected subsequent events at Fort Pillow is a matter of conjecture.[5]

Forrest now fell back to Jackson, Tennessee, leaving most of Buford's troopers in Kentucky to visit their families and find more mounts, with the understanding that they rejoin him within the next ten days. "I have, as far as prudent, allowed my men an opportunity of going home," he reported on April 4. "Am now concentrating and preparing for any move the enemy may make. . . . I am confident of my ability to whip any cavalry they can send against me, and can, if necessary, avoid their infantry. . . . General Chambers is here, and will be kept in readiness for any move that may be made from Memphis. General Buford's division is above [us] . . . ten miles west of Trenton."

Then he added: "There is a Federal force of 500 or 600 at Fort Pillow, that I shall attend to in a day or two, as they have horses and supplies which we need."[6]

That promised day or two extended into several more, during which Forrest conducted diversionary raids near the Union bastion at Memphis, some seventy-five miles to the southwest. Finally, on April 10 all was in readiness. This time with Chalmers's division—the brigades of Colonel McCulloch and Colonel Richardson—in the lead, he advanced due west fifty-five miles to Fort Pillow, located on the Mississippi River forty miles above Memphis, intending to neutralize the post. He could not know that the fighting there, rightly or wrongly, would become infamous.

Fort Pillow's garrison consisted of some 560 men under the command of Major L. F. Booth. Roughly half were blacks, principally elements of the 6th U.S. (Colored) Heavy Artillery, whom the Rebels instinctively despised; the rest were units of the 13th Tennessee (Union) Cavalry led by Major W. F. Bradford, whose conduct in the area had made his men pariahs. "Under the pretense of scouring the country for [Confederates]," reported Forrest's historians, "Bradford and his subalterns had traversed the surrounding country . . . robbing the people of their horses, mules, beef cattle . . . wearing apparel, money, and every moveable article of value . . . besides venting upon the wives and daughters of Southern soldiers the most opprobrious and obscene epithets."[7]

The fort itself was a horseshoe-shaped affair, perched on a bluff where the Mississippi met Cold Creek, with deep ravines on its southern and eastern fronts. A ditch twelve feet wide and eight feet deep led to its parapet, which was six feet high and extended for 120 yards. At a half dozen places in the walls, there were openings through which cannon could be fired. In the river below, to the west, the Federal gunboat *New Era* offered the garrison further support, although its guns would be relatively useless—lacking a clear sight line, they could not do substantial damage to the enemy on the heights.

Toward this redoubt at dawn on April 12, Colonel McCulloch and his dismounted troopers made their way from the south, taking heavy fire but moving within three hundred yards of their objective. Forrest arrived on the scene a few hours later, and after a reconnaissance during which his mount was shot from under him, quickly grasped the significance of the terrain. If he could advance his troops into the two ravines, the enemy would not to be able to *depress* his cannon enough to reach them. "He asked me what I thought of capturing the barracks and houses which were near the fort and [the ravine]," said Colonel McCulloch. "I replied that if I could get possession of the houses I could silence the enemy's artillery."

"Go ahead and take them," Forrest ordered.

The resulting charge was successful, and soon McCulloch's sharpshooters, finding cover in the abandoned houses, were riddling the defenders. "The barracks had previously been ordered to be destroyed," said one Union officer, "but after severe loss . . . our men were compelled to retire. From these barracks the enemy kept up a murderous fire. . . . Owing to the close proximity of these buildings to the fort, and to the fact that they were on considerably lower ground, our artillery could not be sufficiently depressed to destroy them or even to render them untenable."

Next, from the east, Forrest threw forward Tyree Bell's Brigade of Tennesseans—Buford's division—toward the Cold Creek ravine. "[He] had at once realized . . . that if he could get his men in that sharp depression," said one contemporary, "they would be so far beneath the fort that the artillery could not . . . strike them." Moving Bell's line into position, however, proved arduous. "It was finally accomplished under a heavy body of sharpshooters, which, as Bell's troops would rush across the exposed places, would open in lively fashion at any men of the garrison who would show their heads . . . to fire upon the advancing line."[8]

With the noose drawn tight and the fort completely invested, Forrest about 3 p.m. called upon Major Booth to surrender, not knowing that earlier he had been killed and superseded by Major Bradford. "I demand the unconditional surrender of this garrison, promising you that you will be treated as prisoners of war. My men have received a fresh supply of ammunition, and from their present position can easily assault and capture the fort. Should my demand be refused, I cannot be responsible for the fate of your command."

In the midst of these negotiations, while a truce was in effect, one or more transports loaded with Federal reinforcements could be seen in the distance, steaming up the river from Memphis. Bradford now resorted to delaying tactics, not only signing Booth's name to his reply, but also asking for an hour's grace. The aggressive Forrest, however, was not to be deprived of his prize.

"You have twenty minutes from the receipt of this note," he rejoined. ". . . If at the expiration of that time the fort is not surrendered, I shall assault it. I do not demand the surrender of the gunboat."[9]

Meanwhile, to keep Federal troops on the lead steamer, the *Olive Branch*, from landing, he dispatched an aide, Captain Charles Anderson, with a squadron of riflemen around the southern end of the fort. There they took up a position on a bluff overlooking the river, where their fire quickly forced the steamer to reverse engines. The gunboat *New Era*, for the most part, would remain a spectator in these proceedings.

Forrest at this juncture received a second note from Bradford, who was still passing himself off as Booth. "Your demand does not produce the desired effect," it read enigmatically.

Nathan reacted violently. "This will not do," he told an aide. "Send it back, and say to Major Booth that I must have answer in plain English—Yes or No!"

During this time, report Forrest's campaign historians, "the parapets of the fort were thronging with Negro soldiers, intently watching the course of events. . . . And so close were the Confederate lines, that the white men of both sides were bantering each other from their respective positions, while some of the Negroes indulged in provoking, impudent jeers."

Bradford, following a council of war, now made a calamitous decision. *I will not surrender*, he announced.

Forrest promptly resumed hostilities. "At the first blare of the bugle, the Confederate sharpshooters, at all points, opened a galling fire upon the hostile parapets," continue the historians, "to which the garrison replied, for a few moments, with great spirit. But so deadly was the aim of the Confederates, from their enfilading positions, that their enemies could not rise high enough from their scanty cover to fire over at their foes, nor use their artillery. . . . Consequently there was little resistance when . . . the main force, as with a single impulse surged onward, like a tawny wave, and crowning the parapet poured over, on all sides, into the works."[10]

Major Bradford, it appears, nonetheless had a contingency plan. "[He] had arranged with the captain of the gunboat [Captain Marshall] that, if beaten at the breastworks, the garrison would drop down under the bank, and the gunboat would come to their succor, and shelter them with its cannister. The proposed signal was now given and the garrison, en masse, white and black, for the most part with arms in their hands, broke for the place of refuge . . . leaving the Federal flag still aloft on its staff and turning repeatedly . . . to return the fire opened upon them."

At this critical moment, however, the *New Era* was not in the appointed place. Sum up the historians: "Captain Marshall gives, as an excuse for his course, that he was fearful the Confederates 'might hail in a steamboat from below, capture her, put on four or five hundred men and come after me.' " Marshall was also mindful, of course, that if he came too close to the landing, the fort's cannon, now in the hand of the Rebels, could blast him out of the river. "He was apprehensive . . . if he attempted to go down to the fort . . . and engage in the fight, the Confederates would sink him."[11]

The bloodletting that ensued, during the overrunning of the redoubt and the flight to the water, would be fearful to behold. Daniel Stamps of the 13th (Union) Tennessee quickly was taken prisoner, only to find himself in mortal peril. "I heard a Rebel officer shout out an order . . . to the men who had taken us and . . . asked [a soldier] what the officer had said. He repeated it to me. It was, 'Kill the last damn one of them.' The soldier replied that we had surrendered. . . . The officer replied, seeming crazy with rage that he had not been obeyed, 'I tell you to kill the last God-damned one of them.' He then turned and galloped off. . . . I saw two white men shot down. . . . They had their hands up . . . and were begging for mercy. I also saw . . . at least twenty-five Negroes shot down. . . . They had also surrendered."

Stamps survived, but many others did not. Sergeant Achilles Clark of Forrest's 20th Tennessee later admitted, in a letter home: "Negroes would run up to our men, fall upon their knees and with uplifted hands scream for mercy, but they were ordered to their feet and then shot. . . . The white men fared but little better. . . . Blood, human blood, stood about in pools and brains could have been gathered up in any quantity."

Southerners, trying to explain the senseless killings, would point out that Colonel Bradford had never struck the Union flag. Moreover, they claimed, large numbers of the garrison were liquored up. "They acted like a crowd of drunken men," said Colonel Clark Barteau of the 2nd Tennessee. "They would at one moment yield and throw down their guns, and rush again to arms . . . and renew the fire. If one squad was left as prisoners . . . it was soon discovered they could not be trusted . . . for taking the first opportunity they would break loose again."[12]

Before the shooting ended, some 230 of Fort Pillow's 560-man garrison would be slain, a disproportionate number of them black, more than a hundred wounded, and the rest captured. Confederate losses were fourteen killed and some eighty-five wounded.

Forrest, in the immediate aftermath of the fight, was jubilant. "Men, if you will do as I say, I will always lead you to victory!" he told his troopers. "I have taken every place that the Federals have occupied in West Tennessee and North Mississippi except Memphis, and if they don't [take care] I'll have that place too."[13]

The next day, April 13, brought on a truce for the business of burying the dead and caring for the wounded. Federal officers and men, landing from the steamer *Silver Cloud*, were appalled by what they saw, and their accounts, magnified by wartime emotions, were soon trumpeted with understandable indignation in the Northern press. (Southern newspapers, covering the story from their own point of view, initially all but celebrated the carnage.)

Captain John Woodruff of the 113th Illinois Infantry, visiting the battleground in the company of General James Chalmers, would deliver one of the more restrained reports. "Some of [the Negroes] were burned as if by powder around the holes in their heads, which led me to conclude they had been shot at very close range," he said. "One of the gunboat officers . . . asked General Chalmers if most . . . were not killed after they [the rebels] had taken possession. Chalmers replied that he thought that they had been, and that the men of Forrest's command had such a hatred for the armed Negro that they could not be restrained. He said they were not killed by General Forrest's or his orders . . . that both Forrest and he stopped the massacre as soon as they were able. . . . He said it was nothing better than we could expect as long as we persisted in arming the Negro."

How much at fault, then, was Forrest for the massacre? Certainly he had demanded unconditional surrender, stating he otherwise could not be responsible for the fate of Major Bradford's command. Whether he called for the ensuing killings, however, or whether his men could not be controlled, is unclear. In point of fact, some combatants—Federals as well as Confederates—maintain they saw him in the midst of the melee, trying to stop the bloodshed, and that the loss of life would have been all the greater had he not intervened.

What we do know is that Forrest, the former slave trader, was a fierce warrior, with a hair-trigger temper, and could easily be branded as a brutal oppressor of blacks. But he was also a man of honor, whose self-imposed code made it unlikely he would shoot, or condone the shooting, of a disarmed foe, whether white or black. Consider his brusque exchange with one Charles Fitch, who identified himself as Fort Pillow's surgeon while the violence was raging, and asked for his protection.

"You are the surgeon of a damn nigger regiment!" Forrest spit out.

"No, I'm not!" Fitch retorted.

"You are a damn Tennessee Yankee then."

"I'm from Iowa."

"What the hell are you down here for? I have a mind to have you killed for being down here!" With that last rejoinder, Forrest recovered himself, beckoned to an aide, and directed that Fitch be kept safe.[14]

One last vignette is in order. Major Bradford, taken unhurt at Fort Pillow, soon violated his parole. According to Forrest's campaign historians: "He was placed for the night in the custody of Colonel McCulloch, who gave him a bed in his own quarters and shared with him his supper. . . . Taking advantage of the darkness and his knowledge of the locality, when his host was asleep, he effected his escape."

A day or two later, while trying to reach Memphis, Bradford was re-captured and sent to a prison camp at Brownsville, Tennessee. "On the way, he again attempted to escape, soon after which one of the men shot him. It was an act in which no officer was concerned [and] mainly due . . . to private vengeance for well-authenticated outrages committed by Bradford and his band upon the defenseless families of the men of Forrest's cavalry. . . . Had there been a wish to slay the man particularly, there was ample opportunity . . . at Fort Pillow."[15]

FOUR

THE WEST, MAY-SEPTEMBER: CAVALRY IN THE ATLANTA CAMPAIGN

William Tecumseh Sherman's advance into Georgia from Chattanooga, in the aftermath of the Federal triumph there the previous November, began on May 7. Ulysses S. Grant, now general-in-chief, was entrusting his chief lieutenant with the taking of Atlanta, even while he moved East to face Lee, a campaign we will explore in a later chapter. "Cump" Sherman, commanding some 100,000 men, had a distinct advantage over the Rebels, who numbered only 65,000. But in the cautious Joseph Johnston, who had replaced Braxton Bragg, he was facing an officer who possessed several tactical strengths.

First and foremost was the terrain of northern Georgia. A series of steep ridges and mountains had to be turned, and formidable creeks and rivers forded, before Atlanta, no more than 100 miles away as the crow flies, could be invested. Moreover, Johnston could choose where he wanted to fight, and if forced to fall back he would grow only stronger, since his troops could be consolidated and his supply lines shortened. Sherman's numbers, on the other hand, would lessen as he advanced, since troops would have to be detached to guard his own supply lines, which were anchored by the Western & Atlantic Railroad.

Despite these difficulties, Sherman persisted, and through the spring and into the summer he engaged the Rebels in one spirited fight after another, either flanking them or pushing them back. The actions first were at Dalton, Resaca, and the Etowah River; then at Dallas, New Hope Church, and Pickett's Mill; then at Marietta, Pine Mountain, and Kennesaw Mountain; finally at Smyrna Church and the Chattahoochee River, the crossing of which in mid-July brought the Federals within eight miles of the Georgia capital.

Here Jefferson Davis, frustrated by the long retreat, relieved Johnston and replaced him with John Bell Hood, a hero of the Army of Northern Virginia. "If the Army of Tennessee were found unable to hold positions . . . like those at Dalton, Resaca, Etowah and the Chattahoochee," he lamented, "I could not reasonably hope it would be more successful on the plains below Atlanta, where it would find neither natural nor artificial advantages."[1]

Hood's far more aggressive forays against Sherman, however, proved equally futile, and after three consecutive July defeats outside Atlanta, on July 28 he withdrew into the city's fortifications, knowing he was only delaying the inevitable.

Through the early part of this campaign, the cavalry on both sides—plagued alternately by mountains and waterways—played only a minor role, confining itself to guarding the flanks and reconnoitering. Only in July and August would certain notable raids be launched, with the Federals taking the lead. Sherman, who had as many as 12,000 troopers at his disposal, was in effect his own cavalry leader, perhaps because, a crusty infantryman at heart, he never fully trusted the mounted branch. His particular peeve was that the cavalry took too long saddling up and getting into the fray.

"Get out of here quick!" he had shouted at one top-ranking officer in the midst of a dustup.

"What shall I do?" asked the man, who was accustomed to more formal orders.

"Don't make a damn bit of difference," he was told, "so [long as] you get out of here and go for the Rebs!"[2]

Sherman's cavalry divisions were four, and were headed by Major General George Stoneman, the senior officer, and by Brigadiers Hugh Judson Kilpatrick, Kenner Garrard, and Edward McCook. Stoneman and Kilpatrick, both refugees from the Army of the Potomac in the East, we already know—Stoneman for his ill-conceived raid during Chancellorsville, and Kilpatrick, most recently, for his fruitless attempt to free Federal prisoners in Richmond. Garrard, a West Pointer whose grandfather had been twice elected governor of Kentucky and whose stepfather was a justice of the U.S. Supreme Court, was reserved and quiet, and without field experience. McCook, one of the fifteen brothers and cousins who comprised the "Fighting McCooks" of Ohio, was a garrulous and impulsive Midwest politician.

Opposing these men was the dutiful Confederate horseman Joseph Wheeler, whose elevation to command of the Army of Tennessee's cavalry had so provoked the irascible Forrest. Wheeler at this point led from 9,000 to 10,000 troopers, but because of a shortage of mounts his effective force was perhaps two-thirds that number.

The first Federal expedition, however, involved none of these commanders. Instead it was undertaken in July by Union Major General Lovell Rousseau, who from his headquarters in Nashville commanded the District of Tennessee. Rousseau, who was feeling deskbound, had been corresponding with Sherman for weeks, seeking permission to assemble a makeshift cavalry division and lead it from the West on a wide arc below Atlanta, attacking rail lines and supply depots as he went.

"The movement I want you to study," Cump had told him, just before authorizing the raid, ". . . should start from Decatur [Alabama], move slowly to Blountsville and Ashville, and if the way is clear, cross the Coosa at the Ten Islands or the railroad bridge . . . then move rapidly for Talladega or Oxford, and then for the nearest ford or bridge over the Tallapoosa. That passed, the [column] should move . . . on the [Atlanta & Montgomery] Railroad between Tuskegee and Opelika, breaking up the road. . . . If no serious opposition threatens, it should threaten Columbus, Ga., and then turn up the Chattahoochee to join me between Marietta and Atlanta."[3]

One of twelve children, the forty-six-year-old Lovell Rousseau had been born in poverty on a farm near Stanford, Kentucky. Through grit and determination he had become one of the state's foremost lawyers, as well as a member of the Kentucky senate, where he had made a name for himself representing the downtrodden and condemning the anti-immigrant policies of the Know-Nothing party. When war broke out, he was one of the men instrumental in keeping Kentucky in the Union, and thereafter he led a brigade at Shiloh and a division at Perryville. Though without formal military training, he was a natural soldier. "When he showed himself on the battlefield," said one admirer, ". . . encouraging or urging [his troops] into the fight, his influence over them was unbounded. . . . His fine physique, noble bearing . . . caught their eyes and aroused their enthusiasm. [Yet] he was without ostentation."[4]

Within days of getting the go-ahead, Rousseau was in Decatur, assembling a strike force and commandeering horses, supplies, and weapons—such as seven-shot Spencer carbines—with a bluntness that brooked no opposition. The lead elements of his 2,700-man division left the city on July 10, heading southeast toward the Coosa River. One brigade, led by Colonel Thomas Harrison, eventually would be comprised of the 2nd Kentucky, 8th Indiana, and 9th Ohio. The other, headed by Colonel William Hamilton, would include the 5th Iowa and 4th Tennessee.

No impediments were met during the column's early progress, as it passed through Somerville, Blountsville, and Ashville—except the complaints of farmers losing crops and livestock to Rousseau's foragers, and the barbs of locals who could not believe Yankees would venture so far South.

"You'uns are no Yankees," insisted one woman.

"Yes, we are, ma'am."

"I know you are not. You'uns have no horns."

"We are young Yankees," one forager answered. "Our horns haven't grown yet."[5]

On the morning of July 14, however, while getting his troopers across the Coosa in two locations—at Green's Ferry and four miles downstream at the Ten Islands ford—Rousseau found his way blocked by 200 men of the 6th and 8th Alabama under Colonel James Clanton. The Federals at Green's Ferry used their carbines to blast away the opposition, but those at Ten Islands, where the Coosa surged over large rocks at white-water speed, became pinned down.

Here Lieutenant Colonel Fielder Jones of the 8th Indiana, who had reenlisted despite severe wounds that made riding tortuous, volunteered to lead a flanking movement.

"You are too valuable," said Rousseau. "I can't spare you."

"My life is worth no more than any private," said Jones, brushing the objection aside. In short order he found a ford upstream from the Rebels, and his men, with whoops and shouts, aided by their comrades coming down from Green's Ferry, turned the enemy and put them to flight.[6]

Next the raiders passed south through Eastaboga, and about 8 a.m. on July 15, they arrived in Talladega, crossing the Alabama & Tennessee Railroad as they did so. There, sixty miles deep into Confederate territory,

they put to the torch the depot and huge stores of food, clothing, and tobacco. They then resumed the march, seizing fresh horses and mules as
they went, and leaving exhausted animals in their place. All along the
way, enthusiastic slaves rushed from their plantations, cheering them on.
"The rate of marching was too rapid for [most] to keep along on foot,"
said a Union officer. ". . . Nevertheless a number succeeded. . . . They
would trudge along uncomplainingly, riding when they could get an animal . . . and if asked where they were going, the invariable answer was,
'Goin' with you all!' "[7]

The next morning, with Major Harlan Baird's 5th Iowa in the lead, the
column galloped into Soccopatoy. Here Rousseau ordered a brief rest while
he and some aides visited a plantation owned by one Patrick McKinney.
They were all sitting down with some glasses of ice water on McKinney's
front porch, making small talk with their host—the dust on their uniforms
making him think they were Confederates—when Rousseau noticed a
number of sturdy mules in a nearby corral.

"My good sir, I fear I must take some of your mules," he said.

The planter protested, explaining that only last week he had given some
mules to Confederate General Philip Roddey's command.

"Well, in this war you should be at least neutral," said Rousseau, "that
is, you should be as liberal to us as to Roddey."

"Ain't you on our side?" asked a bewildered McKinney.

"No, I am General Rousseau, and all these men you see are Yanks."

"Great God! Is it possible?" said the planter. "Are these Yanks? Who-
ever supposed [you] would come way down here in Alabama?"

Naturally, Rousseau got his mules.[8]

Before sundown the Federals were at the swift and deep Tallapoosa,
where Colonel Charles Hamilton, who had given up brigade command to
restore discipline in the straggling 9th Ohio, forced a black man, who understandably feared for his safety, to lead the way in making a crossing. "I
ordered him to . . . come quickly or it would be the worse for him," said
the no-nonsense Hamilton. "He begged piteously, but I told him the boys
would shoot if he did not go."

Traversing the river in the ensuing darkness was a harrowing challenge,
but by 3 a.m. on July 17 the last of the Federals were across, some with
badly scraped shins and painful bruises, but without the loss of a uni-
formed man. "Ever after," said Hamilton, "we referred to the
crossing . . . with a shudder, for the thought of it was as unpleasant as that
of any battle."[9]

Hour after hour the column pushed on, passing through one village after another, until by day's end—at Loachapoka—it reached its main objective, the Atlanta & Montgomery Railroad. The weary troopers had come some 240 miles, and now were poised to cut a major supply line between the Deep South and Atlanta.

Much to his surprise, Rousseau found Loachapoka undefended even though, as one officer noted, it contained "the largest amount of quartermaster and commissary stores any of us ever saw." The men helped themselves to harness, rifles, and food, and then destroyed the rest.

Quite soon, however, Rousseau had them hard at work on the business at hand: tearing up rail track with gusto. "The kind of timber used in [the road's] construction greatly facilitated the [wreckage]," he said. "The cross-ties were of pitch pine, and into these were sunken stringers of the same kind of wood, and a light bar of iron [was] spiked on the top through holes in a projection or flange. The wedges by which the string timbers were fastened into the cross-ties were driven out, and from 50 to 100 feet of the track raised from the ties at once by the use of fence rails as levers."

Rails and timbers from one side of the road were then piled on the other side and put to the torch. "The dry pine burned so readily and produced such an intense heat that the iron was warped and rendered worthless, and the ties burned off where the track rested on them, making the destruction complete." By daylight on July 18, six miles of track were heaps of blackened ruins.[10]

Rousseau now sent part of his command under Colonel Harrison a few miles south toward Chehaw Station and distant Montgomery, with orders to extend the wreckage as they progressed. It was at Chehaw about noon that some 1,000 Rebel militia, rushed into action, brought the Federals up short. Rather than take further casualties, Rousseau promptly broke off the action and sounded the recall, muttering "I shouldn't have got into this affair."

"There's no reason to be uneasy about Harrison, General," said an aide, pointing out that the withdrawal was orderly and without panic.

"Uneasy about Harrison!" retorted Rousseau. "Tom Harrison can whip all the militia in Alabama. But what shall I do with my poor wounded boys? We are a thousand miles from home."

Soon the Federal commander's entire force was moving north along the railroad toward Atlanta, passing through towns like Auburn, Opelika, and Rough and Ready, again tearing up track and burning government stores, but for the most part respecting civilian property. In Auburn, for instance, where troopers took over the hotel, they did little damage other than demanding food and forcing the harried kitchen staff to work overtime. "It would be better . . . to get the things and cook them up," the hotel owner told his employees, "rather than have the soldiers go in & hull everything about."

By the afternoon of July 19, learning from scouts that a large Rebel contingent was in their path, the raiders diverged from the railroad and continued north on a parallel route west of the Chattahoochee. The next day they left Alabama and entered Georgia, heading for Marietta rather than Atlanta.

The need for food and fresh mounts at this juncture was imperative, causing Rousseau and his men, who hitherto had behaved reasonably well, to invade private farms and homes and seize whatever they could. In Carrollton, for instance, William Bell lost the contents of his barns and smokehouse, and his mules and horse as well. His neighbor, Dr. James Thomason, suffered similarly. When Mrs. Thomason protested, a soldier told her that he and his comrades were starving. "This must have been true," she later conceded, "for they would stand around and eat raw bacon quite greedily."[11]

Rousseau reached the safety of Marietta on July 22. In twelve days of hard riding, he had covered some 400 miles, destroyed a critical 30 miles of track, and done damage in the tens of millions of dollars to Rebel supply depots and factories. In so doing, he lost no more than twelve men killed and wounded, and thirty-five taken prisoner. His exploit merits comparison with that of Benjamin Grierson, whose earlier raid through Mississippi caused similar consternation in the South. Here Rousseau fades from our story, back to the relative obscurity of Nashville and command of the District of Tennessee, but not before he had a memorable meeting with Sherman.

"That was well done, Rousseau, well done," said Cump, laughing over the plight of the Soccopatoy planter who had mistaken the raider for a Confederate officer. "But I didn't expect to see you back."

"Why not?"

"I expected you to tear up the road, but I thought [the Rebs] would gobble you up."

"You are a pretty fellow," said Rousseau, feigning indignation, "to send me off on such a trip."

"You proposed it yourself," Sherman rejoined with a smile. "Besides, I knew they wouldn't hurt you, and I thought you would pay for yourself."[12]

Rousseau's severing of the Atlanta & Montgomery, combined with Kenner Garrard's minor but successful expedition about the same time against the Georgia Railroad, left one major supply line into Atlanta: the Macon & Western. Sherman now devised a pincer movement to cut this last artery, instructing George Stoneman to take his own cavalry division and Garrard's (6,000 men) and gallop south from Decatur, Georgia, attacking the railroad from the east around Lovejoy's Station. Simultaneously, Edward McCook, with 2,800 troopers on a slightly longer route, was to skirt Atlanta and close in on the Macon & Western from the west. Together the bluecoats should have no trouble routing Joseph Wheeler's outmanned command and achieving their objective.

Before leaving on the raid, Stoneman approached Sherman with a proposition. Once he cut the railroad, might he not continue south to the Confederate prison camps in Macon and Andersonville, freeing the 30,000 Federals held there? Sherman acquiesced. "There was something most captivating in the idea. . . . I consented that after the defeat of Wheeler's cavalry . . . and breaking the road he might attempt it with his cavalry proper, sending that of General Garrard back."

Stoneman's 2,200-man column left Decatur early on July 27, with Kenner Garrard's 4,000 troopers close behind. Around 1 p.m. the two men met and briefly conferred, with Garrard being told, as a diversionary tactic, to advance to Flat Rock near the South River, some miles from the railroad. Stoneman would move forward on a separate route, join him there the next day, and together they would close on Lovejoy's Station.

But Stoneman never did make the agreed-upon rendezvous. Either he did not intend to go to Flat Rock from the get-go, or during the hours after he left Garrard, he chose to reinterpret his orders. One historian believes the latter was the case. "Thinking things over before [meeting] Garrard at Flat Rock [and joining] forces later with McCook . . . he decided these intermediate steps could be dispensed with. His ultimate goal was Andersonville and the liberation of the prisoners. This single act would embellish his career, so far branded a 'distinguished failure.' Why bother with the preliminaries? Garrard and McCook could take care of demolishing the Macon & Western."[13]

Whatever his thinking, Stoneman on the night of July 27–28, when he should have been pursuing a junction with Garrard, was plunging due south toward Macon and Andersonville, fully fifty miles *away* from Lovejoy's Station. Consider the debacle his decision created. What would have been an overpowering Union cavalry force, some 9,000 troopers, now was divided. McCook was approaching the railroad from the west, Garrard was bedding down at Flat Rock to the east, and in the days to come, neither would have any idea where Stoneman was or what he was doing.

Joseph Wheeler, meanwhile, alerted by his pickets, was taking full advantage of the enemy's disarray, racing in the darkness with a force of some 3,500 troopers toward Flat Rock to confront and lay down heavy fire on Garrard, even while sending three brigades of cavalry under Brigadier Alfred Iverson after Stoneman. The next morning, July 28, he confidently sent forward an officer to demand Garrard's surrender.

"My men do not know what surrender is, and I will not teach them such a lesson!" the Union commander indignantly replied. "Tell your general that as soon as I get ready I will *walk* out of here!"

Garrard was as good as his word. When the Rebels, underestimating the firing power of the opposition's Spencer repeaters, made a dismounted frontal assault, the Federals sent them reeling under a hail of lead. "We opened up on them with our Spencers," said Sergeant Ben Magee of the 72nd Indiana, "killed a few and captured others. They were taken so completely by surprise that many of them never even fired a single round."

Despite this temporary success, Garrard now thought it prudent that he disengage, and this he did during the course of the afternoon, falling back some five miles to Latimer's Crossroads. There he waited through the rest of the day and the next, anticipating another attack that never came. "We seem to be taking things rather coolly," said Magee. "We wonder why the Rebels do not pay us their respects."[14]

Garrard was also wondering, of course, where Stoneman was. By the morning of July 30, deciding he could wait for him no longer, he withdrew unimpeded, back to the main Union lines.

Wheeler during this time, learning that McCook was on his way to Lovejoy's Station, was disengaging himself, turning west to protect the railroad, leaving only a token force to watch Garrard.

Delayed by logistical problems, McCook was running a day behind schedule, not crossing the Chattahoochee until July 28, and then passing through Palmetto, where he paused briefly to upend sections of the Atlanta & Montgomery Railroad. Later, pushing down the Fayetteville Road at nightfall, he came upon a cavalryman's dream—600 Rebel supply wagons and teams. "We marched slowly through the camp," explained one Federal trooper, "the rear guard doing most of the work of killing the mules, burning wagons and taking prisoners. It was strange to hear, in the darkness . . . a mule groan when a saber was thrust into him."

Early the next morning, east of Fayetteville, the 1st (Union) Tennessee in McCook's van seized and destroyed another 500 supply wagons. "It was my fortune to capture the Chief Quartermaster of Gen. [William] Loring's corps . . . with his chest of [Confederate] funds," said Captain Moses Wiley. "I stuffed my pockets full. . . . When I would meet with an officer I was acquainted with, I would make him a present of a few thousand dollars by way of a joke."

Soon the Federals were galloping into Lovejoy's, where through the rest of the morning they wrecked the depot, derailed two freight trains, and tore up several miles of Macon & Western track, but did little permanent damage. Meanwhile, a puzzled McCook was keeping an eye peeled for dust clouds in the distance. Where, he wondered, were Stoneman and Garrard?

Shortly after midday, pickets advised him that horsemen were indeed approaching. They were not bluecoats, however, but Wheeler's command—and they were reportedly in great strength. McCook now felt he had no choice but to withdraw in haste. Thinking that militia and bushwhackers would be lying in wait if he went back the way he had come, he opted to return on the Panhandle Road, pass south of Fayetteville, and proceed to Newnan, a hospital town for wounded Rebels, and thereafter recross the Chattahoochee.

Wheeler's lead elements caught up with the Federal rear guard about 2 p.m., just as it was entering the Panhandle Road. There Colonel Joseph Dorr, in peacetime an editor of the *Dubuque Herald,* massed his battalion of the 8th Iowa and ordered a charge, trying to buy time until the 1st Tennessee and the rest of the 8th Iowa could form line of battle. He succeeded in doing so, but at a cost, taking a bullet in his right side and seeing two of his officers killed beside him.

Hour after hour, this tableau repeated itself. On every occasion that Wheeler's men drew too close, McCook's rear guard would turn, bloody their tormentors, and then fall back anew. "Up to [now] our raid had been a picnic . . . ," said Captain Wiley. "But from this time on it was not so funny."[15]

McCook had expected no opposition in Newnan, on whose outskirts he arrived on July 30, but such was not to be. Some 600 cavalrymen under General Philip Roddey, on their way to reinforce Hood in Atlanta, were in the town with the sick and wounded, and Roddey was spoiling for a fight. Hearing the Federals were coming, he leapt on his horse, "without taking time to saddle the animal or don his uniform," according to nurse Kate Cumming, and rallied both convalescents and attendants—anyone who could pick up and fire a weapon—behind makeshift barricades. "Evidently they expected to surprise [us]," said nurse Fanny Beers, "but, finding themselves opposed by a force whose numbers they were unable to estimate, they hastily retreated."[16]

The bluecoats veered to their right, making for the high ground above Brown's Mill. But here their plight worsened. The delay at Newnan had enabled Wheeler to close in on his prey. Together with Roddey's ragtag force, plus other units rushed to the neighborhood, the Rebels about 4 p.m. attacked McCook from several directions, all but surrounding him. Here it appears the Union commander lost his composure.

"What shall we do? What shall we do?" he asked aloud.

Colonel John Croxton of the 4th (Union) Kentucky, a Yale graduate, glared at his chief. "Why, god damn it, fight them! Fight them!" he shouted.

Soon the situation grew even more precarious. The last of the Federal reserves had been committed, and artillery shells and rifle ammunition were all but exhausted. McCook called together some key officers and declared he would have to surrender.

"You can all surrender and be damned," said Colonel James Brownlow of the 1st Tennessee, youngest son of the state's Union governor. "I am going out with my regiment."

"What will you do?" McCook asked.

"I can and will cut my way out. I would about as soon be killed in the attempt as to be captured and sent to Andersonville. . . . They treat us Southern soldiers worse in those prisons than they do you Northern soldiers."[17]

Following this exchange, McCook took heart, giving his brigades permission to cut their way out of the trap independently. Here Colonel Dorr of the 8th Iowa, continuing to serve despite his wound, was once again ordered to protect the withdrawal. This he did with stoic calm, permitting McCook and most of his command to reach and cross the Chattahoochee. In making their escape, however, the Federals lost some 1,200 of 3,000 men, their pack train, two cannon, and several hundred horses.

Further bad news would be coming from Stoneman, who reached the vicinity of Macon on July 30 and, to his surprise, found it well fortified and garrisoned by Georgia militia—augmented by hundreds of boys, old men, and the wounded—under General Howell Cobb.

"We went into line of battle in a swamp," said Campbell Tracy, a Rebel soldier who hobbled forward on crutches, ". . . all well posted behind trees. . . . The venerable Dr. [David] Wells, pastor of the First Presbyterian Church, was on my right; and . . . the Reverend J. E. Evans, Mulberry Street Methodist Church, was on my left. . . ." Stoneman's first advance was repulsed, as was the second. "On their third advance a Yank got a shot at me as I leaned against my tree . . . the shock knocking me off my crutches."

Wells and Evans ran to his aid, even as Tracy began doing some serious cussing. "Ain't you afraid to take the name of the Lord in vain," the Rev. Evans asked, "right here in the presence of death?" Just then a shell burst came close, and the clergymen dropped him and ran for the rear.

Tracy swore some more, and eventually his friends came back and helped him take cover. "You like to have broke my wounded leg! Don't you try that stunt again!" he berated them.

Stoneman by late afternoon found the Confederate resistance too strong, and broke off the fighting. Meanwhile in adjacent Camp Oglethorpe, where 1,500 Union officers were imprisoned, the inmates groaned in frustration as the sounds of battle died, realizing their comrades would not be freeing them.

The Union commander at this point was faced with a choice: swinging around Macon and moving on less fortified Andersonville, some sixty miles farther south, and then, whether or not he was successful in freeing the prisoners there, escaping westward into Alabama—or returning to the Union lines around Atlanta. "Had [he] pushed on . . . he could have done the Confederacy tremendous and irreparable damage, but he hesitated and lost," wrote a contemporary. "He realized that he had made a great mistake to ride away without McCook or Garrard. . . . [Now] he resolved to retrace his steps, and go back from whence he had come."[18]

In so doing, Stoneman the next day rode straight into the advance of the pursuing Alfred Iverson. (He did this despite the protests of his officers, some of whom felt, perhaps uncharitably, that their chief's need to take the shortest route back to Atlanta was dictated by his recurring hemorrhoids.) The meeting took place north of Macon at Sunshine Church, and instead of taking evasive action, Stoneman made a stand. It would be an unwise decision. The enemy slashed at his flanks, and threw his men into confusion. Like McCook at Brown's Mill, within hours he was all but surrounded; and running low on ammunition.

Here Stoneman decided to surrender. Silas Adams and his brigade of Union Kentuckians nonetheless managed to cut their way out of the trap, as did elements of the brigades of Horace Capron's and James Biddle's Midwesterners. Colonel Thomas Butler of the 5th Indiana, meanwhile, tried to change Stoneman's mind.

"I said to him that I would rather sacrifice the regiment in an effort to escape than to have them made prisoner and die in those prison pens," Butler stated, "and that our friends at home would honor me for it. His reply was 'that they would condemn me for it.'" Later Butler repeated his plea.

"Be a man and surrender," Stoneman said.

"You are a liar and a coward!" retorted his furious subordinate.

"Colonel Butler," said Stoneman, turning away, "I want you to understand I am in command."[19]

Iverson in due course accepted the Federal surrender. Stoneman, who suffered a total of 1,300 killed, wounded, and captured in his 2,200-man force, would never be disciplined, oddly enough, by Sherman or anyone else for disobeying orders and precipating the expedition's failure. Indeed, he never admitted to any fault at all. Muddying the waters further, he even suggested that he should be praised for surrendering, and that those who cut their way out of the trap at Sunshine Church should be vilified. From his cell in Macon he wrote, "I feel better satisfied with myself to be a prisoner, much as I hate it, than to be amongst those who owe their escape to considerations of self-preservation."[20]

With the main body of Confederates now under siege within Atlanta, John Bell Hood in early August decided to send Wheeler's cavalry into eastern and middle Tennessee, with an eye toward cutting the enemy's supply lines. "Wheeler and Iverson having thus thoroughly crippled the Federal cavalry," he said, referring to the Stoneman raid, "I determined to detach all the troops of that arm that I could possibly spare, and expedite them . . . against Sherman's railroad to Nashville . . . and also that General Forrest be ordered . . . into Tennessee for the same object." (Forrest's June-August operations will be discussed in the next chapter.)

Hood would be much criticized for this order, because he was depriving himself of the cavalry's eyes and ears at a critical time. "I could not have asked for anything better," Sherman chortled. But the Rebel general was facing a dilemma. Without the strength to repel his opponents, he felt he had little choice but to go after their food and ordnance.[21]

Wheeler left Covington, Georgia, with 4,000 troopers on August 10, hitting the railroad north of Marietta, again at Calhoun, and again south of Dalton. Wrote a Wheeler biographer: "Dalton now being reinforced by cavalry and infantry, [he] wasted no time in a siege of the place. Instead he instituted a game of 'fox and goose' with [Union General James] Steedman. Riding away from Dalton, Wheeler made a demonstration toward Chattanooga, Steedman in close pursuit. Having thus drawn the Federals away . . . he faced his men about and rode toward Dalton. Again Steedman took up the pursuit. For three days this game was kept going, while the railroad was left unrepaired."

Wheeler now proceeded to Tennessee, leaving detachments along the way with instructions to tear up rails every night on a continuing basis. He demonstrated against Cleveland, captured Athens, and tore up more track at Loudon. Skirting Knoxville, he turned west into middle Tennessee, routing a small Union garrison at McMinnville on August 29 and breaking rail and telegraph communication with Murfreesboro. Later he moved still farther north to Nashville but did not attack, knowing it was too well defended.

Now he fled southward, galloping through Franklin and Columbia with the enemy on his heels. On September 10 he crossed the Tennessee River and reached safety in Tuscumbia, Alabama. Despite his best efforts he had achieved little, the enemy laying down new track as fast as he had torn it up. "The raid had no significant effect on Sherman's operations," wrote one expert in disapproval, "other than to remove the Confederate cavalry from his front and facilitate his maneuvering to turn Hood."[22]

In truth, Wheeler's absence did enable another major Union expedition against Hood's rear. On August 18 our old friend Judson Kilpatrick, recovered from a wound he had incurred at the start of the Atlanta Campaign, was sent by Sherman to Jonesboro, Georgia, in a second attempt to cut the Macon & Western. Besides his own division, he had with him two of Garrard's brigades—in all, some 4,500 men.

"Will the raid succeed?" Sherman had asked.

"It [is] not only possible," replied Kilpatrick, who never lacked for confidence, "but comparatively easy."

"Kilpatrick would display so much zeal and activity," Sherman would enthuse, "that I was attracted to him at once."[23]

Brushing aside minor resistance en route, the Federal column arrived at Jonesboro about 4 p.m. the next day. In short order, Kilpatrick's horse artillery scattered the defenders, and his men set about ripping up track.

Through the ensuing darkness they toiled, and at first it appeared they would be successful in their mission. "It was a wild night," one trooper remembered, ". . . the sky lit up with burning timbers . . . the continuous bang of carbines, the galloping of staff officers . . . the terrified citizens peering out of their windows."

Kilpatrick was elated. "Damn the Southern Confederacy!" he yelled as he watched the work, waving his hat exuberantly. "I can ride right through it!"

Hearing him, Lieutenant Joseph Hedges of the 4th Regulars urged caution. "We may sing a different tune tomorrow," he said.

"What's that, my man?" Kilpatrick asked sharply.

"When infantry comes down from Atlanta, we will not have it all our own way."

"We will not fight their infantry—we will run away from it!" Kilpatrick insisted. "But we can lick hell out of their cavalry!"[24]

The Rebel infantry did not wait for the next morning, instead coming into the Jonesboro area on boxcars and attacking about 11 p.m. Within hours it became apparent their weight could not be resisted. Kilpatrick then left the depot, moving east, but instead of turning north and withdrawing, he turned south, aiming to resume his destruction of the railroad at Lovejoy's Station.

When he reached the depot about 10 a.m. on August 20, however, he quickly learned that the Rebels, again using rolling stock, had anticipated his maneuver and were lying in wait. His skirmishers were sent reeling, and with the arrival of enemy cavalry, he soon was caught in a trap.

"A fierce battle seemed now to be going on in every direction, but which was the front or main point I could not for the life of me tell," said Lieutenant William Webb, leading a battalion of the 4th Regulars. "Artillery and musketry were pouring their deadly missiles into our front, rear and both flanks. I could find for a moment no one to report to, and was uncertain and bewildered as to what I should do with my handful of men."

Just then a Kilpatrick aide galloped up and directed him to pile up some fence rails on a nearby hill and get behind them for cover.

"Which way shall I face?"

"Suit yourself," the aide yelled as he rushed away.

Though the situation was dire, Kilpatrick had no intention of surrendering like Stoneman, or of allowing his regiments and brigades, like McCook, to slash their way out independently. His command, by God, had gone into the fight together, and it would escape together! Sometime in the afternoon, he called for Colonel Robert Minty, who led Garrard's 1st Brigade.

"We are surrounded," he said. "You know what is in our front; [William] Jackson with 5,000 cavalry is in rear of our left, and Pat Cleburne with 10,000 infantry is closing on our right. . . . You will form [battle] line on the right. . . . Colonel [Eli] Murray will form on the left; you will charge simultaneously."

Minty studied the ground, an open field crisscrossed with several gullies and fences. "If it were left to me," he said, "I would never charge in line over this ground. When we strike the enemy, if we ever do so, it will be a thin, wavering blow that will amount to nothing."

"How, then, would you charge?" Kilpatrick asked.

"In column, sir. Our momentum would be like that of a railroad [train] where we strike. Something has to give."

Kilpatrick, to his credit, accepted the advice. "Form in any way you please," he directed.[25]

With the 4th Regulars, 4th Michigan, and 7th Pennsylvania side by side in column of fours, Minty fell on Rebel Brigadier Lawrence Sullivan Ross's Texans with irresistible force, opening a gaping hole in the enemy's cordon. In charge after charge, the rest of the Federals followed, each unit in turn relieving the one in front and serving as a rear guard. By sundown the bluecoats were fleeing east to McDonough and then, the next day, proceeding northeast to Peachstone Shoals.

Kilpatrick and his tired, bedraggled troopers arrived in Decatur the morning of August 22, having lost no more than 300 men in their narrow escape. "I destroyed three miles of the road about Jonesboro," he reported, "and broke pieces for about ten miles more, enough to disable the road for ten days." This latter estimate, of course, was one of Kilpatrick's many big lies. Even as he rode into Decatur, the road was repaired, and supply trains were rolling into Atlanta from the South, as their cheery whistles attested. "Two days after his return," a Union general would marvel, "one would hardly [know] that he had been defeated at all."

Sherman eventually would sever the Macon & Western, but with infantry not cavalry, and Hood would abandon Atlanta, leaving the city on September 1. Soon Kilpatrick, far better known for his vigor than his victories, would be named by Cump as his chief of cavalry. Only when his performance is compared to that of Stoneman, McCook, and Garrard (the capable Major General Rousseau being needed in Nashville) can the case for his promotion be made. "I know Kilpatrick is a hell of a damn fool,"

Sherman would admit, "but I want just that sort of man to command my cavalry." Then he compounded the slur. "If I used such language, it [was] because that was what a good many of [my] officers were in the habit of [saying]."[26]

Sherman had many gifted cavalry officers at the regimental and brigade level, such as the aforementioned Colonel Minty. Why he did not jump them to higher rank, in view of the woeful showing of many of his key subordinates in the Atlanta Campaign, is one of the war's mysteries. Perhaps he was hamstrung by Army politics, perhaps by interference from Washington. The fact remains that his cavalry, on the whole, was not well led.

FIVE

THE WEST, JUNE-AUGUST: FORREST IN MISSISSIPPI AND TENNESSEE

While the preceding events were taking place in Georgia, Nathan Forrest remained a persistent irritant in northern Mississippi and western Tennessee—so much so that in early June some 8,000 Federal troops and eighteen cannon were dispatched from Memphis to bring him to bay. They were led by Brigadier Samuel D. Sturgis, a West Pointer whose previous commands in the West had been relatively untaxing. Sturgis's troops consisted of 3,000 cavalry under Benjamin Grierson and 5,000 infantry under Colonel William McMillen.

Forrest had 4,800 troopers and twelve guns to oppose this force, principally the division of Abraham Buford—the division of James Chalmers having been taken from him for duty in Alabama. Buford's brigades consisted of Hylan Lyons's Kentuckians, W. A. Johnson's Alabamians, Edward Rucker's Mississippians, and Tyree Bell's Tennesseans. With 2,800 men, Bell's unit was by far the largest.

The two sides would meet near Brice's Crossroads, a dozen miles west of Ripley, Mississippi, country that Forrest knew well. Despite the odds against him, he was, as usual, sanguine that he would prevail. "I know [the enemy] greatly outnumber the troops I have at hand," he told Colonel

Rucker, "but the road along which they will march is narrow and muddy; they will make slow progress. The country is densely wooded and the undergrowth so heavy that when we strike them they will not know how few men we have. Their cavalry will move out ahead of the infantry, and should reach the crossroads three hours in advance. We can whip their cavalry in that time. As soon as the fight opens they will send back to have the infantry hurried up. It is going to be hot as hell, and coming on a run for five or six miles . . . their infantry will be so tired we will ride right over them. . . . I will go ahead with Lyon and the escort and open the fight."[1]

The skirmishing with Grierson's cavalry began about 9 a.m. on June 10, but it was not until two hours later that three of the Rebel brigades—from left to right, Rucker, Lyons, and Johnson—were dismounted and in line of battle west of the crossroads. Though Bell's large command, together with John Morton's artillery, was not yet up, Forrest characteristically went on the attack.

Rucker's 7th Tennessee took the lead, bursting from a thicket and engaging the 7th Indiana as it crouched behind a rail fence. "The fire was so terrific that the regiment staggered for a moment," said one Tennessean, and some of the men fell flat upon the earth for protection." Nonetheless, the Confederates persevered. "So close was this struggle that guns fired were not reloaded, but used as clubs; and pistols were brought into play, while the two lines struggled with the ferocity of wild beasts."

For the combatants, the fighting was mean and personal. "Sergeant John D. Huhn . . . came face to face with a Federal, presented his gun, and ordered the Union soldier to throw his weapon down. Several Federal soldiers rushed to [help] their comrade. With clubbed guns they broke Sergeant Huhn's arm and struck him over the head until he fell senseless. Privates Lauderdale and Maclin . . . ran to his aid, shot two of his stout-hearted assailants, and drove the others away."[2]

The charge cracked the 7th Indiana's line, exposing the rest of the bluecoats to enfilading fire and necessitating a three-quarter-mile withdrawal to reform. Grierson, believing he was badly outnumbered, now sent a courier back to McMillen, urging him to rush the infantry forward.

Not until 1:30 p.m. did the foot soldiers arrive on the scene, after double-quicking for five miles, and when they arrived they were in deplorable condition. "One-third of my men," said Lieutenant Colonel George Clarke of the 113th Illinois, "were so completely exhausted as to be scarce able to stand; several were sunstruck." Grierson, his troopers running out of ammunition, at this juncture again fell back, retiring behind the infantry to regroup and refit.

Everything was going as Forrest had foreseen. Not only had the enemy weakened himself through clumsy maneuvering, but Bell's brigade now was on hand after a twenty-five-mile gallop, bringing the Rebels to full strength, and John Morton's cannon likewise were rolling into the lines.

Here Forrest, giving the Federal infantry little time to rest, increased the pressure. First he sent forward Morton, unscreened by skirmishers, to decimate the bluecoats with double-shotted cannister at point-blank range. Then, even as Lyon and Johnson under Buford advanced on the right, he hurled Bell into the fray on Rucker's left, intent on turning the Federal flank. To support this tactic, he also dispatched Colonel C. R. Barteau's 2nd Tennessee even farther on the left, with orders to swing wide and get in the enemy's rear.

Pistol in hand, he next proceeded with his escort into the midst of the fighting. "If we moved too slow he would curse, then praise, then threaten to shoot us himself if we were so afraid the [enemy] might hit us," said one trooper. ". . . The Yanks espied him, and then what a deluge of . . . ricochet shots plowed up the ground. . . . I expected every moment to see Forrest and horse torn into fragments."[3]

With the lines surging back and forth in charge and countercharge, Barteau's 2nd Tennessee tipped the balance about 4 p.m. "I succeeded in reaching the Federal rear just as the fighting seemed heaviest in front," he said. "I at once deployed my men . . . had my bugler ride up and down sounding the charge at different points, and kept up as big a show as I could."

The Federals, believing themselves trapped, fell back in a panic. "Order gave way to confusion," said General Sturgis. ". . . The army drifted toward the rear and was beyond control. The road became crowded and jammed with troops; wagons and artillery sank into the deep mud." Meanwhile Morton, pushing his cannon forward by hand, continued his deadly fire. "The havoc was ghastly," reported Forrest's campaign historians, "and . . . as the enemy crowded back along the Ripley Road, toward Tishomingo Creek, the bridge over which, still standing, was blocked by wagons . . . [many] were killed or wounded. . . . Finding their way thus barred, the enemy rushed into the creek on both sides of the bridge; but as they emerged from the water . . . the Confederate artillery played upon them for half a mile, killing or disabling large numbers."[4]

———

Forrest would keep crowding the fleeing Federals through the evening and into the night, adding to the damage. Almost 2,300 of 8,000 Union troops would be lost, including all the enemy's artillery, wagons, and ammunition. Sturgis was to argue the case that Nathan had 15,000 to 20,000 men—not 4,800, which was the real figure—but Sherman knew the true reason for the rout. "Forrest is the very devil," he wrote Secretary of War Edwin Stanton, "and I think he has got some of our troops under cower."

The deeper he went into the South, Sherman realized, the more vulnerable he was to the Rebel cavalryman's raids on his supply lines. Soon he would give the task of containing him to General Andrew Jackson Smith, a tough, seasoned veteran of the Trans-Mississippi theater. "I will order [him] to make up a force and go out and follow Forrest to the death," he said, "if it costs 10,000 lives and breaks the Treasury. There never will be peace in Tennessee until Forrest is dead."[5]

Smith's expedition would consist of 14,000 men—11,000 infantry, the rest cavalry—and twenty guns. It left La Grange, Tennessee, in late June, burning and pillaging as it moved South, and by July 13 was at Harrisburg near Tupelo, Mississippi, well dug-in and, in effect, daring the Rebels to attack. Opposing Smith was Forrest with almost 10,000 men, mostly cavalry, under the command of Stephen D. Lee (no relation to the Virginia Lees). That worthy, who technically headed all the forces in the area, including horse soldiers, had just been named lieutenant general, a development that may have rankled Major General Forrest. Though Lee asked the Tennessean to take field command, he demurred, citing illness. While it was true that Forrest had pushed himself to the point his body was rebelling—he was plagued with boils—the real reason for his begging-off seems to have been disagreement with Lee's tactics for the upcoming battle. Stephen Lee, believing he had to take on Andrew Jackson Smith as soon as possible, was insisting on a head-on attack against a well-fortified position. Forrest wanted to wait out the Union general, cut off his supplies, and then, when he vacated his lines, take him in a series of flanking attacks.

To back up his intuition, Nathan initiated a daring personal reconnaissance on the night of the 13th, taking an aide, Lieutenant Samuel Donelson, and riding into the enemy stronghold. Recounted one of his men: "[They] soon found themselves among the Union wagons and teams. The . . . darkness concealed the Confederate uniforms and, keeping well away from the campfires, the two . . . officers rode through nearly every portion of the enemy's camp." What Forrest saw confirmed his opinion: too many men would die taking on Smith frontally.

Just as he and Donelson were taking their leave, some sentries challenged them. "Riding directly up to these men, General Forrest, affecting intense anger, said, 'How dare you halt your commanding officer?'—and, without further remark, put spurs to his horse . . . quickly followed by Lieutenant Donelson." Later, safe in his own camp, he told the story amid whoops and laughter, saying that "a bullet might have done him good, as it might have opened one of his boils, which would have been a relief."[6]

Though Forrest made a second plea that the battle be delayed, Lee would not be deterred. Early the next day the Confederates formed up for the assault. In the first line, Abraham Buford's division with Tyree Bell and Hinchie Mabry was on the left, with Edward Crossland (filling in for Lyons, who was leading the infantry) holding the center, joined by Lee. Philip Roddey (still two weeks away from taking on McCook south of Atlanta) was on the right, joined by Forrest and his escort.

Chalmers's division—now consisting of Edward Rucker and McCulloch—formed the second line, Lyons with the infantry the third.

Lee had ordered a simultaneous attack—Bell, Mabry, Crossland, and Roddey advancing in unison—but such was not to be. "It so happened that [Crossland's] Kentucky brigade debouched into the open space considerably [ahead] of Bell and Mabry," wrote a contemporary historian, "and these gallant spirits, believing themselves invincible when Forrest was on the field, eager to close in upon the enemy in hand-to-hand combat, could not be restrained." Explained Crossland: "Raising a shout, they charged forward. . . . Within two hundred yards, the enemy suddenly opened an enfilading fire from both flanks." His troopers were decimated.

Seeing Crossland's plight, Buford threw Mabry's Mississipians and Bell's Tennesseans into the fray, hoping to ease the pressure on him. Mabry's fate, however, was equally horrific. "Within three hundred yards of the works, a terrific fire of small arms was opened upon me. I ordered a charge, but the heat was so intense and the distance so great that some men and officers fell exhausted . . . while the fire . . . was so heavy and well-directed that many were killed and wounded, leaving my line almost like a line of skirmishers."[7]

Bell's men likewise fell in droves. All told, Buford's three brigades lost one-third of their number in casualties.

Here Forrest had a choice: to send Roddey's troopers on the right forward, almost surely sealing their doom as well, or to keep them back to fight another day. He elected the latter course. Crossland, understandably, would resent this decision. "[The] failure of Roddey's division to advance, and thus draw the fire of the enemy on my right flank, was fatal to my men. . . . They were literally mowed down."[8]

Uncaring for his personal safety, however, Forrest now dashed into Crossland's lines, seizing a battle flag, reassuring the troops, and restoring a semblance of order. Soon a general withdrawal was sounded, with the Confederates falling back to the positions held by Chalmers and Lyons.

Thus the day passed, with the Rebels expecting Smith to follow up on his triumph, and the Union general staying in his Harrisburg works, content with the damage he had wrought. That evening Stephen Lee held a council of war. Forrest, described by one soldier as being "so mad he stunk like a pole-cat," at first declined to attend. A second message made his appearance mandatory.

"We are in a bad fix," Lee told him.

"We are in a hell of fix," replied Forrest, fuming over what he believed were senseless losses. Despite his fearsome repute he held dear the lives of his troopers. "He knew both men and horses; knew how to treat them; knew the full measure of the capacity of each; [knew] the utmost level of endurance," an aide would say.

The other officers present, who knew the cavalryman's black moods, edged away.

"General Forrest," persisted Lee, "have you any ideas?"

"I've always got ideas," erupted Forrest, perennially skeptical of professional soldiers, "and I tell you one thing, General Lee, if I knew as much about West Point tactics as you, the Yankees would whip hell out of me every day! I've got five hundred empty saddles and nothing to show for them!"

Lee took this bit of insubordination calmly, turning the talk to other matters. He was a good officer, and he had made a mistake. There was no point compounding it, he must have felt, by quarreling with his most valuable subordinate.[9]

The next morning, much to the Confederates' surprise, the situation changed for the better. Electing not to continue the battle, Smith abruptly fell back from Harrisburg and retreated whence he had come, claiming he was running low both on food and ammunition. "My troops were so exhausted with the heat, fatigue and short rations that it was not possible to press them farther," he would report. "It became a matter of necessity to return."[10]

Though the bloodied Rebels organized a pursuit, it was more to keep track of Smith's whereabouts than to bring on another fight. During the chase Forrest suffered a minor but painful foot wound, and was reduced to riding in a horse and buggy. There he persisted in brooding about his casualties—and no wonder. Some 1,300 men had been lost in killed and wounded, three of his brigade commanders had been severely wounded, and almost all of his colonels killed or wounded. Harrisburg had been a humbling experience.

In early August, Andrew Jackson Smith made a second foray into Mississippi, this time with an even larger force: 20,000 men, mostly infantry. At this juncture, Forrest, who with the departure of Stephen Lee to the Atlanta defenses was in sole field command, had no more than 5,000 troopers to block the enemy's progress. Soon it became apparent that the Federals were crossing the Tallahatchie and making for Oxford, a town some forty-five miles west of the area where the earlier battle had been fought. There the two sides faced each other for a rainy ten days, while Smith accumulated supplies and Forrest pondered his next move.

Knowing it would be suicide to take on the enemy directly, Nathan decided on a bold diversion, one that would take him behind Smith's lines and into Union-occupied Memphis. Leaving James Chalmers behind to cope with the enemy as best he could, he left Oxford with 2,000 troopers on the night of August 18 and quickly galloped west and then north, with Smith none the wiser.

Forrest's column—now 1,500 men because of horses that had broken down during the enforced march, leaving their riders without mounts—arrived outside Memphis at 3 a.m. on August 21. Forrest had no thoughts of taking on the 5,000-man garrison in any substantial way. Instead his plans called for capturing several high-ranking officers, whom informants had told him were lodging in hotels and private houses, and creating a panic that would force Smith's recall.

Captain William Forrest with forty picked men was to take the lead, dealing with the enemy's pickets and racing to the Gayoso Hotel, where Major General Stephen Hurlbut, who led the 16th Corps, was staying. Colonel Thomas Logwood, close behind, was to secure the intersection at Main and Shelby Streets, as well as the wharf on the Mississippi. Lieutenant Colonel Jesse Forrest was to gallop into Union Street, where Major

General Cadwallader Washburn, head of the West Tennessee Department, had his headquarters. Other Rebel units were dispatched elsewhere, while Forrest himself, along with elements of Tyree Bell's brigade, remained in the city's suburbs, ready to cover the expedition's withdrawal.

Just before dawn, Captain Forrest and his detachment encountered a Yankee sentry.

"Who goes there?"

"A detachment of the 12th Missouri, with Rebel prisoners," Forrest replied.

"Dismount and come forward alone on foot."

Forrest instead spurred forward, drew his revolver, and within seconds clubbed the sentry to the ground. Soon he and his men were past the pickets and galloping up to the Gayoso, where without dismounting he cantered into the lobby. *Where is Hurlbut?* he demanded of the stunned clerk.

Hurlbut was not in the hotel that night, having accepted the hospitality of a friend. But other Union officers were not so fortunate. Billy Forrest's men ran through the halls, bursting open doors, creating havoc. Several Federal officers were killed while trying to resist; many others were captured.

Colonel Logwood, meanwhile, was clattering through the streets, scattering small groups of surprised Yankees in one meeting after another and rousing the residents. "Women and children . . . were shouting and clapping their hands as they recognized the muddy Rebels," said one Confederate. "Memphis was the home of many of Forrest's daredevil riders, and as they dashed by, women young and old . . . threw open their doors and windows and ran forth with cheers."[11]

Colonel Jesse Forrest, whose task it was to capture General Washburn, arrived at his Union Street digs just minutes before the latter, still in his nightclothes, fled through the back alleys to the safety of the garrison's lines. Washburn, it seems, had been roused from slumber by one of the few vigilant bluecoats, Colonel Starr of the 6th Illinois Cavalry. Instead Jesse had to settle for his quarry's uniform and personal effects, together with a handful of Washburn's aides.

With the enemy regrouping, the Rebels in early morning began to withdraw from the city, moving south toward Hernando, Mississippi. Here Colonel Starr, leading the pursuit, was mortally wounded in hand-to-hand combat with Nathan Forrest, who personally was directing the rear guard. "Colonel Starr was no more in the hands of General Forrest than a butterfly would be in the claws of an eagle," said a Confederate officer. "Forrest ran his saber entirely through his body."[12]

Though Hurlbut and Washburn escaped, the raid achieved its purpose. Smith down in Oxford was ordered to get back to Memphis posthaste, as the fire-breathing cavalryman might return at any time. "So widespread was the feeling of panic in the city," a contemporary historian said, "that two days after Forrest had left, and in fact when he was well beyond the Tallahatchie, a stampede was caused by the rumor that he was returning in force."

From Hernando, Nathan would report: "I attacked Memphis at 4 o'clock this morning, driving the enemy to his fortifications. We killed and captured four hundred, taking their entire camp, with about three hundred horses and mules. Washburn and staff escaped in the darkness of the early morning, Washburn leaving his clothes behind."

Later, under flag of truce, he would send Washburn back his dress uniform, possibly to show him that, off the field of battle, he could be as chivalrous as any cavalier. Not to be outdone, Washburn called in Nathan's prewar Memphis tailor, placed a rush order, and soon thereafter gifted his foe with a resplendent dress uniform of his own—for which, we are told, he was most grateful.[13]

SIX
* * * *

THE EAST: MAY-JULY: MOSBY STEPS UP HIS RAIDS

While Sherman in early May was beginning his movement toward Atlanta, General-in-Chief Ulysses S. Grant in the East was embarking on the Overland Campaign, sending his 120,000-man army into the Wilderness. In the days that followed, he would push south against Robert E. Lee in a series of bloody battles to Spotsylvania, the North Anna River, and Cold Harbor, all with the ultimate goal of taking Richmond. Simultaneously he would send thousands of troops west into the Shenandoah Valley, hoping once and for all to pacify that region and deny Lee its bountiful livestock and crops.

Soon the Federals would get bogged down in both these efforts, becoming embroiled in a lengthy siege of Richmond and Petersburg, and enduring in the short term some surprising reversals in the Shenandoah.

Contributing greatly to the enemy's problems during this May-July period were John Mosby and his Rangers, still at any one time no more than 200 to 300 strong, but making an impact far beyond their numbers. From their base east of the Blue Ridge, they continued to harass the enemy's supply lines to Richmond almost at will. Meanwhile, when they moved west into the Shenandoah, they created equal consternation. Union cavalry trying to keep order in Mosby's Confederacy, wrote one of his biographers, "saw outlined in the sky silhouettes of mysterious riders . . . sitting, motionless, on the surrounding hills. It was useless to fire on the Rebels because they were just out of range. They were at home and equally familiar with every byway."

The interlopers not only had to steel themselves again the threat of sniper fire—"A horse or a man would fall, wounded or dead, creating the stress of constant alert"—but also of capture. "[They] knew that Mosby's men were watching. . . . When a horse staggered or broke down and a man fell behind, he was gobbled up."[1]

The Rebel leader at this juncture had four companies in his command. Companies A and D, under Joseph Nelson and Richard Montjoy, respectively, primarily were charged with pestering Grant's rear as he rolled south; companies B and C, under Adolphus "Dolly" Richards and William Chapman, usually operated in the Shenandoah. These men, it seems, were all Mosby's mirror images—young, smart, and fearless—well suited to conduct quick, slashing raids and ambushes.

On the night of May 8, for instance, Mosby with fifty troopers from Nelson's and Montjoy's group descended on a train of twenty wagons as it left Belle Plain, Grant's supply base on the Potomac, and hastily diverted half of them onto a side road.

"Who the hell has stopped these wagons?" demanded a Union officer, not thinking there was a Confederate anywhere in the vicinity.

"Colonel Mosby," said Sergeant Ben Palmer, pointing his revolver in the man's face. Soon the horses and mules were unhitched and led away, the wagons looted, with the rest of the train none the wiser.[2]

Companies under Chapman and Richards, meanwhile, were in the Shenandoah. There on May 9, Chapman scattered the guards and looted a wagon train near Berryville. For his part, Richards that night near Westchester took on a unit of the 21st New York, capturing a dozen men in the van before retreating.

Further such actions ensued, with one of the more notable occurring on the 22nd at Guard Hill, near Front Royal in the valley. There Lieutenant Sam Chapman, Mosby's adjutant, led an attack at dawn on 200 sleeping Yankees, capturing only a handful but putting the rest to flight and seizing about seventy-five horses. Union Captain Michael Auer, who was in charge of the pickets but who had been ailing and staying at a nearby farmhouse, now rode onto the scene. Not quite knowing what was going on, he swiftly became a prisoner.

"What the hell does all this fuss mean!" he shouted.

"It means Mosby's got you," rejoined a smiling Sam Chapman.

Auer was stunned. A dutiful and courageous officer who had been wounded in the foot when serving in the infantry at Antietam, he had been medically discharged, but had reenlisted in the cavalry, only to be wounded again three months before in a skirmish with the Rangers.

"Well this beats hell, don't it?" he remarked.[3]

The Federals were not entirely helpless, of course. They continued to strike where they could, riding up to farms and private houses and harshly interrogating any male of service age. In this manner several dozen of Mosby's men were arrested in May and June, most by his chief opponent, Colonel Charles Russell Lowell. One such prisoner was Charles Beavers, whom Lowell accused, rightly as it turned out, of violating the amnesty he had been granted by taking a loyalty oath. Beavers was hung on the spot.

By late June, nonetheless, Mosby still had some 260 men reporting for duty, and a welcome acquisition as well: his first cannon, a 12-pound howitzer sent to him from Richmond. Putting the artillery piece to good use, he captured Duffield's Station on the Baltimore & Ohio Railroad, near Harpers Ferry, on the 29th and, before burning it, waited fruitlessly for an incoming train he could shell and board. He then returned to his base in Fauquier County.

Robert E. Lee in Richmond meantime would send Jubal Early with 10,000 seasoned infantry into the Shenandoah, where he would oust the Federals and later proceed down the valley to cross the Potomac and threaten Washington. "On July 4, hearing of General Early's movement [against Washington]," said Mosby, ". . . I moved with my command east of the Blue Ridge for the purpose of cooperating with him and crossed the [river] at Point of Rocks, driving out the garrison (250 men, strongly fortified). . . . I thought the best service I could render would be to sever all communication both by railroad and telegraph between that point and Washington, which I did, keeping it suspended for two days."[4]

What Mosby did not mention was that, in the aftermath of the fight, in which the howitzer again was used to advantage, his men went through the stores and transport boats in and around Point of Rocks like so many Huns. Liquor, cigars, and food delicacies, even ribbons, bonnets, and bolts of cloth soon were stuffed into saddlebags or draped around sweaty bodies, giving the column, for the nonce, a decidedly nonmilitary appearance.

The next day, Mosby continued his cutting of the Union communication lines, even while loading the booty into wagons and sending it back to his base. Then on July 6, just before recrossing the Potomac, he learned that a Yankee cavalry force was at Leesburg. "I immediately hastened to meet them," he said. "At Leesburg I heard that they had gone on toward Aldie, and I accordingly moved . . . to intercept them . . . meeting them at Mount Zion Church."

The enemy were some 150 men of the 13th New York and 2nd Massachusetts, Lowell's brigade, under the command of Major William H. Forbes, a tough fighter and a member of a prominent Boston family. Mosby had a slightly larger force and a cannon as well, and he intended to show no mercy.

Skirting the Federals while they were taking a lengthy break to feed their mounts, he set up an ambush near the church, placing the gun on a crest and packing the road with his men in column of fours. Forbes, resuming his march, soon was alerted to their presence by his advance guard. He drew up his command in line of battle, confident his Spencer repeaters gave him the firepower to repel any attack. He had not, however, taken into account Mosby's howitzer.

One cannon shot was all it took to create bedlam among Forbes's horse soldiers, their mounts rearing and bolting, defying all attempts to maintain order. During these minutes of chaos, Mosby sounded the charge, hurling his troopers forward in a rare head-on assault. "Mosby and his Rangers [instantly] were upon us," said one Yankee, "swooping down like Indians, yelling like fiends, discharging their pistols with a fearful rapidity." Remembered Ranger John Munson: "We swept into their line like a hurricane, each man with a drawn six-shooter."

Forbes tried desperately to rally his men. "Form in the woods! Form in the woods!" he cried out again and again.

"It was a mass of struggling, cursing maniacs," said Munson, each striving to slay his antagonist."[5]

Seeing Mosby in the midst of the fray, Forbes spurred his horse toward him, thrusting forward with his saber. But Thomas Richards, Dolly's brother, wheeled his mount between them, taking the blade in his shoulder and simultaneously firing his revolver in Forbes's face. The bullet went awry, killing the horse instead, and pinning its rider underneath as it crashed to the ground.

When the fighting finally stopped, Mosby had one killed and seven wounded. The Federals, on the other hand, had forty-one killed and wounded, and fifty-five captured, including Forbes—almost three-quarters of the command. Out of this bitter clash, ironically, would be born a close relationship, with the two men becoming fast postwar friends.

Mosby's subsequent efforts to coordinate with Early in the valley would not always run smoothly. Jubal was a difficult, contumacious man, who did things his own way, and he made it obvious—in the case of a partisan—that like Fitzhugh Lee the previous year, he wanted little contact with the Rangers. But Mosby persisted through July in his small-size, hit-and-run attacks wherever he saw a Federal weakness, tying up sizable numbers of the enemy in defensive postures. To him much credit should be given for facilitating Early's July 11–12 advance on Washington and his July 24 triumph at 2nd Kernstown.

Mosby's repute among Southern sympathizers now swelled the ranks of volunteers, making it necessary for him to create a fifth Ranger unit, Company E, and name Samuel Chapman, a brother of William and a former divinity student, as its captain. Mosby would need all of these troopers, and all of his skills, in the difficult months in and around the Shenandoah that lay ahead.

SEVEN

THE EAST, MAY 11: YELLOW
TAVERN

When General-in-Chief Ulysses S. Grant moved East to supervise the
Overland Campaign against Robert E. Lee and the Army of Northern Virginia, he left the command structure of the Union forces in the West, now
under William Tecumseh Sherman, virtually intact. One of the few officers Grant brought with him was Major General Philip Sheridan, an infantryman who had distinguished himself in fights in Kentucky and
Tennessee, and who had caught his attention leading the charge up Missionary Ridge at Chattanooga. Grant named the bellicose Sheridan the
Army of the Potomac's chief of cavalry, replacing the adequate but less aggressive Alfred Pleasanton.

From the start, as the Federals during May pushed south through the
Wilderness and Spotsylvania, the newcomer chafed at taking orders from
George Meade, the victor at Gettysburg, who under Grant's watchful eye
remained head of the Army of the Potomac. Part of Sheridan's problem
was a fundamental disagreement with Meade as to how the cavalry
should be used, with the former thinking he should be allowed to hit the
enemy whenever and wherever opportunity presented, and the latter insisting the mounted branch stay close at home, guarding wagon trains and
doing reconnaissance.

The relationship between the two men worsened when Sheridan did not handle his command properly during the Wilderness fighting, allowing some of his troopers to be cut off and nearly captured, and when Meade, during the Spotsylvania fighting, countermanded some of his orders, thereby botching a promising operation.

In the aftermath of the Spotsylvania affair, on May 8, the two officers got into an expletive-filled argument. "Meade was possessed of an excitable temper which under irritating circumstances became almost ungovernable," said a headquarters aide. "He had worked himself in a towering rage . . . and when Sheridan appeared [he] went at him hammer and tongs, accusing him of blunders." Little Phil—he was no more than five-feet-five, weighing 115 pounds—was equally fiery, and "smarting under the belief that he was being unjustly treated, all the hotspur in his nature was aroused." He shouted at Meade that he had created the problem himself, by canceling his orders without cause, and "declared with great warmth he would not command the cavalry any longer under such conditions, and said that if he could have matters his own way he would concentrate the cavalry, move out in force against [Jeb] Stuart's command, and whip it."

Meade soon afterward reported the incident to Grant, including Sheridan's wish to leave the lines and take on Stuart.

"Did Sheridan say that?" said Grant disingenuously, ignoring his protégé's near insubordination. "Well, he generally knows what he is talking about. Let him start right out and do it."[1]

The thirty-three-year-old Sheridan, whose Irish immigrant parents had settled in Somerset, Ohio, when he was an infant, seemed born for warfare. Direct, uncomplicated, brooking no nonsense, he saw the battlefield as a checkerboard, where the moves must be simple and fast. Far from being rash, however, he believed in ample intelligence as to the enemy's intent, and he took care, whenever possible, to see that his men arrived on the field rested and well fed. "Put your faith in the common soldier," he would say, "and he will never let you down." Coarse-featured, with a predatory look, he could be as short-tempered and apt to use his fists as any ruffian. In fact, before graduating from West Point, he served a one-year suspension for assaulting an upper classman, a Virginian he believed was talking to him in a disrespectful manner.

Eight years of service on the frontier followed. With the outbreak of war he was commissioned a brigadier, later fighting at Perryville in Kentucky and Murfreesboro in east Tennessee. At Chickamauga his command suffered 1,500 casualties out of 4,000 men engaged. Then came Chattanooga and a measure of fame. Whether he now could add to that luster in the East, and as a cavalryman at that, was still open to question.

Grant nonetheless felt he knew his man. Told by someone that Sheridan seemed "rather a little fellow" to head the cavalry, the general-in-chief brushed the comment aside like so much cigar ash, "You will find him big enough for the purpose," he promised.[2]

By early morning on May 9, Sheridan was leaving Spotsylvania and cantering on a single road south to Richmond, his three divisions of 10,000 troopers stretched out in a thirteen-mile column. Wesley Merritt's unit was in the lead, then James Wilson's, then David McMurtrie Gregg's. They were young men in their late twenties and early thirties, as were most of their brigade commanders, and were eager to take on any challenge.

Brigadier Wesley Merritt, thorough and professional, was leading the 1st Division in place of the ailing Alfred Torbert; his brigade chiefs were the dashing George Armstrong Custer, newly married to his beloved Elizabeth "Libbie" Bacon; Colonel Thomas Devin, who had risen through the ranks of the New York militia; and Colonel Alfred Gibbs, heading Merritt's old outfit.

David Gregg of Pennsylvania, leading the 2nd Division, was as rock solid as he had been at Gettysburg; his brigade heads were his cousin John Irvin Gregg and Henry Davies Jr. of New York. Commanding the 3rd Division was General James H. Wilson, a onetime Grant aide who had been in charge of the Cavalry Bureau in Washington, where he lobbied successfully for Union troopers to be issued the seven-shot Spencer repeaters. Colonels John McIntosh and George Chapman led his brigades.

Sheridan's lieutenants, despite some mutterings that Wilson had little field experience, were well regarded. "Torbert had already distinguished himself"—from the Seven Days to Gettysburg—"as an infantry commander," said one cavalry officer.

"Gregg . . . possessed the confidence of the whole corps for good judgement and coolness. Wilson . . . was very quick and impetuous; Merritt . . . was with cavalry virtues well proportioned. Custer was the meteoric *sabreur;* McIntosh, the last of a fighting race; Devin, the 'Old War Horse'; Davies, polished, genial, gallant; Chapman, the student-like; Irvin Gregg, the steadfast."[3]

While Sheridan was intent on getting in Lee's rear and raiding the Richmond defenses, his true purpose, as we have seen, was to lure Stuart in pursuit. Jeb took the bait, but unaccountably left behind Wade Hampton's brigades, giving Little Phil a better than two-to-one advantage. Perhaps Stuart still felt one Rebel could lick two or more Yankees; perhaps his other troopers were dispersed too quickly to give chase; perhaps Lee, remembering how blinded he had been by Jeb's absence the first two days at Gettysburg, had insisted some cavalry be left with him.

By dusk Sheridan had crossed the North Anna River and was at Beaver Dam Station on the Virginia Central Railroad, where the Confederates had an immense supply depot. Scattering the few guards, he burned two trains, a million and a half rations, and irreplaceable medical stores, leaving the place in ruins. The next day, with one of Stuart's brigades nipping at his heels, he deliberately covered only eighteen miles, bedding down on the South Anna and letting the other two brigades of the hard-riding enemy circle to his front.

Riding into smoldering Beaver Dam Station on May 10, Stuart reacted with bitter resolve. He dispatched James B. Gordon's North Carolinians down the Mountain Road to harass Sheridan's rear, and then with Fitz Lee's two brigades of Virginians—under Williams Wickham and Lunsford Lomax—swerved east down the Telegraph Road, racing during the day and most of the night to interpose himself between the enemy and Richmond. "He was more quiet than usual, softer and more communicative," said his aide Henry McClellan. "It seems now that the shadow of the near future was already upon him."[4]

Jeb arrived at Yellow Tavern, an abandoned inn at a fork where the two roads met, about 10 a.m. the next day. Here, ignoring the odds, he planned to assail Sheridan's left flank as he moved on Richmond, no more than a half dozen miles away. He placed Lomax to the east of the Telegraph Road, Wickham to the west, with the two dismounted lines forming an inverted V. His men shared his optimism. "Our only fear was that Sheridan would get away," remembered W. W. Burgess of the 1st Virginia. "That we would not whip him if we caught up with him did not enter our minds." Meanwhile, Stuart sent McClellan to the capital to tell the authorities what was happening and to inquire whether the defenses would hold. The aide was assured they would, but did not return with the welcome news until the cavalry fight was under way.[5]

The Federal van was led by Colonel Devin, who around noon, instead of galloping past, changed direction and directly attacked the Rebel lines, seizing the crossroads and threatening the Rebels' left flank. This was accomplished despite fierce enfilading small arms and horse artillery fire on his own left from Wickham and Lomax. Sheridan was showing that he could be just as aggressive as Stuart.

Initially the heaviest fighting occurred on Lomax's front, where the open fields offered little protection. In the midst of the melee was Colonel Henry Clay Pate of the 5th Virginia who, through a series of misunderstandings, was on no better terms with Stuart than Grumble Jones had been. During a lull in the skirmishing, Jeb rode over to evaluate the situation.

"You have done all any man could do," he said. "How long can you hold this position?"

"Until I die, General," was the answer.

The two men then shook hands, all differences healed in the heat of battle.[6]

Sheridan's overwhelming numbers, however, all but guaranteed success. The bluecoats inexorably pushed forward, and at 2 p.m. turned the Rebel left flank, forcing a withdrawal and opening the way to Richmond. Pate fell with a bullet in his head even as his Virginians were huddling in the roadbed, wondering how best they could retreat to the cover of the woods without being picked off. "The question was whether to remain in the ditch where we were safe . . . and surrender," said one survivor, "or take the hazard of crossing a newly plowed field in front of their whole line." Like most of his comrades, Leiper Robinson of the 5th Virginia chose to run the gamut. Racing for safety, he saw the man ahead of him grazed by a bullet. "He yelled out and seemed to redouble his speed," Robinson said. "He left me away behind."[7]

Gordon's North Carolinians meantime on May 11 continued to harass the rear of Sheridan's centipede-like column, doing what they could to slow his march to Yellow Tavern, but with inconclusive results. One such engagement began at dawn at Goodall's Tavern, a country inn some eighteen miles from Richmond. "The enemy filled the old hotel and all its outhouses, stables, barns with sharpshooters," said Colonel William H. Cheek of the 1st North Carolina. "Without artillery we could not dislodge them. The fight . . . lasted several hours."

Finally the Rebels flanked the sharpshooters and fell on Sheridan's rear. "We had the most desperate hand-to-hand conflict I ever witnessed," said Cheek. "The regiment we met was the 1st Maine, and it had the reputation of being the best cavalry in the Army of the Potomac. Saber cuts were given thick and fast on both sides. The staff of my colors received two deep cuts while the sergeant was using it to protect himself from the furious blows of a Yankee trooper."

Cheek's men drove the 1st Maine from the field, but then were brought up short by a battery of artillery and a second mounted line, posted at Ground Squirrel Church. "Here we had another hand-to-hand fight, which resulted in our breaking and hurling them back. . . . Here it was that, while I was pursuing a fleeing foe with the point of my saber in his back, his companion sent a bullet crashing through my shoulder."

Colonel Cheek was taken prisoner, even as the two sides disengaged and caught their breath. The skirmishing in Sheridan's rear, to all intents, was at an end.[8]

Pushed back north of Yellow Tavern in the aftermath of Pate's death, Stuart reorganized his troops in the woods on either side of the Telegraph Road, with Wickham's regiments still on the Rebel right and Lomax's on the left, and awaited Sheridan's next assault. Protected by his artillery, located on a commanding ridge, he remained optimistic, sending a second messenger to Richmond to ask that infantry be rushed from the city to attack the Federals in flank. If this were done, he insisted, "I do not see how [the enemy] can escape."

Before the request could be acted upon, however, the battle resumed about 4 p.m. The irrepressible George Custer, knowing that the Rebel cannon had to be silenced, would touch off the fighting. "From a personal examination of the ground," he said, "I discovered that a successful [assault] might be made upon the enemy's battery by keeping well to the right."

Riding over to his division commander, he told him what he had seen. "Merritt, I am going to charge that battery," he concluded.

"Go in, General," Merritt replied. "I will give you all the support in my power."

Barely had Custer left to rejoin his men when Sheridan cantered up to Merritt and learned what was happening. "Bully for Custer!" he enthused.[9]

The 1st Michigan would make the charge, with the 5th and 6th Michigan, dismounted, surging forward on either side. Lieutenant Asa Isham of the 7th Michigan remembers: "My attention was diverted by what appeared to be a tornado sweeping in the rear. It was the 1st Michigan Cavalry, in column of squadrons, moving at the trot. It wheeled upon my flank as a pivot with beautiful precision, and came to a halt a little in advance of me, squarely in front and in full view of the Rebel guns. . . . In squadron front it covered over two hundred and fifty feet by one hundred and twenty in depth, and it formed a weight of six hundred tons that was about to be hurled across the fields and ravines upon that battery."

Taking his place at the column's head, Custer, a striking presence with his long blond hair and black and gold velvet uniform, sounded the advance. Away the 1st Michigan went at the trot, soon to be swallowed up in dust and smoke, with exultant cries filling the air and the ground shaking under the horses' hoofs.

Five fences had to be dismantled, and a narrow bridge crossed in column of threes, before the Federals got within 200 yards of the cannon. This took about twenty minutes, and all the while shell and canister were roaring and whistling overhead. Luckily for the Michiganders, most of the fire was harmless, because the Rebel gunners, strive though they might, could not depress their guns sufficiently to meet the close-up challenge.

Now the troopers pounded forward at the gallop, and within seconds were among the cannon, hacking away at the crews. The Rebel center was being breached, and collapse was imminent.[10]

Here Stuart rushed to the scene, calling for a rally. Captain Gus Dorsey of the 1st Virginia was there. "The enemy's charge captured our battery . . . and drove back almost our entire left. Where [I] was stationed . . . about eighty men had collected, and among these the general threw himself, and by his personal example, held them steady while the enemy charged entirely past their position." Soon the Michiganders came staggering back, temporarily put to flight by a countercharge of the 1st Virginia. "Give it to them! Give it to them!" cried Stuart, emptying his pistol into the fleeing bluecoats.

"As they retired," continued Dorsey, "one man who had been dismounted in the charge, and was running out on foot, turned as he passed the general . . . discharging his pistol." The shot came from close range, and Stuart had no chance. He reeled in the saddle, his plumed hat falling to the ground. The bullet had struck him in the stomach, severing blood vessels and puncturing his intestines.

"Are you wounded badly?" someone asked.

"I am afraid I am," Stuart replied, "but don't worry, boys; Fitz will do as well for you as I have done."

Even before Stuart could be taken to the rear, Fitz Lee was at his side. "Go ahead, Fitz old fellow," Stuart said, turning over command. "I know you will do what is right."[11]

Though the engagement at Yellow Tavern would be a crushing Confederate defeat, with Wickham and Lomax losing perhaps one-quarter of their commands, it blunted the impact of Sheridan's raid. Fitz Lee and his cavalry would fall back and rejoin the main body of Confederates; the Federals would for almost two weeks thereafter prowl on the outskirts of Richmond until, fearful of meeting infantry, they too withdrew and rejoined their comrades.

Jeb Stuart died the next day in the capital, even before Flora and their children could come to his bedside. "General, how do you feel?" asked Jefferson Davis as he came into the bedchamber. "Easy, but willing to die," Stuart answered, "if God and my country think I have fulfilled my destiny and done my duty."

Lee learned by telegraph of Stuart's passing. "He never brought me a piece of false information!" he would tell his staff. Later he would say of his surrogate son, "I can scarcely think of him without weeping."

Grant, however, was well pleased. In the lethal business of warfare, there was little time for sentiment over a fallen foe, and Sheridan had made good his boast. Grant greeted his protégé with heavy humor: "Now Sheridan evidently thinks he has been clear down to the James River," he told his officers, ". . . and even getting a peep at Richmond; but probably this is all imagination. . . . I don't suppose he seriously thinks he had made such a march."

Knowing he had proven himself, Sheridan joined in the bantering: "Well, after what General Grant says, I do begin to feel doubtful as to whether I have been absent at all."[12]

EIGHT
* * * *

THE WEST, JUNE: MORGAN'S LAST KENTUCKY RAID

Following his escape from a Yankee prison and his Christmas Day reunion with Mattie, John Hunt Morgan spent the early months of 1864 agitating for a new command. This was no small undertaking, for the Richmond authorities were understandably chagrined that he had overstepped his orders in making the Indiana-Ohio Raid and lost most of his cavalry. Eventually, however, he was assigned to the Department of Southwestern Virginia in Abingdon, with orders to guard the vital lead and salt mines there. With typical energy, he straightaway began the work of issuing clarion calls for volunteers and assembling a new brigade.

By May 1, he had formed up some 2,000 troopers, which he organized into three regiments. The first, led by Colonel D. Howard Smith, included Morgan hands who had been left behind in Tennessee during the Indiana-Ohio Raid, as well as the remnants of the storied 2nd Kentucky who had survived the debacle. The second, under Colonel Henry Giltner, was the 4th Kentucky, which had been serving in the Abingdon area; the third, under Lieutenant Colonel Robert Martin, with Lieutenant Colonel Robert Alston as his second-in-command, was a dismounted unit—as of yet, there were not enough horses for everyone. Smith and Alston recently had been exchanged for Union prisoners of similar rank; Giltner was a newcomer;

Martin, an old standby, had been detached to fight under Nathan Forrest at Chickamauga.

Tom Quirk, Tom Hines, and George "Lightning" Ellsworth, among others, also rejoined Morgan's ranks.

Trouble nonetheless lurked in the command. "The raiders were predominantly Kentuckians; about half of them had been with Morgan before, and most were honorable men," said one of his biographers. ". . . Even so, discipline was a problem . . . and especially among the wild [volunteers] who had wandered in from all over the country. . . . On earlier raids Morgan had had a harmonious team of handpicked officers, and the enlisted men had generally volunteered in companies with friends. . . . They were acquainted with each other and were dedicated and loyal to [him]." Now many of his officers, including Basil Duke, were still in prison, and many of the troopers were riding with him only to loot. "On this raid he was less able to weld his troops into a finely honed fighting machine. This deficiency was especially felt on the company commander level."[1]

Morgan at this juncture, despite instructions to stay in Virginia, again began to exhibit rash behavior. Hearing that Federal troops under General Stephen Burbridge were advancing from Kentucky into his area, he resolved that he would move into Burbridge's territory, rationalizing that this would force his recall. Besides, he insisted, the foray would enable him to commandeer all the horses and equipment he could wish. What he ignored was that other Federals were just then advancing into the Shenandoah, and the absence of his cavalry would contribute to the defeat—and death—of William "Grumble" Jones in the upcoming clash at Piedmont.

Richmond did not learn of Morgan's departure on June 1 until he had crossed the Cumberlands and entered Kentucky through Pound Gap, and could do nothing to prevent it. Braxton Bragg, now serving as military advisor to President Davis, called it "a most unfortunate withdrawal of forces from an important position at a very critical moment." Replied Secretary of War James Seddon, "Unfortunately I see no remedy for this movement."[2]

The Rebel column, with Colonel Martin's 800 dismounted men bleeding from excruciating foot wounds but somehow managing to keep up, reached Mount Sterling, Kentucky, on June 8. There the raiders surprised and captured the 300-man garrison and plundered their camp, feasting on their foodstuffs and providing themselves with new boots. Private George Mosgrove went even further. "In the tents we found a number of officer's trunks filled with 'biled shirts,' fine clothing, etc.," he said. ". . . I found a trunk, and without any conscientious scruples jumped upon it with both feet and smashed the top to smithereens. . . . The owner had the key in his pocket and was probably miles away with General Burbridge. . . . I forthwith discarded my 'old clothes' and 'dressed up' in elegant habiliments."[3]

Clusters of Morgan's men, ignoring or evading their officers, subsequently went into the town, freely helping themselves to merchandise in the stores and, in some cases, robbing citizens and breaking into homes. The most egregious of these crimes occurred when one or more men entered the Mount Sterling Bank and took $60,000 in cash and coins. This was not government money, whose confiscation would have been legal, but local deposits.

Morgan first learned of the theft in the early afternoon, when a delegation of citizens came to him and protested, explaining most of the money belonged to Kentuckians who were Southern sympathizers. The group produced an order, ostensibly written by Captain Charles Withers, one of his aides, informing the bank manager the town would be set afire if he did not open the vaults.

"What does this mean?" asked Morgan, turning to Withers and showing intense anger.

The aide swore that he had given no such instructions, backing up his assertion by showing his chief that the order was not in his handwriting. One of the citizens then mentioned that the trooper visiting the bank had a blond beard and spoke with a German accent. This description applied to only one man in the command, Surgeon R. R. Goode. Morgan immediately sent for Goode, but the doctor was missing. He would never be found, nor would the money.[4]

By 4 p.m., Morgan was preparing to move out, heading with Colonel D. Howard Smith's regiment for nearby Lexington, whose capture—however brief—he knew would both dismay his foes and provide him with hundreds of fresh mounts. Giltner's and Martin's regiments he temporarily left behind, with orders to complete the sacking of the Federal camp and follow the next morning. Smith, however, sought to persuade Morgan to delay his departure, saying a more thorough investigation of the bank robbery was needed.

"I have just heard of it," Morgan answered, brushing aside Smith's concerns. "I have no time to attend to it now, but will."[5] This decision, while necessary from a tactical standpoint, would serve to perpetuate the notion that the Kentuckian was involved in, or at least covering up, the theft. Moreover, it would drive a wedge between Morgan and his lieutenants.

General Burbridge, meanwhile, had indeed abandoned his drive into Virginia, and was fast backtracking into Kentucky, hot on the raider's trail. Marching through the night on June 8, he descended on Giltner and Martin at Mount Sterling with some 1,800 men at 4 a.m. the next morning, scattering unwary pickets and galloping into the main bivouac while the men were still in their blankets. Luckily for the Rebels, the predawn darkness and a heavy fog slowed the attackers, and though the Confederates lost perhaps 300 troopers, they were able to regroup and fall back toward Lexington. Burbridge at this point, having ridden his horses to exhaustion, could only swear in frustration. His mounts would need twenty-four hours to recover.

Giltner and Martin would catch up with Morgan, and the three regiments would be reunited. But the two officers in future days would be disgruntled, choosing to believe it had not been their carelessness that had permitted their camp to be overrun, but their chief's impetuosity in embarking on the expedition. Robert Alston already had quarreled with Morgan and left his command; now all his lieutenants, to one degree or another, were showing signs of petulance.

At 2 a.m. on July 10, with Tom Quirk's scouts in the van, the Rebels entered Lexington. "I volunteered to test the enemy by going [in] under a flag of truce," said Captain John Castleman. With him went his brother, Humphrey, and Key Morgan, the general's youngest brother. "Bearer of a flag of truce!" Castleman called out repeatedly as he rode through the streets, trying to get someone's attention. Finally a woman opened her window and told him a Federal gun emplacement was just around the corner. "I advised the boys to pull their horses well up on the sidewalk," Castleman said, "and we halted and [shouted out] our mission with unusual vehemence."

Finally a confused Union officer appeared and asked what they wanted.

"To demand the surrender of Lexington," he was told.

The officer refused to surrender, but it was obvious he commanded only a handful of men and his reply was sheer bravado. Castleman duly reported this information back, and Morgan's troopers soon were sweeping through the city, setting the rail depot and Federal storehouses ablaze. With the coming of daylight came the taking of hundreds of badly needed horses, just as Morgan had anticipated. "My entire command," he said, "was then elegantly mounted, and the greater portion clothed and shod."

These horses, of course, came not only from Federal army corrals, but from private breeders. Compounding such borderline thievery was the conduct of a lawless minority of the Rebels, who again showed their propensity for looting. Citizens in some instances were robbed at gunpoint; $10,000 was stolen from the local bank. Once more Morgan chose to ignore these crimes, perhaps laboring under the delusion that he was liberating Kentucky, and thereby achieving a greater good.[6]

The column swept on to Cynthiana, where it arrived early on July 11. When the small enemy garrison there took refuge in private buildings, Morgan routed them by setting the structures afire. Then about 2 p.m., even as his officers were urging him to leave the town before the relentless Burbridge came on the scene, the cavalry leader heard the sounds of an approaching train. It bore a second Federal force, that of General Edward Hobson, one of the officers who had brought him to grief in Ohio. Hobson had hurriedly assembled a group of militiamen in Cincinnati, perhaps as many as a thousand, and was keen on giving battle.

This time, however, it would be Morgan who was the victor, as he personally led a flanking attack against the enemy as they were leaving the train, throwing them into panic and inducing surrender. Negotiations as to what to do with the prisoners now further delayed his departure, though he showed little concern. In his mind, the raid thus far had been a smashing success, a feat that would restore his reputation. It did not even trouble him that his men were running out of ammunition for their Enfields, and that the captured cartridges did not fit his rifles.

Scouts meanwhile reported that Burbridge, now leading a force more than double Morgan's, was no more than fifteen miles away.

"Gentlemen," he told his officers, "we will fight the enemy in the morning."

Men like Colonel Giltner, nonetheless, were greatly worried. "I very much fear there is a serious disaster ahead," he confided to an aide. "General Morgan is a very likeable man, and a genius in raiding; but he is such an optimist. I have advised him to leave [Cynthiana] at once, but he persists in remaining and fighting Burbridge's command with near-empty guns."[7]

The Federals struck before dawn, and from the start the set-to was no contest. Many Rebels simply threw down their empty Enfields. Others in squads and companies skedaddled east across the Licking River. Some 250 men were killed, wounded, and captured—in the last category was Lightning Ellsworth—and the rest were so dispersed that weeks would pass before they could be reorganized. Morgan, the canny, calculating gambler, it appeared, was losing his appreciation of the odds, or perhaps he was tiring of the game.

Private George Mosgrove would notice his chief's almost casual behavior during the chaos of the retreat: "I saw General Morgan skimming along at an easy pace, looking at our broken lines and—softly whistling. I was glad to see him getting away, for had he been captured he would doubtless have fared badly."[8]

The summer months would see Richmond and Petersburg coming under siege and, on August 30, Morgan suspended from his Virginia command and facing a court of inquiry—not for going off on the expedition but for the bank robbery at Mount Sterling during its progress. Robert Alston, who believed his chief had ordered the theft, was the main accuser. Giltner, Smith, and Martin, perhaps to cover up their own inaction, also pointed fingers. One theory had it that Morgan intended to use the money to buy the freedom of Confederate prisoners, and that Surgeon Goode had wrecked the plan by absconding. Another suggested that the Kentuckian, preoccupied with the tactics of the raid, was guilty of no more than nonfeasance.

Morgan, who placed great store in camaraderie and comradeship, was deeply hurt by his officers' charges. Basil Duke, newly exchanged and reporting for duty at Abingdon, at this point found his brother-in-law an upset and changed individual. "His face wore a weary, care-worn expression," he said, "and his manner was totally destitute of his former ardor and enthusiasm. He spoke bitterly, but with no impatience, of the clamor against him."[9]

Just about this time, however, came word that a Federal column was advancing from Tennessee through the Cumberlands, into Morgan's department. Even though he had been relieved, and doubtless hoping that a smashing victory would help his cause, he moved west with 1,600 men to meet the threat.

By September 3 he was at Greeneville, Tennessee, bedding down for the night at an elegant mansion owned by Mrs. Catherine Williams. Though a Southern sympathizer, with two sons fighting for the Confederacy, she also had a third son, Joseph, who was a Union officer and whose wife, Lucy, was staying with her. Mrs. Williams was delighted to have Morgan in her home—she was a relative of his wife Mattie by marriage—but she warned him that, by staying in the house, which was a short distance away from his main camp, he was putting himself in danger. Yankees were in the vicinity and could strike the town at any time.

Shortly before dinner was served, Lucy Williams excused herself, saying she was going to the family farm to bring back watermelon and other produce. She did not return, but rain by now was coming down heavily, and everyone assumed she was staying overnight at the overseer's home. Morgan and his aides ate well, inspected the picket lines, and then went to bed.

The next morning, Morgan slept past his customary 4 a.m. wake-up in the field. Only at dawn was he roused, when the sounds of rifle fire crackled in the air. Yankee attackers were encircling Mrs. Williams's house.

"Where are they?" he demanded, as he and his aides, half-dressed, rushed down to the main floor.

"Everywhere," answered Mrs. Williams.

Morgan and his aides ran out into the extensive gardens, searching for an escape route. Almost all of his staff eventually would be captured. Morgan for his part, however, was not giving up. Charles Withers, his assistant adjutant, urged him to return to the house and barricade himself in one of the rooms until help came.

His chief shook his head. "It's no use," he said. "The boys cannot get here in time. [But] the Yankees will never take me prisoner again."[10]

Morgan ended up with Captain James Rogers, another aide, in a small vineyard adjacent to the gardens, just as Union Captain C. C. Wilcox, commanding the assailants, and several of his men rode up and spotted them.

Here accounts of the ensuing moments vary. Some of Morgan's people would claim that Wilcox's men opened fire with no warning, and that Morgan never had a chance. "I've killed the damn horse thief!" one Yankee rejoiced. The Federals would maintain that Morgan was given every opportunity to surrender, as Captain Rogers did, but instead turned and ran, refusing orders to halt. Private Andrew Campbell of the 10th Tennessee (Union) Cavalry, the man who would say he killed Morgan, insisted he even delivered a second warning, but "he still disregarded me. [Then] I deliberately aimed at and shot him. He dropped in his tracks. . . . But I did not know at that time, or even had the least idea, who it was I had shot."[11]

Whatever the truth, one of Morgan's aides soon made positive identification and asked that the body be returned to the Williams house, where it could be washed and prepared for burial. The request was summarily denied, with Captain Wilcox saying, "My orders are to take him out, dead or alive, and as he is dead, there is no other way to take him." Morgan's body was slung over a horse, and ignominiously brought to Federal headquarters.

When Morgan's main force arrived at Mrs. Williams's house, his body was long gone. The two sides then clashed briefly, but soon his leaderless troopers disengaged and withdrew back toward Virginia. Their opponents, elated by the news of Morgan's death, were only too happy to see them go.[12]

The aftermath of his passing, however, created shock waves in East Tennessee, some of which, unfortunately, enveloped Lucy Williams. Since she was absent from the household at Greeneville the night before the Union assault, and was married to a bluecoat, she was accused of informing on Morgan. The charges would destroy her. She would be ostracized in local society, forced to move to Knoxville, get divorced, and ultimately end up in Texas.

In actuality, the informant was a twelve-year-old boy named James Leddy, who raced on his mare with the news of the Rebel presence in Greeneville some eighteen miles west to the Federal camp in Bulls Gap. There about 9 p.m. on September 3 he sought out Union colonel J. W. Scully, with whom he was acquainted. Young Leddy, who lived with his widowed mother, had a grievance. Some of Morgan's men had stolen a bag of cornmeal from him and tried to take his horse. Now he was having his revenge. "I at first doubted his story," said Scully, "but finally concluded to awake General [Alvan] Gillem, who was asleep in the next tent to mine."

Gillem took immediate action, mobilizing his command. One of his regiments, under Lieutenant Colonel William Ingerton, was sent into Greeneville proper, to get in rear of the nearby Confederate camp; the main force advanced on its front.

"The night was pitch dark," remembered Scully. "One of the most fearsome thunder storms [I] ever witnessed prevailed for several hours, and had it not been for the constant flashes of lightning we could not have continued our march." Once the Federals arrived in the Greeneville area, however, there occurred a bit of serendipity. Though they knew, courtesy of Jimmy Leddy, where the enemy camp was, they did not know that Morgan was sleeping apart from his men. "Colonel Ingerton, having been successful in getting in the rear of the enemy, was awaiting developments," said Scully, "when a Negro boy rode up and told him that Morgan and staff were asleep at Mrs. Williams' house."

Ingerton quickly dispatched Captain Wilcox and two companies to capture the Kentuckian. Recounts Scully: "This force surprised the premises at six o'clock, and the soldiers began firing from their horses over the high board fence that enclosed the gardens. It was from this fire that General Morgan received his death wound. The bullet entered his back, penetrating his heart, and death was instantaneous."[13]

Thus passed away a volatile, almost incandescent, cavalier. Had he brought about his own death by refusing to surrender? It seems likely. The war was wearing him down, and the prospect of a return to a Yankee prison must have been daunting. His body eventually was placed on a caisson, brought back to Mrs. Williams's, and decently cared for. Subsequently it was taken under flag of truce back to Virginia. Those in the ranks who had been with him longest mourned his death the hardest. "Anyone of us—all of us—would gladly have died in his defense," Lieutenant Kelion Peddicord would say. ". . . So much was he trusted that his men never dreamed of failing him."[14]

NINE

THE EAST, JUNE 7 – 28: SHERIDAN V. HAMPTON AT TREVILIAN STATION

In the East, meanwhile, cavalry movements proceeded apace. Following the Battle of Cold Harbor, to divert attention from his pending movement with the main army across the James River against Petersburg, Ulysses Grant on June 7 sent Sheridan with 8,000 troopers far to the north and west toward Trevilian Station on the Virginia Central. Sheridan had orders to wreck the railroad and then unite with Federal forces in the Shenandoah.

Little Phil's two divisions were led by Alfred Torbert and David Gregg, both dependable, hard fighters, well liked by their men. (The third Federal division, that of James Wilson, was held back on the James.) Torbert's brigades consisted of Wesley Merritt's Regulars and Pennsylvanians, George Custer's Michiganders, and Thomas Devin's New Yorkers; Gregg's included J. Irvin Gregg's Pennsylvanians and Henry Davies' multistate Volunteers.

Learning of the march, Robert E. Lee promptly dispatched Wade Hampton, recovered from his wound at Brandy Station, with his own cavalry division and that of Lee's nephew Fitz Lee—some 5,000 men—to block the incursion. (The third Rebel division, that of his son Rooney Lee, now exchanged and freed from prison, the commanding general kept at Richmond.) Both Hampton and Fitz Lee were actively competing to replace the slain Jeb Stuart, a decision that Robert E. Lee, fearing divisiveness in his cavalry, was trying to postpone. On this occasion, however, with two officers operating so far afield, one or the other had to be in charge. Hampton was senior by date of his commission, so Lee gave him the nod.

Hampton's brigades included Matthew Calbraith Butler's South Carolinians (he was back in the saddle with a cork foot after being maimed at Brandy Station), Pierce Manning Young's Georgians (temporarily under Colonel Gilbert J. Wright), and Tom Rosser's Virginians. Fitz Lee's two all-Virginia brigades were led by Lunsford Lomax and Williams Wickham.

By the night of June 10, Hampton's division had reached Trevilian Station on the Virginia Central. Fitz Lee's division, in the rear of the column, was five miles to the east at Louisa Court House. Here scouts told Hampton that Sheridan had crossed the North Anna at Carpenter's Ford and would be advancing south toward Trevilian the next day. Hampton resolved to meet him head-on. His plan called for Butler's and Wright's brigades to move north on one road toward Clayton's Store, while Fitz's division, on their right, advanced on a second route and merged with them there. Rosser's brigade, on the Confederate left, would be kept in reserve.

Whether Hampton clearly explained these tactics to Fitz Lee that night or the next morning, stressing the need for a punctual movement on June 11, is open to debate. Certainly it is clear that an hour after dawn, his subordinates closer at hand were still uninformed.

"Butler," asked Rosser, "what is Hampton going to do today?"

"Dammed if I know," was the reply. "We have been up mounted since daylight. . . . My men and horses are being worsted by non-action."

The two men then rode over to ask Hampton for instructions. "General," asked Rosser, "what do you propose to do?"

"I propose to fight!" replied Hampton, giving them their orders.[1]

Butler touched off the affair. "We had advanced but a short distance from the railroad," he said, "when we were met by Captain Mulligan's squadron, of the 4th South Carolina, who had been on picket, retiring before the enemy. . . . General Hampton then [instructed] me to . . . attack at once, telling me he was expecting to hear Fitzhugh Lee's guns on my right, on his way up by another road from Louisa Court House." Butler soon ascertained the Federals, in the person of Torbert's division, were moving upon him in force. "I thereupon dismounted squadron after squadron until [almost] my entire command was on foot, and we were soon driving the enemy before us in the very thick woods."[2]

Then the Federals began to assert themselves. Colonel B. Huger Rutledge, 4th South Carolina, sent Butler an urgent message: "I am being flanked!"

"Flank back!" he was told.

Later, riding into Rutledge's sector to lend encouragement, Butler saw a group of soldiers breaking for the rear. Losing his habitual savoir-faire, he became enraged. "You damn rascals!" he shouted. "If you don't turn back, I will [kill] the last damn one of you!" His anger stopped them in their tracks, and they shamefacedly returned to the fight.[3]

Hampton in the late morning pushed Wright's Georgia brigade into action, and for the nonce, the Confederate front stabilized. But where was Fitz Lee? Couriers must have been sent to find him and to urge him to hasten his advance, but no contact appears to have been made.

Then sometime about noon disaster loomed. With Lee not moving north with sufficient speed from Louisa, Butler's entire right became exposed. The opportunistic Custer, scarcely believing his good fortune, galloped down the wide-open corridor and captured the Rebels' supply wagons, as well as some 800 led horses. A rout was in the making.

"On the arrival of the head of Colonel Wright's column," said Butler, ". . . I directed him to Colonel Rutledge . . . and paid little attention to my right . . . as I supposed it was protected by Lee's division. . . . While we were thus struggling with a superior force in my front, and the stubborn fight had been kept up at close quarters for several hours, I received information from the rear that Custer . . . had moved by an open road to my right."[4]

Butler now had little choice but to disengage, falling back toward the railroad and doubtless hoping for a miracle.

That stroke of good fortune came in the person of Brigadier Tom Rosser who, alerted to Custer's presence by a fleeing trooper, rushed eastward from his reserve position toward the captured wagons. "Not expecting trouble from the direction from which I came," he said, "Custer had not taken the precaution of putting pickets on that road, and thinking when he saw the head of my column that it was only a scouting party, he wheeled so as to meet [my] charge."

Rosser crashed into the Michigander's ranks, breaking up and scattering his squadrons, inflicting many casualties, and recapturing the wagons and horses. In the midst of the melee, just before retreating, Custer behaved with his usual panache. "His color sergeant was shot down at his side, by Major Holmes Conrad," Rosser remembered with admiration, ". . . [and he] grabbed the staff to save his flag. But the death-grip of the sergeant would not release it, so, with a quick jerk, Custer tore the flag from its staff and . . . carried it off."[5]

The battle would continue until nightfall, with Gregg's division joining the action and Hampton's harried troopers forming a defensive line parallel to the railroad. During this time, Rosser received a severe leg wound, and was replaced by Colonel Richard Dulany. Custer meanwhile remained an irritant. Though he had been thrown back from the wagons, he continued to hold his position between Hampton and Fitz, preventing the merging of the two commands.

"[The] day's operations ended disastrously to our arms," said Butler. "I venture to believe that I am not claiming too much for [my] gallant troops . . . when I say that they bore the brunt of the fight, and but for their . . . courage must have been annihilated. In making this claim"—and here he surely was referring to Fitz Lee—"I do not wish to be understood as disparaging others."[6]

Well before dawn on June 12, Hampton issued new orders. Whatever the truth of the matter, the South Carolinian believed that Fitz, upset about serving under him, had been guilty of foot-dragging. To reassert his control, he placed Butler in charge of his own division and instructed Fitz to swing south around Custer posthaste and join him at Trevilian. Once he had his reluctant subordinate in his presence, he must have felt, he could insure that the two divisions would act in concert.

Fitz Lee did not arrive at Trevilian until noon. Luckily for Hampton, however, Sheridan was in no hurry to continue the battle, perhaps thinking the Rebels were no longer a threat. He spent the morning and the early afternoon tearing up track, choosing not to follow up his advantage. "Sheridan *supposing* the battle was over," said one of Rosser's troopers. "Hampton *knowing* it had not been fought yet."

Not until 3 p.m. did the Federals attack. Butler was sitting on some rail ties, talking to Rutledge, when an enemy marksman sent a bullet past his head. "*That* is the opening of the ball," he said, rising and walking toward the front.[7]

Both sides, for the most part, would fight dismounted. "The bugles would sound the charge, but there was no *horseback* charge by the Yankees that day," said Private Edward Wells of the 4th South Carolina. "They would prepare for the charge, [then] the fire from our long Enfield rifles would create such consternation [that] they would come to a halt and disappear behind a body of woods, then reappear and try the process again and again. . . . Prisoners captured the next day stated that our fire was so great that it was thought we had been reinforced by infantry."

While these preliminaries were going on, Hampton placed Fitz Lee on Butler's left, with instructions to anchor the Confederate line and position himself to deliver enfilading fire when the Federals advanced on foot.

Wesley Merritt led the first such assault, and was sent reeling back. "Those raw men didn't know anything . . . about being whipped," said Rebel Frank Myers, "and had no idea of anything but killing all the Yankees in sight. . . . [They] made their rail piles look as if they were on fire, so incessantly did they burn their powder."[8]

Torbert sent Merritt forward again, and then Devin, and then Custer, with similar results. "Six charges were made by the enemy," said Private Wells, "and all [were] repulsed. After each, however, the foe had retired to a lesser distance, so that after the sixth unsuccessful attempt . . . he was . . . perilously close to the Confederate line. . . . Moreover, he had managed to put some sharpshooters in a farmhouse, from the upper windows of which they were able to shoot down with considerable effect. Worse still, six guns had been brought into action . . . These pieces were capitally served, and were doing severe execution."

Here Butler called for Captain James Hart's horse artillery. "Hart took two of his guns, all that could be spared," said Wells, "and galloped to the point indicated. He concentrated [his] fire . . . with short-range fuses upon the house, and in less than one minute . . . he had the building in flames and the sharpshooters scurrying out for their lives. Then turning to the Federal battery, he poured into it so rapid and accurate a fire that it was driven away."[9]

With the sun going down, Sheridan made one last desperate attempt to crack the Confederate line, concentrating on the 4th and 5th South Carolina. Trooper Wells remembered one Yankee unit marching straight toward his position, "with beautiful precision, in close order, shoulder to shoulder, the rifles, Spencers or Winchesters, held horizontally at the hip, and shooting continuously. On they came, and a few steps in advance . . . strode the leader, a large fine-looking man. . . . His right arm was bent holding his cocked revolver pointing upward at the 'Ready!' . . . He presented a fine mark, but somehow no bullets, it seemed, could hit him."

Then one shot found its mark. "This brave fellow had almost reached the rail breast-work, when suddenly he stopped; very slowly the right arm descended. . . . He made an effort as if striving to brace up, and then all at once the legs gave way, and [he] collapsed upon the ground. . . . Immediately his men broke and ran."

One of Hart's shells at this juncture exploded an ammunition wagon, throwing the enemy into further confusion. "At that . . . the whole Confederate line leaped to their feet, sprang over the temporary breast-work with an exultant yell, and charged. The foe was driven back in disorder pell-mell . . . and at the same time Fitz Lee was seen pushing steadily forward . . . doubling-up their right flank."[10]

That night, under cover of darkness, Sheridan began withdrawing, his mission incomplete. Even his damage to the railroad soon would be repaired. He would retreat in a meandering manner northeast, toward Washington rather than the James, until he reached Spotsylvania. Then he would turn southeast, not rejoining Grant until June 28. Hampton, though he followed, would not be able to bring him to bay.

Trevilian Station was a costly affair, the bloodiest all-cavalry battle of the war. Some 1,100 Confederates (of 5,000 engaged) were casualties; 1,000 Federals (of 8,000) were lost. "It was a spirited infantry-style attack and a stubborn infantry resistance," said Rosser. "Sheridan showed no skill in maneuvering; it was simply a square stand-up fight, man to man, and Hampton whipped him—defeated his purpose and turned him back."[11]

The South Carolinian took little pleasure in the victory. He was, at forty-six, a man of amazing strength and stamina, but he was also a mature man, fifteen years or more older than most cavalry leaders, and had never been a firebrand. "We gain successes but after every fight there comes to me an ominous paper, marked 'Casualties,' 'Killed and Wounded,' " the wealthy planter wrote his sister. "Sad words which carry anguish to so many hearts. And we have scarcely time to bury the dead as we press on in the same deadly strife. I pray for peace. I would not give peace for all the military glory won by Bonaparte."

Observed the Army of Northern Virginia's foremost historian: "A man who had that view of war, but displayed on the field of battle highly intelligent leadership and the most unflinching courage, could not fail to impress his soldiers. Increasingly he won favor as the best possible successor to the lamented 'Jeb.' "[12]

Sergeant B. J. Haden of the 1st Virginia Cavalry, Wickham's Brigade, tells us how he believed Stuart and Hampton differed in their tactics: "What General Stuart was going to do, he would do before General Hampton got ready. But when Hampton got ready, he was there. Stuart did his work with a rush, while Hampton never made an attack until he had made thorough preparation, and consequently, was generally successful, unless he was contending with overwhelming numbers. . . . I am unable to say which . . . would have accomplished the most in the end."[13]

Hampton's promotion to head of cavalry would continue to be delayed, and he would not be named to that post until August 11. Meanwhile he rejected all suggestions, by Butler and Rosser among others, that he ask for a court of inquiry regarding Fitz Lee's conduct at Trevilian, saying he had too much respect for Robert E. Lee to bring such charges against his nephew.

TEN
* * * *

THE EAST, JUNE 22-JULY 1: THE
WILSON-KAUTZ RAID

By the night of June 18 the Federal movement south of the James to take
Petersburg by storm had ground to a halt, but Grant still hoped to avoid a
drawn-out seige. On June 22, therefore, he sent James Wilson, commanding his own cavalry division and a smaller force from the Army of the
James under August Kautz—some 5,500 men and twelve guns—in a
sweeping arc southwest of the city, with orders to disrupt one or more of
the railroad supply lines. One such line, the Petersburg & Weldon, which
ran directly south to North Carolina, was not Wilson's target. Instead he
was instructed to concentrate on the Southside Railroad, going west as far
as Burkeville Junction, and then to proceed south along the Richmond &
Danville as far as Roanoke.

Though the raid would take him more than ninety miles away from the
main army, Wilson was not apprehensive. His only opposition, he imagined, would come from Rooney Lee's understrength command—1,500
men. One of Lee's brigades, that of John Chambliss and his Virginians,
was elsewhere; the other, that of Rufus Barringer's North Carolinians,
could muster only two regiments. Besides Barringer's troopers, Lee would
have only the loan of James Dearing's small, multistate brigade in any pursuit he might make.

Hampton's and Fitz Lee's divisions, Wilson was assured, were still chasing Sheridan in the aftermath of Trevilian Station, and would not be a factor. Moreover, he was told, Federal infantry would be in control of the Petersburg & Weldon line by the time he returned, affording him a safe escape route.[1]

Moving out in the wee hours of June 22, the Federals with Kautz in the van reached Ream's Station on the Weldon by daylight, wrecked some track and cars, and then continued on their way, passing through Dinwiddie Court House and pillaging the countryside. Reaching the Southside Railroad by 5 p.m., they commenced their real work. "The weather was in the most favorable condition for the destruction of the railroads," said one bluecoat. "[C]lear skies, a burning sun and several weeks of drought had rendered all wood materials intensely burnable."

Miles of track were already smoldering on the 23rd, when Rooney Lee caught up with the enemy rear guard commanded by Colonel George Chapman. The Rebels were "fired with a spirit of revenge, at the sight of these burning ruins, and the tales of woe frightened ladies eagerly poured into their ears," said one, "[and were] eager to overtake the 'robbers' "— who had invaded private homes—"and put an end to some of them, and if possible all."[2]

The fighting would be fierce and last until nightfall, but ultimately be inconclusive. Lee simply lacked the numbers to be more than an annoyance. By the next day the Federals—with Kautz still in the van, while Wilson and Chapman protected the rear—were at Burkeville Junction. There they continued with their mission, some troopers burning ties and twisting rails, others swatting away Rooney Lee's attempts to stop them. So far all was going according to plan.

Turning south along the Richmond & Danville, the column reached Roanoke on the afternoon of June 25, having laid waste to thirty miles of track. Here Wilson found the Staunton River Bridge, his last objective, defended on both its western and eastern banks by 800 to 900 militia, including convalescing veterans, and by six cannon. The relative ease with which the raid thus far had gone now made him careless. Rather than flank the position, he chose to launch a head-on assault.

What he did not know was that Confederate Colonel Eaton Coleman, a skilled engineer, "had moved two hundred and fifty men across to the [eastern] end of the bridge nearest the enemy," the *Richmond Times* would report. "The river bank was steep and high. This he cut down to about four feet, throwing all the earth as removed down the bank, and showing no fresh earth in front. His command was ordered to crouch down, carefully concealed, until the enemy should arrive at point blank. Then at the word they would rise, take good aim and fire."

It was 4 p.m. when the overconfident Wilson sent 2,500 of his dismounted troopers straight into this trap. "No shot was fired . . . as [the Yankees] approached in fine array, until within fifty yards of the bridge, [with] every eye of the assailants fixed upon . . . the men beyond the river, at Coleman's command the force under the bank arose, and . . . poured in their unexpected fire. The centre of the Federal line was torn out—scarce a man of it escaped wounds or death, and the whole force fell back."[3]

Next two cannon on the far side of the bridge, hidden 100 yards above the river, added their roar to the battle. "When we opened up on them with cannister," said Captain J. W. Lewis, "they were thrown into great confusion . . . and in twenty minutes we had them all in a ditch. . . . We never permitted them to form again. Every time they attempted it, we gave them cannister. In that ditch we kept them until darkness enabled them to retreat. They left their dead on the field."[4]

The ensuing days found Wilson in full flight, heading back east toward Ream's Station and the supposed protection of Federal infantry on the Weldon line, even while Rooney Lee tenaciously hung on his rear. But when he galloped on June 28 into Stony Creek Depot, ten miles south of Ream's, he found himself in a second trap. Hampton, having crossed the James and rejoined Lee's army south of Petersburg, was waiting for him, along with John Chambliss's brigade. Here Wilson divided his force, sending Kautz on to Ream's Station to seek infantry support.

Most of the action between Hampton and Wilson at this juncture took place at nearby Sappony Church, where the Federals sought to breach the Rebel roadblock. "General Chambliss dismounted his men and took up a line near the church," said Hampton, "where in a few moments he was heavily attacked. I brought up a portion of the 7th Virginia to reinforce him, and the attack was repulsed. . . . Young's brigade, under Colonel Wright, was then dismounted and put in position—the enemy in the meantime using his artillery and small arms rapidly. . . . The position of the enemy—who had two lines of works—was so strong I could not attack it in front."

Early on the 29th, however, Hampton prevailed. "I threw portions of Butler's and Rosser's brigades on the left flank of the enemy. At the same moment Chambliss advanced the whole of his front, and [soon] we were in possession of both lines of works, and the enemy were in full retreat."[5]

Wilson now again entrusted the redoubtable Colonel Chapman with the task of delaying the foe, while he fled north through the night to Ream's Station. There he found not only Kautz, but also, to his dismay, a full division of Confederate infantry under General William Mahone—victors in a fight for control of the railroad several days before.

Soon Wilson was all but surrounded. "In a twinkling, as it seemed," said one Rebel artilleryman, "the rattling fire of the carbines told us that [Lunsford] Lomax was hotly engaged"—Fitz Lee's division also was joining the fray—"and on the instant the movement in front began—the infantry under Mahone advancing swiftly. . . . For a brief space the confused combat, ever receding, went on—shouts of triumph mingling with the dismal cries of stricken men, ringing pistol shots, the chattering fire of cavalry carbines, the dull roar of the guns."[6]

Caught between Mahone and Fitz Lee on the one hand, and Hampton on the other, a desperate Wilson about 2 p.m. was close to being overwhelmed. He spiked what guns and burned what wagons he could, abandoned his wounded, and ordered his men to cut their way out. This they did, crisscrossing country lanes, woodland, and pastures with frantic abandon. Kautz's troopers had the easier of the escapes, trickling back to the main army about 9 p.m. on June 30. Wilson, making for the Blackwater River, was held up at a half-burned bridge. Hours passed before he could make the necessary repairs, with the result he did not find safety until the next day.

The raid cost Wilson 1,500 casualties (1,000 of them prisoners taken at Ream's Station), all his wagons filled with small arms and ordnance, many hundreds of horses, and thirteen cannon. On the positive side, he had severed for several weeks part of Robert E. Lee's essential supply lines.

One of the side effects of the expedition was that it confirmed, in a hitherto largely undisturbed area, that the war in the East increasingly was punishing civilians. Wilson's men had looted and plundered among them mercilessly, going onto farms and into homes to take not only horses, mules, and food, but even personal items, including women's petticoats and dresses. These last thefts were interpreted, in light of the prevailing mores, as being especially provocative. Growled one Rebel cavalryman: "I wish they were all dead for they have done us [much] damage. . . . in their camps we found all kind of ladies apparel that the rascals had stolen."[7]

ELEVEN

* * * *

THE EAST, AUGUST 6 – OCTOBER 19: SHERIDAN IN THE SHENANDOAH

Just before Ulysses S. Grant pushed the Confederates into a defensive posture inside the Richmond and Petersburg lines, Robert E. Lee audaciously had sent Jubal Early with 14,000 men—almost a third of the Army of Northern Virginia—into the Shenandoah. His orders were to clear the Valley of Federals, safeguard its bountiful crops and livestock, and create havoc, if possible, by crossing the Potomac and bringing the war home to the enemy.

This Early did with a vengeance. On June 18 he routed Union General David Hunter at Lynchburg, driving him down the Shenandoah. By July 6, he was terrifying the citizens of Hagerstown, Maryland, and by July 11–12, he was threatening Washington, forcing Grant to divert troops from Petersburg and rush them north. Later, on July 24, he scored a triumph at 2nd Kernstown, defeating General George Crook, and a week after that, incensed by the pillaging the Federals had done in the Valley, he torched most of Chambersburg, Pennsylvania.

Grant resolved to crush Early. "[The Shenandoah] . . . had been the source of a great deal of trouble to us heretofore . . . partly because of the incompetency of some of our commanders, but chiefly because of interference from Washington. . . . [The authorities kept] any force sent there . . . moving right and left so as to keep between the enemy and the capital. . . . They pursued this policy until all knowledge of the whereabouts of the enemy was lost."

His solution on August 6 was to have Sheridan named as head of the newly formed, 30,000-man Army of the Shenandoah, telling him to pacify the area once and for all. Grant did this over the objections of Secretary of War Edwin Stanton and Chief of Staff Henry Halleck, who thought the thirty-three-year-old too young for the job. "I want Sheridan put in command," he insisted, ". . . with instructions to put himself south of the enemy and follow him to the death. Wherever the enemy goes, let our troops go also."[1]

Sheridan's hurriedly patched-together command consisted of some 22,000 infantry and 8,000 cavalry. The foot soldiers included the Army of the Potomac's 6th Corps under Major General Horatio Wright; the Army of the James's 19th Corps, led by Brigadier William Emory; and western Virginia troops under Major General George Crook. Wright's three divisions were led by Brigadiers David Russell, George W. Getty, and James Ricketts; Emory's two divisions by Brigadiers William Dwight and Cuvier Grover; and Crook's two small divisions by Colonels Joseph Thoburn and Isaac Duval.

Going with Little Phil to the Shenandoah were two of the Army of the Potomac's three cavalry divisions, those of Alfred Torbert and James Wilson—with David Gregg remaining with Grant. Torbert became the new force's cavalry chief; Wesley Merritt took over his division. Merritt's brigades were led by George Custer, Thomas Devin, and Charles Lowell, the last-named officer being John Mosby's longtime foe. Continuing to serve under Wilson, whose division had been refitted after Ream's Station, were Brigadiers John McIntosh and George Chapman.

Torbert also would have a third cavalry division, western Virginia troopers led by William Averell, who had been relieved from duty at Chancellorsville for lack of initiative, and whose record since had been similarly colorless. How he would fare under the hot-tempered Sheridan would be anyone's guess. Colonels James Schoonmaker and Henry Capehart headed Averell's brigades.

Through August and into September, Sheridan conducted a series of probing movements to ascertain Early's whereabouts. He also learned, through a Northern sympathizer in Winchester, a young woman named Rebecca

Wright, that the Rebel commander had been stripped of a crack infantry division and an artillery battalion—troops badly needed in the Richmond-Petersburg lines. Meanwhile, Early was growing overconfident, scattering his forces and leaving them vulnerable to a swift, concentrated blow. "The events of the last month had satisfied me," he would admit, "that the commander opposed to me was without enterprise."[2]

Complicating this feeling-out period was Mosby, some of whose nettlesome but deadly tactics the Federals understandably regarded as criminal. Small groups in civilian clothes would ride up to sentries, suddenly draw pistols, shoot them, and gallop away. Larger units, dressed in Yankee uniforms, would approach whole squadrons and companies, open fire without warning, and send them reeling. On a few occasions, Union soldiers out foraging would be taken prisoner and summarily hung. The Federals would respond similarly, killing and taking vengeance. (We will further explore the Sheridan-Mosby struggle in the next chapter.)

By September 19, Sheridan was ready to strike. His target was Early's base at Winchester, where for the third time during the war a battle would be fought. His plan was to advance at dawn with Wilson's cavalry and the infantry from the east, crossing Opequon Creek and proceeding through Berryville Canyon before reaching the village. Merritt's and Averell's cavalry, under Torbert, were to circle to the north, in an effort to turn the Rebel left flank. If he moved quickly enough, Sheridan would be on top of Early before he could consolidate his troops.

Two impediments, however, slowed the Federal progress. The first was the canyon itself: a narrow, two-mile-long passage that soon became clogged with trudging infantry. The second was the inexplicable behavior of Horatio Wright, who insisted on keeping his wagon trains with him despite Sheridan's orders to the contrary, further delaying the advance. "The scene in the swarming gorge was one not easily forgotten," said one Union soldier. "The road was crowded with wagons, ambulances, gun carriages and caissons. . . . On the right and on the left endless lines of infantry struggled through underbrush and stumbled over rocks and gutters."[3]

Not until Sheridan, in a flaming rage, ordered Wright's wagons dumped into roadside ditches was the pace accelerated. The upshot was that Early was given time—several hours—to mass his forces.

Through the late morning, then, and into the afternoon, the main infantry and artillery battle raged east of Winchester, with fierce charges and countercharges commonplace. Though greatly outnumbered, Early's division heads—Dotson Ramseur, Robert Rodes, and John Brown Gordon—were among the best in the Rebel army, and they were implacable foes. "Getty and Ricketts [Wright's corps] made some progress toward Winchester in connection with Wilson's cavalry," Sheridan would say of the confusing ebb and flow, "and as they were pressing back Ramseur's infantry . . . [Cuvier] Grover attacked from the right with decided effect. Grover in a few minutes broke up [Clement] Evans' brigade of Gordon's division, but his pursuit of Evans destroyed the continuity of my general line."

Observing this widening interval, Sheridan tried to fill the gap, but was too late. "Both Gordon and Rodes struck the weak spot where the right of [Wright] and the left of [William Emory] should have been in conjunction, and succeeded in checking my advance by driving back a part of Ricketts' division and most of Grover's."

Here Sheridan ordered David Russell's reserve into action. "Just as the flank of the enemy's troops in pursuit of Grover was presented, [Emory] Upton's brigade, led in person by both Upton and Russell, struck it in a charge so vigorous as to drive the Confederates back in turn to their original ground. . . . The charge of Russell was most opportune, but it cost many men in killed and wounded. Among the former was the courageous Russell himself."[4]

Meanwhile, Merritt's and Averell's horsemen, who had been told to sweep north and test the enemy left, also were meeting strong resistance. "My division reached the fords of the Opequon . . . at dawn," said Wesley Merritt. "Here I found a force of cavalry supported by [General John] Breckinridge's infantry. After sharp skirmishing the stream was crossed at three different points, but the enemy contested every foot of the way beyond."

Later, while these firefights were continuing, the main attack on Winchester began. "Hearing Sheridan's guns, and knowing the battle was in progress, [the cavalry] was satisfied with the work it was doing in holding from Early a considerable force of infantry," said Merritt. "The [fighting] here continued for some hours, the cavalry making charges on foot or mounted according to the nature of the country, and steadily though slowly driving the enemy's force toward Winchester."[5]

Sometime about 3 p.m., he and the less aggressive Averell, together with Torbert, drew near the Martinsburg Pike north of the village. There they would have a climactic clash with Early's cavalry, led by Fitz Lee—commanding his own division and Lunsford Lomax's Valley troopers. George Custer, Merritt's division, describes the action: "The enemy had effected a junction of his entire [force]. . . . No obstacles to the successful maneuvering of large bodies of cavalry were [present]; even the forests were so open as to offer little or no hindrance to a charging column. Upon our left and in plain view could be seen the struggle now raging between the infantry of each army. . . . At that moment it seemed as if no advantage could be claimed by either."

Now Torbert's cavalry would decide the battle's outcome. Both his and Fitz's troopers raced toward each other at the gallop, met with visceral fury, and soon became hopelessly entangled. Curses, gunfire, and cries of pain filled the air. "[We] were so closely connected that a separate account of the operations of a single brigade or regiment is almost impossible," said Custer. "The enemy relied wholly upon the carbine and pistol; my men preferred the saber. A short contested struggle ensued."[6]

Within minutes, the Federals prevailed. Fitz Lee fell back about three-quarters of a mile and tried to form a new line, but failed. Three horses had been shot from under him. Now he suffered a crippling thigh wound, and his men, seeing their leader brought down, lost heart and fled for the imagined safety of the lines at Winchester.

With the infantry battle east of the village still at stalemate, Sheridan about 4 p.m. sent forward George Crook's 8,000-man reserve corps to pressure the Rebel left. Originally he had meant to use Crook, along with James Wilson's troopers, on Early's right to cut off his retreat. Now the reserve was needed across the field. Simultaneously, Sheridan ordered Torbert's cavalry down from the north along the wide-open Martinsburg Pike. "The ground which [the enemy] was holding was open," he said, "and offered an opportunity such as seldom has been presented during the war for a mounted attack, and Torbert was not slow to take advantage of it."[7]

Key to the Federal horse soldiers' success was the fact that Breckinridge's small and beleaguered infantry force, on the Confederate left, was much distracted by Crook's determined advance.

With Custer in the van, the cavalry fell on their foes toward day's end with irresistible force. Harris Beecher, assistant surgeon of the 114th New York, tending the wounded in front of Winchester, would remember: "To the right a dull thunder arose. Looking in the direction of the setting sun our men saw the most impressive and soul-stirring sight it was ever their lot to witness. Custer's cavalry was making a charge . . . pouring down at a keen gallop upon the already discomfited enemy. . . . Sabers glistened and quivered over their heads. . . . Chargers threw up a great cloud of dust. . . . It was glorious to see how terror-stricken the Rebels were. . . .

They broke and ran in perfect dismay. The cavalry poured upon and rushed through a great herd of stampeding Rebels, capturing prisoners, cannon and flags—striking here and striking there."[8]

Merritt, who with Custer and Tom Devin and Charles Lowell was in the thick of the fighting, sent forward his brigades in charge after charge, pausing only to reform his lines. "The cavalry charged repeatedly into Early's infantry," he said, "first striking it in rear, and afterward face to face as it changed front to repel the attack. [Now] the Union infantry advanced along the entire line and the enemy fled in disorder from the field, and night alone . . . saved Early's army from capture."

Recalled one Federal officer, who had been taken prisoner and had a bird's-eye view of the chaos: "The confusion, disorder, and actual rout produced by the successive charges of Merritt's division would appear incredible did not [I] actually witness them. To the right a battery with guns disabled and caissons shattered was trying to make it to the rear . . . to the left, the dead and wounded, in confused masses, around their field hospitals; directly in front, an ambulance . . . while six men in great alarm were carrying to it the body of [the slain] General Rodes."

In the battle's aftermath, Torbert rejoiced. "This day [Brigadier General Merritt] alone captured 775 prisoners, about seventy officers, seven battle flags, and two pieces of artillery," he reported. Just as importantly, his cavalry had gained that rarest of triumphs—a victory over infantry.[9]

Though Sheridan had won at Winchester, he had suffered 5,000 casualties and was too bloodied immediately to pursue. That night found Early digging in fifteen miles to the south on Fisher's Hill, a high ridge fronted by a fast-running creek. It was a solid defensive position, three and one-half miles long, extending from the Massanuttens on the east to Little North Mountain on the west.

On September 22, Sheridan renewed the attack. While Horatio Wright and William Emory demonstrated on Early's front, George Crook moved unnoticed through the mountainous woodland on his left. Here Early had posted one of his weakest units, Lomax's depleted and dismounted Valley troopers. When Crook's battle line surged out of the woods in late afternoon, the Confederates crumbled. What began as an orderly withdrawal turned into a second rout. Early's army would not rally for several days, until it was well up the Valley near Staunton.

Despite the victory, Little Phil was livid. He had sent Tom Devin to pursue the enemy, with the expectation that Averell would push forward his division and join in harassing the retreat. But, said Sheridan, "It turned out that [Averell] was not near at all and, moreover, that without good reason . . . had gone into camp and left to the infantry the work of pursuit." Without fanfare, he soon would relieve the derelict officer of command, replacing him with Colonel William Powell.

In the days that followed, Sheridan chose not to chase Early farther up the Shenandoah and into the passes of the Blue Ridge, believing that the effort would substantially weaken his command and leave his rear vulnerable to the hit-and-run tactics of Mosby's Rangers. Instead on October 6 he began withdrawing his army down the Valley from Harrisonburg to Strasburg, pillaging and burning as he went. During this time too, James Wilson left his command, transferred to head William Sherman's cavalry in Georgia, Alabama, and Tennessee. Replacing him was George Custer.

"The cavalry as we retired was stretched . . . from the Blue Ridge to the eastern slope of the Alleghenies," Sheridan said, "with orders to drive off all stock and destroy all supplies. . . . The infantry preceded the cavalry, passing down the pike, and as we marched the many columns of smoke from burning stacks, and mills filled with grain, indicated that the adjacent country was fast losing the features which hitherto had made it a great magazine of stores."[10]

Watching this destruction with gritted teeth was Rebel General Tom Rosser and the men of the Laurel Brigade, many of whom were natives of the Shenandoah. Rosser had been sent to reinforce Early and, now that Fitz Lee was incapacitated, to lead his cavalry. On the afternoon of the 7th, he fell on Sheridan's rear guard, the 1st Vermont, hacking them up and taking thirty-four prisoners. These men were part of Custer's new command, and he took their mishap as a personal insult.

Let me turn around and teach those Rebs a lesson! he begged Torbert.

No! No! he was told. *We're here to tear up the valley, not to be distracted by pipsqueaks!*

The next day was worse. Rosser sliced in several times on the new rear guard, the 18th Pennsylvania Cavalry, killing and wounding a dozen troopers, and capturing five more.

Let me turn around! Custer entreated.

No! No! again was the answer.[11]

That evening Sheridan, who had been riding at the head of the column, learned what had been happening. Worse, he even got the idea that a wagon and some cannon had been lost. Incensed, he burst into Torbert's mess just as he and his staff were finishing a hearty meal. "Well, I'll be damned! If you ain't sitting here stuffing yourselves—general, staff and all—while the Rebels are riding into our camp! Having a party, while Rosser is carrying off your guns! Got on your nice clothes and clean shirts!"

Then he turned his temper directly on his cavalry chief.

"Torbert, mount quicker than hell will scorch a feather! I want you to go out there in the morning and whip that Rebel cavalry or get whipped yourself!"[12]

At dawn on October 9, with Sheridan watching intently, the Federals turned on their foes at Tom's Brook, near Strasburg. There Custer, while diverting Rosser's attention with skirmishers and artillery fire on his center, sent regiments on two routes around the enemy's left flank. "Rosser superintending the left became heavily engaged at the ford," said Colonel Thomas Munford, one of his officers. "[He] repulsed the first attack . . . which was intended as a feint." Just as the bluecoats fell back, a second column, unobserved by Rosser, passed behind a hill to his left and pushed rapidly to his rear. When Custer subsequently assailed the center in force, the Confederates were caught in a pincers.

They had little choice but to flee for their lives, abandoning their wagons and all their artillery. "We fell back under fire until we reached a body of timbers which afforded shelter," said Munford, "after which the enemy retired."[13]

Though casualties were minor, the loss of guns and supplies was galling. Nor could Custer, who was a classmate of Rosser's at West Point and a close friend, later resist poking fun at his rival. Finding the six-foot-two Rosser's dress coat in one of the wagons, the shorter Custer pranced around camp in the oversized garment, drawing appreciative whoops of laughter.

Thereafter he wrote his wife, Libbie: "Darling little one, Yesterday, the 9th, was a glorious day for your Boy. . . . He signalized his accession to a new command by a brilliant victory. . . . Genl. Torbert has sent me a note beginning 'God bless you.' "[14]

Now it was Sheridan's turn to become overconfident. He and the Army of the Shenandoah on October 10 went into bivouac on the north side of Cedar Creek, near Middletown, continuing their work of destruction and not thinking that Early could mount an attack. But the crusty Rebel, who had reorganized his command and been reinforced—though he was still badly outnumbered—was making plans to do just that. By the evening of October 13, following some probes, he was back in his old lines on Fisher's Hill, within striking distance of Cedar Creek.

Pressure from above, meantime, was building on Sheridan, perhaps distracting him from the business at hand. He had convinced Grant he should stop at Staunton and then retrace his steps, laying waste to the Valley as he went. The sooner he returned with the bulk of the army to the Petersburg lines, he felt, the quicker Lee would be crushed. But Grant at this juncture was having second thoughts about the matter, believing that if Sheridan renewed his drive south and moved through the Blue Ridge, more might be accomplished. "General Grant wishes," read a communiqué from headquarters on October 14, "a position taken far enough south to serve as a base for future operations upon Gordonsville and Charlottesville. . . . Some point in the vicinity of Manassas Gap would seem best suited."[15]

Sheridan hemmed and hawed over this order for several days, with the inevitable result that there came, via Secretary of War Edwin Stanton, a second order that he come to Washington and discuss the strategic situation further. This he did, arriving in the capital on the 17th.

That same day Confederate General John Brown Gordon climbed to the top of the Massanuttens, where he observed, far below, the Federal position at Cedar Creek. Protecting the enemy right was Torbert's cavalry; protecting the left was the northern end of the Massanuttens, at whose base ran the North Fork of the Shenandoah River, off which Cedar Creek was a tributary. A flanking attack seemed all but impossible, and the center was too strong to storm.

But then Gordon made a startling discovery. "A dim and narrow pathway was found [along the mountainside]," he explained, "along which but one man could pass at a time; but by beginning the movement at nightfall the entire corps could be passed before daylight."

Later, at a council of war, Early took up the Georgian's proposal and devised a three-pronged assault. Gordon's corps would march all night, wend its way along that narrow path, and cross the North Fork at McInturff's and Bowman's Fords. Then at daylight, while diversions were being staged by Joseph Kershaw's and Gabriel Wharton's divisions against the Federal center and right along Cedar Creek, he would assail and hopefully turn the enemy's left.

On October 19 the attack began. William Payne's Virginia cavalry led off Gordon's onslaught, driving in the enemy videttes. Then his infantry advanced on the double-quick, adding to the chaos and, said Gordon, rushing upon "the unprepared and unsuspecting Federals, great numbers of whom were still asleep in their tents. Even those who had been aroused by Payne's sudden eruption . . . [next] were thrown into the wildest terror by Kershaw's simultaneous assault in front. . . . The intrepid Wharton was soon across with his superb division, adding momentum."

The surprise was complete. "Two entire corps [Crook's] 8th and [Emory's] 19th, broke and fled, leaving the ground covered with arms, accoutrements, knapsacks and the dead bodies of their comrades. Across the open fields [they] swarmed, heedless of all things save getting to the rear." By 7:30 a.m. hundreds of Federals had been killed, some 1,300 taken prisoner, and eighteen cannon captured.[16]

Gordon's and Kershaw's forces now merged, pushing the broken ranks of the enemy toward and then past Middletown. Only Wright's 6th Corps, which had been in a relatively rearward position, held firm. The fighting was heavy, and a captain in a Vermont brigade would never forget the bloodletting: ". . . splashes of blood, and zigzag trails of blood, and bodies of men and horses. I never on any battlefield saw so much blood as on this of Cedar Creek. The firm limestone soil would not receive it, and there was no pitying summer grass to hide it."[17]

Gordon about 9:30 a.m. was preparing to assail Wright's 6th Corps ("It stood like a granite breakwater . . . but it was also doomed"), when Early arrived on the front.

"Well, Gordon, this is glory enough for one day," he said. "This is the 19th," he added, thinking of the flight from Winchester. "Precisely one month ago we were going in the opposite direction."

"We have one more blow to strike," replied Gordon, pointing toward Wright's position.

"No use in that," said Early. "They will all go directly."

"That is the 6th Corps, General. It will not go unless we drive it from the field."

"Yes, it will go, too."

For the rest of the morning and into the late afternoon, Early made no concerted effort to follow up his advantage. It would be a terrible blunder.[18]

That morning at 9 a.m., Sheridan, unaware of the Rebel attack, was just leaving Winchester, where he had spent the night en route from Washington, following his conference with Stanton. He had barely covered a couple of miles when he began encountering panic-stricken refugees from the 8th and 19th Corps. "I felt," he said, "that I ought to try to restore their broken ranks, or failing in that to share their fate."

Leaving his escort and, later, a cavalry detachment to stem the flow down the Valley Pike as best they could, he put his mount in a canter toward Middletown and Cedar Creek, waving his hat and shouting words of encouragement. "Boys, if you don't want to fight yourselves, come back and look at others fighting!" he yelled. "We will whip them out of their boots by 4 o'clock."

Soon the troops, buoyed by his optimism, began to cheer and slowly turn back. Sheridan then increased his efforts, galloping in all directions to deliver the same message. "Boys, I am glad to see you looking so well," he told large groups of the 114th New York Infantry. "This thing would never have happened if I had been [there]. . . . We're going to get the tightest twist on those rascals. . . . We're going to take supper in our old camps. Our cannon will all be [retaken] this evening. . . . [The Rebs] will be the sickest lot of devils you ever saw."[19]

By 10:30 a.m., Sheridan was at the front, greeting Wright and his other lieutenants.

"What are you doing way back here?" he inquired of his close friend Crook, throwing his arms around him. Now a blood-splattered Wright, as he and Sheridan clasped hands, murmured an apology for the debacle. "We've done the best we could."

"That's all right, that's all right," Sheridan assured him.

Only when William Emory reported that the 19th Corps, reduced but restored, was prepared to cover the retreat did he bridle. "Retreat, hell!" he roared. "We'll be back in our camps tonight!"[20]

In the hours that followed, Sheridan must have been puzzled, like all his officers, as to why Early did not advance. But he used the time to advantage, strengthening his lines with returning soldiers. Summed up Major Aldace Walker of the 8th Vermont: "No more doubt or chance for doubt existed; we were safe, perfectly and unconditionally safe, and every man knew it."

Finally, at 4 p.m., orders went out to counterattack. Emory drove down the Valley Pike on the right in a swinging maneuver. Wright advanced more deliberately in the center. Crook's command, still badly mauled, was asked only to hold the left and act as the pivot of the assault. Sheridan's purpose was to turn Gordon's strung-out left in open ground, and this, with his superior numbers, he soon succeeded in doing. "Regiment after regiment . . . in rapid succession was crushed," the latter would say, "and, like hard clods of clay under a pelting rain, the superb commands crumbled to pieces."[21]

Early's irresolution had proved fatal. "My whole line as far as the eye could see," Sheridan exulted, "was now driving everything before it, from behind trees, stone walls, and all such sheltering obstacles." Harassed by Custer's and Merritt's cavalry, the Rebels fled south across Cedar Creek, tried in vain to make a stand at Fisher's Hill, and ended up the next day at faraway New Market.[22]

Early would stay in the upper Valley with a token force through the winter, but most of his shattered command would return to the Richmond-Petersburg area. "The Yankees got whipped; we got scared," was the way he would describe the stunning reversal. Here he may have been using "we" to mean himself. Four years of war, against great odds, were taking their toll.

Sheridan, on the other hand, was ebullient. "You have done it for me this time, Custer!" he shouted that night, pulling his curly-haired protégé from his horse and pummeling him good-naturedly. Custer responded in kind, seizing Sheridan around the waist, raising him off the ground, and repeatedly whirling him about. "By God, Phil," he rejoiced, "we've cleaned them out of their guns—and gotten ours back!"[23]

To all intents and purposes, the organized Rebel presence in the Shenandoah now was at an end.

TWELVE
* * * *

THE EAST, AUGUST–DECEMBER: MOSBY RETALIATES

The quick-hitting incursions of John Mosby's men on either side of the Blue Ridge during the latter part of 1864, though they did not frustrate Sheridan's ultimate triumph in the Shenandoah, made his task all the more difficult. From their base in Fauquier and Loudoun counties, the Ranger battalion ranged far and wide, sending raiding parties west into the Valley and east toward Washington, threatening both Federal supply lines and unwary bluecoats. "We lived on the country," Mosby would say, ". . . and drew nothing from Richmond except the gray jackets my men wore. We were mounted, armed, and equipped entirely off the enemy."[1]

One such foray, called the Great Wagon Raid, occurred on August 13. Sheridan, who was just beginning to pursue Jubal Early up the Valley, was trailed by 500 wagons—a column stretching for five miles, its tail end at Berryville and its van at Winchester. Mosby and his scouts, seeing that only raw infantry and a handful of cavalry protected its rear, decided it was there they would strike. During the night, while the enemy was pausing for rest at Buck Marsh Creek near Berryville, he posted two cannon on a hill and then, at 6 a.m. on the 13th, shelled their camp. Minutes later Dolly Richards and William Chapman and their troopers, revolvers blazing, dashed down upon them.

Completely demoralized, the teamsters and most of the Union troops panicked and fled through the woods, offering only token resistance. During the action, the Rangers killed and wounded a dozen men, and took 200 prisoners, at a minuscule cost of two dead and three wounded. More importantly, they looted and burned some forty of Sheridan's supply wagons—helping themselves to food, forage, and weapons—and seized 500 horses and mules and 200 cattle.

"My command reached the highest point of efficiency as cavalry," Mosby later would reflect, "because they were well-armed with two six-shooters and their charges combined the effect of [gun]fire and shock. We were called bushwhackers, as a term of reproach, simply because our attacks were generally surprises, and we had to make up by celerity for lack of numbers. I never resented the epithet of 'bushwhacker'—although there were no soldiers to whom it applied less—because bushwhacking is a legitimate form of war, and it is just as fair and heroic to fire at an enemy from behind a bush as a breastwork."[2]

The affair at Berryville would force Sheridan to assign a crack 1,800-man brigade of infantry as wagon-train guards, permanently taking them away from the front. Soon the bitterness between the two sides would escalate further, with Mosby believing his tactics were perfectly legitimate, and Sheridan and his men believing they were criminal.

The Rangers and the Union cavalry renewed their skirmishing on August 17, with Dolly Richard's company catching one of Charles Lowell's squadrons unawares, and in the process killing or capturing two dozen men. Told that one trooper had escaped, Mosby expressed wry satisfaction, remarking that he hoped the man would "tell Sheridan what happened to the rest of them." The next day Lieutenant Alfred Glascock with fifteen Rangers scored another success. Wearing ponchos over their uniforms because of rain, they misled a gullible Yankee detachment into thinking they were friends. Quickly drawing their revolvers, they captured thirty men.

Ranger Lieutenant Joseph Nelson, meanwhile, was intent on showing that enemy pillaging had a price. Stealing up on a Union soldier skinning a sheep, he killed him forthwith, cut one of the hooves off the animal, and shoved it into the man's mouth. Then he pinned a message on the body, reading, "I reckon you got enough sheep now."[3]

Similar rough treatment was dealt out on the 19th, when William Chapman with some 100 men surprised 30 members of the 5th Michigan cavalry at Berryville. The Yankees were burning down houses, on Custer's orders, in retaliation for the death of a comrade they believed had been ambushed. Some were killed in the ensuing fighting, but Chapman ordered that those who surrendered should be shot on the grounds that they were torching private homes. "Wipe them from the face of the earth! No quarter, no quarter! Take no prisoners!" yelled the Rebels. Stated *The New York Times* subsequently, "Mosby has . . . raised the black flag."[4]

These killings understandably enraged Sheridan and his lieutenants. "All able-bodied male citizens under the age of fifty who may be suspected of aiding, assisting, or belonging to guerilla bands now infesting the country will be immediately arrested," he announced. Wesley Merritt went further, telling his brigade commanders to "stir up and kill as many of the bushwhackers as possible who are between you and the river." Alfred Torbert chimed in, sending out the 1st Rhode Island on reconnaissance with orders "to bring in no prisoners."[5]

Sheridan at this point created a special 100-man force under Captain Richard Blazer, giving it a single task: killing or capturing Mosby and the Rangers. Blazer, a thirty-five-year-old Ohioan who had made his reputation hunting guerrillas in western Virginia, threw himself into the assignment. He made himself familiar with the countryside, interrogated captured Rangers, and developed a network of informers. Like many Union cavalry units, his men were armed with short-barreled Spencer carbines, which was both a plus and a minus. They could get off seven shots without reloading, but the weapon was better suited to fighting on foot than in the saddle. Mosby's revolver-toting men, if they could close in fast enough, would have the advantage.

Blazer was not long in making his presence felt. On the afternoon of September 4, alerted by informers, he closed in on two companies of the Rangers who were encamped on the east bank of the Shenandoah near Charlestown and Harpers Ferry. Mosby was not with his command; he had gone ahead to scout, leaving Lieutenant Joseph Nelson in charge. That worthy had all his pickets facing the river, not thinking there would be any threat in his rear.

The Federals, moving in dismounted, made good use of their Spencers, cutting down the Rangers from a distance and forcing them into a defensive posture. Before the Confederates managed to withdraw, they suffered thirteen killed, six wounded—including Nelson—and five captured. Mosby, hearing later of the reversal, was unsympathetic. "You let the Yankees whip you? I'll get hoop skirts for you!"[6]

Just about this time, two other Ranger companies under newly promoted Captain Sam Chapman also became engaged. Near Berryville they came upon Major William Beardsley's dismounted 6th New York Cavalry, strung out in a fence-enclosed field next to the road. Chapman promptly divided his command, sending one company wide to turn the enemy through a gate, while he led the other in a quick charge. Confused and shaken, the Federals broke and tried to withdraw, only to find that the fence they had thought a barricade was now a holding pen. Before they found a second gate through which they could flee, they incurred more than forty casualties. Chapman's losses were minimal.

On September 14, just five days before the battle of Winchester, Mosby himself was wounded. He and two of his men were scouting in Fairfax County near Centreville when they turned a bend in the road and found themselves face-to-face with five members of the 13th New York. "As we were all within a few yards of each other," he said, "we all fired at the same time." Then the Rebels turned their horses and bolted, with the enemy in hot pursuit.

Minutes later, Mosby and his companions suddenly reined up, faced about, and delivered a barrage from their revolvers. Two horses went down, together with their riders, and the three remaining Federals turned tail. But Corporal Henry Smith, pinned beneath his dead horse, now got off his last round. The bullet ricocheted off something, perhaps the pommel of Mosby's saddle or the handle of one of his pistols, and entered his groin. Faint with pain, he managed to ride on with his men to The Plains, where a surgeon decided the bullet was too close to an artery to be removed. It would stay in his body the rest of his life.

Subsequently, Mosby noted, "I was carried, for safety, to my father's home near Lynchburg. Captain William Chapman commanded my battalion during my absence." He would not return to duty for three weeks, and then on crutches.[7]

During his absence, there occurred still another clash, which resulted in the cold-blooded killing, hours after the end of hostilities, of six Confederate prisoners. On September 23, Sam Chapman with some 100 men found a lightly guarded ambulance train moving toward Front Royal and launched an attack. What his reconnaissance did not reveal was that the train was being followed by two whole brigades of Sheridan's cavalry: Charles Lowell's and George Custer's.

Chapman soon realized his mistake, and he and almost all his men eventually made their escape, racing out of the Valley through Snicker's Gap but leaving behind six comrades as prisoners. During their flight, however, they fatally wounded Lieutenant Charles McMaster, who, by some accounts, claimed before dying that he had been shot after surrendering. The Rangers would always deny this, saying their pell-mell withdrawal gave them no chance to take prisoners, even if a Yankee *had* wanted to throw up his hands.

But Tee Edmonds, a Mosby sympathizer who often hid Rangers in her home near Paris, would make the denial suspect. Shortly after the incident, she would write in her diary: "Our men had captured a Colonel [she could have been referring only to Lieutenant McMaster] and were overtaken, surrounded by the enemy. Our men shot the Colonel . . . after his begging and pleading with them not to kill him. He lived long enough to tell . . . what they did."[8]

The captured Rangers were brought forthwith to Front Royal, even as the news of McMaster's shooting was traveling through the Federal cavalry ranks, fostering cries for revenge. The result was predictable. Two of the troopers, David Jones and Lucien Love—natives of Fredericksburg, Virginia—were taken by enraged bluecoats behind the Methodist church and shot. A third man, Thomas Anderson of Fauquier County, was marched by other captors to a nearby farm and similarly executed.

Seventeen-year-old Henry Rhodes of Front Royal, the fourth prisoner to be shot, was not a Ranger at all. Learning that Mosby's men were planning to launch an attack, he had impulsively borrowed a horse and joined them. Two of Custer's horsemen dragged him through the streets between them, his hands tied to their saddles. When his widowed mother tried to intervene, they brushed her aside. Rhodes was taken to an open field, where a trooper, said one onlooker, "emptied his pistol upon him."[9]

The remaining two prisoners, William Overby and a man named Carter, both of whom hailed from the Deep South, were taken before Alfred Torbert, who that day was leading Custer's and Lowell's brigades. "Take them to that tree and hang them," he said brusquely, pointing to a large walnut tree on the side of the road. The order was carried out, even as a band played the dirge, "Love Not, The One You Love May Die." Reported the onlooker: "They bore themselves like heroes, and endured the taunts of their captives with proud and undaunted mien."

Torbert, meanwhile, having learned of Sheridan's victory at Fisher's Hill the previous day, now reversed his course, moving south up the Valley to rejoin the main army. Before the Federals left, however, one trooper scrawled out a macabre notice and left it on Overby's body: "Such is the fate of Mosby's Men."[10]

Recovered from his wound, Mosby during October initiated a series of strikes against Sheridan's 100-mile-long supply lines, whose protection at this time, much to Little Phil's displeasure, was requiring the detachment of some 6,000 infantry from his command. One such foray involved the Manassas Gap Railroad, which the enemy was feverishly trying to rebuild. It came on October 5, when Mosby attacked with 200 men and two cannon at Salem, scattering the work crews and sending their infantry guard scurrying. The Washington authorities responded by scraping together some 2,000 cavalry and sending them to confront the Rangers. Instead Mosby simply melted away in his usual will-o'-the wisp manner, and then on the 10th hit again, pulling a rail loose near The Plains and derailing an incoming train. Killed in this crash was M. J. Mc-Crickett, the road's superintendent.

Next, on the night of the 14th, the Rangers moved against the Baltimore & Ohio Railroad in two nearly simultaneous attacks. In what came to be known as the Great Greenback Raid, Mosby with eighty men derailed a train near Duffield's Station as it sped toward Martinsburg. Soon they were stomping through the cars, demanding money and valuables from the shaken passengers. One trooper, West Aldridge, made the biggest haul of all when he came upon an army paymaster and confiscated a metal box containing $173,000, money the troopers later would divide.

Mosby remained outside the wreck, gallantly helping women exit from the train and telling the passengers to leave before he put it to the torch. One whole carload of German immigrants, not understanding English, refused to leave. "Burn the Dutch, if they won't come out," he said, briefly losing his savoir-faire. Stacks of newspapers, set afire and tossed into the car, soon got the message across.[11]

William Chapman meanwhile with another eighty men was crossing the Potomac and assailing the B&O at Adamstown, Maryland. No trains were running—Mosby's attack at Duffield's Station had disrupted the schedule—so Chapman contented himself with burning canal boats, cutting telegraph lines, and looting stores.

There would be bad news as well. On the 14th also, Ranger John Lunceford deserted and informed the Federals where the command's cannon were hidden. That night, elements of the 13th New York Cavalry climbed Little Cobbler Mountain, near Piedmont, and took the guns without incident.

More to Mosby's liking was the capture on October 25 of General Alfred Duffie, whom we last saw at Brandy Station. Mosby was on the Valley Pike near Winchester, waiting in vain to ambush a wagon train, when Duffie rolled into view in a horse and buggy, escorted by a handful of bluecoats. Sheridan had just relieved him of command, having found his ways too pedantic, and Duffie, possibly in a huff, was galloping for a training camp assignment at Hagerstown, Maryland, ahead of his main escort. With much hooting, the Rangers quickly dispersed the few men who were with him and took the dapper Frenchman into custody. "I think him a trifling man and a poor soldier," said Sheridan unsympathetically when he heard the news. "He was captured by his own stupidity."[12]

In the midst of these events there occurred other controversial killings. On October 3, Lieutenant John Meigs and two aides were returning to their camp at Harrisonburg after a mapmaking expedition. They were well within Union lines, and thought nothing of it when three other horsemen joined them. All six were wearing ponchos against the rain, concealing their uniforms. The newcomers, however, were Tom Rosser's cavalrymen—regulars from Jubal Early's army—and at some point each side made this discovery, shots rang out, and Meigs fell dead.

Though wounded, the aides made it back to camp and reported the Rebels had blasted away without giving Meigs a chance to surrender. (Rosser's men, in turn, would claim that Meigs had fired first.) The lieutenant, who had graduated number one in the West Point class of 1863, was a favorite of Sheridan's, who promptly called his death a murder and told Custer to burn all homes within five miles of the scene. Several homes were torched the next day, but then Sheridan canceled the order, realizing that most residents in the area were Mennonite pacifists. The Rangers had nothing to do with Meigs's killing, but the rumor mills had it that they did.

Then on October 11, two more of Sheridan's aides were slain, increasing his frustration. They were Chief Quartermaster Lieutenant Colonel Cornelius Tolles and Medical Inspector Emil Ohlenschlager, and they were riding in an ambulance with a small escort when Dolly Richards and some thirty Rangers ambushed them. The two men, ignoring cries that they surrender, jumped from the wagon and fled on foot, only to be gunned down. Subsequently, lamenting the deaths, one of Ohlenschlager's fellow surgeons, Alexander Neil, wrote that he had heard Mosby's men were killing all prisoners. "But there are two sides that can play this game and our boys remember. . . . But tis best to tell no tales."[13]

Such retribution came on the 13th when Colonel William Powell, commanding one of Sheridan's cavalry divisions, captured a Ranger named Absalom Willis. Powell believed that Mosby had ordered the "willful and cold-blooded murder of a United States soldier by two men (Chancellor and Meyers, members of Mosby's gang of cutthroats) . . . a few days previous." The guerrilla leader subsequently would contend that neither Chancellor nor Meyers were Rangers, that the dead soldier was a spy dressed in civilian clothes who was being taken to the Confederate authorities, and that he was killed while trying to escape.

No matter. Powell had the unfortunate Absalom Willis hung, and for good measure had a placard placed on the body as it dangled from a tree: "A. C. Willis, member of Company C., Mosby's command, hanged by the neck in retaliation for the murder of a United States soldier."[14]

These violations of the rules of war reached a peak on November 6, when Mosby ordered twenty-seven prisoners in Rectortown marched out of the village and brought to Goose Creek. Nearly all were from Custer's command, which he primarily blamed for the six Rebel killings at Front Royal. "The [captives] were drawn up in single rank, and for each a bit of paper was prepared," said an eyewitness, "but seven only of them were numbered. They were then all put into a hat, and each prisoner was required to draw one of them. Those who drew blanks were to be sent to Richmond as prisoners of war, but those who drew numbers were to be hung."

During the process, the faces of the captives ran the gamut of emotions, from impassivity to hesitation to outright fear. "As each hand was taken from the hat an expression of joy and relief would brighten the countenance, or a groan of anguish or a cry of despair would burst from the line."[15]

A drummer boy, one of two such youngsters among the prisoners, all but became hysterical as the hat was placed before him. "Oh God, spare me!" he entreated

His slip of paper was blank.

"Damn it! Ain't I lucky!" he shouted, his face now wreathed in a smile.

His fellow drummer boy was not so fortunate, drawing one of the marked slips. Seregeant Major Guy Broadwater informed Mosby, who had absented himself from the proceedings. "I didn't know there was a drummer boy in the lot," said Mosby. "I immediately ordered his release and lots again to be drawn."[16]

Finally the seven victims were selected and taken for hanging at Beemer's Woods, near Berryville. But even then the tension was not over. On the way the guard detail and captives met Ranger Captain Richard Montjoy, his Masonic pin glinting on the lapel of his uniform coat, who was returning from a raid with prisoners. Two of the condemned Yankees, members of the order, saw the pin and gave the Masonic distress signal. In short order, Montjoy saved them from hanging, substituting two of his own captives whom he knew to be Custer's men.

Later he admitted to Mosby what he had done. "I want you to understand my Command is not a Masonic lodge," was the only rebuke he received.[17]

When the guard detail reached Beemer's Woods early on November 7, they soon showed they would rather be elsewhere, "like men who preferred not to do what they had been ordered to do." Mosby had idiosyncratically instructed them to shoot four and hang three of the captives, just as the troopers at Front Royal and Absalom Willis had been executed. But one Yank escaped into the woods by dropping to his knees in feigned prayer, loosening his bonds and running for his life, and another got away when a revolver misfired, enabling him to knock down his captor. Two others were shot, but not fatally, and the guards had no stomach for checking their handiwork. Local residents found them and got them medical treatment.

Three other prisoners, not so fortunate, ended up swinging in the wind. On the body of one was pinned the inevitable note: "These men have been hung in retaliation for an equal number of Colonel Mosby's men hung by General Custer. . . . Measure for measure."[18]

On November 11, Mosby signaled that he was ready to end the tit-for-tat violence. "General," he wrote Sheridan, "Sometime in the month of September . . . six of my men . . . were hung and shot in the streets of Front Royal . . . in the immediate presence of Brigadier-General Custer. Since then, another (captured by Colonel Powell) . . . shared a similar fate. . . .

"Since the murder of my men, not less than 700 prisoners, including many officers of high rank, captured from your army by this command, have been forwarded to Richmond; but the execution of my purpose of retaliation was deferred in order, as far as possible, to confine its operation to the men of Custer and Powell. According, on the 6th instant, seven of your men were, by my order, executed on the Valley Pike—your highway of travel.

"Hereafter, any new prisoners falling into my hands will be treated with the kindness due to their condition, unless some new act of barbarity shall compel me reluctantly to adopt a line of policy repugnant to humanity.[19]

Sheridan sent Mosby a written reply, but it does not survive. While no repetition of Front Royal and Beemer's Woods occurred in the ensuing fighting, how much this was due to the exchange of letters, and how much it was due to Sheridan's dominance in the Valley after Cedar Creek, is a matter of conjecture. One thing is certain: with Jubal Early's army broken and bleeding, Mosby's 43rd Battalion was the only Rebel presence west or east of the Blue Ridge.

That presence again asserted itself on November 18, when the Rangers and Captain Richard Blazer, their longtime nemesis, met in a climactic firefight near Myerstown. There Dolly Richards pretended to retreat with part of his 200-man command, luring Blazer into the open, and then fell on his right flank with the rest of his men, who raced out from concealment behind a hill. "Richards' attack was like a dynamite explosion at close range," said Rebel John Munson, "inasmuch as it was entirely unexpected." Blazer's seventy-five men were decimated, taking fifty-five casualties. Their leader was clubbed from the saddle and captured by Ranger Sydnor Furguson, an eighteen-year-old from Fauquier County."[20]

To punish Mosby's supporters, Sheridan from November 28 to December 3 embarked on a campaign of devastation against civilians, sending Wesley Merritt from the Valley to Loudoun County and its environs. "This section," he said, "has been the hot-bed of lawless bands."

There the Federals—day after day in villages like Paris, Upperville, and Snickersville, in Piedmont, Rectortown, and Middleburg—burned hundreds of acres of haystacks and crops, made off with thousands of horses and livestock, and destroyed countless barns, mills, and sometimes homes—though private dwellings supposedly were to be spared. Even Union sympathizers and pacifists suffered. "If old Satan himself had thrown open the gates of hell and turned loose all the devils," one Ranger would say of the fervor with which the bluecoats went about their work, "they could not have inflicted greater misery and woe than . . . Merritt's [men] inflicted . . . in this raid."[21]

Hopelessly outnumbered, the Rangers could only watch from afar. On December 4, with organizational matters pending, Mosby journeyed to Petersburg, where he had dinner with Robert E. Lee, and asked that his command, "in order to secure greater efficiency," be divided into two battalions, one under William Chapman and the other under Adolphus "Dolly" Richards, with both men raised to the rank of major. Lee and Secretary of War James Seddon approved the proposal, and the 43rd Virginia Battalion soon became the 43rd Virginia Regiment, with Mosby promoted to full colonel.[22]

December 21 found Mosby attending the wedding of Jake Lavender, his ordnance sergeant, to Judith Edmonds, in a ceremony near Piedmont. During the reception he was told that some Union cavalry were at Salem. With scout Tom Love by his side, he rode off to investigate, and learned the force was bedding down at Rectortown. Sensing an opportunity for a surprise daylight attack, he located a courier and sent him back to Chapman and Richards, ordering them to join him at dawn.

With rain and sleet coming down heavily, Mosby next sought food and shelter in the home of Ludwell Lake, whose son was serving under him. Love volunteered to stay outside and keep watch, but the guerrilla leader pooh-poohed the idea.

"No, Tom . . . there is no danger," he said.

Soon the two men, their host, and several women were at supper, enjoying spareribs, rolls, and coffee. "I was better dressed that evening than I ever was during the war," Mosby would say. On entering the house, he had been wearing a hat with an ostrich plume, gold cord, and star; a black beaver overcoat; and a gray cape lined with scarlet—all of which he took off and put aside. Now he had on a gray uniform jacket with two stars on the collar to indicate the rank of lieutenant colonel (his promotion had not yet become official); gray trousers with a yellow cord down the seam; and long, black cavalry boots.[23]

Then suddenly, all around Lake's house, came the sounds of thudding hoofbeats, shouted orders, and violent curses. *Yankees!* Mosby and Love shouted, almost in unison. Enemy scouts had seen their tethered horses and encircled the building. With no warning, a bullet came through the dining room window, striking Mosby in the stomach. "My God, I'm shot!" he cried out, seeing the blood spurting from the wound. He staggered into Lake's bedroom and, aided by one of the women, removed his jacket with its two stars and hid it under the bed mattress before falling to the floor.

Major Douglas Frazar and men of the 13th New York Cavalry now rushed into the house. Tom Love threw up his hands in surrender, and Frazar went on to the bedroom, where an ashen-faced Mosby was writhing in pain.

"Who are you?"

"Lieutenant Johnson, 6th Virginia Cavalry," Mosby gasped, hoping his reply would be taken at face value. "As I knew the feeling of the North against me and the great anxiety to kill or capture me, I was sure I would be dragged away as a trophy."

Frazar cursorily examined the wound and pronounced it mortal. Two other officers agreed. Mosby was stripped of his boots and pants, and left to die. "He won't last through the night," someone said.

The Federals left as quickly as they had come, taking Love with them. "I listened to hear them getting away . . . rose from the pool of blood in which I was lying and walked into the room where Lake and his daughter were sitting by the fire. . . . They were as astonished to see me as if I had risen from the tomb." A check of the wound revealed little. "My own belief was that [it] was mortal; that the bullet was in me; that the intestines had been cut."[24]

Mosby was taken by oxcart to a safe haven near Rectortown, where the next morning William Dunn, his surgeon, removed the bullet. It had not entered the abdominal wall after all, which almost certainly would have caused fatal peritonitis, but had somehow passed around the abdomen. Weak from the loss of blood and a subsequent fever, Mosby would not return to command until February.

THIRTEEN
* * * *

THE WEST, SEPTEMBER–DECEMBER:
FORREST IN ALABAMA AND
TENNESSEE

Forrest had caused such panic in his bold raid on Memphis in August that General Cadwallader Washburn had hurriedly recalled Sooy Smith's army to protect the city, in effect freeing northern Mississippi from Federal occupation. Now from his headquarters in Grenada he was asking permission to move into neighboring northern Alabama and then into Tennessee. His aim would be to cut the supply lines to Sherman in Georgia and force him to divert troops to protect them, easing the pressure on John Bell Hood, who would soon be evacuating Atlanta.

Jefferson Davis thought well of the proposal, with the result that on September 4 Forrest arrived in Meridian to discuss the matter further with General Richard Taylor, commanding the East Louisiana–Mississippi–Alabama Department.

Taylor, the son of former President Zachary Taylor and the brother-in-law of Davis, was meeting Nathan for the first time. Despite his elitist credentials, he was a hard-nosed fighter who had earned the praise of the exacting Stonewall Jackson during the First Shenandoah Campaign, and was initially taken aback by Forrest's demeanor. "To my surprise, [he] suggested many difficulties. . . . How he was to get over the Tennessee

[River] . . . how he was to get back . . . how he was to be supplied . . . I began to think he had no stomach for the work."

But then, Taylor continued, "having isolated the chances of success from causes of failure, with the care of a chemist experimenting in a laboratory, he rose and asked for Fleming, the superintendent of the railway, who was on the train by which he had come. Fleming appeared . . . and at once stated what he could do in moving supplies on his line, which had been repaired up to the Tennessee boundary."

Forrest's whole manner now changed. "In a dozen sharp sentences he told his wants, said he would leave a staff officer to bring up his supplies, asked for an engine to bring him twenty miles north to meet with his troops, [and] informed me he would march with the dawn, and hoped to give an account of himself in Tennessee."[1]

Over the next two weeks, Forrest prepared for what would be the first of three incursions into enemy-occupied territory. Leaving James Chalmers in Grenada with a single brigade—Robert McCulloch's Mississipians and Texans—he folded Edward Rucker's brigade of Tennesseans into Abraham Buford's division, composed of Hylan Lyon's Kentuckians and Tyree Bell's Tennesseans. On September 18 he arrived at Cherokee Station, Alabama, just below the Tennessee border. Altogether, with John Morton's cannon, his force numbered some 3,500 troopers.

Forrest next moved eastward, soon to be joined by 1,000 men from Philip Roddey's division under Colonel William Johnson. Late on the 23rd, he neared Athens, Alabama, where a strong Union fort guarded the Nashville & Decatur Railroad. There the following morning he tore up five miles of track and laid siege to the 600-man garrison, pounding them for two hours with Morton's guns.

Then he sent forward a flag of truce. "Knowing it would cost heavily to storm and capture the enemy's works," he said, ". . . I determined to see if anything could be accomplished by negotiations. Accordingly, I sent Major [J. P.] Strange of my staff . . . demanding the surrender of the fort."

Colonel William Campbell, who commanded the garrison, the 110th U.S. Colored Infantry, quickly rejected the proposal. Forrest, perhaps having no wish for a repeat of the Fort Pillow massacre, then requested a personal meeting. "Colonel—I desire an interview with you outside the fort, at any place you designate. . . . My only object is to stop the effusion of blood that must follow the storming of the place."[2]

During the ensuing parley, Forrest repeated his demand that Campbell surrender, saying that he had 10,000 troops and, if he had to launch an all-out attack, he could not be responsible for the bloodbath that would result. He even offered to give the Union commander a tour of his lines to show him how badly outnumbered he was.

Campbell returned to the fort, consulted with his officers, and came to the conclusion that if the Rebels indeed "had eight or ten thousand troops, it would be worse than murder to attempt to hold the works." Subsequently he "rode round [the] entire line, satisfying myself . . . that there were at least 10,000 men and nine pieces of artillery. It was now 11 a.m. I had been 'dilly-dallying' with General Forrest since 8 a.m., expecting reinforcements would be sent from Decatur. Believing they could not reach me, I ordered the surrender of the fort."

How Nathan pulled off this deception was classic sleight of hand. Dismounted troops were passed off as infantry, horse-holders pretended to be cavalry, and all concerned swiftly were put on the move after Campbell passed, only to pop up elsewhere as he made his rounds. Two batteries of artillery similarly were rolled in motion, "until the whole [encirclement] seemed to be swarming with enthusiastic troops and bristly with guns."[3]

Reinforcements, meanwhile, were nearer at hand than realized. Earlier Forrest had sent the 7th Tennessee, a detachment from Bell's Brigade under Lieutenant-Colonel Jesse Forrest, and elements of the 15th Tennessee along the railroad toward Decatur to intercept Federal troop arrivals. Now, just as the surrender was taking place, the sound of gunfire farther to the south could be heard, as these men blocked a train carrying members of the 18th Michigan and 102nd Ohio Infantry. The Rebels triumphed, after a desperate struggle at close quarters, taking 400 prisoners but losing Jesse Forrest with a severe thigh wound in the process.

Forrest followed up Campbell's surrender by attacking two more nearby forts. One immediately gave up, but the other resisted, the German-born officer in charge telling the Rebel negotiator to return to his lines before "[I] shoot your damned head from your shoulders off." Nathan now reverted to type, seeing red and swearing a blue streak. "Well, I'll blow him up, then," he told his artillery officer. "Give him hell, Morton, as hot as you've got it." After taking one direct hit, the defenders waved a white handkerchief, and Morton ceased fire.

"Go on, John, go on!" Forrest urged. "That was bully. Keep it up!"

Morton pointed to the handkerchief. "Keep on firing," his chief responded. "It'll take a sheet to attract my eye at this distance." Luckily the defenders soon produced a larger white flag, and the action ended.[4]

All in all, Forrest reported to General Taylor, "My force captured this place [Athens] this morning, with thirteen hundred officers and men, fifty wagons and ambulances, five hundred horses, two trains of cars loaded with quartermaster's and commissary stores, with a large quantity of small arms and two pieces of artillery. My troops in fine spirits. My loss, five killed and twenty-five wounded."[5]

On September 25, Forrest topped off these successes with an assault on the heavily guarded blockhouses at the 300-foot-long Sulphur Springs trestle, one of the most important bridges on the Nashville & Decatur. Placing his long-range guns on an elevation, and the rest on all sides of the fort, he swiftly dominated the 1,000-man Federal defenses, pouring some 800 rounds on the enemy. When his dismounted troops raced forward, few bluecoats dared raise their guns above the works, and victory was inevitable. Soon both the forts and trestle were ablaze.

Besides capturing the garrison, the Rebels at Sulphur Springs added to their plunder, taking possession of 700 stands of small arms, two pieces of artillery, a score of wagons and ambulances, 300 horses, and untold quantities of supplies.

These developments were not unnoticed by the Union high command. Wired Ulysses Grant from the Petersburg lines to Sherman in Georgia about this time: "It will be better to drive Forrest from Tennessee as a first step." Replied Cump: "Have already sent one division (General Newton's) to Chattanooga and another (Corse's) to Rome. Our armies are much reduced, and if I send back more I will not be able to threaten Georgia much. There are men enough to the rear to whip Forrest, but they are necessarily scattered to defend the road."[6]

September 26 found the Rebel column still farther north along the railroad, destroying the rail trestle and blockhouses on the Elk River, and the next day nearing Pulaski, Tennessee. Finding the town too well defended, Forrest swerved east toward Fayetteville, intending to assail and damage the Nashville & Chattanooga Railroad, Sherman's main lifeline. His scouts soon informed him, however, that large numbers of Federals—as many as 30,000—were flooding into the area, making such an attack impossible.

Forrest at this point decided to divide his depleted troopers, whose ranks had been thinned by the need to escort prisoners and captured stores back to Cherokee Springs. One detachment of 1,500 men, along with his wagons and cannon (his artillery ammunition was all but exhausted), he placed under General Buford, with orders to move south to Huntsville, Alabama, and tear up track of the Memphis & Charleston Railroad. Hoping to draw off pursuit from Buford, meanwhile, he proceeded with another 1,500 men north through Mulberry and Lewisburg to Spring Hill, Tennessee, which he reached on October 1.

Here and elsewhere in the area he captured and set afire still more blockhouses and trestles on the Nashville & Decatur, even while tapping the telegraph line to learn the routes the enemy was taking to converge on him.

The following day Forrest began his withdrawal south, marching through Mount Pleasant and Lawrenceburg and on October 5 arriving in Florence, Alabama, where he rendezvoused with Buford. There the entire command, with horses swimming alongside, made a perilous but successful crossing of the rain-swollen Tennessee River in small boats and makeshift rafts. During the passage, Forrest again showed off his famous temper. With all the occupants of his boat feverishly thrusting with oars and poles to propel the craft, he noticed a young lieutenant doing nothing.

"Why don't you take hold of an oar and help get this boat across?" he demanded.

"I'm an officer," was the reply. "There are plenty of private soldiers to do this kind of work."

This answer did not please Forrest, who himself was tugging away with a pole at the time. He gave the lieutenant a sharp, backhand slap that sent him sprawling over the gunwale and into the river. Within minutes, however, the slacker was pulled back into the boat.

"Now, damn you, get hold of the oars and go to work! If I knock you out of the boat again, I'll let you drown!"

By October 6, Forrest was back at Cherokee Station. Soon thereafter, at nearby Eastport, he culminated this first raid by ambushing two Federal gunboats and three transports belatedly coming up the Tennessee to intercept him. Colonel David C. Kelley with 500 men and a section of artillery, well concealed, disabled one gunboat, riddled the troops on the transports, and sent the entire flotilla packing.

Reported Forrest: "During the expedition I captured 86 commissioned officers, 67 government employees, 1,274 non-commissioned officers and privates, 933 negroes, besides killing and wounding an aggregate of 3,360, being an average of one to each man I had in the engagements. In addition to these I captured about eight hundred horses, [eight] pieces of artillery, two thousand stands of small arms . . . [and] a large amount of medical, quartermaster's and commissary stores. . . . The greatest damage done to the enemy was the complete destruction of the railroad from Decatur to Spring Hill."[7]

Forrest, tired and worn as he and his troopers were, already was planning another incursion, this one into west Tennessee. On October 12, he wrote General Taylor: "It is my present design to take possession of Fort Heiman, on the west bank of the Tennessee River, below Johnsonville, and thus prevent all communication with Johnsonville by transports. It is highly important that this line be interrupted, if not entirely destroyed, as I learned during my recent operations in middle Tennessee that it was by this route that the enemy received most of his supplies at Atlanta. . . . The great, predominating, absorbing desire is to cut Sherman's line of communication."[8]

One week later Forrest's column left Corinth, Mississippi, heading north to Jackson, Tennessee, and thence to Huntingdon. By the 28th, the van, led by Abraham Buford, was digging in both at Paris Landing on the Tennessee and at nearby Fort Heiman, a onetime but now abandoned Confederate garrison. Forrest's 3,000-man force consisted of Buford's division (Hylan Lyon's Kentucky and Tyree Bell's Tennessee brigades) and James Chalmers's patched-up division (Edward Rucker's Tennesseans, plus woefully small remnants from the brigades of Robert McCulloch and Hinchie Mabry). Four batteries of artillery were led by John Morton.

Early on October 29th, all was in readiness to intercept the Federal transports moving south, or upriver, to unload their cargo at Johnsonville. Forrest and Chalmers were not yet on the scene, but Buford and Morton, having concealed their troops and cannon along the bank at Fort Heiman and Paris Landing, were chaffing at the bit. Their patience was rewarded at 9 a.m., when the steamer *Mazeppa* with a barge in tow, both heavily laden, passed the battery at Fort Heiman. "A section of Morton's guns . . . was immediately opened upon her, followed promptly by the heavy Parrotts," said Forrest's campaign historians, "and with such effect that, her machinery being disabled, she became unmanageable, and drifting to the opposite shore, was deserted by her crew."

Stripping down to the buff and tying a revolver around his neck, Captain Frank Gracey of the 3rd Kentucky promptly mounted a plank and hand-paddled his way across the river. The *Mazeppa*'s captain, who had remained aboard, provided a yawl to bring a work detail across the water. A hawser was attached to the disabled boat and its barge, and in short order they were pulled to the west bank.

Crammed with food, shoes, and blankets, the *Mazeppa* was a welcome prize, and Buford quickly doled out some of the booty to his men. When he found a two-gallon jug of choice Kentucky bourbon, however, he reserved it for himself.

"Hold on, General!" someone shouted. "Save some whiskey for us!"

"Plenty of shoes and blankets for the boys!" he responded with a broad smile. "But just whiskey enough for the General!"[9]

Most of the *Mazeppa*'s stores would be sent on to John Bell Hood's ragtag troops in Georgia, and unloading the food and clothing for the long journey consumed the better part of the day. Just as the task was ending, about 5 p.m., three Federal gunboats approached from Johnsonville. The Rebel cannon triumphed in the ensuing fight, with the result that the ships hurriedly retreated whence they had come, and during the night both the steamer and the barge were set ablaze.

The following morning, the 30th, the transport *Anna* came north, or downriver, from Johnsonville, and Buford decided to shell and perhaps capture empty supply boats as well, thus denying the enemy their use. "She was allowed to pass the Paris Landing batteries and fell into the snare," said Captain Morton. "As she approached Ft. Heiman a few well-directed shots . . . caused her to raise the white flag. . . . Hearing the pilot ringing his signal bell top land, I ordered the firing to cease."

Buford and Morton went down to the river to accept the surrender, but soon saw that the *Anna*'s pilot was flimflamming them. "She hugged the bank as if to stop," Morton continued, "but instead of landing she raised steam and hastened by us. I ordered the batteries to reopen. She was, however, so close to us . . . that our guns could not be sufficiently depressed to effect serious damage until out of range. [Nonetheless] her chimney, masthead and pilothouse were knocked down, and she floated helplessly with the stream. . . . We subsequently learned from our cavalry, which followed her, that the pilot was killed."[10]

Later, about 10 a.m., with Chalmers's division and cannon now reinforcing Buford, the Union gunboat *Undine* approached from Johnsonville, trailed by the transport *Venus* and two barges, and by the transport *J. W. Cheeseman*. Not ironclad but tinclad, the *Undine*, despite its eight howitzers, before long was getting the worst of it from the Rebel batteries. "Soon a white flag in the hands of a lady was seen waving through a porthole," said Morton. "Our firing ceased for an instant, when the flag was snatched down. The firing was instantly resumed. . . . It was [thereafter] ascertained that the flag was raised by the wife of the Captain of the gunboat, who had been killed, and was [taken] down by the second in command."[11]

Caught between the guns at Fort Heiman and those at Paris Landing, the *Undine* and *Venus*, riddled by shellfire, could only flounder about, able neither to proceed farther north nor to return to Johnsonville. In desperation they huddled at a bend in the river, seeking relief from the Rebel cannon. Sometime around noon Colonel David Kelley with two companies would storm the *Venus* and then use the transport to capture the *Undine*, which at the last moment sped to the east bank, where its officers and crew scattered and sought safety. Both vessels, their engines and hulls still intact, subsequently would be taken to Paris Landing.

The *Cheeseman* meanwhile took even greater punishment. "Hardly a shot failed to find its mark," said Morton. "She was irreparably damaged and drifted ashore. . . . We boarded her, and found that dinner had just been served. Without special invitations . . . we seated ourselves and partook of 'the first square meal' for many a day." Judged a hopeless wreck, the *Cheeseman* and the two barges was put to the torch.[12]

Forrest, who did not arrive at Paris Landing until October 31, now revealed his master plan: taking and destroying the Johnsonville depot. Reconnoitering the town, he saw that its wharf "was lined with transports and gunboats . . . while several acres of the shore were covered with every description of army stores." A redoubt overlooking the depot "was situated on a high hill and in a commanding position." His challenge would be getting his cannon in position near Johnsonville before the enemy divined his intent, and before they could forestall it.[13]

The *Undine* with its eight howitzers, and the *Venus* with its storage facilities, Forrest believed, could play a role in the upcoming clash, helping the land-based troopers and guns as they moved south along the Tennessee's west bank toward the depot. Accordingly, he placed Captain Gracey, who had been a riverboat pilot, in charge of the *Undine* and Colonel William Dawson of the 15th Tennessee in command of the *Venus*, giving the latter overall responsibility for the improvised flotilla. Crewmen were drawn from cavalry volunteers, and a few hours during the afternoon were devoted to a crash course in seamanship.

Dawson, who had no waterway credentials at all, expressed apprehension about his assignment. "You must promise me," he told Forrest, "that if I lose the fleet you won't give me a cursing when I wade ashore."

"No, Colonel," was the reply, "you will do the best you can. That is all I want."

Nathan realized, of course, that his fleet did not stand a chance against the U.S. Navy, which besides the three gunboats at Johnsonville had six more north of Fort Heiman at Paducah, Kentucky. But there was every chance, he felt, that in trying to recapture the boats the enemy would become careless and venture too close to the riverbank, where his batteries would have the advantage.[14]

That hope would be short-lived. November 1, the opening of the joint Rebel advance by land and river was uneventful, but the next day proved Dawson's fears were justified. That afternoon, north of Johnsonville, the *Undine* and the *Venus*, steaming too far ahead of Forrest's batteries, came under heavy fire from two enemy gunboats. The *Venus* quickly was rendered helpless. Dawson ran her nose into the bank, and he and his men, after setting the vessel afire, sought refuge on land. The *Undine*, more fortunate, made her escape, falling back under the protection of the Rebel guns.

On the 3rd, Gracey tried once more to lure Federal gunboats close to the bank, taking up a position with the *Undine* in the strait formed by Reynoldsburg Island, four miles north of the depot. But the enemy did not bite.

The following morning saw the climax of the water battle. Federal gunboats, prodded by rumors of Forrest's movements, steamed up and down the Tennessee from north and south. Here the *Undine*, still in the strait, made a magnificent stand. Backed up by the Rebel gunners on shore, she held off nine enemy warships for several hours until running out of coal. Gracey then turned toward the bank, soaked some bedding in kerosene and, once his men were clear of the ship, blew her out of the water.

It was now about 11 a.m. The Federal gunboats at this juncture, far from being victorious, were both bloodied and bowed. The ones coming down from Johnsonville, having suffered debilitating hits, retreated to the town. The ones coming up from Paducah, also wounded, did not dare push through the strait, lest they be sunk.[15]

During the night of November 3, while leaving one battery of Morton's cannon in the Reynoldsburg Island area, Forrest had placed the other three sections opposite Johnsonville, some 800 yards across the river, and carefully masked their presence. At 2 p.m. the next day, with the battle in the strait long over, he launched his attack on the depot. Perhaps because they thought Forrest would not attack them in their fortified stronghold, the enemy was curiously complacent. "Straggling [Union] troops were sauntering about . . . or pacing the parapet of the redoubt," said Forrest's historians. "Laborers were at work landing stores from transports and barges. . . . It was apparent there was not the least suspicion of the impending tempest."

Then all hell broke loose. "Ten pieces, carefully trained upon the gunboats at the landing, were discharged with such harmony, that it could not be discerned it was more than one report. . . . Immediately steam and smoke poured forth from the boats. . . . Only one returned the fire, but the redoubt burst forth with a storm of shells. . . . Two disabled gunboats were now wrapped with flames, and the commander of the third . . . unable to endure it any longer, ran her ashore."

Morton next turned his cannon on the redoubt, swiftly neutralizing the threat. "By this time, the burning gunboats having drifted against some loaded barges, these were quickly in flames. . . . And [other] guns, being turned upon two transports and some barges lying somewhat above the landing, soon succeeded in setting them ablaze. Then their cables burning, they went adrift and were carried by the current downstream, in contact with another transport to which the fire was communicated, and thence spread . . . to the other transports and barges." By 4 p.m. every vessel on the river was ablaze.

Nor did the stores ashore escape destruction. "Discovering a large pile of hay, a few deftly-exploded shells kindled it into a consuming fire that soon spread to vast heaps of corn and bacon adjoining. And descrying higher up the slope a large pile of barrels under tarpaulins, suspecting that they contained spirits . . . [shells] were thrown with the happiest effect, for a blue blaze, unmistakably alcoholic, was quickly seen."[16]

Warehouses stuffed with supplies similarly were ignited, with the enemy helpless to protect them. Forrest himself subsequently turned gunner, as Buford and other officers crowded around him. When an aide, posted as an observer, reported that one of his shots had fallen short, he doubled over with laughter. "Rickety shay! Rickety shay!" he roared. "I'll hit her next time. Buford, elevate the breech of that gun!" Toward evening, when he signaled a cease-fire and drew back his troopers from the riverbank, the depot and its environs were a smoldering ruin.[17]

By November 10, Forrest was back in Corinth, Mississippi. "I captured and destroyed four gunboats, fourteen transports, twenty barges, twenty-six pieces of artillery, $6,700,000 worth of property, and captured one hundred and fifty prisoners," he would report. ". . . My loss during the entire trip was two killed and nine wounded."

Despite these deprivations, however, the raid at Johnsonville would have little impact on Sherman's March to the Sea through eastern Georgia and South Carolina, which began on the 15th. Such was the huge Federal superiority in stores and ordnance that they earlier had established additional—and well-stocked—supply bases.[18]

Forrest, meanwhile, was ordered to report to John Bell Hood, who was lurking in Sherman's rear, and take command of all the cavalry of the Army of Tennessee; Joseph Wheeler, with a token force, was left in Georgia to harass Cump's movements. Southern strategy at this desperate juncture called for Hood to ignore the Federals who had bested him at Atlanta. Instead he was instructed to invade Tennessee, speedily defeat the Union forces there under General George Thomas, and thereafter join with Lee at Petersburg in whipping Grant.

The bureaucrats on Hood's headquarters staff soon learned about Forrest's temper firsthand. Some paper-pusher had sent him an order reducing the number of mules per wagon and demanding the surplus animals be turned over to the quartermaster. He ignored it, and when Major A. L. Landis asked him why no mules were forthcoming, he showed his temper.

"The atmosphere was blue for a while," said Captain Morton. "Stripped of General Forrest's bad words, he said to Major Landis: 'Don't you come here again or send anybody here again about mules. . . . If [the quartermaster] bothers me any further . . . I'll come down to his office, tie his long legs in a double bow knot around his neck, and choke him to death with his own shins. It's a fool order, anyway. General Hood had better . . . overhaul his wagons, rid them of all surplus baggage . . . reduce the number of his wagons instead of the strength of his teams. . . . If he knew the road . . . this order would be countermanded.' "[19]

Moving in advance of the 33,000-man Rebel infantry, Forrest on November 21 left Florence, Alabama; crossed the Tennessee River; and brushing aside enemy cavalry resistance amid freezing rain and snow, proceeded eighty miles north to the outskirts of Columbia, Tennessee, which he reached on the 24th. His 6,000 troopers consisted of three divisions—those of the stalwarts Buford and Chalmers—and that of William Jackson, many of whose men had previously served under Nathan and cheered his arrival.

The Union forces in Tennessee now were widespread. John M. Schofield, serving under George Thomas, had some 30,000 men at Pulaski and Columbia, well south of the latter's 25,000-man Nashville garrison, and was susceptible to being flanked and cut off.

Finding Columbia strongly defended by infantry, Forrest held his position for three days until Hood's force caught up with him, and later, on the afternoon of November 28, crossed the Duck River. His intent was to get in the rear of Schofield's command, even while Hood was assailing the Federal front, and keep him from joining Thomas. His target was Spring

Hill, a village on the Columbia-Franklin Turnpike that effectively controlled the route north to Franklin and Nashville.

The tactic might well have worked. Only the next day, at the last moment, did Schofield begin his withdrawal and dispatch infantry to protect his means of egress through Spring Hill, blunting Forrest's initiative. Even so, had Hood's infantry subsequently moved up with vigor, the town might have been taken and the pike severed. But a mix-up in communications held them back, making the matter moot. During the night, however, Forrest did all he could to harass the retreating Federals. "[William] Jackson had possession of the pike and fought the enemy until near daylight," he would report. "But receiving no support, he was compelled to retire, after killing a large number of horses and mules, and burning several wagons."[20]

By dawn on November 30, Schofield's column had passed through Spring Hill, and a few hours later, it was in Franklin, feverishly throwing up breastworks and barricades.

Here Forrest and Hood, two of the South's most relentless fighters, had a difference of opinion. To be fair, the latter realized time was running out. If he did not smash Schofield forthwith, and allowed him to unite with Thomas, the game would be up.

"The position of the enemy is exceedingly formidable," Forrest advised Hood, "and it cannot be taken by direct assault, except after great loss of life."

"I do not think the Federals can withstand strong pressure from the front," was the reply. "The show of force they are making is a feint to hold me back from a more determined assault."

"General," Forrest persisted, "if you will give me one strong division of infantry with my cavalry, I will flank the Federals from their works within two hours' time."[21]

His request was denied, and about 4 p.m. the Rebel infantry was sent on the double-quick toward the enemy lines. Forrest's cavalry would be only a minor factor in the ensuing action, possibly because Hood had split up his divisions and not allowed Nathan his usual freedom to roam. On the left, Chalmers crossed over the Harpeth River, behind Franklin, but then was driven back. On the right, Buford and Jackson under Forrest were similarly stymied. "Forrest may have had in mind attempting what he had suggested to Hood, except without the requested infantry division," said a biographer. "He instinctively knew that the easiest—perhaps only—victory here lay in reaching the Federal rear."

But this was not to be, and in the meantime wave after wave of Rebel infantry, largely unsupported by cannon themselves, were being decimated by entrenched enemy troops and artillery. Hood would suffer 6,000 casualties, including twelve generals; Schofield's losses would total 2,300.

One historian of the Army of Tennessee compares Hood's charge at Franklin with that of George Pickett's at Gettysburg, and shows that the former's was bloodier and more difficult by far. Pickett's losses were some 1,350; Hood's more than four times that. Pickett's assault was made after a two-hour artillery barrage; the one at Franklin was launched without any softening-up to speak of. Pickett moved forward across a mile of open space; Hood's army had to cover twice that distance. The Union forces at Gettysburg had only a low stone wall for protection; Schofield's men had elaborate fortifications. Pickett made his charge but once; Hood kept coming again and again, perhaps as many as thirteen times.[22]

That night, Schofield fell back once more, entering the defenses at Nashville on December 1 and uniting with Thomas, who now took personal command. During the days that followed, both sides paused to regroup, with Hood taking a position just south of the city and the Cumberland River. To say that he was regrouping is something of a misnomer. The truth is he did not know what to do other than stand pat and throw up breastworks of his own. He had not half the strength of Thomas, but to withdraw back into Georgia was completely against his nature. He chose to stand his ground, hoping that raw courage would win out.

Thomas took two weeks before assailing the Rebels at Nashville, much to Grant's displeasure, and during this cold, icy interval, Hood ineptly ordered Forrest (with Buford and Jackson) east to the Murfreesboro area. There, assisted by infantry, he launched a series of minor attacks against rail and telegraph lines, and the blockhouses protecting them, hoping to sever communications with Chattanooga.

When Thomas did push forward on December 15, therefore, Forrest was not on the scene, and only Chambers's horse soldiers were at Hood's disposal. Perhaps Nathan would have made a difference, perhaps not. Certainly the Federal cavalry, commanded by Major General James Wilson (he had been dispatched by Sherman to help Thomas cope with Forrest), had a field day in his absence.

Substantially through Wilson's efforts, the Confederate left flank, guarded by Chalmers, was turned that day and driven back about four miles, even as the Union infantry pounded the center, necessitating a general retreat. Hood formed a new line on the 16th, anchored by Shy's Hill on the west and Overton's Hill on the east, but here Wilson's dismounted troopers, outnumbering Chalmers's men more than four to one, again prevailed.

Not that the Rebels submitted tamely. Late that evening, with the battle still raging, Colonel George Spalding of the 12th Tennessee (Union) Cavalry found that out firsthand as he led a sally against a desperate foe. "A running fight took place, charge and countercharge in quick succession," said a commentator, "in which the shouts of the combatants, the clang of sabres, and the rattle of pistols and rifles made the night one never to be forgotten." Suddenly Spalding found himself face-to-face with Colonel Edward Rucker of Chalmers's division, who had proven himself in many an encounter. "It was so dark both were at a disadvantage. Grappling with each other blindly, each wrested the sabre from his antagonist's hand and renewed the fight with the other's weapon. . . . The issue was doubtful till a stray shot broke Rucker's sword-arm, when he was compelled to surrender."

Rucker's service to his cause did not end there. Taken to the rear and questioned by one of Wilson's officers, he insisted reinforcements were at hand. "Forrest has just arrived with all the cavalry and will give you hell tonight! Mark what I tell you!" This bit of bravado in part convinced the Federals to halt the pursuit, possibly saving Hood's army from complete disaster.[23]

Forrest did not rejoin the main Rebel body until December 18, when the dispiriting retreat was well under way. Subsequently, in a council of war at Columbia, he convinced Hood he had no choice, despite the bad winter roads, than to evacuate Tennessee and return to Alabama.

"Give me 4,000 infantry," he said, asking for the command of the rear guard, "and I will give you the time and the opportunity to escape across the Tennessee."

On this occasion, Hood accepted his advice, though he sent Nathan less than 2,000 infantry, many without shoes, under Major General Edward Walthall. Nathan loaded them in wagons, to be disembarked when needed, and helped by Morton's eight cannon, his depleted 3,000 horsemen took up their new responsibilities. Coming after him would be Federal cavalry and infantry totaling some 40,000 men.

In the ensuing days, the clashes and skirmishes ran one into the other. Forrest would make temporary stands on favorable ground, lay ambushes, throw off shells from hidden artillery, and then, having delayed the pursuit for the nonce, would fall back to fight again. Reported George Thomas:

"[Hood's] army had become a disheartened and disorganized rabble of half-armed and barefooted men. . . . The rear-guard, however, was undaunted and firm, and did its work bravely to the last."

The Confederate main body crossed the Tennessee to eventual refuge on a pontoon bridge December 26, and Forrest, after laying a last ambush, followed them the next day. "The part which he took in the Hood retreat from Nashville," Colonel David Kelley would say, "in directing almost every movement of the army, suggesting the roads that should be taken, the manner in which the artillery and baggage-trains were to be moved, sending messengers every few hours to General Hood, giving the minutest practical details, showed him fully capable of handling an army of any size."[24]

Tennessee, once and for all, was lost to the Confederacy. But Forrest and his cavalry would remain a factor in the West, fighting on with superb courage.

FOURTEEN

THE EAST, SEPTEMBER 16–OCTOBER 27: CATTLE RAIDS AND HATCHER'S RUN

Grant's activities in the Richmond-Petersburg area at this juncture had settled into a mind-numbing siege. Though he made occasional forays against the capital, his main effort was south of the James against Petersburg. There he strove to push ever westward, hoping to stretch Lee's lines to the breaking point and sever his railroad supply routes. The Confederates, however, were not entirely on the defensive. Whenever the opportunity presented itself, they would leave their breastworks and strike some punishing blows. Two such sallies involved the resourceful Wade Hampton, now officially heading the Army of Northern Virginia's cavalry.

In early September, the South Carolinian learned from Sergeant George Shadburne, a scout who had donned a blue uniform and gone behind Union lines, that the enemy had some 2,500 cattle in lightly guarded corrals at Coggin's Point on the James River, eight miles from Grant's headquarters at City Point. These cattle could feed the half-starving Rebels for weeks, and Hampton resolved to go after them.

By September 14, he had assembled his raiding party: Rooney Lee's division; the brigades of Tom Rosser and James Dearing; and assorted detachments. Altogether, they totaled some 4,000 men. Before sunup the troopers were galloping down the Boydton Plank Road southwest of Petersburg to Dinwiddie Court House, skirting the Federal left, and then turning east toward the James.

Late the next day, they arrived at deepwater Blackwater Creek, where Hampton's pioneers rebuilt the bridge the enemy had destroyed, making the waterway passable. "[That] night we crossed over the Blackwater," said one officer of the Horse Artillery, "and were particularly enjoined not to make a noise, and several times the musical men of the column were cut short in attempted songs, which they thoughtlessly began. Nothing was heard but the steady tread of the horses and the rattle of sabres. The guns of the artillery had been muffled by grain-sacks."

About 3 a.m. the troopers took a brief rest. "One by one the men [stepped] down from their horses to the soft grass, overcome by the fatigue following rapid movements. We had now ceased to speculate where we were going. We were too sleepy, and soon most if not all were dozing on the ground with our bridle reins around our elbows. . . . The horses, too, slept, and showed no disposition to disturb their masters."[1]

By 5 a.m. on September 16, everyone had his orders. Rosser was to attack elements of the 1st District of Columbia Cavalry, who were guarding the cattle, at Sycamore Church, no more than a mile from the corrals at Coggin's Point. Rooney Lee, meanwhile, with the largest force was to advance from the left; Dearing, from the right. Their assignment was to block the roads and cut the telegraph lines between the corrals and the main Federal body, giving Rosser a head start in getting away with the cattle.

Routing the 250 men guarding the steers was no problem, and the all-Virginia Laurel Brigade, with much gleeful heehawing, soon was driving the herd southwestward back to the Blackwater. Hearing Rosser's gunfire, Rooney Lee simultaneously assaulted a far more substantial Federal camp, where most of the 1st District of Columbia, together with the 3rd New York and the 11th Pennsylvania, were bivouacking. These men, too, taken by surprise, quickly were scattered and put to flight. "Some, of course, were up and on guard," said the Rebel officer, "but the majority of the Federals were in bed in their little buttoned tents. We ran them out and took them prisoners in their night clothes."[2]

Hours later, the Confederates were crossing Blackwater Creek with their rustled steers—2,486 in number, according to one count—and burning the bridge behind them. "[They] soon found," wrote one contemporary, "that if the cattle were driven in one herd, the difficulties of moving them would be much increased, their speed would be much lessened and the animal in great crowds might become panic stricken, and so with the help of the [Federal] herders and captives, three or four hundred cattle were placed in [bunches]. . . . These were surrounded by the horsemen and forced forward as rapidly as the condition of the beasts would permit."[3]

Brigadier August Kautz, commanding the Union cavalry in the sector, was just beginning to see what was happening. "I found on reaching Sycamore Church," he said, "that Wade Hampton with his entire cavalry force had come upon my line . . . and had swept along [it] about six miles, taking out about three hundred men, and held the ground until they had gotten the beef herd." Throwing together some 500 men, he set out in what would be futile pursuit.

More dangerous was the response of the Union high command, who by now also had learned of the raid. Realizing that Hampton's southwestward route would take him in a wide arc before he regained the works at Petersburg, they dispatched Brigadier Henry Davies Jr. with 2,000 men from their own lines to intercept him. Galloping down the Jerusalem Plank Road, Davies needed to cover only half the distance as his foes.[4]

Hampton met the threat head-on. Even as the cattle were crossing the Nottoway River, he about 2 p.m. interposed the head of his seven-mile-long column between them and Davies, with the skirmishing intensifying, over the course of the afternoon, as more and more of his troopers joined the action.

Rosser took on the Federals first, then Dearing, and finally Rooney Lee. "We made haste to meet him, the enemy, sometimes at a trot, sometimes at a gallop, for fifteen miles," one of Lee's men would remark, "and at full speed came into line of battle just as the sun went down. The enemy was lavishing profuse attention upon us in the way of solid shot and shells, but we faced him resolutely and sent him back screaming and glittering-like meteors shot for shot, seemingly to say, 'Come take your beeves if you can.' "[5]

Nightfall brought the fighting to an end, with both sides disengaging. Early the next morning, both Hampton and the cattle entered the Confederate breastworks, where one famished South Carolina soldier remembered that a comrade "looked at [the steers] until his eyes watered, and his mouth, too, I reckon. I know mine did."

For weeks thereafter, the Rebels continually needled the Federals over the raid, with pickets on the front lines "bawling and bellowing like cattle," and calling out "Hello, Yanks! Want any fresh beef?"

Even Grant endured some subtle criticism. "When do you expect to starve out Lee and capture Richmond?" he was asked.

"Never," admitted the general-in-chief, "if our armies continue to supply him with beef-cattle."[6]

Hampton's second notable service during this period occurred on a rainy October 27 morning, when Grant sent three infantry corps—43,000 men—west toward Hatcher's Run and the Boydton Plank Road, again hoping to cut the Southside Railroad. Gouverneur Warren's 5th Corps and John Parke's 9th Corps were to assail the Rebel works directly, pinning down the enemy, while Winfield Scott Hancock's 2nd Corps was to move circuitously southwest around the Petersburg defenses, and then veer north toward the Southside.

Hancock crossed Hatcher's Run with his infantry and David Gregg's cavalry, and reached the Boydton Road about noon, but swampland and ignorance of the terrain impaired the progress of Warren and Parke, leaving his right flank vulnerable to counterattack. Here about 4 p.m. Confederate infantry under William Mahone and Hampton's cavalry sallied forth, intent on taking advantage of the tactical misstep.

Finding a gap between Hancock and Warren, the brash Mahone rushed into the opening, ripping the Federal lines asunder. "We were completely surrounded," said one New Yorker, "and in so small a cleared spot that the balls from the Rebel lines would pass clear over us or stop in our lines on opposite sides." Ordered by Hancock to have the men dig in, one of his officers asked in desperation, "General, which way will you have them face?"

Mahone's triumph, however, would be only temporary. Lacking reinforcements to expand the wedge he had made into Hancock's numerically superior lines, he soon found himself on the defensive. "It was like one man getting in between four," said one Rebel officer. "After making a brilliant dash, capturing a small number of prisoners, killing many and uttering disorganizing the enemy, Gen. Mahone became surrounded, but cut his way out in a very handsome manner."[7]

Bolstering Mahone in the frenzied fighting before the withdrawal was Hampton, who as usual had little regard for his own safety. Leading the divisions of Matthew Calbraith Butler and Rooney Lee, he pushed forward with his troopers time and again in slashing attacks. His son Preston, an aide, likewise galloped to the front, waving his hat and urging on the men, emulating his father's courage. Suddenly young Hampton took a bullet in the groin and toppled from the saddle. It would be a mortal wound.

His older brother Wade IV rushed to his side, only to be wounded himself, though not fatally.

Hampton now arrived, throwing himself on the ground as minié balls whistled by, and cradling Preston in his arms. The young man was still alive, but could not speak. The father kissed his cheek and whispered in his ear. "My son, my son!" he murmured.

Butler at this juncture joined his chief, who looked up at him with tear-filled eyes.

"Poor Preston . . . Poor Preston," Hampton softly repeated.

The son was carried to a wagon that would take him to the rear, even as a surgeon tried to dress the wound. Hampton watched for a few minutes, then abruptly remounted.

"Too late, doctor," he said. Then he galloped away, once more turning his face to the enemy.[8]

In great grief, Hampton continued the inconclusive fight for the rest of the day, with the Federals finally falling back to their original lines. "Until night he did not even know Wade's fate. He might be dead, too," later wrote Richmond hostess Mary Chestnut, who kept a salon for Confederate officers. "Now [his father] says no son of his must be in his command. When Wade recovers he must join some other division. The agony of that day—and the anxiety and duties of the battlefield—it is all more than a mere man can bear."[9]

With winter coming on, this affair at Hatcher's Run effectively brought to close, for 1864, the engagements around Richmond and Petersburg. But few people in the North doubted that the two strongholds ultimately would fall. Coupled with Sherman's recent capture of Atlanta, the Union's military dominance insured Lincoln's reelection on November 8.

FIFTEEN

THE WEST, NOVEMBER 16 – DECEMBER 21: MARCH TO THE SEA

Sherman moved east from Atlanta on November 16, leaving the city a smoking ruin behind him, eager to cut a swath of destruction through Georgia until he reached Savannah on the seacoast. He had some 60,000 men under his command, of whom about 5,500 were cavalry, and as he marched his front extended, at any given time, an awesome forty to sixty miles. His cavalry commander at this juncture was the amoral Judson Kilpatrick, the "damn fool" he was so quick to disparage, but a man whose courage, Sherman mistakenly believed, outweighed his lack of scruples.

Opposing this Federal juggernaut as best it could was 3,000 Georgia militia and Joseph Wheeler's cavalry corps, who numbered no more than 3,500 effectives.

On November 22, as Sherman's columns were converging on Milledgeville, then the state capital, the Confederate infantry rashly threw themselves on the army's right at nearby Griswoldsville. There some 600 of 2,000 assailants were cut down like wheat before a scythe. Captain Charles Wills of the 103rd Illinois would say: "We all felt that we had a sure thing. . . . By the time the first line had got [up] . . . three other lines emerged. . . . We then let loose on them with our muskets. . . . One after another their lines crumbled to pieces, and they took to the run."

Looking over the battlefield later, he was appalled. "Old gray-haired and weakly looking men and little boys, not over fifteen years old, lay dead or writhing in pain." What had they hoped to accomplish? "My neighborhood is ruined . . . these people are all my [friends]," a wounded Rebel in his sixties told him, gesturing to the bodies around him. Summed up Wills: "I hope we never have to shoot at such men again."[1]

In truth, with Sherman's twenty-four-day march to Savannah only a quarter complete, Georgians already were desperate. "It is evident that our soldiers are determined to burn, plunder and destroy everything in their way," said one Union officer approvingly. Foraging parties descended on homes, plantations, and farms each morning, and they were voracious. "They go where they please, seize wagons, mules, horses and harness, make the Negroes of the plantation hitch up, load the wagons with sweet potatoes, flour, meal, hogs, sheep, turkeys, chickens, barrels of molasses, and in fact everything good to eat, and sometimes considerably good to drink."[2]

Dolly Lunt, the widow of a Covington planter, tells us how the Federals behaved. "Like demons they rush in. My yards are full. To my smokehouse, my dairy, pantry, kitchen and cellar, like famished wolves they come, breaking locks and whatever is in their way. The thousand pounds of meat in my smokehouse is gone in a twinkling, my flour, my meat, my lard, butter, eggs, pickles of various kinds . . . wine, jars and jugs are all gone. My eighteen fat turkeys, my hens, chickens and fowls, my young pigs, are shot down in my yard as if they were Rebels themselves. Utterly powerless I ran out and appealed to the guard.

"I cannot help you, Madam, it is orders."

"A Captain Weber from Illinois came into my house. Of him I claimed protection from the vandals who were forcing themselves into my room. . . . He felt for me, and I gave him and several others the character of gentlemen. . . . I don't believe they would have molested women and children had they had their own way. . . ."[3]

Such violence, of course, was precisely what Sherman condoned. "Unless we can repopulate Georgia, it is useless to occupy it," he had told Grant before leaving Atlanta. "But the utter destruction of its [rail]roads, houses and people will cripple their military resources. . . . I can make the march, and make Georgia howl!"[4]

With Wheeler's Rebel cavalry unable to do more than nibble at their flanks, the Union troops marched into Milledgeville late on November 22 without firing a shot. In short order they burned warehouses, factories, machine shops, and the railroad depot, as well as 2,000 bales of cotton. Public buildings were plundered of anything of value, down to inkwells, and many a private home was ransacked.

There were high jinks as well. The next day bluecoats conducted a sham session of the Georgia legislature, complete with much drinking and laughing. "A number of bills and resolutions were put forward," said one historian, "including one that brought Georgia back into the Union. . . . Someone rushed in, shouting, 'The Yankees are coming!' This produced much '. . . mock panic.' "

Kilpatrick, three sheets to the wind, now took it upon himself to address the assembly. "I am a very modest man who never blows his own horn," he said in stentorian tones, unfailingly self-promoting even while drunk, "but I must tell you that I am the Old Harry on raids!"

"Mr. Speaker," someone called out, "I believe it is the custom to treat the Speaker."

"Indeed," said Kilpatrick, pulling out a flask, "I beg to inform this honorable body that I am going to do just that!" He took a long swallow amid great applause.[5]

November 24 found Kilpatrick east of Milledgeville, camping with his troopers at a large plantation and confiscating 500 horses. When he looked over the herd the next morning and realized the number was far greater than he could use as replacement mounts, he ordered most of the animals killed. His men methodically went among the horses, throwing blankets over their eyes to calm them, then smashing their heads with axes. The plantation owner looked on aghast, dismayed both by the senseless cruelty and by the growing heaps of carcasses, which he had no means of burying and which would soon be rotting in front of his house.

"My God!" he said, "I'll have to move away!"[6]

Kilpatrick's original orders had been to proceed to Millen and free the Union captives in the prison camp there. But the camp had been evacuated, and his new instructions called for him to march still farther east to Waynesborough and then turn north to burn the railroad bridge across Brier Creek.

The new mission was far more dangerous, putting him in an exposed position between the left of Sherman's columns and the Rebels at Augusta, and depriving him of infantry protection. Kilpatrick reacted characteristically, making his main camp the night of November 27 south of Waynesborough, where he though he would be safe, and sending a 200-man detachment under his adjutant, Major Lewellyn Estes, to do the dangerous work of destroying the trestle.

Joseph Wheeler, however, had been watching and waiting. He pounced on Estes and sent him packing, and then followed his retreating force into the Federal camp, which he struck at 1 a.m. on the 28th. Kilpatrick's troopers put up a spirited defense, holding off a series of attacks in dense fog, but their commander was much less sanguine, sending off couriers demanding infantry support. "Wheeler is all around us with a vastly superior force," he wrote, even though his own command, if anything, had the numerical advantage. "Hurry, or all will be lost!"[7]

Reinforcements arrived in early morning, and with their help Kilpatrick during the daylight hours conducted a retreat in echelon, with some of his regiments holding their ground, while others withdrew. Then the first group streamed through the second's protective lines to withdraw still farther. Just before dawn of the 29th, however, after the Union infantry had left, the arrangement broke down. Kilpatrick's regiments continued to fall back in echelon, but he, some aides, and his personal guard did not.

The reason for this oversight was Kilpatrick's dalliance with a black prostitute he earlier had taken into his bed. When Wheeler again struck, boldly charging into the headquarters camp, he created chaos. W. R. Davis, a trooper in the 4th Tennessee, remembered that "Kilpatrick barely escaped capture by mounting a bareback horse caparisoned only with a halter, he being bare-headed, barefooted, and with nothing on but his under clothing, leaving several horses, his gold-mounted sword, a pair of ivory-handled six-shooters, and a handsome saddle—all of which the boys presented to General Wheeler." How the prostitute fared we do not know.[8]

Kilpatrick now retreated to Louisville, Georgia, where he briefly rested and reorganized his command. In a subsequent report, he remained true to form, claiming he had fought his way through a Rebel trap after enduring "one of the most desperate cavalry charges I have ever witnessed."[9]

Oddly enough, the libertine Kilpatrick and the straitlaced Wheeler, who had been classmates at West Point, were both being accused by Georgia citizens of letting their men rob and pillage. In the former's case, of course, this was true; in the latter's, not necessarily so. It would be foolish to maintain that Wheeler's troopers never helped themselves to Southern food and fodder—sometimes they had no other recourse if they were to maintain themselves in the field. But wanton, wholesale theft was another matter.

The countryside was swarming, Wheeler insisted, "with organized [brigands] who do not and never did belong to my command." His immediate superior, General William Hardee, backed him up, writing Jefferson Davis, "The depredations ascribed to his command can be traced to bands of marauders claiming to belong to it." Indeed, Georgia during the Yankee march was a lawless place, where not only the invaders, but also bands of disgruntled men seeking to take advantage of the situation, were compounding the suffering.[10]

Cavalry skirmishes played little part in subsequent events. Taking care to travel with the infantry, Kilpatrick made several forays against Wheeler during early December, but they were minor. Seeing how well he was supported, the Rebel horse soldiers fell back northward to Augusta. By the 4th, Kilpatrick once again was in the Waynesborough area, where this time he succeeded in destroying the railroad trestle at Brier Creek.

His personal conduct during this period was so shameless it was almost farcical. Stopping at one plantation deserted by its owners, he summoned the black butler, Jacob Walker, and demanded to know where the family's valuables were hidden. Told they had been removed to Augusta for safekeeping, he decided to settle for Walker's gleaming shirt studs, which he assumed were solid gold. The butler kept his shirt intact only by convincing him, rightly, that the studs were brass.

Kilpatrick reached Springfield, less than twenty miles from Savannah, on the 8th. All along the way his men had robbed without restraint. Women's clothing and jewelry were particularly cherished. "The dirty, grimy, sweaty, heavily bearded troopers thought it great fun to [don] this finery," one observer said, "and pirouette like burlesque queens on a . . . runway." Georgia women understandably were outraged; Northern photographers, sending back snapshots of the merriment to their newspapers, were delighted.[11]

By December 10, the entire army was on the outskirts of Savannah, which was defended by General William Hardee, and Sherman, doubtless buoyed by the news of the Federal triumph against Hood at Franklin, Tennessee, was preparing to invest the city.

Feeding the army now had become a problem, testimony to the infertile land in the area. Food and fodder would have to be supplied by the Yankee fleet, which was lingering somewhere offshore. Sherman straightaway resolved to take Fort McAllister, just south of the city on Ossabaw Sound, and thereby bring in supplies—as well as siege guns—from the water.

This he did on December 13, sending General William Hazen's division in a successful assault on the redoubt. Hazen sums up the last stages of the attack: "The line moved on without checking, over, under, and through abatis, ditches, palisading, and parapets, fighting the garrison through the fort to the bomb-proofs, from which they still fought, and only succumbed as each man was individually overpowered."

Sherman celebrated by having dinner with Hazen, who had also invited Major George Anderson, the fort's commander, to sup with him. During the meal Anderson was shocked to see one of his slaves was waiting table.

"Bob," he asked, "have you joined the Yankees?"

"I'm working for Mr. Hazen," the man impassively replied.

"General," said Anderson to Cump, "it looks to me as if the game is up."

"Yes," said Sherman. "Slavery is gone, and the Confederacy a thing of the past."[12]

The South would fight on into the following spring, of course, but her cause was doomed. Soon Sherman was receiving his supplies from the sea, and awaiting his siege guns, preparatory to bombarding the city.

In a note of the 17th, he asked for Savannah's surrender. Over the next few days, Hardee procrastinated, and then in the early hours of the 21st, he evacuated the city by crossing the Savannah River via a pontoon bridge into South Carolina.

Kilpatrick, who did not participate in the attack on the fort and whose overall contributions to the campaign were minimal, nonetheless received Sherman's effusive praise. "The operations of the cavalry have been skillful and eminently successful," Cump told him. "You may have it on my signature that you acted wisely and well."

One Rebel soldier put the matter in perspective. "The march from Atlanta to Savannah was so little opposed," he said, "that it was a sort of holiday excursion to the Federals. He who desired to let himself loose had only to leave the ranks. He could rob and burn, and Sherman had no reproofs. The more he destroyed, the greater hero he was."[13]

1865

ONE
* * * *

THE EAST, FEBRUARY-MARCH: CAVALRY IN THE CAROLINAS

Sherman's march through Georgia to the gates of Savannah had inflicted great suffering on the populace, and his progress up South and North Carolina would impose more of the same. His purpose now was to move north and unite with Grant in Virginia, continuing to burn and pillage as he went. In these activities Kilpatrick would be a more than enthusiastic participant, terrorizing and robbing civilians with singular energy as he rode alongside the infantry.

"How shall I let you know where I am?" he had asked Cump upon getting his orders.

"Oh, just burn a bridge or something," Sherman had answered. "Make smoke, as the Indians do on the Plains."[1]

The Federals advanced into South Carolina on February 1, pushing inland toward Columbia, the state capital, and bypassing Charleston, which the enemy soon would evacuate. Sherman's troops remained in the neighborhood of 60,000.

Opposing them, under the command of General Pierre Beauregard, would be a mixed bag: the divisions of Lafayette McLaws and Ambrose Wright (8,000 total); some 3,000 South Carolina militia; Matthew Calbraith Butler's 1,500-man cavalry unit; some 1,500 of Gustavus W. Smith's Georgia militia; 4,000 survivors from the Army of Tennessee under Carter Stevenson; and Wheeler's horsemen, at best 4,500 effectives. The Confederates' strength would be 22,500.

For Kilpatrick at this point, punishing South Carolinians—the people who had begun the war with their firing on Fort Sumter—was the watchword. Galloping into Barnwell on the 6th, he let his men run wild. "They . . . fired Wm. deTreville's office, the Ivestman's store, [and] the Ferguson's barn," said a resident. ". . . Mrs. Oakman screamed, when the Yankees rode up the street."

Later Kilpatrick stabled his horses in the Church of the Holy Apostle. "To show the inhabitants how little he thought of them," said another resident, "the Baptistry . . . was used [as] a watering trough."

There was more violence on the 7th. The courthouse was torched, private homes were ravaged. "[The Yankees] behaved more like enraged tigers than human beings, running all over the town, kicking down fences, breaking in doors and smashing glasses."

That night, even as twenty-seven public and private buildings were burning, a sardonic Kilpatrick staged a ball at Banksia Hall, an estate just outside Barnwell. "Regarding [their invitations] as orders," said a townsman, "[the women] sat like sad ghosts through the whirling mazes of the dance, while their . . . dwellings were in flames. It was the bitterest satire I ever witnessed."[2]

Reporting these goings-on to Sherman, Kilpatrick joked about the destruction. "I changed the name Barnwell to Burnwell," he said.

Cump enjoyed the jest, and repeated it to others, but he may have realized that Kilpatrick was being excessive. "Spare dwellings that are occupied," he said, giving his subordinate advice that would be ignored, "and teach your men to be courteous to women."[3]

On February 11, Kilpatrick moved into Aiken, intending to give that non-strategic town northwest of Barnwell the same treatment, despite Sherman's warnings that he would not provide infantry support. Here Joseph Wheeler again was lying in wait, just as he had been at Waynesborough. The Rebels were positioned, concealed, and dismounted, along Aiken's backstreets, ready to close a trap. Kilpatrick foolishly led the 92nd Illinois right into it, and was fortunate he was not captured. Luckily, his other regiments, following behind, helped him cut his way out.

Never at a loss for words, he would report that he had been "most furiously attacked by Wheeler's entire command," and "fell back, fighting gallantly, disputing every foot." Besides, he subsequently added, "It was not a general fight, but simply a reconnaissance."[4]

Five days later, moving on the infantry's left flank, he had more success at Lexington, a town twenty miles west of Columbia, where he robbed the citizens with abandon. "The Chivalry have been stripped of most of their valuables," Lieutenant Thomas Myer wrote his wife. "Fine gold watches, silver pitchers, cups, spoons and forks . . . are as common in camp as blackberries. . . . I have about a quart of rings, earrings, breastpins."

The booty was divided throughout Sherman's army, explained Myer, according to rank, with commanders and staff taking the top fifth, the field officers the next best fifth, and the enlisted men the rest.[5]

On February 17, Sherman marched into Columbia with only minor incident. Just prior, Wade Hampton had considered making a stand, but soon had seen it would be hopeless. The South Carolinian had been detached from the Army of Northern Virginia and sent to take command of all cavalry in the area, including Wheeler's. Because the bulk of the Rebel infantry had not been able to reach the capital in time, his horsemen were in effect the only defenders—until they withdrew in the face of Sherman's advance.

While Hampton had little choice but to retreat, in view of the Federal numbers, he made two bad decisions before departing. One was to leave thousands of bales of cotton along the city's streets—barricades he had set up, but never used. Nor did he make sufficient effort, despite Mayor Thomas Goodwyn's urging, to get rid of the vast amount of liquor in Columbia.

Sherman was met by Mayor Goodwyn, who surrendered the city and begged him not to sack it. Cump told him not to worry, that only government buildings and arsenals, and the railroads, would be destroyed, "that we did not intend to stay long, and had no purpose to injure the private citizens or private property." He spent the rest of the day and evening in exhausting meetings and inspections, and with the coming of darkness went to bed.

That night, bright lights flickering on Sherman's bedroom wall awakened him, and he soon saw that Columbia was ablaze. "The fire continued to increase, and the whole heavens became lurid. I dispatched messenger after messenger to [my generals], and received from them repeated assurances that all was being done that could be done, but that high wind was spreading the flames beyond control." Not until 3 or 4 a.m. did the wind moderate, and by then 30,000 people were homeless.[6]

This account is notable for what it leaves out. Major Thomas Osborn, chief artillery officer for the Army of the Tennessee, would maintain that Hampton's men had ignited some of the bales before leaving, but thereafter the Federals had caused the catastrophe. "When the [first] brigade occupied the town the citizens and Negroes brought out whiskey in buckets, bottles, and in every conceivable manner treated the men to all they would drink . . . and the entire brigade became drunk. The enemy had taken the cotton out of the storehouses . . . and set it on fire, which the citizens and soldiers, when we entered, were trying to subdue and had nearly accomplished. But when they became thoroughly intoxicated they began to . . . plunder freely."

Then the wind sprang up, reigniting the smoldering flames, with help from tipsy soldiers holding lighted cigars to the cotton. "By this time all parties were willing to assist [the blaze]. . . . The Negroes piloted the men to the best places for [looting], and both men and Negroes by nightfall were setting fires rapidly. . . . The first brigade was relieved. . . . The second brigade was also relieved, as they had also become intoxicated. The third brigade was put to work to stop the fire."

Before the night was over, substantially more Union soldiers would be required to clear the city of their drunken comrades. "Many would not be arrested and were shot," said Osborn. "Forty of our men were killed in this way, many were wounded, and several . . . drunk men were burned to death."[7]

Regardless of who was responsible for the fire, there is little question that Sherman's slash-and-burn tactics were the driving force. Said Captain Charles Wills: "Whiskey and wine flowed like water. . . . This gobbling of things so, disgusts me much. I think the city should be burned, but would like to have it done decently."[8]

Kilpatrick on February 17, meanwhile, still on the army's left flank, was leaving Lexington a blackened ruin, and during the next few days he would create similar mischief in Alston and Monticello. Then on the 22nd, outside Chester, he was told that eighteen of his troopers, who had gone out to forage and loot, had been captured by Wheeler's men and summarily executed. He immediately informed the Rebel cavalryman that a like number of his troopers would be hung in turn.

Before this order could be carried out, Kilpatrick received an urgent note from Wheeler, denying the killings and pledging a prompt investigation. Mollified, he arranged a meeting with his fellow West Pointer on the 27th at Lancaster, for the purpose of exchanging prisoners. "The threats by both to execute captives in retaliation for atrocities committed in the field," explained a Kilpatrick biographer, "had made each anxious for the safety of friends held by the other." The meeting went well, and soon twenty Northerners and twenty Southerners were rejoining their respective commands.[9]

Kilpatrick during this period continued his determined womanizing. Though his conquests generally had been from the lower social classes, he now began a relationship with an elegant young woman named Marie Boozer, whom he befriended in the aftermath of the burning of Columbia. She was beautiful and spirited, and during their stay at Lancaster she insisted on the pretense of separate bedrooms. Upon leaving the town, the happy couple rode off in a commandeered carriage, complete with piles of blankets to ward off the cold.[10]

In early March, the Federals crossed over into North Carolina, heading toward Fayetteville. Called back from retirement and leading the Confederate defense at this juncture was General Joseph Johnston, whom we last saw during the Atlanta Campaign. He and Hampton now resolved to interpose Rebel infantry between Kilpatrick and his foot-soldier support, thereby giving the South Carolinian an opportunity to smash his opposite number.

The clash came at Monroe's Crossroads, outside of Fayetteville, before sunrise on March 10. Butler's men were to dash into the Union camp from the north, Wheeler's from the west, and rout the enemy and seize Kilpatrick, who was sleeping in a private house—with Marie Boozer—to the rear of the bivouac. Suddenly, through a heavy mist, Butler saw more than a hundred Rebels running back toward him. "Suspicion flashed through [my] mind," he said, "that [we] had been repulsed. It turned out that these were Confederates, who [had been] prisoners . . . and [were] running for liberty. One poor fellow . . . seized my leg, embraced and kissed it."[11]

Initially the bluecoats offered little resistance, but they soon rallied among nearby trees, raining bullets on Butler's men, now exposed in the camp clearing. Meanwhile, Wheeler's troopers were nowhere in sight.

Here Joe Wheeler himself rode up to Butler, shouting above the noise of battle, "Where's your command?"

"Scattered [to] hell!" Butler yelled. "Where's yours?"

"Tried to attack from my side but encountered a bog. . . . Couldn't get my men across." Unable to close the trap, Hampton signaled a withdrawal.

Kilpatrick, however, had not waited to see the reversal of fortune.

Wrote E. L. Wells, one of Butler's troopers, who was nearing the Union commander's billet during the early moments of triumph: "Just then there bolted from the door a sorry-looking figure in his shirt and drawers. The fugitive"—who turned out to be Kilpatrick—"made no fight." Several Rebel riders rushed up to him.

"Where's General Kilpatrick?" one demanded.

"There he goes!" Kilpatrick replied, pointing to a Yankee fleeing on a black horse. The riders took off in pursuit, and seconds later Kilpatrick, grabbing a stray mount, was making his own escape.

Wells continues: "Now in wild alarm there emerged from the house, whose weather boards fast were being perforated by chance bullets, a strange apparition, one quite out of place in such wild scenes—a forlorn, forsaken damsel." It was Marie Boozer. "She looked for a moment disconsolately at her carriage . . . as if with the vague idea in her dazed head that it was high time for her to be leaving, and then stood still in mute despair." Here a trooper took her to a drainage ditch, "within which she crouched in safety, as if it had been a riflepit. It was noticed, however, that, in spite of the risk thus incurred, she persisted in lifting her head from time to time . . . to see what was going on."[12]

Hampton, though he had inflicted almost 200 casualties, had not seriously damaged the Federal cavalry. The Confederates dropped back at this point north of Fayetteville, where Johnston began concentrating his meager force in the Averasboro-Bentonville area, hoping to fall on the enemy's left wing before the right could come to its assistance. The first such meeting was at Averasboro on March 15, when the Rebels fenced inconclusively with the oncoming enemy.

More to the point was the ensuing battle near Bentonville, which Hampton and Johnston hoped would be a tactical triumph. Explained Alexander C. McClurg, a Union staff officer: "When Johnston, with skillful strategy . . . massed his scattered troops near the little hamlet of Bentonville, and placed them, unknown to [Sherman] . . . across the road upon which two [Federal] divisions were marching, he proposed to . . . sweep the two divisions from the field, in the first furious onset. . . . Then, with half the army destroyed, with supplies exhausted, and far from any base, he believed General Sherman . . . would no longer be a match for his elated troops."[13]

Hampton's role in this action, besides selecting the site for the ambush—a high, wooded ridge dominating an open field through which the enemy would be marching—was using his cavalry as bait the morning of March 19, drawing the bluecoats into the trap. Leading the Rebel infantry under Johnston at this juncture were Alexander Stewart, holding down the right flank; William Hardee, in the center; and Braxton Bragg, restored to field command, on the left.

In the beginning, all went well. "The plan proposed was that the cavalry should move out at daylight," said Hampton. "The infantry could then be deployed, with one corps across the main road and the other two obliquely in echelon to the right. . . . As soon as these positions were occupied, I was to fall back . . . through the first corps [Bragg's] and, passing to the rear . . . take a position on our extreme right."

Sherman still was unsuspecting. "There is nothing there but . . . cavalry," he told Henry Slocum, who was heading his left wing. "Brush them out of the way."

Slocum soon found otherwise, encountering blistering infantry fire that brought him up short and forced him into a defensive posture. Then about noon, when Stewart on the right was to turn the Union left, the situation began to unravel for the Confederates. Hardee, unfamiliar with the terrain and lacking accurate maps, was late coming up, leaving a gap in the Rebel center. Instead of closing the opening, the timorous Bragg panicked, demanding—and getting—reinforcements even while the Federals were retreating.

Hampton had thinly veiled contempt for Bragg's conduct. "In order to hold the gap until the arrival of Hardee," he said, "I had two batteries of horse artillery . . . placed in the vacant space. . . . All the guns of both batteries were admirably served, and their fire held the enemy in their front until Hardee reached his allotted position."

But the damage had been done. The Federal left had not been turned when it was most vulnerable, and when the Rebels did attack, about 3 p.m., Slocum was in line of battle and ready to fight. Stewart and Hardee charged time and again, but to no avail. Meanwhile, Bragg did nothing, remaining in place. Reported Johnston: "The impossibility of concentrating the Confederate forces to attack the Federal left wing, while in column on the march, made complete success also impossible." Hampton was less circumspect. "Much precious time had been lost by a delay in following up promptly the success gained by [our] troops in their first conflict with the enemy. Bragg should [have changed] the front . . . which movement would have aligned him with the other corps and enabled him to attack."[14]

Some 16,000 men were engaged on each side during the affair, with the Confederates losing 2,600 men and the Federals 1,600.

———

Bentonville would be the last engagement of any consequence in North Carolina. Though cavalry units continued to skirmish in the area, and Lee remained a stubborn holdout on the Richmond-Petersburg front, the end of the war was fast approaching.

TWO

* * * *

THE WEST, MARCH – APRIL:
WILSON V. FORREST IN ALABAMA

The last important clash between the troopers in the West took place in March between the cerebral James Wilson, the onetime Grant aide who had been so successful at Nashville, and the rough-edged, hot-tempered Nathan Forrest, arguably the finest horse soldier in the Western theater. The latter, newly named a lieutenant general, now was in command of all Confederate cavalry in Alabama, Mississippi, and east Louisiana. These men were some 10,000 in number, but were widely dispersed and, in many cases, badly mounted and armed. One of Forrest's first acts, as a morale booster, was to form the troopers into three divisions and, so far as possible, to group them by states.

General James Chalmers was placed in charge of the Mississippians, brigades led by Frank Armstrong, Wert Adams, and Peter Starke (4,500 total). General William "Red" Jackson headed the Tennessee division, the brigades of Tyree Bell and Alexander W. Campbell (substituting for Edward Rucker, captured at Nashville), together with Lawrence Sullivan Ross's Texans (3,800). Abraham Buford had the last division, which with the remnants of the Kentucky troopers under Edward Crossland consisted mostly of the Alabama cavalry under Philip Roddey (1,700). Robert Mc-

Culloch's woefully decimated Missouri stalwarts became part of Forrest's personal guard.

From his headquarters in Verona, Mississippi, Nathan issued a manifesto to his men, calling for "strict obedience to all orders" and promising "prompt punishment . . . for all violations of law." He served particular notice on those deserters and robbers preying on civilians under the guise of being raiders, saying, "their acts of lawlessness and crime demand a remedy, which I shall not hesitate to apply even to extermination."[1]

But the width and breadth of the area Forrest was protecting, as well as his horse and supply problems, were not easily dealt with. Wrote his campaign historians: "He had to recruit his regiments, to disperse his men to procure remounts and secure clothing, to glean the lean Confederate arsenals and armories for weapons and ammunition, to watch a long frontier bristly with foes; in sooth, not only to mould resources into effective form, but in great part to create them."

Meeting with Federal officers during this period to discuss the care of prisoners, Forrest nonetheless showed no concern. "To think quickly and concretely, and to decide likewise, seemed to be his mental habit," said Major Lewis Hosea admiringly. "He speaks of his success with a soldierly vanity, and expresses the kindest feeling toward prisoners and wounded."

Before the conference broke up, Forrest sent off a verbal warning shot. "Jist tell General Wilson that I know the nicest little place down below here . . . and when he is ready, I will fight him with any number from one to ten thousand cavalry, and abide the issue. Wilson may pick his men, and I'll pick mine. He may take his sabers and I'll take my six-shooters."

Wilson at Gravelly Springs, Alabama, in the northwest corner of the state, meanwhile had much the advantage of the situation. His command was concentrated and poised to move south, "well-armed, splendidly mounted, perfectly clad and equipped," and after the rout of Hood at Nashville, quietly confident. "His men [were] all in hand, the vast resources of the arsenals and depots of the United States were at his easy disposition, and so he was left free to give his thoughts and care exclusively to the molding of his force."[2]

The Federals left Gravelly Springs on March 22, some 12,000 mounted men together with 1,500 infantry and guns, and proceeded south in three columns, the better to confuse the enemy, toward Jasper and the Black Warrior River. Their aim was to seize and sack first Selma and then Montgomery, Alabama, two all-important munitions and manufacturing centers, and later to move in Sherman's footsteps through Georgia. Comprising three divisions, led by Edward McCook, Eli Long, and Emory Upton, they made an imposing sight as they clattered along. "Never can I forget the brilliant scene," said Major Hosea, "as regiment after regiment filed gaily out of camp, decked in all the paraphernalia of war, with gleaming arms, and guidons given to the wanton breeze. Stirring bugle sounds woke the slumbering echoes of the woods; cheer after cheer went up from joyful lips."[3]

By the 29th, Wilson had covered 100 miles and was across the Warrior River and approaching the hamlet of Elyton (now the city of Birmingham), sixty miles north of Selma. There he sent John Croxton's brigade, McCook's division, west to Tuscaloosa, again as a diversion, with orders to raze the town.

Forrest during this advance had not been idle, using his scouts to follow Wilson's progress and ordering William Jackson and James Chalmers to meet him near Selma, which he correctly guessed was the invader's main target. If all went well, Chalmers would join him in time to take on Wilson in front, while Jackson, coming up from Tuscaloosa to the west, would attack the bluecoats in rear. With Nathan at this point, besides his personal escort, were only the brigades of Philip Roddey and Edward Crossland.

John Croxton meanwhile on the afternoon of the 31st was blundering into Jackson's own rear, coming between the tail of his mounted column and his guns and supply wagons. A Yale-trained lawyer in civilian life, Croxton was well regarded in the army. But on this occasion, he faltered. Instead of wrecking the cannon and ordnance, and then continuing to Tuscaloosa to inflict like damage on the city, he did neither, deciding instead to tag along behind the Rebel column. "Jackson was for a time entirely ignorant of Croxton's presence," said a contemporary historian, "and had the Union commander moved rapidly westward, he could have captured every gun and wagon."

Jackson soon learned the Federals were behind him, however, and with his far greater numbers, he turned on Croxton savagely, forcing him into ignominious flight and making him a nonfactor in the advance on Selma. "He ran away with such celerity that he soon had Jackson many miles behind him." Croxton did not stop until he was back at the Warrior River, which he recrossed on April 2.[4]

Leaving Elyton's factories in ruins, Wilson with Emory Upton in the van crossed the Cahaba River on March 31 and that afternoon reached Montevallo. Here the Federals had brushed aside a handful of Roddey's men—Jackson and Chalmers still being many miles away—and taken the town. Now, just south of Montevallo, Roddey massed his brigade and waged a second delaying action. "Greatly inferior in numbers, the Confederates were soon worsted, and [again] driven southward . . . to Six-Mile Creek," said Forrest's campaign historians, "where Roddey, being reinforced by Crossland's small brigade of Kentuckians, and the ground being favorable, [made] a stand." But the odds were too great, and the Rebels again were forced to fall back.

During these clashes, which covered some twenty miles, Forrest returned from a scouting mission on the Cahaba River at Centreville. There he had posted a guard at a vital bridge, a span that had to be kept intact if Jackson and Chalmers were to cross the waterway and come up in timely support.

Now, with only seventy-five troopers, he threw himself into the running fight. "Forming his little following—upon each man of whom he could rely—into a column of fours . . . he charged boldly from his covert into the moving mass, and broke through. Turning, he dashed upon the fragment northward of him, and drove it rearward for half a mile. But there his adversary stood drawn up in heavy line of battle."

Changing his direction, Forrest moved south, galloping past dead troopers. Soon he learned that Wilson was ahead of him, pressing Roddey and Crossland back toward Selma. "Being in the very midst of the whole Federal force . . . it was incumbent upon him to withdraw, and find his way speedily to the main body."[5]

This Forrest did, taking a circuitous route. By nightfall, he was back with his men, intent on impeding the Federal advance until Jackson and Chalmers arrived. What he did not know, however, was that Wilson before dawn would intercept his dispatches and, learning his plans, would send McCook to destroy the Cahaba River bridge. Jackson and Chambers would be of little help in the defense of Selma.

"If all the [Confederate] forces had been concentrated, as Forrest intended," said one rueful Rebel, "somewhere between Montevallo and Selma would have been fought the cavalry battle of the ages."[6]

The next day, April 1, at Ebenezer Church some twenty miles north of Selma, an unsuspecting Forrest with less than 2,000 troopers and militia resumed the fight, taking on four times his numbers, still expecting reinforcements. "As soon as Forrest saw [the Federals] riding down upon him with sabers in air, he placed himself in line with his escort and Crossland's Kentuckians," reported an early biographer. "He ordered his men to reserve the fire of their rifles until the enemy arrived within one hundred yards. . . . They were then to draw their revolvers and with one in each hand to ride in and among their assailants and use the weapons at close quarters."

Nathan was in the center of the maelstrom. "I saw General Forrest surrounded by six Federals at one time, and they were all slashing at him," said Lieutenant George Cowan. "One of them struck one of his pistols and knocked it from his hand. Private Phil Dodd was fortunately near, and spurred his horse to the rescue, and shot the Federal soldier, thus enabling General Forrest to draw his other pistol, with which he killed another of the group."

The man slashing at Forrest's arm and hand, and inflicting some bloody wounds, was Indiana Captain James D. Taylor, and Nathan later would admit he had been lucky. "If that boy had known enough to give me the point of his saber instead of its edge," he remarked, "I should not be here to tell you about it."

Remembered another Taylor, Tennessee Captain J. N. Taylor: "The odds were heavily against us, but Forrest told us we must hold them back until he could concentrate the troops near Selma. He was at the front all the time. On one occasion, in a particularly important moment . . . the general called for some volunteers to make a desperate charge, offering to lead them himself. Sergeant Parks said, 'General, if you are going into this charge the escort will leave, but if you stay where you are, we will do whatever you tell us.' The general said, 'All right, boys,' and we accomplished the task."[7]

Despite these heroics, Nathan soon was falling back anew. The Yankee pressure was too great, relieved only by the coming of darkness. By noon on April 2, he was leading his men into Selma and reporting to General Richard Taylor. "Forrest appeared, horse and man covered with blood," said Taylor, "and announced the enemy at his heels, and that I must move at once to escape capture. I felt anxious for him, but he [insisted] he was unhurt and would cut his way through. . . . My engine started toward Meridian, and I barely escaped."[8]

Forrest now positioned some 1,400 troopers from Frank Armstrong's Mississippi brigade—the only men from Chalmers's division to reach him—on the left of the Selma fortifications, and a like number of

Roddey's Alabamians on the right. In the center he placed 2,500 ill-trained militia, hoping the veterans on either side would give them heart. The city's three-mile-long works were formidable, with walls six feet high, protected by abatis, palisades, and ditches. But the Rebels were so strung out that there were gaps of as much as ten feet between each man. The thinness of their lines, along with a shortage of grape and canister, would be their undoing.

Jackson and Chalmers, meanwhile, largely remained absent from the action. The former, delayed by his pursuit of Croxton and the burning of the bridge over the Cahaba at Centreville, never would fall on the Union rear. The latter at this juncture, though he had managed to cross the river farther south at Selma, was bogged down in rain-swollen swamps, unable to reach his chief.

Wilson on April 2 continued to enjoy good fortune. Nearing Selma that morning, he held in his hand a sketch of the city's fortifications, provided by the English engineer who had designed them and who had renounced his Southern sympathies. Supplied with this information, he quickly made his plans. Once the sun was setting, Eli Long was to advance on the Union right against Armstrong's Mississippians, coming over a concealing ridge and covering 600 yards at the double-quick. Simultaneously, Emory Upton was to move through woodland and attack on Long's left, where, as luck would have it, the Rebel militia was posted.

Sometime about 5 p.m., however, the battle began prematurely. Lead elements from Chalmers's division finally came up in Long's rear, harassing his led horses and pack animals. Sending a regiment back to deal with them, the Union commander instinctively moved forward with his main force against the Selma works. "Appreciating that if he halted with his portion of the line . . . the assault might fail . . . ," said a contemporary historian, "Long in person led a desperate charge of his gallant troops upon that portion of the Confederate works defended by Armstrong."

Initially the assault incurred heavy losses. "In less time than it takes to tell," said one Union officer, "over three hundred of Long's men were killed and wounded. Long himself was stricken down"—taking a ball in the head that paralyzed him for two weeks—"together with two of his three brigade commanders and four colonels." Only the lack of grape and canister precluded greater carnage.

Then Upton attacked with his columns, hitting the part of the Rebel line defended by the militia. "These troops . . . fled the field, leaving a gap through which the Union soldiers swarmed," the contemporary went on. "Forrest, seeing these men give way, rushed into the break . . . and endeavored to stem the tide of disaster until Roddey could be moved over to unite with Armstrong. In overwhelming force . . . the Federals swept him back, however, before the new alignment could be made, forcing Armstrong and Roddey to withdraw their troops, with considerable loss, to a second or interior line."[9]

Soon the inner works also were crumbling. "The scene generally was one of the wildest confusion," said Forrest's campaign historians. "The Confederates, beaten from the breastworks, were rushing toward their horses; in the town, the streets were choked . . . with soldiers and citizens hurrying to and fro. Clouds of dust rose and so filled the air, that it was difficult to distinguish friend from foe." Wilson, who was riding with Long's troopers during these climactic moments, was flung to the ground when a bullet grazed his horse, causing it to rear. He picked himself up, remounted, and quickly resumed command.[10]

By nightfall, even as the beleaguered Robert E. Lee in the East was evacuating Richmond and Petersburg, the Federal triumph at Selma was complete. Forrest and a handful of men managed to cut their way out and flee eastward to Plantersville and thence to Marion, but most Confederates were not so fortunate—some 2,700 of them were captured, killed, and wounded.

Wilson at this point did not know that Grant had finally broken Lee's lines and was forcing the Army of Northern Virginia's final retreat toward Appomattox. During the next eight days he set about destroying the city's arsenals, machine shops, and railroads, and reestablishing his communications with McCook and Croxton. He also took the time, on April 7, to meet with Forrest to discuss prisoner exchange. The conference, held in a plantation house near the Cahaba, provided the opportunity for a candid exchange between the two horse soldiers.

"Well, General, you have beaten me badly," said Forrest, "and [it is] the first time I am compelled to make such an acknowledgement."

"Our victory was not without cost," replied Wilson. "You put up a stout fight."

Forrest, candid as ever, shook his head. "If I had captured your entire force twice over, it would not compensate for the blow you've inflicted upon us."[11]

Wilson next proceeded east to Montgomery, the first capital of the Confederacy, which he entered without incident on April 12. There, while sacking and burning the city's military and rail facilities, he heard rumors that Lee had surrendered on April 9 and that Jefferson Davis was on the run but, receiving no fresh orders, he crossed the Coosa River and marched to Columbus, Georgia. Moving into the city on the 16th, he crushed all resistance and continued eastward toward Macon. Not until the 20th would he learn that Sherman had accepted the surrender of Confederate troops under Joseph Johnston in North Carolina and that the war, in effect, was at an end.

Forrest meanwhile, joined at last by Jackson's division and the rest of Chalmers's men, sought to energize his battered command. As late as April 25, he was still telling his troops that he did not believe Lee had surrendered, and that they should be "firm and unwavering." Then, five days later, he was notified by General Taylor that a cease-fire had been declared in the area and, subsequently, that Lee and Johnston had indeed offered up their swords.

Many of Nathan's men wanted to fight on, saying they would never give up as long as they had guns and horses, and urging that he lead them into the Trans-Mississippi to continue the struggle in west Louisiana and Texas. But Forrest demurred. Whatever his feelings, he would not risk his men's lives now that the main Rebel forces and his superiors had surrendered.

On May 8, he and his troopers, many with tears in their eyes, gathered around a storied battle flag, that of the 7th Tennessee. "The old bullet-torn flag, whose blue cross had been triumphantly borne aloft for years at the cost of so much blood and valor, they would never part with," recounted a contemporary. ". . . The men reverently gathered around the staff . . . and, cutting the silk into fragments, each soldier carried away with him a bit of the treasure. The flag had been the gift of a young lady of Aberdeen, Mississippi, made from her bridal dress, and had never . . . been abandoned by the men . . . after it was committed to their guardianship."

The next day, Forrest issued a poignant farewell address, which read in part: "I have never on the field of battle sent you where I was unwilling to go myself, nor would I now advise you on a course which I found myself unwilling to pursue. You have been good soldiers, you can be good citizens. Obey the laws, preserve your honor, and the government to which you have surrendered can afford to be and will be magnanimous."[12]

THREE
* * * *

THE EAST, JANUARY–APRIL:
MOSBY'S LAST HURRAH

Back in northern Virginia in early 1865, John Mosby was slowly recovering from the wound he had received at year's end, and command of the Rangers devolved on Dolly Richards and William Chapman. Richards would stay in the "Confederacy" during the winter, but a scarcity of food and fodder would force Chapman, with about half the force, to migrate to the Northern Neck, the area between the Rappahannock and Potomac Rivers east of Fredericksburg. He would not return until mid-April.

Richards meanwhile stayed on the attack, just as if Mosby was still directing operations. Though General Tom Devin's 2,000-man cavalry brigade was posted in Loudoun County during January and February in an effort to pacify the countryside, the Rebels kept up the pressure. Besides harassing Union sentries and outposts, they succeeded in derailing two freight trains near Duffield's Station on the Baltimore & Ohio during this period, cutting the Federal supply lines and carting away foodstuffs ranging from coffee beans to canned oysters.

Sheridan's men, of course, quickly responded to these incursions, targeting houses where the Rangers might be taking shelter and making sudden overnight strikes. One such foray began at dusk on February 18, when

225 men from the 14th Pennsylvania and 21st New York under Major Thomas Gibson rode into Fauquier County. Directed by two Ranger turncoats, the Federals split into two columns, one under Gibson going to Markham, with the other under Captain Henry Snow moving to Upperville, where they expected to reunite.

Shortly after the columns parted, however, Gibson had second thoughts about where they would rendezvous, and he sent Snow a message to meet him instead at Piedmont. Whether his subordinate received these orders we do not know, but Snow subsequently made no effort to go there.

Once in Upperville, Snow left most of his men in town to conduct searches, and with a small escort rode to the nearby home of Dolly Richards's father. There he came up empty-handed, unable to find the Ranger, who with some comrades was hiding in a small room behind a sliding wall panel. Returning to town, Snow found to his chagrin that his troopers, who in the interim had captured three prisoners, also had laid their hand on some barrels of whiskey. Perhaps one-third were drunk, a few so besotted that they could not get on their horses.

If Snow did know he should have been going on to Piedmont, the condition of his men made the matter moot. He forthwith skedaddled out of Upperville and rode west through Ashby's Gap into the Shenandoah.[1]

Gibson during the early hours of February 19 had been more successful, swooping up eighteen Rangers at Markham and riding on undisturbed to Piedmont. He waited there impatiently for Snow, and then suspecting that his change of orders had not been received, galloped north to rally with him at Upperville. There he was told his subordinate already had returned to Federal headquarters in the Valley.

It was not until midmorning that Major Gibson and his 125 men themselves reached Ashby's Gap, with dire results. The delay had enabled Dolly Richards and some forty Rangers to arrive on the scene. Pistols blazing, they closed with the Federals on a mountain path so narrow that Gibson's men were riding in single file and could not form a line or use their carbines to advantage. Within minutes, the fight was over. Not only did Richards free the prisoners, but he killed, wounded, or captured some 90 bluecoats. "It was the most brilliant thing our men ever did," said Mosby, writing to a friend after the war.[2]

Days later, the Gray Ghost would be back with his men, but facing a new adversary. Sheridan was recalled to Petersburg to participate in the final push against Lee, and was replaced by Winfield Scott Hancock, an able and well-regarded general from the Army of the Potomac.

Though the outlook for the Confederates on all fronts was dismal, Mosby continued his maneuvering against the enemy. The most important of these clashes began on March 21, when he rebuffed a Yankee effort to seal off the "Confederacy" and catch him in a trap. The morning before, Hancock had sent Marcus Reno with 1,000 men—300 of them cavalry—south into Loudoun County to chase him down, simultaneously blocking the escape passes in the Blue Ridge and ordering 500 more cavalry west from Fairfax Court House.

Mosby now gathered together about 130 Rangers and met Reno's cavalry near Hamilton, where he set up a trap of his own. Leaving a score of his men on the road under the command of Jim Wiltshire, he concealed the rest in the woods to their right rear. The 12th Pennsylvania in the Federal van took the bait, sounding the charge even as the Rangers on the road turned tail. When the enemy galloped forward, enfilading fire from the woods withered their ranks just before Wiltshire's men wheeled about and compounded the damage. In all, a score of Yankees were killed and wounded and a dozen taken prisoner.

Pursuing Reno's retreating cavalry into Hamilton, Mosby's men kept up their reputation for looting. One Ranger shot down a Yankee and then noticed the man was wearing a large diamond ring. With bullets flying past, he jumped from his horse and grabbed the dead man's hand. When the ring did not come loose, he pulled out a knife and cut off the finger.[3]

Reno's cavalry that night sought shelter with the infantry and, for the next several days, while enduring constant sniper fire, stayed near them for protection. Marching through Snickersville, Upperville, and Middleburg, the combined force searched houses and farms for Rangers and weapons, but to little effect. In his report, their shaken commander estimated that he had been attacked by at least 500 horse soldiers, testimony to Mosby's evasive, hard-hitting tactics. For his part, Hancock was experiencing what Sheridan and other Union officers had been up against in coping with the Rangers. He could not understand, he would say, why such a strong Federal expedition "accomplished much less than I had expected."[4]

In the opening days of April, Mosby's activities took on a surreal aspect. It was as if he was refusing to admit that the Southern cause was doomed. Not only did he summon William Chapman back from the Northern Neck to carry on the fight, but he organized still another Ranger company. Named to command it was George Baylor, twenty-four, who had served under Turner Ashby and risen to the rank of lieutenant in the 12th Virginia Cavalry.

On April 6, ordered by Mosby to create mischief near Harpers Ferry, Baylor and his fifty men at first scored a signal success. Wearing blue top-coats, they passed through the picket line of the so-called Loudoun Rangers, a much hated Unionist independent unit, and took their enemies completely by surprise. A handful were killed and wounded, some sixty were captured, and the Loudoun Rangers as a body ceased to exist.

Soon, however, Baylor himself came a cropper. The night of April 9, even as Lee was surrendering at Appomattox, the new commander did not post sentries while bedding down near Manassas Junction on the Orange & Alexandria Railroad. Predictably, Federal cavalry—in this case, the 8th Illinois—discovered the camp and the next morning descended on it with a vengeance. Baylor and some veterans fought a desperate holding action, but his company dissolved, most men fleeing for their lives.[5]

In the days after Appomattox, the Federal authorities made stringent efforts to obtain Mosby's surrender as well, in effect offering him and his men paroles if they would give up their arms. Hancock, nonetheless, remained wary, thinking the Rangers might simply disband and melt into the countryside. "All his men have fine animals, and are generally armed with two pistols only," he mused. "They will not give up these things, I presume, as long as they can escape."

Mosby hemmed and hawed during this period, which on April 14 saw the mortal wounding of Lincoln by John Wilkes Booth. Heightening the suspense was that Lewis Powell, a former Ranger, had been one of Booth's accomplices, and many in Washington wondered if the Gray Ghost had been involved in the plot. "If Mosby is sincere," Secretary of War Stanton wired Hancock, "he might do much toward detecting and apprehending the murderers of the President."

The two sides met at Millwood in the Shenandoah on the 18th—the Ranger leader by now having been advised by Robert E. Lee to give up—but the talks proved inconclusive, with Mosby claiming he was awaiting the outcome of the fighting between Joe Johnston and Sherman in North Carolina. A forty-eight-hour extension was agreed upon, but tempers clearly were fraying. "If Mosby does not avail himself of the present truce," Grant bluntly told Hancock, "end it, and hunt him and his men down. Guerillas . . . will not be entitled to quarter."[6]

The second meeting at Millwood was tense. Mosby and a dozen or more officers sat on one side of the room; a like number of Federals led by a colonel sat on the other. No, Mosby was informed, further extensions would be granted. Moreover, unless he promptly surrendered, Hancock would lay waste to Loudoun and Fauquier counties. The warning infuriated him. "Tell General Hancock it is within his power to do it; and it is not in my power to resist," he said. "But I will not accept a parole until Joe Johnston has surrendered."

Just then one of his Rangers interrupted the meeting, shouting that Union cavalrymen were in the woods around the town. "Colonel, the damned Yankees have got you in a trap! There is a thousand of them hid in the woods!"

Though the information would prove false, Mosby did not know this. He reacted to danger the same way he had at the University of Virginia many years before, when he gunned down a threatening classmate. Rising to his feet, he put his hand on his revolver.

"If the truce no longer protects us," he said, "we are at your mercy. But we shall protect ourselves."

The silence in the room was palpable. "It was a scene . . . never to be forgotten," said Aristides Monteiro, the Rangers' surgeon. "Every partisan was prepared for instant death and more than ready for a fight. Had a single pistol been discharged by accident, or Mosby given the word, not one Yankee officer . . . would have lived a minute."

Seconds later, the Gray Ghost turned and led his men outside, where their horses were tethered. "Mount and follow me," he said, heading back toward home.[7]

Within hours, Mosby was having second thoughts. Like Forrest in Alabama, he realized the Confederacy was at an end, and there was no point in sacrificing further lives. On April 21, meeting in Salem with 200 of his men, he officially disbanded the 43rd Virginia Regiment. "Soldiers!" he said. "I have summoned you together for the last time. The vision we have cherished of a free and independent country has vanished. . . . I disband your organization in preference to surrendering it to our enemies."

Subsequently, more than 300 Rangers would ride to various Union stations in the Valley and formally apply for parole. The Federals let them keep their horses, and it is reasonable to assume that many of their revolvers, so long as they remained out of sight, also escaped confiscation.

Mosby, however, pursued a different course. Instead of giving himself up, he traveled to Richmond, and there learned that Johnston had surrendered. Then, through May and into June, with a price on his head, he concealed himself in a series of safe houses. On June 13, he finally applied for parole in Lynchburg. Though he had been led to believe it would be granted, he instead found himself, because of bureaucratic meddling, in danger of imprisonment. "I will not submit to arrest," he said, showing a brace of pistols to the military authorities. "I will kill the first man who attempts it."[8]

The Federals were sympathetic, perhaps because they realized they inadvertently had betrayed his trust, and he was allowed to make a hasty departure. On the 17th he returned to Lynchburg, and on this occasion, through Grant's direct intervention, his parole was granted.

How many Union soldiers Mosby kept from the front lines and on guard duty in northern Virginia we will never know, but the activities of his few hundred men throughout the war had an impact far greater than their numbers. It would be Grant, years later, who admiringly summed up Mosby's value to the Confederacy: "There were . . . few men in the South who could have commanded successfully a separate detachment in the rear of an opposing army, and so near the border of hostilities, as long as he did without losing his entire command."[9]

FOUR

THE EAST, MARCH 31−APRIL 1: DINWIDDIE AND FIVE FORKS

The Union siege of Petersburg was hopelessly stalled during March because of inclement weather and muddy roads, and the inaction was driving Sheridan to distraction. "I can drive in the whole cavalry force of the enemy with ease," he assured some aides after riding into Grant's headquarters on March 30, "and if an infantry force is added to my command, I can strike out for Lee's right, and either crush it or [make] him so weaken his entrenched lines that our troops in front of them can break through and march into Petersburg."

"How do you expect to supply your command with forage if this weather lasts?" asked one officer.

"Forage!" Sheridan cried out. "I'll get all the forage I want. I'll haul it out if I have to set every man . . . to corduroying roads . . . from the [Weldon] Railroad to Dinwiddie. I tell you, I'm ready to strike out tomorrow, and go to smashing things."

Entering Grant's tent, he repeated his wish to go on the attack, exuding conviction. "Knowing as I did . . . of what great value that feeling of confidence to a commander was," said Grant, "I determined to make a movement at once . . . for the purpose of extending our lines as far west as possible toward the enemy's extreme right." The target would be Five

Forks, a vital crossroads near the Southside Railroad. "My hope was that Sheridan would be able to carry Five Forks, get on the enemy's right flank and rear, and force them to weaken their center . . . so that an attack [there] might successfully be made."

Grant did not at this juncture give his cavalry chief infantry support, but assured him he would do so as the turning movement developed. "It is natural to suppose that Lee would understand my design [was] to get to the Southside and ultimately to the Danville Railroad. . . . These roads were so important to his very existence [for supplies] while he remained in Richmond and Petersburg, and of such importance to him even in case of retreat, that he would make the most strenuous efforts to defend them." But Grant and Sheridan would not be content to sever the railroads; they would be aiming to crush Lee's army.[1]

So the stage was set. On March 31, Sheridan departed from Dinwiddie Court House, and with 13,000 cavalrymen galloped northwest toward the Five Forks neighborhood. His second-in-command was Wesley Merritt, and his division chiefs Thomas Devin, George Custer, and George Crook. Once at Five Forks, however, he encountered heavy resistance, Lee having divined his purpose and drained his defensive lines to send 19,000 cavalry and infantry—under his nephew Fitzhugh Lee and George Pickett, respectively—to stop him.

With Hampton dispatched to duty in the Carolinas, Fitz now was in charge of the Army of Northern Virginia's horsemen. His fellow major generals Rooney Lee and Tom Rosser led two of his divisions, and Colonel Thomas Munford headed the third.

Munford, though he had been fighting with distinction since Stonewall Jackson's Valley Campaign in 1862, and then through all the major battles, had long been overlooked for promotion. In large part this was due to Jeb Stuart's belief that he had been tardy in coming forward to meet the Yankee attack at Brandy Station. But Jeb before his death had absolved Munford of blame in the matter, promising that he would recommend him for a brigadier's star. Both Hampton and Robert E. Lee subsequently endorsed the upgrade in rank. Now the promotion papers were in the War Office, awaiting signature.[2]

By midafternoon on the 31st, it was apparent that Sheridan, as yet unsupported by infantry, was outmatched against the combined Rebel force. Retreating from Five Forks under unrelenting pressure, he found himself pushed back to Dinwiddie, where he set up breastworks. Still, neither he nor his men were panicking. "They surrounded [my command] . . . and nearly got me," said Tom Devin, "and would have done so if . . . my gallant lads had wavered for a moment. . . . But all the praise I got from Sheridan was a grin and 'O, I knew you would get out somehow!' " Remembered an officer in the 2nd Massachusetts: "We were *overpowered,* badly whipped but not *driven* nor *routed.*"[3]

The final action of the day occurred about 5 p.m., with George Pickett's infantry, guarded on the right by Rooney Lee and on the left by Munford, advancing on Dinwiddie by two roads. "Accompanied by Generals Merritt and Custer and my staff," said Sheridan, "I now rode along the barricades to encourage the men. Our enthusiastic reception showed that they were determined to stay."

Such bravado encouraged the enemy's fire, with the result that several men in his entourage were shot from their saddles, including a correspondent for the New York *Herald.* "In reply," said Sheridan, "our horse artillery [shelled] the Confederates, but the men behind the barricades lay still till Pickett's troops were within short range. Then they opened up, Custer's repeating rifles pouring out such a shower of lead that nothing could stand against it. The repulse was very quick, and as the gray lines retired to the woods . . . all danger of their taking Dinwiddie . . . was over, at least for the night."[4]

Custer's timely arrival at the front turned the tide. He and his men hitherto had been with Sheridan's wagons, helping pull them through the rain-soaked roads and getting covered with muck in the process. Now, with Devin's and Crook's divisions badly bloodied, he had galloped his own division to the rescue. Over his head flew his personal guidon—red and blue with white crossed sabers. It had been sewn by Libbie, his wife, who had embroidered her name on one of the points.

While his troopers were dismounting and filing into the works, Custer emulated Sheridan, cantering along the lines and seemingly taking delight in making himself a target. Though he emerged unscathed, the resulting Rebel minié balls killed one of the orderlies riding with him and tore Libbie's name out of the flag.[5]

Just as the front at Dinwiddie was stabilizing, Horace Porter, a Grant aide, rendezvoused with Sheridan. "He said he had one of the liveliest days in his experience, fighting infantry and cavalry with only cavalry," Porter recounted, "but that he would hold his position at all hazards. He did not stop there, but declared his belief that with the corps of infantry which he expected to be put under his command, he could take the initiative the next morning, and cut off the whole of the force which Lee had detached."

Despite the rough treatment he had endured, Sheridan remained buoyant. "The [Rebel] force is in more danger than I am," he insisted, noting that a three-mile gap existed between Pickett and the main Confederate lines to the northeast. "If I am [isolated] from the Army of the Potomac, it is cut off from Lee's army, and not a man ought to be allowed to get back. We at last have drawn the enemy . . . out of its fortifications, and this is our chance to attack it." He told Porter he wanted Horatio Wright's corps in support—it had been under his command in the Shenandoah, and its commander was familiar with his hard-fighting ways. But this was impossible; Wright was too far to the east. The only corps that could reach him by daylight was Gouverneur Warren's.

That night Warren with some 15,000 men was ordered west to Sheridan's aid—a distance of a dozen miles. "It was expected that the infantry would reach its destination in ample time to take the offensive about daybreak," said Porter, "but one delay after another was met with, and [the generals] spent a painfully anxious night."[6]

While it was true that Warren was still another deliberate officer, with a style that could be maddening, it also was true he faced many difficulties in coming up in support. Not only did he have to rebuild an important bridge in the dark, but he was the recipient of confusing and contradictory orders, from more than one superior.

When dawn broke on April 1, there were hard feelings all around. Sheridan was fuming and wondering aloud when the devil Warren would arrive, the latter was aggrieved, George Meade (the commander of the Army of the Potomac) was ringing his hands, and most importantly, Grant rightly or wrongly was in no mood for excuses.

"I was so much dissatisfied with Warren's dilatory movements . . . in his failure to reach Sheridan in time, that I was afraid he would fail Sheridan. [Warren] was a man of fine intelligence, and could make his dispositions as quickly as any officer, under difficulties, when he was forced to act. But I had before discovered a defect that was beyond his control. . . . He could see every danger at a glance before he encountered it. He would not only make preparations to meet the danger which might occur, but he would inform his commanding officer what others should do."[7]

Earlier, Pickett and Fitz Lee had learned from a vigilant Tom Munford that Warren's infantry, however slowly, was approaching on their left rear. Fearing that they might be cut off from their main lines, they began retreating from Dinwiddie and moving their commands north, back to

Five Forks. Their withdrawal was unhurried, and the entire force did not reach the crossroads until 9 a.m. There Pickett received an urgent wire from Robert E. Lee: "Hold Five Forks at all hazards. Prevent Union forces from striking the Southside Railroad. Regret exceedingly your forced withdrawal."

Soon the Rebels were drawn up in a two-mile-long line of battle, with Munford—together with a contingent of North Carolinians under William Roberts—on the left, Rooney Lee on the right, and the infantry in between. Tom Rosser's troopers were in reserve, camping in the rear at Hatcher's Run.

Whether Pickett and Fitz Lee fully realized the seriousness of their situation at this juncture is arguable. Certainly, as the morning hours passed, it must have been tempting to think that the Federals were bogged down, that Warren's tardy ways were catching, and that Sheridan would not strike that day. Pickett even believed, he later claimed, that he would be reinforced, though how he could imagine this is mystifying. Nor did he pay much attention to bolstering his breastworks, which were mediocre at best. "Hearing nothing more of the [Federal] infantry's move . . . I thought that the movements, for the time being, were suspended. . . . Our throwing up works and taking position were simply matters of military precaution."[8]

The Federals, however, still were intent on attacking. About 10 a.m., Horace Porter returned to Sheridan's headquarters, sent by Grant to keep him informed of developments. Warren's corps was advancing on Five Forks, it was true, but not fast enough for anyone's liking. About this time, a messenger arrived from Grant and, in Porter's presence, said to Sheridan: "General Grant directs me to say to you that if, in your judgment, the 5th Corps would do better under one of its division commanders, you are authorized to relieve General Warren." The cavalry chief was noncommittal, saying he hoped such a step would not be necessary.

Sheridan's plan of battle called for Merritt with the cavalry, mostly dismounted, to make a feint against the enemy's right and center, even as Warren turned his left, cutting off Pickett from Lee's lines. Spearheading the infantry's drive would be a small division of horse soldiers from the Army of the James under Ranald Mackenzie. These orders were given about 1 p.m., and Sheridan went over them with Warren in detail. "[He] seemed to understand me clearly, and then left to rejoin his command," said Little Phil, "while I turned my attention to the cavalry. . . . Afterward

I rode to Gravelly Run Church and found the head of Warren's column just appearing, while he was sitting on the ground making a rough sketch of the ground."

Incensed that the infantryman was not personally hurrying up his troops, Sheridan resorted to sarcasm. "I expressed to Warren my fears that the cavalry might expend all their ammunition before the attack could be made." He was more concerned, of course, that the daylight hours were being wasted. "Warren did not seem to me at all solicitous; his manner exhibited decided apathy, and he remarked with indifference that 'Bobby Lee was always getting people into trouble.' With unconcern such as this, it is no wonder that fully three hours' time was consumed in marching his corps . . . to Gravelly Run Church, though the distance was but two miles."[9]

The Confederate Tom Rosser, in reserve with a flesh wound at Hatcher's Run, meanwhile was having his infamous shadbake. A big and burly man with an appetite for good food and drink, he had set his troopers to catching and deboning large numbers of shad in the stream, preparatory to having a feast. Then he invited Pickett and Fitz Lee to join him.

About 2 p.m., just as Fitz was about to join the party, Tom Munford rode up with the news that the Yankees were moving on the Rebel left, and at some points were engaging skirmishers. The cavalry leader, anticipating a rare hearty meal, was unimpressed. "Well, Munford," he drawled, "I wish you would go over in person and see what this means and, if necessary, order up your division and let me hear from you." Then he cantered away.[10]

Munford went off to reconnoiter, swinging in a wide arc around the works, and was appalled by what he saw. Not only had the 8th Virginia and Roberts's North Carolinians been pushed back by the energetic Ranald Mackenzie's troopers, but in the distance Warren's infantry could be seen massing, poised to deliver a potentially crushing blow on the Rebel left. He quickly sent messengers to Pickett and Fitz, telling them a climactic fight was in the offing, but "neither of these officers were at their headquarters."[11]

How the two men entrusted by Robert E. Lee to defend Five Forks could have been so indifferent to their danger, and their duties, remains a puzzle. Perhaps Grant's relentless pressure had benumbed them. But they left the lines to join Rosser without telling anyone where they were going, and then for two hours ate and drank in his company, oblivious to the coming storm.

All this time, the Union assault was gathering momentum. "Warren's swarming blue lines were plainly visible . . . forming into line and preparing to assault Pickett's left," said Munford. "Merritt's dismounted cavalry was keeping up a sharp continuous fire along the whole of the infantry front, as if preparing to attack our right, and Custer's mounted division was demonstrating. . . . And I was still without orders."[12]

With Warren at last in position, the attack began at 4 p.m. Despite the absence of Pickett and Fitz, the Rebel left initially laid down a scathing fire on their enemies, bringing the Federal infantry up short. They were greatly helped in this regard by the fact that the divisions of Romeyn Ayres and Samuel Crawford marched forward in diverging columns, opening a gap in the lines.

Whether this was Warren's fault is debatable, but Little Phil clearly thought it was. In a blind rage, he rode his huge black stallion into the breach, shouting for his battle flag. "Sheridan seized the crimson-and-white standard, waved it above his head . . . and made heroic efforts to close up the ranks," said Horace Porter. "Bullets were now humming like a swarm of bees above our heads. . . . A musket ball pieced the battle-flag; another killed the sergeant who had carried it; another wounded an aide."

Sheridan's efforts bore fruit. Within minutes Ayres's and Crawford's men were reforming and renewing the attack, using their great numbers to advantage. "Ayres, with drawn saber, rushed forward once more with his veterans, who now behaved as if they had fallen back only to get a 'good ready,' " said Porter, "and with fixed bayonets and a rousing cheer dashed over the earthworks, sweeping everything before them, and killing or capturing every man in their immediate front."[13]

The Confederate left was collapsing. Sheridan and other officers now jumped their mounts over the works, adding to the enemy's panic. "Where do you want us all to go to?" one terrified fellow entreated, hands in the air. Little Phil's battlefield rage quickly turned to heavy-handed humor. "Go right over there," he said, pointing to the Federal rear. "Get right along. . . . You'll all be safe over there. . . . Are there any more of you? . . . We want every one of you fellows."[14]

Next to feel the weight of the Federal onslaught was the Confederate center, where Tom Devin and George Custer were facing the bulk of Pickett's infantry. "We are going to take those works," Custer told the 2nd Ohio, urging on the troopers, "and we will not come back until we get them!" His dismounted men surged forward, covering half the distance with a rush. Then, just before the Rebels opened fire, he ordered the bugler to sound the call to hit the ground. "We all hugged America," said one Buckeye. "As we did so, a most terrible fire went over us, from both infantry and artillery."

The Yanks sprang to their feet, closing with the enemy before they could reload and discharging their repeating carbines with abandon. Custer led the charge, like Sherman leaping his mount over the barricades. Enthused a bluecoat: "About half of the men behind the works ran, the rest we captured, and many of those who got away left their guns."[15]

On the Rebel right, only Rooney Lee with some 1,200 troopers, supported by Montgomery Corse's infantry brigade, offered the Confederates hope. Following his success in the center, Custer had regrouped his men and now was attempting to turn Rooney's flank. If he had done so, the disorganized enemy not only would have been routed but completely surrounded.

As Custer galloped forward with the commands of Henry Capehart and William Wells—New Yorkers, West Virginians, and Vermonters—Rooney's pickets fell back to the main body. "Boys, we are going to catch hell," they told their comrades. Remembered another Rebel: "The voices of Custer and his officers rang out in clarion tones, orders that every old cavalryman in that little field distinctly heard and knew to mean our utter destruction if implemented."

Richard Beale's Virginians, dismounted, hunkered down with Corse's infantry, holding their fire until the last moment. Then the order came, and volley after volley blasted the oncoming Federals. Simultaneously Rufus Barringer's North Carolinians charged. "The shock of the collision was terrible," said one trooper. ". . . Sabers rang on each other with a cold steel ring that only the bravest veterans can stand. Pistol shots here and there and everywhere emptied saddles. . . . Each side knew what was at stake, and this saber slashing lasted longer than I ever saw one."[16]

Rooney stopped Custer in his tracks, and then fought an impressive delaying action, giving the remnants of Pickett's force the chance to fall back toward the Petersburg lines. "We were engaged from all three directions, our front and right by cavalry and our left by infantry," a trooper would say of the covering movement. "One squadron would charge and check the enemy in their efforts to surround us, and [then] rally and reform in the rear. That uncovered another squadron, formed and ready for action, which shortly repeated the same operation, always presenting, in each of the three directions, an effective fighting front. . . . It was grand! It was magnificent!"[17]

Pickett, whose storied charge at Gettysburg had failed so disastrously, first realized the seriousness of the 4 p.m. attack when Union skirmishers materialized at Hatcher's Run seemingly out of nowhere. He leaped on his horse and made it back to the lines as the sun was going down, but by then the damage had been done. Rebel casualties totaled between 4,500 and 5,000, most of them prisoners; the Southside and Danville Railroads soon would be severed; and the Federal triumph was complete. Fitz Lee that day never did get back to his cavalry, the Yankees having gotten between him and his command. Subsequently, neither he nor Pickett would be disciplined for his absence from the fighting.

Sheridan was more unforgiving. Not having seen Warren once the battle began, Little Phil worked himself into a fit, choosing to believe that his subordinate had kept himself out of the conflict.

"By God, sir!" he thundered at an aide. "Tell General Warren he wasn't in the fight! Tell him he wasn't in the fight!"

The aide was dumbstruck. He could not take such a message to Warren, he said, unless it was in writing.

"Take it down, sir! Tell him, by God, he was not at the front!" Then Sheridan rode off in search of Charles Griffin, who headed Warren's reserve division. When the two men met, he peremptorily informed Griffin that Warren had been relieved and he was now in charge of the 5th Corps.

Later, Warren approached Sheridan in the gathering darkness, the order relieving him clutched in his hand.

"Will you not reconsider?" he asked.

"Reconsider, hell!" was the reply. "I don't reconsider my decisions. Obey the order!"

With that, Gouverneur Warren was dismissed. He had been wounded during the Peninsula Campaign, fought at second Bull Run and Antietam, blocked the Confederate threat to Cemetery Ridge the second day at Gettysburg, and fought through the bloody Overland Campaign. But Grant and Sheridan had found him wanting. He would spend the rest of his life trying to clear his name.[18]

Sheridan's victory at Five Forks led the next day to the breaching of the Rebel lines and Robert E. Lee's evacuation of Richmond and Petersburg. The gallant Army of Northern Virginia was breathing its last.

FIVE

THE EAST, APRIL 6–9: SAILOR'S CREEK AND APPOMATTOX

The Confederates left their besieged and broken strongholds the night of April 2–3 on several parallel routes, heading west toward Amelia Station on the Danville Railroad, with the enemy in close pursuit. There Lee expected to find boxcars filled with food and fodder, and then to turn south, uniting his command with Joseph Johnston in North Carolina. But the supplies never arrived, and he was forced to halt for twenty-four hours to scour the countryside in a futile search for food. "The delay was fatal," he later acknowledged, "and could not be retrieved."

On the 5th, pushing farther west to Jetersville, the half-starved army found the enemy in its path. Lee handled this impasse by looping north on a night march and then, despite strong harassment, continuing west toward Farmville, hoping to be resupplied from Lynchburg via the Southside Railroad. James Longstreet, with the strongest divisions, led the way; Richard Anderson and Richard Ewell, with the weakest units, were in the center, encumbered as well by the wagon train; and John Brown Gordon's tough command comprised the rear guard.

Even for the indefatigable Gordon, the trek was a nightmare. "On and on, hour after hour, from hilltop to hilltop, the lines were alternately forming, fighting and retreating, making one almost continuous shifting battle."[1]

Early on April 6, still distant from Farmville, the Rebel column was strung out for ten miles. Predictably, Sheridan's cavalry remained a constant irritant. On one sally, the bluecoats captured half an artillery battalion, led by Colonel Frank Huger. Remembered a Confederate officer: "The two leading guns had reached the top of a long ascent of bad road, when Custer's brigade . . . [charged] down upon them. The two guns quickly unlimbered & fired two rounds each of cannister, when Custer's men were in between them, cutting & shooting."

Huger blasted one noncom from his horse, and with another shot laid open the cheek of a major. "But another fellow rode up & held a carbine to his head & said, 'Surrender, damn you!' . . . Custer & Huger had been great friends & classmates [at West Point] & Custer made him ride along all day . . . & sleep with him that night, & treated him very nicely." Even the officer whom Huger had wounded came to see him, "with his face sewed up and bandaged, & expressed his sincere thanks for the glorious furlough he was about to enjoy."[2]

Confederate horsemen that morning also were active. The rivals Tom Rosser and Tom Munford, who had little regard for each other, were sent ahead of the column by Fitz Lee to clear the enemy from High Bridge, a crossing of the Appomattox River near Farmville. In a spirited action, they did just that, the former taking the foe in flank while the latter moved on him frontally. "In a piece of woods opposite us, the enemy's infantry was distinctly seen," said Munford. "Our skirmishers opened up . . . and the enemy responded, vigorously. We could see Rosser's mounted men charging and we pushed on, losing some valuable men."

Because many officers in Munford's command had been killed and wounded, the cannoneers Lieutenant Colonel R. Preston Chew and Major James Breathed temporarily had been assigned to him. This was their first battle as horse soldiers, and he must have been concerned how they would fare. He need not have worried. Chew charged at the head of his men as if it was second nature, and Breathed instinctively headed where the firing was heaviest.

Breathed's enthusiasm, in fact, was almost his undoing. Closing with two Yanks waving sabers, he was knocked from his mount before he could fire his pistol, and for a brief moment, before his boot came off and freed him from the stirrup, dragged along the ground. While lying prone, he snapped off a shot that killed one of his assailants, even as an aide dispatched the other. Munford was impressed. "In a moment Breathed was back in the saddle with only one boot, and again joined in the fight."[3]

So bold were Sheridan's raids on the Rebel column's center becoming, however, that about 11 a.m. Richard Anderson and Richard Ewell halted to swat them away, then waited a while longer to let the wagons go past that were separating them from Gordon. Unfortunately, this opened up a dangerous gap between Longstreet's rear and Ewell's front that Sheridan took full advantage of, rushing his troopers into the breach and, around 2 p.m., setting up a roadblock.

Compounding the problem, Ewell sent the wagons on a northerly fork in the road without telling Gordon, who followed them, leaving him without support. With the Federal infantry close behind, Anderson and Ewell now were caught in a pincer.

Desperate fighting began about 5 p.m. The Yankee foot soldiers moved across Little Sailor's Creek, a tributary of the Appomattox, from the north against Ewell, while Wesley Merritt's cavalry—Crook, Devin, and Custer, from left to right—came up from the south against Anderson. Soon Ewell's lines began to crumble. "Quicker than I can tell it, the battle degenerated into a butchery," said one Rebel officer. ". . . I saw numbers of men kill each other with bayonets and the butts of muskets, and even bite each other's throats and ears and noses."[4]

One mile to the southwest, Dick Anderson likewise was in trouble. Trying to crack the roadblock, he succeeded in roughing up Crook, but quickly found himself repulsed, and then overrun, by Devin and Custer. In short order, his dispirited corps all but dissolved, most men throwing down their arms.

The Federal troopers surged through Anderson's ranks, subsequently coming up on Ewell's men from the rear and enveloping them. One Rebel officer, General Joseph Kershaw, recognizing the flamboyant Custer, ordered his command to concentrate its fire on him. Though he was reluctant to kill a man "so brave, good and efficient," he knew "it was my only hope."

Custer nonetheless ended the day unscathed, and Kershaw became one of thousands of Confederate prisoners. "My God," Lee would say, looking back on the debacle from a hilltop vantage point, "has the army dissolved?"[5]

Following the battle, Kershaw like many Rebel officers enjoyed Custer's hospitality. "After supper," he remembered, "we smoked and talked over many subjects . . . dwelling, however, almost wholly on the past. The future to us was not inviting, and our host with true delicacy of feeling avoided the subject. We slept beneath the stars, Custer sharing his blankets with me."

Later he noticed that many of the troopers in the cavalryman's entourage carried Confederate battle flags. "It is my custom after a battle to select for my escort . . . those men of each regiment who most distinguish themselves," Custer explained, "bearing, for a time, the trophies they have taken from the enemy."

"I counted them," said Kershaw, who was one of Lee's hardest-fighting generals. "There were 31 captured banners representing 31 of our regiments killed, captured or dispersed. . . . It was not comforting to think of."[6]

The surviving Confederates, with James Longstreet and John Brown Gordon closing up the infantry column, and Fitz Lee guarding the flanks, reached Farmville on April 7. There they found much needed rations awaiting them, and briefly halted for rest.

For the Army of Northern Virginia, the end was near. The next day, as they approached Appomattox Court House, the air grew still. "Until now the sound of musketry and the boom of occasional guns could always be heard in some direction," said one Rebel. "But today's march was free from any flank attack, & we had such a head start . . . that there was but little heard from the rear."[7]

During this time, the two commanders—Grant and Lee—were exchanging notes regarding the possibility of surrender. Not until the morning of the 9th, however, after a failed effort by Gordon and Fitz Lee to break through the converging enemy lines, would Lee agree to a meeting. It was set for 1:30 p.m.

In the interim, even though Grant and Lee had agreed to a truce, Union officers in the field were not sure they should observe one. Gordon now ordered forward Colonel Green Peyton, one of his aides, to insure a cessation of hostilities. Peyton protested that he had no flag of truce.

"Well," said Gordon, "take your handkerchief, tie it on a stick, and go!"

"General, I have no handkerchief."

"Then tear your shirt, sir, and tie that on a stick."

"General, I have on a flannel shirt, and I see you have [too]. I don't believe there is a white shirt in the army."

"Get something, sir, get something and go!"[8]

Colonel Peyton galloped toward the enemy front, then returned with George Custer.

"I am General Custer," he haughtily told Gordon, "and bear a message to you from General Sheridan. "The general desires me . . . to demand the immediate and unconditional surrender of all the troops under your command. . . . If there is any hesitation . . . he has you surrounded and can annihilate you within an hour."

Gordon coolly replied that if Major General Sheridan decided to continue the fighting, the responsibility for the bloodshed would be his.

Soon another white flag approached. "Under it was Philip Sheridan," said Gordon, "accompanied by a mounted escort as large as one of Fitz Lee's regiments. Sheridan was mounted on an enormous horse, a very handsome animal. . . . Around me at the time were my faithful sharpshooters, and as General Sheridan and his escort came within easy range of the rifles, a half-witted fellow raised his gun as if to fire."

Gordon told the man to lower his gun. "He did not obey my order cheerfully. . . . In fact, he was again in the act of raising his gun to fire at Sheridan when I caught [the barrel] and said, with emphasis, that he must not shoot men under flag of truce."

"Well, general, let him stay on his own side," the soldier protested.

Sheridan, after a brief discussion, agreed to a cease-fire while Grant and Lee were conferring. Dismounted, he then made some small talk. "We have met before, I believe," he needled Gordon, "at Winchester and Cedar Creek in the Valley."

Gordon replied that he had been there. "I had the pleasure of receiving some artillery from your government," Sheridan went on, "consigned to me by your commander, General Early."

"That is true, and I have this morning received from your government artillery consigned to me through General Sheridan," Gordon retorted, alluding to some cannon captured hours before.

While this banter was going on, Custer encountered Longstreet. "I have come to demand your immediate surrender!" he called out, pushing his luck. "We are in a position to crush you, and unless you surrender at once, we will destroy you!"

Longstreet dismissed the threat. "General Lee is in communication with General Grant. We will certainly not recognize any subordinate."

"Oh, Sheridan and I are independent of Grant today," Custer answered.

Longstreet became enraged. "I suppose you . . . have violated the decencies of military procedure because you know no better. . . . Now go and act as you and Sheridan choose and I will teach you a lesson you won't forget! Now go!" Custer backed off, saying little more.[9]

Subsequently, meeting in a private home at Appomattox belonging to one Wilbur McLean, Grant and Lee signed the surrender documents. The Army of Northern Virginia's armed and organized troops at this juncture totaled no more than 7,900; the addition of prisoners, the weaponless, and the sick would within days swell the number to some 28,000.

Fitz Lee, together with some of Munford's and Rosser's troopers, made their escape shortly before the official surrender, only to give up within days. Rooney Lee, with a sense of noblesse oblige, remained with his father to the end, helping him bear the agony of defeat.

EPILOGUE

Let us now take a look at the principal survivors of these Civil War cavalry actions, more or less in the order that they first appeared in our story, and see how they fared in the years thereafter.

Among the Confederates, *Fitzhugh Lee,* the general-in-chief's nephew, and *William Henry Fitzhugh "Rooney" Lee,* his middle son, quickly took their places among the Virginia elite.

For twenty years the outgoing Fitz, the "laughing cavalier" so similar in personality to Jeb Stuart, would farm at Richlands, his inherited estate in Stafford County. "Stuart and Fitzhugh were alike in temperament and as devoted as brothers," said a fellow officer. "Both were full of fun, and their gaiety never forsook them." Subsequently, Fitz turned to politics, using his gregarious nature to advantage. He served as Virginia governor from 1885 to 1889, but lost a bitter race for the U.S. Senate when he took a stand against the railroad interests, whom he felt were robbing the state treasury.

Some lean times followed, but in 1896 he was named general consul to Havana and, three years later, when the Spanish-American War broke out, was commissioned a major general in charge of the U.S. 7th Corps in Cuba, though he saw no action. "He had fairly won the hearts of the country and . . . become one of its most popular citizens," the officer commented. Back in the United States, Fitz became military commander of the

Department of Missouri. He retired from the army in 1901 and, returning to Virginia, died four years later.[1]

Quiet and self-effacing Rooney Lee, who had lost his first wife to a wasting illness in the middle of the war, returned to White House, the Custis family estate on the Pamunkey River he had inherited from his maternal grandfather. There he restored the devastated plantation, remarried, and sired several children, including a firstborn he named Robert. His interest in scientific farming led him to the presidency of the Virginia Agricultural Society and to the board of directors of Virginia Agricultural and Mechanical College now the Virginia Polytechnic Institute.

Rooney and his family moved to a second inherited estate, Ravenswood in Fairfax County, in 1874. "Virtue and common sense," he would counsel his children, "bring content and happiness in this world." He served as a state senator from 1875 to 1878, and as a U.S. congressman from 1886 to 1891, the year he died. "He never put himself forward except when duty prompted," said one friend, and then he did nothing for display."[2]

For *Nathan Bedford Forrest,* the postwar years in Tennessee were not financially rewarding. "I went into the army worth a million and a half dollars," this fierce warrior would say, "and came out a beggar." Several business ventures failed, he lost his substantial landholdings to creditors, and by 1868 was filing for bankruptcy. Nothing daunted, he raised money for the building of the Memphis & Selma Railroad, becoming its president. This undertaking, after a number of years, also proved unsuccessful, and by 1875 he was reduced to living on leased land, running a prison farm that was worked by convicts.

Reacting to the Reconstruction policies of the radical Republicans, he played a major role in the spread of the Ku Klux Khan, briefly becoming its first grand wizard, and contributed to the slow but steady revival of the Democratic party in the South. Though criticism of the Fort Pillow massacre in the Northern press was unrelenting, his military rivals acknowledged his genius. Recounted Sherman: "He always seemed to know what I was doing or intended to do."

Regardless of his monetary woes, Forrest remained a Confederate icon. When he died in 1877, the funeral procession following his casket to Memphis' Elmwood Cemetery was two miles long.[3]

Joseph Wheeler, the Braxton Bragg favorite with whom Nathan had a falling-out, initially also had financial problems. But by 1870 they were behind him, and he and his wife settled in Lawrence County, Alabama, where the circumspect Wheeler became a well-to-do lawyer-planter and, through most of the 1890s, a U.S. congressman.

The 1898 Spanish-American War found him a major general of volunteers. "How does it feel, General, to wear the blue again?" one of his aides asked the former West Pointer.

"I feel as if I have been on three-week furlough," Wheeler replied.

Once in Cuba, he participated in the victory at San Juan Hill, and later saw action in the Philippines. He retired from the army in 1900, and died six years afterward.[4]

Patrician *Wade Hampton* returned to his native South Carolina in 1865, where even though he had not yet received a Federal pardon, his fellow citizens attempted to elect him governor—an honor he insisted he could not accept. Instead he turned his energies to rebuilding his plantations. But his wealth was gone, along with the Confederate bonds he had purchased to support the war, and his debt load in 1869 forced him into bankruptcy.

For the next half dozen years he helped guide the Southern Life Insurance Company, an enterprise that ultimately failed, and pursued other employment ventures. Then in 1872, his pardon granted, Hampton at last turned to politics.

Running in 1876 on a Democratic anticarpetbagger (and, yes, limited black suffrage) ticket, he became embroiled in a hot dispute as to whether he or a Republican had won the South Carolina gubernatorial race. Republican presidential candidate Rutherford B. Hayes, who needed South Carolina's electoral votes in his own contested 1876 election, then brokered a deal to get them in exchange for Federal troops leaving the state. Soon thereafter, Hampton's Republican opponent gave up his claim to office, and Wade became governor.

Reelected handily in 1878, he resigned from office in 1879 to enter the U.S. Senate, where he served for almost a dozen years. Despite these positions, he never did become financially secure. His Columbia, South Carolina, neighbors came to his rescue, buying him a retirement home. The gift "touched my heart," he would say. He died in 1902.[5]

Hampton's chief lieutenant, *Matthew Calbraith Butler,* divided his immediate postwar time between Edgefield, South Carolina, and Columbia—practicing law, improving his finances, and testing the political waters. Unlike Wade, he was totally unyielding on black suffrage, a trait that led to an estrangement between the two men during Hampton's 1876 gubernatorial race. He was also a womanizer who, despite having a wife and family, fathered children out of wedlock. Sighed a granddaughter, "He was a bit of a rounder, but that is the fate of a handsome man."

Butler's stature in the state Democratic party was such, nonetheless, that in 1877 he was named to the U.S. Senate. He served three consecutive terms, but then in 1894 lost a bid for a fourth, and set up a law office in Washington. With the coming of the Spanish-American War, like Fitz Lee and Joseph Wheeler, he sought and received a major general's commission.

"You rode a white horse," the secretary of war at the time, a former Civil War adversary, told him, "which made you a mark for many of my Michigan riflemen."

"I'll go into [this] war on a less conspicuous horse," Butler rejoined.

He took no part in the Cuba fighting, and returned to Washington, where he resumed his law practice. Then in 1905, his life entered a new phase. Not quite seventy and five years a widower, he married Nancy Whitman, a wealthy widow twenty-four years younger, and settled on an estate in North Augusta. But the end was near. He died in 1909, converting to Catholicism on his deathbed.[6]

Once his parole finally was granted, *John Singleton Mosby* returned to practicing law, and for a few years was quite successful, with many people in "Mosby's Confederacy" coming to him for legal services. Then in 1868 he publicly endorsed Grant for president, believing his decision would help bring about reconciliation. Grant was elected, of course, but Mosby's backing brought the former Ranger nothing but vilification from Democrats and most white Virginians. He was unmoved. "I know very well the measure of denunciation which the expression of [my] sentiments will receive from the people in whose cause I shed my blood and sacrificed the prime of my life," he said. "So be it. I wait on time for my vindication."

Though his law business dried up, his connections with the Republicans in Washington—and a surprising friendship with Grant—made him a Federal patronage broker, and a man to be courted, by state politicians. Nonetheless, the bad-mouthing in Virginia continued, so much so that in 1875 he wrote Grant he thought it would be best for all concerned if he no longer visited the White House.

From 1879 to 1885, he served as U.S. consul in Hong Kong, and thereafter comfortably supported himself by writing and lecturing, though many in the South continued to censure him for his links with the Republicans. He died in 1916.[7]

Thomas Rosser after the end of hostilities went west, where he became chief engineer for a railroad being built through the Indian Territory. There he encountered George Custer, whose army unit was deployed to protect the construction, and the two men resumed their friendship. Later, Rosser returned to Virginia and became a gentleman farmer. He died in 1910.

Thomas Munford, who long resented—with good reason—Rosser's promotion over him, settled in Uniontown, Alabama, where he lived quietly and raised cotton. He died in 1918, shy of his eighty-seventh birthday.

Federal cavalrymen *William Averell, George Stoneman*, and *Alfred Pleasanton*, who had been found wanting to various degrees during the war, all eventually left the army.

Averell resigned in 1865 and was named U.S. consul general to Canada. A few years later he became head of a large manufacturing facility, where his innovations in areas ranging from steel to electrical power made him a rich man. He died in 1900.

Stoneman did not give up his commission until 1871. He then moved to California, where he took up residence near Los Angeles. He served subsequently as the state's railroad commissioner and, in 1882, as its governor. He lived until age 72.

Pleasanton left the service in 1868, when a reorganization resulted, in effect, in his demotion. He worked for a while in the Internal Revenue Service, and later became a railroad executive. He died in Washington in 1897.

The largely unsung *Benjamin Grierson*, whose raid through eastern Mississippi so facilitated Grant's capture of Vicksburg, remained in the regular army for the rest of his career. Despite his distaste for horses, he was named head of the 10th Cavalry, fighting Indians in Arizona and New Mexico. He retired in 1890 and died twenty-one years later in the Midwest.

Philip Sheridan was, of course, the leading Federal horse soldier of the conflict. During Reconstruction, when he was assigned to duty in Louisiana and Texas, his occupation policies were so draconian that his transfer to Missouri by a less vengeful President Andrew Johnson elicited little protest in the North—even among radical Republicans. "If I am disliked, it is because I cannot and will not cater to Rebel sentiment," he said. "The more I see of these people the less I see to admire."

In 1869, when Grant became president, Sheridan was named lieutenant general, reporting to William Sherman. Thereafter until 1883, with time out to marry a woman half his age, he fought the Indians in the West on a give-no-quarter basis, becoming something of a pariah in the East in church and humanitarian circles.

The next year, upon Sherman's retirement, he nonetheless became general-in-chief, and a few months before his death of heart disease in 1888, was raised to full general. His Catholic funeral mass was held at St. Matthew's Church in Washington, with the battle flag he had waved at Cedar Creek at the head of his coffin.[8]

Wesley Merritt, David McMurtrie Gregg, George Armstrong Custer, Alfred Torbert, and *James Wilson,* young Turks all, comprised the backbone of the Federal cavalry.

Continuing in the army for some thirty years, Merritt served in the Indian wars, became superintendent at West Point, and commanded various departments. In 1898, he led U.S. troops into the Philippines and, subsequently, with Admiral George Dewey, forced the surrender of Manila. He retired in 1900 and settled in Natural Bridge, Virginia, where he died ten years later. "Highly competent, and at the same time modest and agreeable" was the way he was characterized.[9]

David Gregg's abrupt resignation, while the war was still raging in February 1865, never has been explained. He had fought with distinction in one bloody battle after another; perhaps he could take no more. Moving to Milford, Delaware, he engaged in farming, and then in 1874, briefly served as U.S. consul in Prague. Subsequently, he put down roots in Reading, Pennsylvania, where he participated in numerous municipal and charitable activities. He died in 1916.

George Custer was given command of the 7th Cavalry in the West, and in 1867, took part in an expedition against the Sioux and Cheyenne. For the next nine years he fought almost continually against the Indians. Those who served under him, whether in the Civil War or the West, were unanimous in their praise. "He never ordered his men to go where he would not lead," said one officer, "and he never led where he did not expect his men to follow. He probably shared with the private soldier the danger of the skirmish line oftener than any officer of his rank." Custer's last battle came in Montana at Little Big Horn in 1876, when he and his 276 troopers were massacred by Sitting Bull and the Sioux. His wife Libbie survived him for fifty-seven years, extolling his virtues to all who would listen.[10]

Alfred Torbert resigned in 1866, disappointed that his role in the peacetime army had been substantially reduced. He became U.S. minister to Central America in 1869, was named consul general to Havana two years later, and served as consul general to Paris from 1873 to 1878. Subsequently, he pursued business interests in Mexico. In 1880, he drowned while a passenger aboard the steamer *Vera Cruz,* which was shipwrecked off the coast of Florida.

James Harrison Wilson transferred to the engineers, then left the army in 1870 to engage in several well-paying railroad ventures. From 1883 on, he settled in Wilmington, Delaware, devoting himself to writing, travel, and public affairs. Fifteen years later, with the outbreak of the Spanish-American War, he reentered the army as a major general, serving in Puerto Rico and Cuba. He then helped put down the Boxer Rebellion in China and, in 1902, represented President Theodore Roosevelt at the coronation of Britain's Edward VII. During the early 1900s, he published biographies of several Civil War comrades-in-arms, and in 1912 produced his most notable work, *Under the Old Flag,* a two-volume autobiography. He lived until 1925, and at age eighty-eight was the last surviving member of the West Point class of 1860.

Thomas Devin, who was a dozen or so years older than the aforementioned "boy generals" and a non–West Pointer as well—having coming up through the ranks of the New York City militia—should not be forgotten. He continued in the regular army, commanding cavalrymen until 1878, the year he died. "[He] knew how to take his men into action," remarked one contemporary, "and also how to bring them out."[11]

But what of Hugh Judson Kilpatrick, the rash braggart and self-aggrandizer? He took leave from the army in 1865, campaigned to help the Republicans win the New Jersey governor's seat, and was named ambassador to Chile as a reward. Soon thereafter he left the service. A widower, his wife having died during the war, he turned his attentions in Santiago to Louisa Valdivieso, daughter of a prominent family and niece of the Catholic archbishop of that country. They were married in 1866.

Kilpatrick would have been happy to remain as ambassador to Chile; he had visions of using Louisa's family connections to make his fortune. But such was not to be. Grant, once he became president, made it clear that Kilpatrick's days in that post were numbered. By 1870 he was back in America.

For the next ten years he devoted himself to the lecture circuit, where his oratorical skills—some might say bombast—made him an instant success.

Such topics as "Sherman's March to the Sea" and "The Battle of Gettysburg," with Kilpatrick's heroics dominating the recital, fascinated gullible audiences. On one occasion, however, he found himself challenged.

"The woods were swarming with Rebels," he was saying about Chancellorsville, a battle in which he was not engaged. "I had two horses shot from under me."

"What did you do then?" someone asked.

"I jumped on a mule. A ball knocked me off, but the mule charged right into the Rebel ranks and had its head shot off."

"I saw that mule," a voice called out.

The speaker was John Mosby, and Kilpatrick at first was pleased by his seeming support.

"I'm glad to have my words confirmed. You saw his head shot off?"

"No," guffawed Mosby, "he died from mortification!"

By 1881, Kilpatrick and Louisa were back in Chile, the result of his reappointment as ambassador by President Chester Arthur, and he must have anticipated, by fair means or foul, amassing great wealth. His hopes were dashed. He died in December of that year, only forty-five years old.[12]

NOTES

PROLOGUE

1. Richard N. Current, ed., *Encyclopedia of the Confederacy,* Simon & Schuster, 1993, vol. 1, p. 266; W. T. Sherman, *Memoirs,* Library of America, 1990, p. 363.
2. W. W. Blackford, *War Years with Jeb Stuart,* Louisiana State University Press, 1993, p. 26; Current, *Encyclopedia,* vol. 1, p. 270.
3. *War of the Rebellion, Official Records of the Union and Confederate Armies,* 128 vols., Washington, D.C., 1880–1901 (henceforth known as O.R.); vol. 39:2, p. 121; all citations are from Series I unless otherwise noted.
4. Edward G. Longacre, *Lee's Cavalrymen,* Stackpole Books, 2002, p. 44.
5. John Thomason, *Jeb Stuart,* Mallard Press, 1992, p. 91.

1862

1. THE EAST, MARCH 23–JUNE 6: ASHBY IN THE SHENANDOAH

1. Christopher Anderson, *Blood Image,* Louisiana State University Press, 2002, p. 189; Jedediah Hotchkiss to Sara Hotchkiss, April 2, 1862, Hotchkiss Papers, Library of Congress.

2. *O.R.,* vol. 12:1, p. 712; Henry Kyd Douglas, *I Rode with Stonewall,* University of North Carolina Press, 1968, pp. 82–83.

3. Harry Gilmor, *Four Years in the Saddle,* New York, 1866, p. 13; Robert K. Krick, *Conquering the Valley,* William Morrow, 1996, p. 25.

4. Jedediah Hotchkiss, *Make Me a Map of the Valley,* Southern Methodist Press, 1973, p. 15; Anderson, *Blood Image,* p. 63.

5. Thomas Ashby, *Life of Turner Ashby,* New York, 1914, p. 35.

6. Ibid., pp. 45–49.

7. Clarence Thomas, *General Turner Ashby,* Winchester, 1907, pp. 191–93.

8. William Thomas Poague, *Gunner with Stonewall,* Wilmington, 1987, p. 14; Robert L. Dabney, *Life and Campaigns of Lieutenant General J. T. (Stonewall) Jackson,* Richmond, 1866, pp. 261, 327.

9. Hotchkiss to Sara Hotchkiss, April 20, 1862, Hotchkiss Papers; Douglas, *I Rode with Stonewall,* p. 83; Anderson, *Blood Image,* p. 170.

10. Rev. James B. Avirett, *The Memoirs of General Turner Ashby and His Compeers,* Baltimore, 1867, p. 177; *O.R.,* vol. 12:3, p. 880.

11. Avirett, *Memoirs,* pp. 187–88.

12. Dabney, *Life and Campaigns,* pp. 371–73; *O.R.,* vol. 12:1, p. 703; *Southern Historical Society Papers,* 52 vols., Richmond, 1876–1959 (henceforth known as *SHSP*), vol. 7, p. 524.

13. Dabney, *Life and Campaigns,* p. 381.

14. Samuel Carter III, *The Last Cavaliers,* St. Martin's Press, 1979, p. 47; William Allan, *History of the Campaign of Gen. T. J. (Stonewall) Jackson in the Shenandoah Valley of Virginia,* Philadelphia 1880, p. 137; *O.R.,* vol. 12:1, p. 711.

15. Dabney, *Life and Campaigns,* p. 398.

16. Anderson, *Blood Image,* p. 6; Krick, *Conquering the Valley,* p. 27.

17. Charles L. Dufour, *Nine Men in Gray,* University of Nebraska Press, 1993, p. 73.

18. Munford Manuscript, as cited in Donald C. Pfanz and Richard S.

Ewell, University of North Carolina Press, 1998, p. 204; Clement Evans, ed., *Confederate Military History,* Atlanta, 1899, vol. 2, p. 78; Dabney, *Life and Campaigns,* p. 400.

19. Krick, *Conquering the Valley,* p. 32; O.R., vol. 12:1, p. 712.

2. THE EAST, JUNE 12–15: STUART'S RIDE AROUND McCLELLAN

1. Clifford Dowdey and Louis H. Manarin, *Wartime Papers of Robert E. Lee,* Little, Brown, 1961, p. 192.
2. *SHSP,* vol. 1, p. 100.
3. Blackford, *War Years,* p. 32; Emory M. Thomas, *Bold Dragoon,* Harper & Row, 1986, p. 95.
4. Alexander K. McClure, ed., *Annals of the War,* Blue & Grey Press, 1996, pp. 674–75.
5. H. B. McClellan, *Campaigns of Stuart's Cavalry,* Blue & Grey Press, 1993, p. 59.
6. John Esten Cooke, *The Wearing of the Gray,* New York, 1867, pp. 169ff.; McClellan, *Campaigns,* p. 56; Mary Bandy Daughtry, *Gray Cavalier,* DaCapo Press, 2002, p. 69.
7. *SHSP,* vol. 26, pp. 248–50.
8. Cooke, *Wearing of the Gray,* pp. 174ff.; Heros von Borcke, *Memoirs of the Confederate War,* New York, 1938, vol. 1, p. 43.
9. McClellan, *Campaigns,* pp. 63–65; Cooke, *Wearing of the Gray,* pp. 180–86.

3. THE WEST, JULY 6–27: FORREST'S FIRST TENNESSEE RAID

1. John Allan Wyeth, *That Devil Forrest,* Louisiana State University Press, 1989, p. 45; Albert T. Goodloe, *Confederate Echoes,* Nashville, 1907, p. 179.
2. Mark Mayo Boatner III, *The Civil War Dictionary,* David McKay, 1959, p. 289.
3. Andrew Nelson Lytle, *Bedford Forrest and His Critter Company,* J. S. Sanders, 1992, pp. 21–22; Wyeth, *Devil Forrest,* pp. 15–16.
4. Robert S. Henry, *As They Saw Forrest,* Jackson, Tennessee, 1956, p. 25; as cited in Jack Hurst, *Nathan Bedford Forrest,* Knopf, 1993, p. 17.
5. Wyeth, *Devil Forrest,* p. 18.

6. Hurst, *Nathan,* p. 54; Wyeth, *Devil Forrest,* p. 20.

7. Thomas Jordan and J. P. Pryor, *The Campaigns of General Nathan Bedford Forrest,* New Orleans, 1868, pp. 52–54.

8. Wyeth, *Devil Forrest,* p. 54; *Battles and Leaders of the Civil War,* 4 vols. (henceforth known as *B&L*), vol. 1, p. 426.

9. Wyeth, *Devil Forrest,* p. 64; Jordan and Pryor, *Campaigns,* pp. 146–48.

10. Lytle, *Bedford Forrest,* p. 91.

11. Ibid., pp. 93–94.

12. Jordan and Pryor, *Campaigns,* p. 170; Lytle, *Bedford Forrest,* p. 97.

13. Wyeth, *Devil Forrest,* pp. 77–78.

14. *O.R.,* vol. 16:1, p. 809; Jordan and Pryor, *Campaigns,* p. 175.

15. Wyeth, *Devil Forrest,* pp. 84–85.

4. THE WEST, JULY 4–22: MORGAN'S FIRST KENTUCKY RAID

1. Basil W. Duke, *History of Morgan's Cavalry,* Cincinnati, 1867, p. 129; *Cincinnati Gazette,* March 14, 1862; *Richmond Enquirer,* April 28, 1862.

2. Carter, *Last Cavaliers,* p. 54; James A. Ramage, *Rebel Raider,* University Press of Kentucky, 1986, p. 60.

3. Ramage, *Rebel Raider,* p. 58.

4. Ibid., pp. 82–83.

5. Virginia French Diary, Tennessee State Library, Nashville, March 13 and March 22, 1863.

6. Dee Alexander Brown, *Morgan's Raiders,* New York, 1959, pp. 70–72, 77–78; Duke, *History,* pp. 180–81.

7. Carter, *Last Cavaliers,* p. 81; Brown, *Morgan's Raiders,* p. 81; Ramage, *Rebel Raider,* pp. 95–97.

8. Carter, *Last Cavaliers,* pp. 82–83; Edison H. Thomas, *John Hunt Morgan and His Raiders,* University Press of Kentucky, 1985, pp. 41–42; Brown, *Morgan's Raiders,* p. 84.

9. Thomas, *John Hunt,* pp. 43–44; Brown, *Morgan's Raiders,* pp. 85–86.

10. Duke, *History,* pp. 200–02.

11. Bennett Young, *Confederate Wizards of the Saddle,* Boston, 1914, pp. 122–25.

12. Brown, *Morgan's Raiders,* pp. 109–10; Ramage, *Rebel Raider,* pp. 115–16; Carter, *Last Cavaliers,* pp. 84–85.

13. Ramage, *Rebel Raider*, p. 116; Duke, *History*, pp. 218–21; O.R., vol. 16:1, p. 871.

5. THE EAST, AUGUST 22–23: STUART AT CATLETT'S STATION

1. Blackford, *War Years*, p. 97; Douglas Southhall Freeman, *Lee's Lieutenants*, Scribner's, 1943, vol. 2, pp. 59–60; John J. Hennessy, *Return to Bull Run*, Simon & Schuster, 1993, p. 48.
2. Blackford, *War Years*, pp. 99–101.
3. Ibid., pp. 102–03.
4. Ibid., pp. 103, 107.
5. Ibid., pp. 104–05; McClellan, *Campaigns*, pp. 94–95; Douglas, *I Rode with Stonewall*, pp. 133–34.
6. Blackford, *War Years*, p. 108.

6. THE WEST, SEPTEMBER 4–NOVEMBER 1: MORGAN REVISITS KENTUCKY

1. Carter, *Last Cavaliers*, p. 86; Duke, *History*, pp. 229–33; Brown, *Morgan's Raiders*, pp. 122–23; Ramage, *Rebel Raider*, pp. 121, 103.
2. Brown, *Morgan's Raiders*, pp. 123–24; Ramage, *Rebel Raider*, pp. 6–7.
3. Ramage, *Rebel Raider*, p. 121.
4. Duke, *History*, pp. 257–58; here and infrequently in the following pages I have taken the plain intent of the original source and in part created dialogue, using italics instead of quotation marks to make the distinction.
5. Brown, *Morgan's Raiders*, pp. 126–29; *Louisville Journal*, October 2, 1862.
6. Ramage, *Rebel Raider*, p. 123.
7. Duke, *History*, pp. 282–86.
8. Ibid., pp. 288–90.

7. THE EAST, OCTOBER 9–12: STUART'S CHAMBERSBURG (PA.) RAID

1. O.R., vol. 19:2, p. 55; Blackford, *War Years*, p. 154.
2. Blackford, *War Years*, p. 155; McClure, *Annals*, pp. 666, 668.

3. Freeman, *Lee's Lieutenants,* vol. 2, p. 286.

4. Edward G. Longacre, *Gentleman and Soldier,* Rutledge Press, 2003, pp. 82–84; Daughtry, *Gray Cavalier,* pp. 5, 49–50; Henry Adams, *The Education of Henry Adams,* Modern Library, 1931, p. 57.

5. Blackford, *War Years,* p. 51; William Woods Hassler, *Colonel John Pelham,* University of North Carolina Press, 1960, pp. 2, 5, 28.

6. *O.R.,* vol. 19:2, p. 52; Blackford, *War Years,* p. 165.

7. Blackford, *War Years,* pp. 166–68.

8. *O.R.,* vol. 19:2, p. 57; Edward G. Longacre, *Mounted Raids of the Civil War,* University of Nebraska Press, 1994, pp. 36–37; McClellan, *Campaigns,* p. 141.

9. McClellan, *Campaigns,* p. 148; Blackford, *War Years,* pp. 169–70.

10. Blackford, *War Years,* pp. 173–75.

11. McClellan, *Campaigns,* p. 156.

12. Ibid., pp. 157–58.

13. Blackford, *War Years,* pp. 176–78.

14. Abraham Lincoln, *Speeches and Writings, 1859–1865,* Library of America, 1989, p. 379; Burke Davis, *Jeb Stuart: The Last Cavalier,* Burford Books, 2000, p. 235.

8. THE WEST, DECEMBER 11–JANUARY 3: FORREST'S SECOND TENNESSEE RAID

1. Wyeth, *Devil Forrest,* pp. 96–97.

2. Ibid., p. 94; Jordan and Pryor, *Campaigns,* p. 198.

3. Lytle, *Bedford Forrest,* p. 123.

4. *O.R.,* vol. 17:1, p. 567.

5. Ibid., p. 587.

6. Wyeth, *Devil Forrest,* pp. 108–10; *O.R.,* vol. 17:1, pp. 596–99, 569.

7. Lytle, *Bedford Forrest,* p. 135; Wyeth, *Devil Forrest,* p. 116; *O.R.,* vol. 17:1, p. 584.

8. Wyeth, *Devil Forrest,* pp. 119, 121.

9. Ulysses S. Grant, *Memoirs and Selected Letters,* Library of America, 1990, p. 289.

9. THE WEST, DECEMBER 20: VAN DORN CUTS GRANT'S SUPPLY LINE

1. Longacre, *Mounted Raids,* p. 47; McClure, *Annals,* p. 460.

2. *A Soldier's Honor: With Reminiscences of Major-General Earl Van*

Dorn, by His Comrades, New York, 1902, p. 28; Robert G. Hartje, *Van Dorn,* Vanderbilt University Press, 1867, p. 60.

3. *A Soldier's Honor,* p. 125.

4. Hartje, *Van Dorn,* p. 119; *Battles and Leaders of the Civil War* (hereafter referred to as *B&L*), New York, 1884–1888, vol. 1, p. 275.

5. *O.R.,* vol. 8, p. 202; Hartje, *Van Dorn,* p. 153; McClure, *Annals,* p. 462.

6. Mildred Throne, ed., *The Civil War Diary of Cyrus F. Boys,* Louisiana State University Press, 1998, p. 72; Hartje, *Van Dorn,* p. 227.

7. William M. Lamers, *The Edge of Glory,* Louisiana State University Press, 1999, p. 148; Throne, *Civil War,* p. 75; Hartje, *Van Dorn,* p. 245.

8. Hartje, *Van Dorn,* pp. 255, 258; *SHSP,* vol. 6, pp. 156–57.

9. *SHSP,* vol. 6, pp. 157–58; *Register and Advertiser,* December 27, 1862; January 7, 1863.

10. *SHSP,* vol. 6, pp. 158–59; Hartje, *Van Dorn,* p. 263.

11. Grant, *Memoirs,* p. 292.

10. THE WEST, DECEMBER 21–JANUARY 1: MORGAN'S THIRD KENTUCKY RAID

1. Duke, *History,* p. 322; Carter, *Last Cavaliers,* p. 89.

2. Young, p. 426.

3. Brown, *Morgan's Raiders,* pp. 146–48.

4. Young, p. 432; Brown, *Morgan's Raiders,* p. 151.

5. Ramage, *Rebel Raider,* p. 140.

6. Young, p. 433; Ramage, *Rebel Raider,* p. 140.

7. *O.R.,* vol. 20:2, p. 236; Young, pp. 437–38; Brown, *Morgan's Raiders,* pp. 153–54; Ramage, *Rebel Raider,* pp. 142–43; John Wyeth, *With Sabre and Scalpel,* New York, 1914, p. 187.

8. Young, pp. 443–44.

9. *SHSP,* vol. 10, pp. 514–18.

10. Carter, *Last Cavaliers,* pp. 91–92.

11. Ibid., p. 91.

11. THE EAST, DECEMBER 26–31: STUART AND HAMPTON ON THE RAPPAHANNOCK

1. Douglas Southall Freeman, *Robert E. Lee,* Scribner's, 1934–1936, vol. 2, p. 457.

2. Samuel J. Martin, *Southern Hero*, Stackpole, 2001, pp. 61–62.
3. Longacre, *Gentleman and Soldier*, p. 113.
4. *O.R.*, vol. 21, p. 696.
5. Freeman, *Lee's Lieutenants*, vol. 2, pp. 497–98; Thomas, *John Hunt*, p. 194.
6. McClellan, *Campaigns*, pp. 200–01.
7. Freeman, *Lee's Lieutenants*, vol. 2, p. 405.
8. Longacre, *Gentleman and Soldier*, p. 123; Freeman, *Lee's Lieutenants*, vol. 2, pp. 405–06.
9. Thomas, *John Hunt*, p. 199.

1863

1. THE EAST, JANUARY–JUNE: MOSBY'S RANGERS

1. Jeffrey D. Wert, *Mosby's Rangers*, Simon & Schuster, 1990, p. 70; *O.R.*, vol. 252, p. 857.
2. Henry Steele Commager, *The Blue and the Gray*, Bobbs-Merrill, 1950, pp. 327–28.
3. Wert, *Mosby's Rangers*, p. 75.
4. James A. Ramage, *Gray Ghost*, University Press of Kentucky, 1999, pp. 18, 21, 30; Wert, *Mosby's Rangers*, pp. 26–27.
5. John S. Mosby, *Memoirs*, Little, Brown, 1917, pp. 51–52, 149; John W. Munson, *Reminiscences of a Mosby Guerilla*, Zenger, 1983, p. 15.
6. Mosby, *Memoirs*, pp. 150, 152.
7. Ramage, *Gray Ghost*, p. 61; Mosby, *Memoirs*, p. 151.
8. Mosby, *Memoirs*, pp. 172–76, 178–79; Ramage, *Gray Ghost*, p. 69.
9. Wert, *Mosby's Rangers*, p. 46; Mosby, *Memoirs*, pp. 181–84.
10. Mosby, *Memoirs*, pp. 193–95; Ramage, *Gray Ghost*, pp. 81–82.
11. Mosby, *Memoirs*, pp. 196–99.

2. THE EAST, MARCH 17: FITZ LEE V. AVERELL AT KELLY'S FORD

1. McClellan, *Campaigns*, pp. 206–09.
2. Ibid., pp. 209–12.
3. *O.R.*, vol. 21:1, p. 62.
4. Freeman, *Lee's Lieutenants*, vol. 2, p. 453.

5. Thomas, *Bold Dragoon*, p. 206; Davis, *Last Cavalier*, pp. 272–74; Harry Gilmor, *Four Years in the Saddle*, New York, 1866, pp. 64–74.
6. Davis, *Last Cavalier*, p. 274; Thomas, *Bold Dragoon*, p. 206.
7. Blackford, *War Years*, p. 201; *O.R.*, vol. 25:2, p. 675; John Thomason, *Jeb Stuart*, Scribner's, 1930, p. 360.
8. Freeman, *Lee's Lieutenants*, vol. 2. p. 466.

3. THE WEST, APRIL 7–MAY 3: FORREST V. STREIGHT

1. *O.R.*, vol. 23:2, p. 225; Carter, *Last Cavaliers*, p. 135.
2. *O.R.*, vol. 23:2, p. 232.
3. Wyeth, p. 169.
4. *O.R.*, vol. 23:2, p. 338.
5. Jordan and Pryor, *Campaigns*, pp. 251–54.
6. Carter, *Last Cavaliers*, p. 141.
7. Wyeth, pp. 179–80; Longacre, *Mounted Raids*, pp. 82–84; Carter, *Last Cavaliers*, pp. 142–43; *SHSP*, vol. 25. p. 47.
8. Wyeth, p. 181; *SHSP*, vol. 25, p. 48.
9. Jordan and Pryor, *Campaigns*, p. 264; *O.R.*, vol. 23:1, p. 290; Wyeth, pp. 184–85.
10. Wyeth, pp. 185–89; Jordan and Pryor, *Campaigns*, pp. 267–69; Carter, *Last Cavaliers*, pp. 143–44.
11. Wyeth, *Sabre*, pp. 190–92.
12. Carter, *Last Cavaliers*, pp. 144–46; Wyeth, pp. 194–95; *O.R.*, vol. 23:1, pp. 290–92.
13. Hurst, *Nathan*, pp. 123–24; Longacre, *Mounted Raids*, p. 88; Lytle, *Bedford Forrest*, pp. 172–73.
14. *SHSP*, vol. 25, p. 54.

4. THE WEST, APRIL 17–MAY 2: GRIERSON'S RIDE

1. Dee Alexander Brown, *Civil War Anthology*, Clear Light, 1998, pp. 91–92; Tom Lalicki, *Grierson's Raid*, Farrar, 2004, pp. 11–13; Longacre, *Mounted Raids*, p. 92; Carter, *Last Cavaliers*, pp. 108–09.
2. Carter, *Last Cavaliers*, p. 110; Brown, *Civil War Anthology*, p. 89.
3. James R. Arnold, *Grant Wins the War*, John Wiley, 1997, p. 84; Lalicki, *Grierson's Raid*, p. 51.
4. Lalicki, *Grierson's Raid*, pp. 59, 63.

5. O.R., vol. 24:1, p. 522ff.

6. Larry D. Underwood, *The Butternut Guerillas*, Dageforde Press, 1994, p. 27; Richard W. Surby, *Grierson's Raid*, Chicago, 1865, p. 33; Arnold, *Grant Wins*, p. 86.

7. Surby, *Grierson's Raid*, p. 36.

8. O.R., vol. 24:1, p. 522ff.; Lalicki, *Grierson's Raid*, p. 93.

9. O.R., vol. 24:1, p. 522ff.

10. John C. Pemberton, *Pemberton: Defender of Vicksburg*, University of North Carolina Press, 1942, p. 112.

11. O.R., vol. 24:1, p. 522ff.; Dee Alexander Brown, *Grierson's Raid*, University of Illinois Press, 1954, p. 162.

12. Carter, *Last Cavaliers*, p. 128; O.R., vol. 24:1, p. 522ff.

13. Commager, *Blue*, p. 661; Carter, *Last Cavaliers*, p. 130; Lalicki, *Grierson's Raid*, p. 163.

14. Brown, *Civil War Anthology*, pp. 102–03; Carter, *Last Cavaliers*, p. 131; Lalicki, *Grierson's Raid*, pp. 169–70.

15. Lalicki, *Grierson's Raid*, p. 174; Brown, *Grierson's Raid*, p. 191.

16. O.R., vol. 24:1, pp. 522ff., 33.

5. THE EAST, APRIL 29–MAY 8: STONEMAN AT CHANCELLORSVILLE

1. O.R., vol. 25:1, p. 1066.

2. Daughtry, *Gray Cavalier*, p. 117; Longacre, *Mounted Raids*, p. 160.

3. O.R., vol. 25:1, p. 1072.

4. Longacre, *Mounted Raids*, p. 164; Gary Gallagher, ed., *Chancellorsville*, University of North Carolina Press, 1996, p. 75.

5. O.R., vol. 25:1, p. 1060.

6. Shelby Foote, *The Civil War*, vol. 2, Random House, 1963, p. 289.

7. O.R., vol. 25:1, p. 1060; Gallagher, *Chancellorsville*, p. 83.

8. Gallagher, *Chancellorsville*, pp. 84–86; Longacre, *Mounted Raids*, pp. 166–69; Henry R. Pyne, *History of the First New Jersey Cavalry*, Trenton, 1871, pp. 144–45; Willard Glazier, *Three Years in the Federal Cavalry*, New York, 1873, pp. 181–82; James Moore, *Kilpatrick and Our Cavalry*, New York, 1865, pp. 50–51.

9. Ben F. Fordney, *Stoneman at Chancellorsville*, White Mane Books, 1998, pp. 34–37; Gallagher, *Chancellorsville*, p. 87; Longacre, p. 170; O.R., vol. 25:1, pp. 1082–83.

10. Gallagher, *Chancellorsville*, p. 89.

11. Daughtry, *Gray Cavalier*, p. 119.

12. Gallagher, *Chancellorsville*, pp. 93–94.
13. Ibid., p. 96; Longacre, *Mounted Raids*, p. 173.
14. Fordney, *Stoneman*, pp. 43–44.
15. Ibid., pp. 50–51.

6. THE EAST, JUNE 9: BRANDY STATION

1. Blackford, *War Years*, p. 212.
2. Edward G. Longacre, *The Cavalry at Gettysburg*, University of Nebraska Press, 1986, pp. 48–50.
3. Ibid., p. 51; McClellan, *Campaigns*, p. 266.
4. Carter, *Last Cavaliers*, p. 153; Longacre, *Gettysburg*, p. 69.
5. McClellan, *Campaigns*, p. 268.
6. Freeman, *Lee's Lieutenants*, vol. 3, p. 9.
7. Cooke, *Wearing of the Gray*, p. 18; McClellan, *Campaigns*, p. 270.
8. McClellan, *Campaigns*, p. 271; Blackford, *War Years*, p. 215; John N. Opie, *A Rebel Cavalryman with Lee, Stuart and Jackson*, Chicago, 1899, p. 154.
9. McClellan, *Campaigns*, p. 277; Carter, *Last Cavaliers*, pp. 157–59; G. W. Beale, *A Lieutenant of Cavalry in Lee's Army*, Boston, 1943, pp. 95–96.
10. Daughtry, *Gray Cavalier*, pp. 134–36; Beale, *Lieutenant*, p. 223.
11. U. R. Brooks, *Butler and His Cavalry*, Germantown, Tenn., 1994, pp. 151–52; McClellan, *Campaigns*, p. 286.
12. McClellan, *Campaigns*, pp. 287–91.
13. Ibid., p. 292.
14. Ibid., p. 294; *Richmond Sentinel*, June 12, 1863; William Woods Hassler, ed., *One of Lee's Best Men*, University of North Carolina Press, 1965, p. 246.

7. THE EAST, JUNE 25–JULY 2: STUART'S GAMBLE

1. O.R., vol. 27:3, pp. 913, 923.
2. McClellan, *Campaigns*, pp. 321–23; Freeman, *Lee's Lieutenants*, vol. 3, p. 63.
3. Blackford, *War Years*, pp. 223–24.
4. Ibid., p. 224.
5. McClellan, *Campaigns*, pp. 326–27; Longacre, *Gettysburg*, p. 157.
6. McClellan, *Campaigns*, pp. 327–28.

7. Blackford, *War Years,* pp. 226.

8. Samuel J. Martin, *Kill-Cavalry, The Life of Union General Hugh Judson Kilpatrick,* Stackpole Books, 2000, p. 109.

9. McClellan, *Campaigns,* pp. 329–30; *SHSP,* vol. 11, p. 323; James L. Morrison Jr., ed., *The Memoirs of Henry Heth,* Westport, Conn., 1974, p. 174.

10. Davis, *Last Cavalier,* pp. 331–32.

11. Ibid., p. 334.

12. *SHSP,* vol. 22, pp. 123–26; Manly Wade Wellman, *Giant in Gray,* Morningside, 1988, pp. 115–16.

13. *SHSP,* vol. 22, p. 126.

14. *O.R.,* vol. 27:2, p. 321.

8. THE WEST, JULY 2–26: MORGAN'S INDIANA-OHIO RAID

1. Carter, *Last Cavaliers,* p. 177; Duke, *History,* pp. 406, 411.

2. Longacre, *Mounted Raids,* p. 178; *SHSP,* vol. 35, p. 110; George Dallas Mosgrove, *Kentucky Cavaliers in Dixie,* Jackson, Tenn., 1957, p. 129.

3. Ramage, *Rebel Raider,* p. 160; Cecil F. Holland, *Morgan and His Raiders,* New York, 1942, p. 222.

4. *SHSP,* vol. 35, p. 110; Longacre, *Mounted Raids,* p. 178.

5. Young, *Confederate Wizards,* pp. 370–71.

6. Brown, *Morgan's Raiders,* p. 180.

7. Commager, *Blue,* pp. 679–80; Carter, *Last Cavaliers,* p. 178.

8. Commager, *Blue,* pp. 680–81; Brown, *Morgan's Raiders,* p. 184.

9. Ramage, *Rebel Raider,* p. 164.

10. Ibid., pp. 165–66; *Louisville Journal,* July 13, 1863.

11. Lester V. Horwitz, *The Longest Raid of the Civil War,* Farmcourt, 2001, p. 43.

12. Ibid., pp. 48–49; Brown, pp. 189–90.

13. Brown, pp. 192–94; Carter, *Last Cavaliers,* p. 181.

14. Horwitz, *Longest Raid,* pp. 87–96; Brown, 198–200.

15. Horwitz, *Longest Raid,* p. 101.

16. Ibid., pp. 108–09.

17. *SHSP,* vol. 35, p. 117; Carter, *Last Cavaliers,* p. 183.

18. Commager, *Blue,* p. 683.

19. Adam R. Johnson, *The Partisan Rangers of the Confederate States Army,* Louisville, 1904, p. 147.

20. Brown, p. 213; McClure, *Annals,* pp. 254–55.

21. McClure, *Annals,* pp. 255–56.

22. Brown, pp. 217–18.

23. Ibid., p. 219; Johnson, *Partisan Rangers,* p. 148.

24. Horwitz, *Longest Raid,* pp. 301, 305.

25. Brown, pp. 224–26; Horwitz, *Longest Raid,* pp. 332–34; Ramage, *Rebel Raider,* pp. 178–79; Carter, *Last Cavaliers,* p. 187.

26. Ramage, pp. 186–89; Brown, pp. 238–39.

27. Horwitz, *Longest Raid,* p. 356; Commager, *Blue,* pp. 704–05.

28. Commager, *Blue,* p. 706.

29. Ibid., pp. 706–07; Horwitz, *Longest Raid,* p. 360.

9. THE EAST, JULY 1: BUFORD HOLDS THE LINE

1. *SHSP,* vol. 4, p. 157.

2. Edward Longacre, *General John Buford,* Combined Books, 1995, p. 20.

3. Ibid., pp. 78–79.

4. Ibid., pp. 83–85.

5. Ibid., pp. 183; Foote, *Civil War,* vol. 2, p. 467; Edwin B. Coddington, *The Gettysburg Campaign,* Scribner's, 1968, pp. 265–66.

6. Commager, *Blue,* p. 600; Foote, *Civil War,* vol. 2, p. 468.

7. Foote, *Civil War,* vol. 2, pp. 468–69; Coddington, *Gettysburg,* p. 269; James I. Robertson Jr., *General A. P. Hill,* Random House, 1987, p. 208.

8. Edward Longacre, *The Cavalry at Gettysburg,* University of Nebraska Press, 1993, pp. 190–91; Coddington, *Gettysburg,* pp. 308–17.

9. Longacre, *Buford,* p. 246.

10. THE EAST, JULY 3: STUART V. GREGG

1. Gregory J. W. Urwin, *Custer Victorious,* Blue & Grey Press, 1983, p. 58.

2. Ezra J. Warner, *Generals in Blue,* Louisiana State University Press, 1964, p. 109.

3. McClure, *Annals,* p. 474.

4. Ibid., pp. 477–79; Urwin, *Custer,* pp. 75–76.

5. Eric J. Wittenberg, ed., *At Custer's Side: The Civil War Writings of James Harvey Kidd,* Kent State University Press, 2001, pp. 22–25.

6. McClure, *Annals,* p. 480.

7. *B&L*, vol. 3, pp. 404–05.
8. McClellan, *Campaigns*, p. 341.
9. Carter, *Last Cavaliers*, p. 172; *B&L*, vol. 3, p. 394.
10. *B&L*, vol. 3, p. 395.
11. Ibid., pp. 395–96; Martin, *Kill-Cavalry*, p. 118.

11. THE WEST, JUNE–DECEMBER: FORREST BEFORE AND AFTER CHICKAMAUGA

1. Wyeth, pp. 200–02; Hurst, *Nathan*, pp. 127–30; italics are used because quotes are at variance.
2. Wyeth, pp. 212–13.
3. O.R., vol. 30:4, pp. 507–10; Lytle, *Bedford Forrest*, pp. 192–93.
4. Jordan and Pryor, *Campaigns*, pp. 318–19.
5. Wyeth, pp. 226–27.
6. Lytle, *Bedford Forrest*, p. 216.
7. Jordan and Pryor, *Campaigns*, pp. 341–44.
8. Wyeth, p. 229.
9. G. Moxley Sorrel, *Recollections of a Confederate Staff Officer*, New York, 1905, p. 196; *B&L*, vol. 3, p. 662; Wyeth, pp. 236–39; Lytle, *Bedford Forrest*, p. 233.
10. O.R., vol. 30:4, p. 710; Wyeth, pp. 242–44.
11. O.R., vol. 31:3, p. 789; Wyeth, p. 254.
12. Carter, *Last Cavaliers*, p. 221; O.R., vol. 31:3, pp. 789, 797, 817.
13. Lytle, *Bedford Forrest*, p. 249; Hurst, *Nathan*, p. 144; Wyeth, pp. 261–62.
14. Jordan and Pryor, *Campaigns*, pp. 379–80.

12. THE WEST, OCTOBER 1–9: WHEELER AT CHATTANOOGA

1. Wyeth, p. 127.
2. Jordan and Pryor, *Campaigns*, p. 228.
3. Wyeth, pp. 131–32.
4. John P. Dyer, *From Shiloh to San Juan: The Life of "Fightin' Joe" Wheeler*, Louisiana State University Press, 1992, p. 17.
5. Longacre, *Mounted Raids*, p. 206.
6. George B. Guild, *A Brief Narrative of the Fourth Tennessee Cavalry Regiment*, Nashville, 1913, p. 35.

7. John Allan Wyeth, *The Destruction of Rosecrans' Great Wagon Train: The Photographic History of the Civil War,* Blue & Grey Press, 1987, pp. 160–62.
8. Ibid., pp. 162–64.
9. O.R., vol. 30:20, pp. 724–27.
10. Ibid., pp. 727–28.
11. Dyer, *Shiloh to San Juan,* p. 106.
12. Ibid., p. 107; Longacre, *Mounted Raids,* p. 224.

13. THE EAST, OCTOBER 19:
STUART V. KILPATRICK AT BUCKLAND

1. James Harvey Kidd, *Personal Recollections of a Cavalryman,* Black Letter Press, 1969, p. 214; Urwin, *Custer,* p. 109.
2. Davis, *Last Cavalier,* p. 366; McClellan, *Campaigns,* p. 394.
3. Carter, *Last Cavaliers,* p. 192; Martin, *Kill-Cavalry,* pp. 59–62.
4. Urwin, *Custer,* pp. 109–11; Kidd, *Recollections,* pp. 216–20.
5. Blackford, *War Years,* p. 241; McClellan, *Campaigns,* pp. 394–95.
6. O.R., vol. 29:1, p. 438ff.; Martin, *Kill-Cavalry,* p. 143; Kidd, *Recollections,* p. 226.

14. THE EAST, JULY–FEBRUARY: MOSBY'S CONFEDERACY

1. Stephen Z. Starr, *The Union Cavalry in the Civil War,* vol. 2, Louisiana State University Press, 1981, p. 51.
2. Ramage, *Gray Ghost,* p. 99.
3. Ibid., p. 108.
4. Mosby, *Memoirs,* p. 259.
5. Ramage, *Gray Ghost,* p. 110; Munson, *Reminiscences,* p. 215.
6. Wert, *Mosby's Rangers,* pp. 92, 95; O.R., vol. 27:2, p. 652.
7. Wert, *Mosby's Rangers,* p. 97; Ramage, p. 116.
8. Ramage, p. 117; J. Marshall Crawford, *Mosby and His Men,* New York, 1867, p. 128; Mosby, *Memoirs,* pp. 263–64.
9. Ibid., p. 262; Ramage, p. 122; O.R., vol. 29:1, p. 495.
10. James J. Williamson, *Mosby's Rangers,* New York, 1909, p. 110.
11. Ibid., pp. 111–12.
12. Ibid., pp. 126–27; Munson, *Reminiscences,* pp. 241–42; Crawford, *Mosby,* p. 163; O.R., vol. 33, p. 15; Mosby, *Memoirs,* pp. 267–69; Wert, *Mosby's Rangers,* p. 134.

13. Williamson, *Mosby's Rangers,* pp. 127–28, 486; Munson, *Reminiscences,* p. 242; Crawford, *Mosby,* pp. 163–65.

14. Mosby, *Memoirs,* p. 270; *O.R.,* vol. 33, pp. 1081–82.

15. Crawford, *Mosby,* pp. 173–77; *O.R.,* vol. 33, p. 568; Williamson, *Mosby's Rangers,* pp. 134–35; Wert, *Mosby's Rangers,* p. 141.

16. Crawford, *Mosby,* pp. 177–79.

17. Munson, *Reminiscences,* p. 83; Williamson, *Mosby's Rangers,* pp. 139–40.

18. Ibid., pp. 84–85, 141–43.

19. Wert, *Mosby's Rangers,* pp. 147–49; Munson, *Reminiscences,* pp. 86–97; Williamson, *Mosby's Rangers,* pp. 144–49.

1864

1. THE WEST, FEBRUARY: FORREST V. SOOY SMITH

1. Wyeth, p. 273.

2. William Tecumseh Sherman, *Memoirs,* Library of America, 1990, p. 418.

3. Wyeth, pp. 276–80; Carter, *Last Cavaliers,* p. 223.

4. Lytle, *Bedford Forrest,* pp. 263–64.

5. Hurst, *Nathan,* p. 151; Wyeth, pp. 283–84; Jordan and Pryor, *Campaigns,* pp. 393–94.

6. *B&L,* vol. 4, p. 417.

7. John W. Morton, *The Artillery of Nathan Bedford Forrest,* Nashville, 1909, p. 152.

8. Wyeth, p. 291; Lytle, *Bedford Forrest,* p. 267.

9. *O.R.,* vol. 32:1, p. 354; Wyeth, *Destruction,* p. 292.

10. Jordan and Pryor, *Campaigns,* pp. 400, 398.

11. *B&L,* vol. 4, p. 418; Sherman, *Memoirs,* pp. 422–23.

12. *O.R.,* vol. 32:1, p. 354.

13. Carter, *Last Cavaliers,* p. 224.

2. THE EAST, FEBRUARY 28–MARCH 4: THE KILPATRICK-DAHLGREN RAID

1. Martin, *Kill-Cavalry,* p. 149; Longacre, p. 231; *O.R.,* vol. 33, p. 172;

Vigil Carrington Jones, *Eight Hours Before Richmond*, Henry Holt, 1957, p. viii; *O.R.*, vol. 33, p. 172; Jones, *Eight Hours*, p. 29.

2. Bruce Catton, *A Stillness at Appomattox*, Fairfax Press, 1984, pp. 464–65.

3. Rear Admiral John A. D. Dahlgren, *Memoir of Ulric Dahlgren*, Philadelphia, 1872, pp. 204–10.

4. H. P. Moyer, *History of the Seventeenth Regiment Pennsylvania*, Lebanon, Pa., 1911, p. 233; Jones, *Eight Hours*, pp. 46–52.

5. James H. Kidd, *Personal Reminiscences of a Cavalryman*, G. P. Putnam's, 1928, p. 246; Catton, *Stillness*, p. 467.

6. *SHSP*, vol. 13, p. 518; Longacre, *Mounted Raids*, pp. 247–48; Catton, *Stillness*, p. 468.

7. *SHSP*, vol. 13, p. 519.

8. Ibid.

9. Catton, *Stillness*, p. 468; Martin, *Kill-Cavalry*, p. 160.

10. *O.R.*, vol. 33, p. 185.

11. *SHSP*, vol. 13, pp. 524–25; Moyer, *History*, p. 243.

12. *SHSP*, vol. 13, p. 539.

13. Ibid., vol. 34, pp. 186–87.

14. Ibid., vol. 13, pp. 541–43, 545–46, 549–51, 556–60.

15. *O.R.*, vol. 33, pp. 178, 180.

16. Martin, *Kill-Cavalry*, p. 171; Jones, *Eight Hours*, p. 128.

3. THE WEST, APRIL 12: FORREST AND FORT PILLOW

1. Jordan and Pryor, *Campaigns*, p. 406.

2. Ibid., p. 408; Wyeth, pp. 302–03; *O.R.*, vol. 32:1, p. 503.

3. *O.R.*, vol. 32:1, p. 547.

4. Wyeth, p. 305.

5. *O.R.*, vol. 32:1, p. 548; Jordan and Pryor, *Campaigns*, p. 413.

6. Wyeth, pp. 306–07.

7. Jordan and Pryor, *Campaigns*, p. 422.

8. Wyeth, pp. 316–18.

9. Ibid., pp. 319, 322.

10. Jordan and Pryor, *Campaigns*, pp. 433–37.

11. Ibid., pp. 437–38.

12. *O.R.*, vol. 32:1, p. 531; Bob Womack, *Call Forth the Mighty Men*, Alabama, 1987, p. 347; Hurst, *Forrest*, p. 173; Carter, *Last Cavaliers*, p. 228.

13. R.R. Hancock, *Hancock's Diary,* Nashville, 1887, p. 364; Hurst, *Forrest,* p. 174.

14. *O.R.,* vol. 32:1, p. 558; Brian Wills, *A Battle from the Start,* New York, 1992, p. 188; Hurst, *Forrest,* pp. 175–76.

15. Jordan and Pryor, *Campaigns,* pp. 440, 455.

4. THE WEST, MAY–SEPTEMBER: CAVALRY IN THE ATLANTA CAMPAIGN

1. Jefferson Davis, *Rise and Fall of the Confederate Government,* vol. 2, D. Appleton, 1881, p. 556.

2. Foote, *Civil War,* vol. 3, p. 402.

3. *O.R.,* vol. 38:4, p. 648.

4. David Evans, *Sherman's Horsemen,* Indiana University Press, 1996, pp. 32–33.

5. Ibid., p. 104.

6. *National Tribune,* May 2, 1901, p. 5.

7. Evans, *Horsemen,* p. 126; Sherman, *Memoirs,* p. 540.

8. Sherman, *Memoirs,* p. 541.

9. William Hamilton, *Recollections of a Cavalryman in the Civil War,* Columbus, Ohio, 1915, pp. 133–34.

10. Evans, *Horsemen,* p. 136; *O.R.,* vol. 38:2, p. 907.

11. Evans, *Horsemen,* pp. 151, 154, 170.

12. Ibid., p. 174.

13. Carter, *Last Cavaliers,* pp. 252, 255.

14. Evans, *Horsemen,* pp. 213–15.

15. Ibid., pp. 228, 230, 237.

16. Carter, *Last Cavaliers,* p. 254.

17. Evans, *Horsemen,* pp. 264, 268.

18. Ibid., p. 319; Young, *Confederate Wizards,* p. 592.

19. Evans, *Horsemen,* pp. 337–38.

20. Dyer, *Shiloh to San Juan,* p. 145.

21. Carter, *Last Cavaliers,* p. 257.

22. Dyer, *Shiloh to San Juan,* p. 149; Mark Mayo Boatner III, *The Civil War Dictionary,* David McKay, 1959, p. 911.

23. *O.R.,* vol. 38:5, pp. 526, 548.

24. Stephen Z. Starr, *Union Cavalry in the Civil War,* vol. 3, Louisiana State University Press, 1979, p. 478; William W. Webb, "Kilpatrick's Great Raid," *Leslie's Monthly,* December 1889, p. 731.

25. Webb, "Great Raid," p. 732; *National Tribune,* January 22, 1903, p. 6.

26. *O.R.*, vol. 38:5, p. 628; Oliver Otis Howard, *Autobiography*, vol. 2, Baker and Taylor, 1907, p. 29; James H. Wilson, *Under the Old Flag*, vol. 2, Appleton, 1912, p. 13.

5. THE WEST, JUNE–AUGUST: FORREST IN MISSISSIPPI AND TENNESSEE

1. Wyeth, p. 350.
2. J. P. Young, *The Seventh Tennessee Cavalry (Confederate): A History*, Nashville, 1890, pp. 90–93.
3. Brown, *Civil War Anthology*, p. 196; Henry, *As They Saw Forrest*, pp. 119–20.
4. Wyeth, pp. 363–366; Jordan and Pryor, *Campaigns*, pp. 474–75.
5. Carter, *Last Cavaliers*, p. 245.
6. Morton, *Artillery*, pp. 205–07.
7. Wyeth, pp. 389–91.
8. *O.R.*, vol. 39:1, p. 336.
9. Lytle, *Bedford Forrest*, pp. 312, 314–15.
10. Wyeth, p. 396.
11. Ibid., p. 413; *SHSP*, vol. 36, pp. 188–89.
12. *SHSP*, vol. 36, p. 191.
13. Wyeth, pp. 415–18.

6. THE EAST, MAY–JULY: MOSBY STEPS UP HIS RAIDS

1. Ramage, *Gray Ghost*, p. 166.
2. Williamson, *Mosby's Rangers*, p. 164.
3. John H. Alexander, *Mosby's Men*, Neale, 1907, pp. 60–61.
4. Mosby, *Memoirs*, p. 275.
5. Ibid., p. 276; Wert, *Mosby's Rangers*, pp. 174–75; Munson, *Reminiscences*, p. 97.

7. THE EAST, MAY 11: YELLOW TAVERN

1. Horace Porter, *Campaigning with Grant*, University of Nebraska Press, 2000, pp. 83–84.
2. Ibid., p. 24.
3. *B&L*, vol. 4, p. 188.
4. McClellan, *Campaigns*, p. 411.

5. Davis, *Last Cavalier,* p. 400.

6. Thomas, *Bold Dragoon,* p. 291.

7. Gary W. Gallagher, ed., *The Spotsylvania Campaign,* University of North Carolina Press, 1998, p. 143.

8. Davis, *Last Cavalier,* p. 397.

9. *SHSP,* vol. 9, p. 138; *O.R.,* vol. 36:1, p. 818; Urwin, *Custer,* p. 140.

10. William O. Lee, ed., *Personal and Historical Sketches and Facial History of and by Members of the Seventh Regiment Michigan Volunteer Cavalry,* Detroit, 1901, p. 224.

11. McClellan, *Campaigns,* p. 413; *B&L,* vol. 4, p. 194; *Confederate Veteran,* vol. 19, p. 531; *SHSP,* vol. 1, p. 102.

12. McClellan, *Campaigns,* p. 417; *SHSP,* vol. 37, p. 68; Thomas, p. 297; Porter, *Grant,* p. 144.

8. THE WEST, JUNE: MORGAN'S LAST KENTUCKY RAID

1. Ramage, *Rebel Raider,* p. 216.

2. *O.R.,* vol. 39:1, p. 66.

3. Mosgrove, *Kentucky Cavaliers,* p. 138.

4. Ibid., p. 140; Brown, *Morgan's Raiders,* p. 259.

5. *O.R.,* vol. 39:1, p. 67; Brown, *Morgan's Raiders,* p. 260.

6. John B. Castleman, *Active Service,* Louisville, Ky., 1917, pp. 124–27; *O.R.,* vol. 39:1, p. 68; Brown, *Morgan's Raiders,* pp. 260–61.

7. Brown, *Morgan's Raiders,* p. 262; Ramage, p. 221; G. D. Ewing, "Morgan's Last Raid into Kentucky," *Confederate Veteran,* July 1933, pp. 255–56.

8. Mosgrove, *Kentucky Cavaliers,* pp. 158–63.

9. Duke, *History,* p. 535.

10. Ramage, pp. 235–37; Brown, *Morgan's Raiders,* pp. 268–70.

11. Ibid., pp. 237–38, ibid., p. 270.

12. Ramage, p. 238.

13. *SHSP,* vol. 31, p. 127.

14. Brown, *Morgan's Raiders,* p. 273.

9. THE EAST, JUNE 7–28: SHERIDAN V. HAMPTON AT TREVILIAN STATION

1. Ulysses R. Brooks, *Butler and His Cavalry,* Germantown, Tenn., 1994, p. 239.

2. *SHSP,* vol. 4, p. 237.

3. Brooks, *Butler and His Cavalry,* p. 243; Brooks, "Memories of Battle," *Confederate Veteran,* vol. 22, September 1914, p. 408.

4. *SHSP,* vol. 4, p. 237.

5. Walbrook Davis Swank, *Battle of Trevilian Station,* Shippensburg, Pa., 1994, p. 59.

6. *SHSP,* vol. 4, p. 238.

7. Frank M. Myers, *The Comanches: A History of White's Battalion, Virginia Cavalry, Laurel Brigade, Hampton Division,* Marietta, Ga., 1956, p. 302; Swank, *Battle,* p. 74.

8. Myers, *Comanches,* p. 304.

9. Swank, *Battle,* pp. 75–76.

10. Ibid., pp. 76–77.

11. Brooks, *Butler and His Cavalry,* p. 256.

12. Freeman, *Lee's Lieutenants,* vol. 3, pp. 522–23.

13. Swank, *Battle,* p. 106.

10. THE EAST, JUNE 22–JULY 1: THE WILSON-KAUTZ RAID

1. Edward G. Longacre, *Grant's Cavalryman,* Stackpole Books, 1972, pp. 134–35; Daughtry, *Gray Cavalier,* pp. 187–88.

2. Daughtry, *Gray Cavalier,* p. 189.

3. *SHSP,* vol. 19, pp. 52–53.

4. Ibid., p. 56.

5. *SHSP,* vol. 7, p. 169.

6. *SHSP,* vol. 2, p. 275.

7. Daughtry, *Gray Cavalier,* p. 193.

11. THE EAST, JULY 23–OCTOBER 19: SHERIDAN IN THE SHENANDOAH

1. Grant, *Memoirs,* pp. 614–15.

2. Jubal A. Early, *Narrative of the War Between the States,* Da Capo, 1989, p. 415.

3. Edward J. Stackpole, *Sheridan in the Shenandoah,* Stackpole Books, 1992, p. 201.

4. P. H. Sheridan, *Personal Memoirs,* Da Capo, 1992, p. 292.

5. *B&L,* vol. 4, p. 507.

6. *O.R.,* vol. 43: 1, p. 455.

7. Sheridan, *Memoirs,* pp. 292–94.

8. Harris H. Beecher, *Record of the 114th New York,* Norwich, N.Y. 1866, p. 426.

9. *B&L,* vol. 4, pp. 509–10.

10. Sheridan, *Memoirs,* pp. 304, 310.

11. Urwin, *Custer,* p. 195; again some remarks have been paraphrased and underlined.

12. Ibid., pp. 196–97.

13. *SHSP,* vol. 13, p. 134.

14. Urwin, *Custer,* p. 202.

15. *O.R.,* vol. 43:2, p. 345.

16. John B. Gordon, *Reminiscences of the Civil War,* Scribner's, 1903, pp. 335, 339.

17. Charles C. Osborne, *Jubal,* Algonquin, 1992, p. 361.

18. Gordon, *Reminiscences,* p. 341.

19. Jeffry D. Wert, *From Winchester to Cedar Creek,* South Mountain Press, 1987, p. 222; Urwin, *Custer,* p. 210.

20. Thomas A. Lewis, *The Guns of Cedar Creek,* Harper and Row, 1988, p. 251; George A. Forsyth, *Thrilling Days in Army Life,* Harper and Brothers, 1900, pp. 141–45.

21. Roy Morris Jr., *Sheridan,* Vintage, 1992, p. 216; Gordon, *Reminiscences,* p. 348.

22. Sheridan, *Memoirs,* p. 332.

23. Douglas, *I Rode with Stonewall,* p. 319; Lewis, *Guns,* p. 288.

12. THE EAST, AUGUST–DECEMBER: MOSBY RETALIATES

1. Mosby, *Memoirs,* p. 284.

2. Ibid., p. 285.

3. Wert, *Mosby's Rangers,* p. 195.

4. Williamson, *Mosby's Rangers,* pp. 449–50; *New York Times,* August 25, 1864.

5. *O.R.,* vol. 43:1, p. 843; Ramage, *Gray Ghost,* p. 197.

6. Williamson, *Mosby's Rangers,* pp. 226–28, 302.

7. Mosby, *Memoirs,* p. 298.

8. Wert, p. 214.

9. *SHSP,* vol. 24, p. 109.

10. Ramage, pp. 198–99; *SHSP,* vol. 25, p. 240.

11. Mosby, *Memoirs*, p. 315.

12. *O.R.*, vol. 43:1, p. 186.

13. Morris, *Sheridan*, pp. 207–08; Ramage, p. 211.

14. *SHSP*, vol. 27, pp. 320–21.

15. Ibid., vol. 25, p. 242.

16. Alexander, *Mosby's Men*, pp. 144–45; *SHSP*, vol. 27, p. 319.

17. Munson, *Reminiscences*, p. 150; Ramage, pp. 213–14.

18. Wert, pp. 248–49; Munson, *Reminiscences*, pp. 150–51; *O.R.*, vol. 43:2, p. 566.

19. *SHSP*, vol. 25, p. 244.

20. Munson, *Reminiscences*, p. 120.

21. *O.R.*, vol. 43:1, p. 55; Crawford, *Mosby*, p. 310.

22. *O.R.*, vol. 43:2, p. 937.

23. Mosby, *Memoirs*, p. 337.

24. Ibid., pp. 338–42; Ramage, pp. 234–35; Wert, pp. 266–67. Sources differ; some claim that the enemy that first stormed into the house thought Mosby was a junior officer because he concealed his collar insignia with his hands. What is certain is that he was shot and that he bluffed the enemy into thinking he was all but dead.

13. THE WEST, SEPTEMBER–DECEMBER: FORREST IN ALABAMA AND TENNESSEE

1. Richard Taylor, *Destruction and Reconstruction*, New York, 1879, pp. 198–99.

2. *O.R.*, vol. 39:2, p. 543; Wyeth, p. 431.

3. *O.R.*, vol. 39:2, p. 522; Morton, *Artillery*, p. 227.

4. Morton, *Artillery*, pp. 231–32.

5. *O.R.*, vol. 39:1, p. 544.

6. Wyeth, pp. 436–37.

7. Ibid., pp. 447, 449.

8. *O.R.*, vol. 39:3, pp. 815–16.

9. Jordan and Pryor, *Campaigns*, p. 592; Robert Selph Henry, *"First with the Most" Forrest*, Bobbs Merrill, 1944, p. 372; *SHSP*, vol. 10, p. 263.

10. *SHSP*, vol. 10, p. 264.

11. Ibid.

12. Ibid., pp. 265–66.

13. *O.R.*, vol. 39:1, p. 870.

14. Wyeth, p. 461.
15. Henry, *"First with the Most,"* pp. 375–76; Jordan and Pryor, *Campaigns,* pp. 598–99; Wyeth, pp. 462–63.
16. Jordan and Pryor, *Campaigns,* pp. 602–04.
17. Lytle, *Bedford Forrest,* p. 350.
18. O.R., vol. 39:1, p. 871.
19. Morton, *Artillery,* p. 14.
20. O.R., vol. 45:1, p. 753.
21. Wyeth, p. 480
22. Hurst, *Nathan,* p. 237; Stanley F. Horn, *The Army of Tennessee,* University of Oklahoma Press, 1941, p. 403.
23. Wyeth, pp. 492–94.
24. O.R., vol. 45:1, pp. 657, 46; Wyeth, pp. 507–08.

14. THE EAST, SEPTEMBER 16–OCTOBER 27: CATTLE RAIDS AND HATCHER'S RUN

1. *SHSP,* vol. 22, p. 150.
2. Ibid., p. 151.
3. Young, *Confederate Wizards,* p. 50.
4. Noah Andre Trudeau, *The Last Citadel,* Little, Brown, 1991, pp. 199–200.
5. Daughtry, *Gray Cavalier,* p. 218.
6. Trudeau, *Last Citadel,* p. 201; Daughtry, *Gray Cavalier,* p. 219.
7. Trudeau, *Last Citadel,* p. 245; Willie Pegram to Mother, October 28, 1864, Pegram-Johnson-McIntosh Papers, Virginia Historical Society.
8. Brooks, *Butler and His Cavalry,* pp. 358–60; Wellman, *Giant,* pp. 160–61.
9. C. Vann Woodward, ed., *Mary Chestnut's Civil War,* Yale University Press, 1981, p. 665.

15. THE WEST, NOVEMBER 16–DECEMBER 21: MARCH TO THE SEA

1. Charles W. Wills, *Army Life of an Illinois Soldier,* Southern Illinois University Press, 1996, pp. 323–24.
2. James A. Connolly, *Three Years in the Army of the Cumberland,* Indiana University Press, 1959, pp. 298, 311.
3. Dolly Lunt, *A Woman's Wartime Journal,* Century, 1918, p. 20.

4. *O.R.*, vol. 39:3, p. 162.

5. Lee Kennett, *Marching Through Georgia,* Harper Perennial, 1996, pp. 260–61; David Power Conyngham, *Sherman's March Through the South,* New York, 1865, p. 256.

6. Lloyd Lewis, *Sherman: Fighting Prophet,* Harcourt Brace, 1932, p. 455.

7. Burke Davis, *Sherman's March,* Random House, 1980, p. 83.

8. Martin, *Kill-Cavalry,* pp. 198–99; Lee Jacobs, ed., *The Gray Riders,* Burd Street Press, 1999, p. 80.

9. *O.R.*, vol. 44, p. 364.

10. Dyer, *Shiloh to San Juan,* p. 166.

11. James R. Reston Jr., *Sherman's March and Vietnam,* Macmillan, 1984, p. 76; Martin, *Kill-Cavalry,* pp. 200–01.

12. Howard, *Autobiography,* p. 89; John F. Marszalek, *Sherman,* Free Press, 1993, p. 307.

13. Martin, *Kill-Cavalry,* p. 204; *SHSP,* vol. 10, p. 415.

1865

1. THE EAST, FEBRUARY–MARCH: CAVALRY IN THE CAROLINAS

1. Howard, *Autobiography,* p. 114.

2. Martin, *Kill-Cavalry,* pp. 209–11.

3. Howard, *Autobiography,* p. 114; *O.R.*, vol. 47:2, p. 351.

4. *O.R.*, vol. 47:1, p. 858; ibid., vol. 47:2, p. 450.

5. Martin, *Kill-Cavalry,* p. 214.

6. Sherman, *Memoirs,* p. 759ff.

7. Richard Harwell and Philip N. Racine, eds., *The Fiery Trail,* University of Tennessee Press, 1986, pp. 128–29.

8. Wills, *Army Life,* p. 350.

9. Martin, *Kill-Cavalry,* p. 216.

10. Ibid., pp. 217–18.

11. Martin, *Southern Hero,* p. 152.

12. Ibid., p. 153; *SHSP,* vol. 12, pp. 127–28; Edward L. Wells, *Hampton and His Cavalry,* Richmond, 1899, pp. 406–12; Brooks, *Butler and His Cavalry,* pp. 446–47.

13. Carter, *Last Cavaliers,* p. 303.

14. *B&L,* vol. 4, pp. 703–04; *O.R.*, vol. 47:1, p. 1056.

2. THE WEST, MARCH – APRIL: WILSON V. FORREST IN ALABAMA

1. *O.R.*, vol. 49:1, p. 530.
2. Jordan and Pryor, *Campaigns*, p. 659; Lytle, *Bedford Forrest*, pp. 372–73; Longacre, *Grant's Cavalryman*, p. 201.
3. Longacre, *Mounted Raids*, p. 311.
4. Wyeth, p. 523.
5. Jordan and Pryor, *Campaigns*, pp. 662–64.
6. James Pickett Jones, *Yankee Blitzkrieg*, University of Georgia Press, 1976, p. 70.
7. Wyeth, pp. 531–32; Wilson, *Old Flag*, p. 217.
8. Taylor, *Destruction and Reconstruction*, p. 219.
9. Wyeth, p. 535.
10. Jordan and Pryor, *Campaigns*, p. 675.
11. Jones, *Yankee Blitzkrieg*, p. 99.
12. Wyeth, pp. 540–43.

3. THE EAST, JANUARY – APRIL: MOSBY'S LAST HURRAH

1. *O.R.*, vol. 46:1, p. 463; John Scott, *Partisan Life with Col. John S. Mosby*, Gaithersburg, Md., 1985, p. 447.
2. *O.R.*, vol. 46:1, pp. 464–66; Scott, *Partisan Life*, p. 448; Williamson, *Mosby's Rangers*, p. 349; Ramage, *Gray Ghost*, p. 240.
3. Williamson, *Mosby's Rangers*, pp. 355–58; Alexander, *Mosby's Men*, p. 157; Aristides Monteiro, *Reminiscences by the Surgeon of Mosby's Command*, Gaithersburg, Md., n.d., p. 123.
4. *O.R.*, vol. 46:1, p. 536; Monteiro, *Reminiscences*, p. 155.
5. Crawford, *Mosby*, p. 354; Williamson, *Mosby's Rangers*, p. 367, Munson, *Reminiscences*, pp. 256–57.
6. *O.R.*, vol. 46:1, p. 536; ibid., vol. 46:3, pp. 800, 839.
7. Munson, *Reminiscences*, pp. 266–68; Monteiro, *Reminiscences*, pp. 133ff., 204–07.
8. Wert, *Mosby's Rangers*, p. 288; Ramage, *Gray Ghost*, p. 269.
9. Grant, *Memoirs*, p. 486.

4. THE EAST, MARCH 31–APRIL 1: DINWIDDIE AND FIVE FORKS

1. Porter, *Campaigning,* p. 428; Grant, *Memoirs,* pp. 696–97; Bruce Catton, *Grant Takes Command,* Little, Brown, 1968, p. 441.
2. Freeman, *Lee's Lieutenants,* p. 667n.
3. Edward G. Longacre, *The Cavalry at Appomattox,* Stackpole Books, 2003, p. 72.
4. Sheridan, *Memoirs,* p. 369.
5. Urwin, *Custer,* p. 236.
6. Porter, *Campaigning,* pp. 432–43.
7. Grant, *Memoirs,* pp. 701–02.
8. Freeman, *Lee's Lieutenants,* pp. 661, 664.
9. Porter, *Campaigning,* p. 435; Sheridan, *Memoirs,* pp. 373–74.
10. Freeman, *Lee's Lieutenants,* p. 667; Thomas T. Munford, "The Last Days of Fitz Lee's Division of Cavalry, Army of Northern Virginia, 1865," Virginia Historical Society, p. 34.
11. Munford, "Last Days," p. 35.
12. Freeman, *Lee's Lieutenants,* p. 671.
13. Porter, *Campaigning,* pp. 437–40.
14. Joshua L. Chamberlain, *The Passing of the Armies,* Bantam, 1993, p. 113.
15. Urwin, *Custer,* p. 241; *SHSP,* vol. 22, p. 71.
16. Daughtry, *Gray Cavalier,* pp. 257–58.
17. Ibid., p. 259.
18. Sheridan, *Memoirs,* p. 376; Chamberlain, *Passing,* pp. 107, 114.

5. THE EAST, APRIL 6–9: SAILOR'S CREEK AND APPOMATTOX

1. *O.R.,* vol. 46:1, p. 1276; Gordon, *Reminiscences,* p. 423.
2. Edward Porter Alexander, *Fighting for the Confederacy,* ed. Gary W. Gallagher, University of North Carolina Press, 1989, p. 522.
3. Longacre, *Cavalry at Appomattox,* pp. 142–43.
4. Robert Stiles, *Four Years Under Marse Robert,* R. Bemis, 1995, p. 333; the waterway and battle have different spellings; to avoid confusion, I have chosen *Sailor's Creek,* not *Sayler's Creek.*
5. Urwin, *Custer,* p. 245; Freeman, *Lee's Lieutenants,* p. 711.
6. Urwin, *Custer,* pp. 248–49.
7. Alexander, *Fighting for the Confederacy,* p. 528.

8. Gordon, *Reminiscences,* pp. 438–39.

9. Ibid., pp. 439–42; Freeman, *Lee's Lieutenants,* p. 736.

EPILOGUE

1. *SHSP,* vol. 35, pp. 143, 138.

2. Daughtry, *Gray Cavalier,* pp. 294, 311.

3. Hurst, *Nathan,* pp. 342, 383.

4. Dyer, *Shiloh to San Juan,* p. 221.

5. Longacre, *Gentleman and Soldier,* p. 276.

6. Martin, *Southern Hero,* pp. 188, 293.

7. Ramage, *Gray Ghost,* p. 282.

8. Morris, *Sheridan,* p. 296.

9. Boatner, *Civil War Dictionary,* p. 545.

10. Urwin, *Custer,* p. 272.

11. Warner, *Generals in Blue,* p. 124.

12. Martin, *Kill-Cavalry,* p. 254.

INDEX

2/11   5   12/10
7/16   (14) 6/16